Communications in Computer and Information Science   **749**

Commenced Publication in 2007
Founding and Former Series Editors:
Alfredo Cuzzocrea, Xiaoyong Du, Orhun Kara, Ting Liu, Dominik Ślęzak,
and Xiaokang Yang

More information about this series at http://www.springer.com/series/7899

Rafael Valencia-García · Katty Lagos-Ortiz
Gema Alcaraz-Mármol · Javier Del Cioppo
Néstor Vera-Lucio · Martha Bucaram-Leverone (Eds.)

Technologies and Innovation

Third International Conference, CITI 2017
Guayaquil, Ecuador, October 24–27, 2017
Proceedings

Springer

Editors
Rafael Valencia-García
Universidad de Murcia
Murcia
Spain

Katty Lagos-Ortiz
Universidad Agraria del Ecuador
Guayaquil
Ecuador

Gema Alcaraz-Mármol
Universidad de Castilla la Mancha
Toledo
Spain

Javier Del Cioppo
Universidad Agraria del Ecuador
Guayaquil
Ecuador

Néstor Vera-Lucio
Universidad Agraria del Ecuador
Guayaquil
Ecuador

Martha Bucaram-Leverone
Universidad Agraria del Ecuador
Guayaquil
Ecuador

ISSN 1865-0929   ISSN 1865-0937 (electronic)
Communications in Computer and Information Science
ISBN 978-3-319-67282-3   ISBN 978-3-319-67283-0 (eBook)
DOI 10.1007/978-3-319-67283-0

Library of Congress Control Number: 2017953422

Printed on acid-free paper

This Springer imprint is published by Springer Nature
The registered company is Springer International Publishing AG
The registered company address is: Gewerbestrasse 11, 6330 Cham, Switzerland

Preface

The Third International Conference on Technologies and Innovation (CITI 2017) was held during October 24–27 2017, in Guayaquil, Ecuador. The CITI series of conferences aim to become an international framework and meeting point for professionals who are mainly devoted to research, development, innovation and university teaching, within the area of computer science and technology applied to any important field of innovation. CITI 2017 was organized as a knowledge-exchange conference consisting of several contributions about current innovative technology. These proposals deal with the most important aspects and future prospects from an academic, innovative, and scientific perspective. The goal of the conference was the feasibility of investigating advanced and innovative methods and techniques and their application in different domains in the field of computer science and information systems, which represents innovation in current society.

We would like to express our gratitude to all the authors who submitted papers to CITI 2017, and our congratulations to those whose papers were accepted. There were 68 submissions this year. Each submission was reviewed by at least three Program Committee (PC) members. Only the papers with an average score of 1.0 or higher were considered for final inclusion, and almost all accepted papers had positive reviews or at least one review with a score of 2 (accept) or higher. Finally, the PC decided to accept 24 full papers.

We would also like to thank the PC members, who agreed to review the manuscripts in a timely manner and provided valuable feedback to the authors.

October 2017

Rafael Valencia-García
Katty Lagos-Ortiz
Gema Alcaraz-Mármol
Javier Del Cioppo
Néstor Vera-Lucio
Martha Bucaram-Leverone

Organization

Honorary Committee

Martha Bucaram Leverone	Universidad Agraria del Ecuador, Ecuador
Javier Del Cioppo	Universidad Agraria del Ecuador, Ecuador
Néstor Vera Lucio	Universidad Agraria del Ecuador, Ecuador
Teresa Samaniego Cobo	Universidad Agraria del Ecuador, Ecuador

Organizing Committee

Rafael Valencia-García	Universidad de Murcia, Spain
Katty Lagos-Ortiz	Universidad Agraria del Ecuador, Ecuador
Gema Alcaraz-Mármol	Universidad de Castilla-La Mancha, Spain
Javier Del Cioppo	Universidad Agraria del Ecuador, Ecuador
Néstor Vera Lucio	Universidad Agraria del Ecuador, Ecuador
Martha Bucaram Leverone	Universidad Agraria del Ecuador, Ecuador

Program Committee

Jacobo Bucaram Ortiz	Universidad Agraria del Ecuador
Martha Bucaram Leverone	Universidad Agraria del Ecuador
Rafael Valencia-García	Universidad de Murcia, Spain
Miguel Ángel Rodríguez-García	King Abdullah University of Science and Technology, Saudi Arabia
Eugenio Martínez-Cámara	Technical University of Darmstadt, Germany
Antonio A. López-Lorca	University of Melbourne, Australia
José Antonio Miñarro-Giménez	Medical University Graz, Austria
Catalina Martínez-Costa	Medical University Graz, Austria
Lucía Serrano-Luján	Imperial College London, UK
Chunguo Wu	Jillin University, China
Giner Alor-Hernández	Instituto Tecnológico de Orizaba, Mexico
José Luis Ochoa	Universidad de Sonora, Mexico
Ana Muñoz	Universidad de Los Andes, Venezuela
Gema Alcaraz-Mármol	Universidad de Castilla-La Mancha, Spain
Ricardo Coelho Silva	Federal University of Ceará, Brazil
Francisco M. Fernandez-Periche	Universidad Antonio Nariño, Colombia
Alejandro Rodríguez-González	Universidad Politécnica de Madrid, Spain
Carlos Cruz-Corona	Universidad de Granada, Spain
Dagoberto Catellanos-Nieves	Universidad de la Laguna, Spain
Juan Miguel Gómez-Berbís	Universidad Carlos III de Madrid, Spain

Viviana Yarel Rosales Morales	Instituto Tecnologico de Orizaba, Mexico
José Javier Samper-Zapater	Universidad de Valencia, Spain
Claudia Victoria Isaza Narvaez	Universidad de Antioquia, Colombia
Raquel Vasquez Ramirez	Instituto Tecnologico de Orizaba, Mexico
Janio Jadán Guerrero	Universidad Indoamérica, Ecuador
Severino Feliciano Morales	Universidad de Guerrero, Mexico

Local Organizing Committee

Andrea Sinche Guzmán	Universidad Agraria del Ecuador, Ecuador
Maritza Aguirre Munizaga	Universidad Agraria del Ecuador, Ecuador
Vanessa Vergara Lozano	Universidad Agraria del Ecuador, Ecuador
Karina Real Avilés	Universidad Agraria del Ecuador, Ecuador
Mayra Garzón Goya	Universidad Agraria del Ecuador, Ecuador
María del Pilar Avilés	Universidad Agraria del Ecuador, Ecuador
Raquel Gómez Chabla	Universidad Agraria del Ecuador, Ecuador
Mariuxi Tejada Castro	Universidad Agraria del Ecuador, Ecuador
Carlota Delgado Vera	Universidad Agraria del Ecuador, Ecuador
Elke Yerovi Ricaurte	Universidad Agraria del Ecuador, Ecuador
Karen Mite Baidal	Universidad Agraria del Ecuador, Ecuador
Jorge Hidalgo Larrea	Universidad Agraria del Ecuador, Ecuador
William Bazán Vera	Universidad Agraria del Ecuador, Ecuador
Wilson Molina Oleas	Universidad Agraria del Ecuador, Ecuador
Roberto Cabezas	Universidad Agraria del Ecuador, Ecuador
Teresa Samaniego Cobo	Universidad Agraria del Ecuador, Ecuador

Sponsoring Institutions

http://www.uagraria.edu.ec/

http://www.springer.com/series/7899

Contents

Cloud and Mobile Computing

Migrating SOA Applications to Cloud: A Systematic Mapping Study

Miguel Botto-Tobar[1,2(✉)], Richard Ramirez-Anormaliza[3],
Lorenzo J. Cevallos-Torres[1], and Edwin Cevallos-Ayon[3]

[1] Universidad de Guayaquil, Guayaquil, Ecuador
{miguel.bottot,lorenzo.cevallost}@ug.edu.ec
[2] Eindhoven University of Technology, Eindhoven, The Netherlands
m.a.botto.tobar@tue.nl
[3] Universidad Estatal de Milagro, Milagro, Ecuador
{rramireza,ecevallosa}@unemi.edu.ec

Abstract. Cloud Computing has emerged as an economical option to use IT resources when needed without considerations about where they are allocated or how they are delivered. Cloud Computing expands the SOA capabilities by adding scalability, elasticity and other relevant quality attributes. In this context, many companies have started to migrate their SOA applications to Cloud environments without proper support. We conducted a systematic mapping study to gather the current knowledge about existing strategies for migrating SOA applications to cloud computing. 105 papers were identified and the results show that most of the approaches follow a semi-automated (conventional) strategy for migrating to the Cloud (93%) and that most of the reported works follow a hybrid deployment model (60%). We additionally identify several research gaps such as the need for more technology-independent solutions, a common definition for concepts and resources, tool support, and validation.

Keywords: SOA · Migration · Cloud computing · Systematic mapping

1 Introduction

Cloud computing is a paradigm shift that enables scalable processing and storage over distributed, networked commodity machines [1]. The main characteristics of cloud services are: on-demand self-service, ubiquitous network access, location independent resource pooling, rapid elasticity, and measured service [2]. Cloud computing technology is classified into Infrastructure as a Service (IaaS), Platform as a Service (PaaS) and Software as a Service (SaaS). And their deployment models as public, private, community and hybrid [2].

The use of cloud services enables companies to pay only for what they use with regard to computing and network resources, rather than having to invest in IT resources, and staff to support all the hardware and software needs. Cloud computing has associated benefits and also challenges. One of these challenges

© Springer International Publishing AG 2017
R. Valencia-García et al. (Eds.): CITI 2017, CCIS 749, pp. 3–16, 2017.
DOI: 10.1007/978-3-319-67283-0_1

is related to its adoption, more specifically, the migration of existing application to cloud computing. There are few studies as reported in [3, 4] that present the evaluation of different cloud platforms for performance indicators. Nevertheless, there is not sufficient literature available to support on process for migrating existing applications to cloud.

The paper is organized as follows: Sect. 2 discusses related work. Section 3 presents the protocol we defined. Section 4 describes the results obtained. Section 5 discusses the threats to the validity of the results, and finally, Sect. 6 presents our conclusions and suggest areas for further investigation.

2   Related Work

Cloud computing is a relatively new field in software engineering, this may be a reason why there are few secondary studies related to cloud migration. Yunus presents costs and risks of application migration [5], while Louridas [6] discussed the migration of applications to the cloud examining key features of cloud offerings based on the taxonomy from [7]. Khajeh-Hosseini et al. [8] illustrated the potential benefits and risks associated with the migration of an IT system to Amazon EC2 from a broad variety of stakeholder perspectives across the enterprise, thus transcending the typical, yet narrow, financial and technical analysis offered by providers.

Kothari and Arumugam introduce guidelines to assess the feasibility of migrating applications to the cloud and suggest a general migration strategy for applications [9] while Sattaluri discusses different aspects that need to be considered during application migration [10]. On the other hand, Mossburg lists four important points that lead to a successful cloud migration [11].

All these studies are different from our work in the sense that they provide general instructions or technology-specific issues related to cloud migration and do not gather knowledge from other sources. Furthermore, these approaches are focused on the IaaS level and not to PaaS nor SaaS levels.

With respect to methodologies, cloud service providers such as Microsoft, Amazon, and Cisco also provide guidelines for migrating legacy applications to their platforms [4, 12–14]. Tran et al. [15] presented a taxonomy of critical factors emphasizing that a migration to cloud platforms is not an easy task: some changes need to be made to deal with differences in software environments, such as programming model and data storage APIs, as well as varying performance qualities.

Andrikopoulos et al. [16] focus on the challenges and solutions for each layer when migrating different parts of the application to the Cloud. They categorized different migration types and identify the potential impact and adaptation needs for each of these types on the application layers. They also investigate various cross-cutting concerns that need to be considered for the migration, and position them with respect to the identified migration types.

In our previous work [17], we conducted a similar study with fewer criteria, the results indicated research into cloud computing migration is still in its early stages. We identified research gaps: (i) MDD approach had been rarely used in the process to migrate SOA applications to Cloud environments; and (ii) Some quality characteristics which we consider relevant in applications (reliability, maintainability, portability) had not received appropriate coverage.

Finally, there are several works about how to migrate SOA and other legacy applications to the cloud but there is a need of gathering this knowledge and to identify the existing research gaps and those aspects that are well-addressed in practice.

3   Research Method

We have performed a systematic mapping study by considering the guidelines that are provided in works as those [18–20]. A systematic mapping study is a means of categorizing and summarizing the existing information about a research question in an unbiased manner. The study was performed in three stages: Planning, Conducting, and Reporting. The activities concerning the planning and conducting stages of our systematic mapping study are described in the following sub-sections and the reporting stage is presented in Sect. 4.

3.1   Planning Stage

In this stage, we performed the following activities in order to establish a review protocol: (1) Establishment of the research question; (2) Definition of the search strategy, (3) Selection of primary studies, (4) Quality assessment, (5) Definition of the data extraction strategy, and (6) Selection of synthesis methods. Each of them is explained in detail as follows.

Research question. The goal of our study is to examine the current use of strategies of migration of SOA applications to Cloud Computing environments from the point of view of the following research question: How researchers and practitioners migrate their SOA applications to Cloud Computing environments and which is the effect on the quality? Since our research question is too broad, it has been decomposed into more detailed sub-questions: RQ1: Which strategies are used to migrate Service-Oriented Architecture applications to Cloud computing environments? RQ2: Which are the consequences of the migration on the product quality? RQ3: Which type of support is used to migrating SOA applications to Cloud Computing environments? RQ4: How is addressed the academic and industry research on migrating SOA applications to Cloud Computing environments?

Search strategy. The main digital libraries that were used to search for primary studies were: IEEEXplore, ACM Digital Library, Science Direct, and Springer Link. We also manually searched on relevant conference proceedings: Cloud Computing, and IEEE CLOUD. In order to perform the automatic search of the selected digital libraries, we used a search string (see Table 1). It was carried out in March 2017, and the period reviewed included studies published from

2006 to 2016 (inclusive). This starting date was selected because 2006 was the year in which Amazon Inc. officially launched Amazon Web Services [21], and after following up the references of the preliminary studies Cloud Computing has started to appear in the Web Engineering field.

Selection of primary studies. Each study was evaluated in order to decide whether or not it should be included (considering the title, abstract and keywords). The studies that met at least one of the following inclusion criteria were included: (1) Papers presenting migration strategies SOA applications to the Cloud. (2) Papers presenting examples or empirical studies (e.g., study cases, experiments) about migration strategies to Cloud Computing environments.

Table 1. Search string applied.

Concept	Alternative terms or synonyms	
Migration	(migra* OR evolv* OR adopt* OR reus* OR mov*)	AND
Services	(soa OR service*)	AND
Cloud	cloud	

The studies that met at least one of the following exclusion criteria were excluded:

- Introductory papers for special issues, books or workshops.
- Duplicate reports of the same study in different sources.
- Papers with less than five pages.
- Papers not written in English.

Quality assessment. In addition to general inclusion/exclusion criteria, it is considered critical to assess the quality of primary studies. A three-point Likert-scale questionnaire was designed to provide a quality assessment of the selected studies. The questions were:

1. The study presents strategies to migrate SOA applications to the Cloud.
2. The study has been published in a relevant journal or conference.
3. The study has been cited by other authors.

The possible answers to these questions were: I agree (+1), Partially (0), and I do not agree (−1).

Data extraction strategy. It was based on providing the set of possible answers for each research sub-question that had been defined. The possible answers to each research sub-question are explained in more detail as follows.

With regard to RQ1 (Strategies used to migrate SOA applications to Cloud), we consider the following C1–C5 extraction criteria:

- C1: Migration strategies: we consider 2 migration strategies.
  1. Conventional: if the paper uses a manual migration strategy.
  2. MDD: if the paper uses a strategy based on models and transformations [22].
- C2: Migration approaches: we consider 4 migration approaches [23].
  1. Rehost: migration of the application without changing its architecture.
  2. Refactor: migration of the application to a different hardware environment and/or change the application infrastructure configuration without changing its external behavior.
  3. Revise: migration to modify or extend the existing base code to support legacy modernization requirements.
  4. Rebuild: migration to rebuild a solution, discarding the code of the existing application and re-architecturing the application.
- C3: Migration types: we consider 4 migration types [16].
  1. Replace components: one or more (architectural) components are replaced by cloud services.
  2. Partially migrate: to migrate some of the application functionality to the cloud, such as application layers, and architectural components.
  3. Migrate the whole software stack: to move the application that is encapsulated in VMs and run it on the cloud.
  4. Cloudify: to complete migrate the application to the cloud.
- C4: Deployments model: we consider 4 model deployments [2].
  1. Private: provisioned for exclusive use by a single organization comprising multiple consumers.
  2. Community: provisioned for exclusive use by a specific community of consumers from organizations that have shared concerns.
  3. Public: provisioned for open use by the general public.
  4. Hybrid: provisioned as a composition of two or more distinct cloud infrastructures (private, community, or public).
- C5: Service models: we consider 3 service models [2].
  1. Software as a Service (SaaS): the capability provided to the consumer is to use the provider applications running on a cloud infrastructure.
  2. Platform as a Service (PaaS): the capability provided to the consumer is to deploy onto the cloud infrastructure consumer-created or acquired applications created using programming languages, libraries, services, and tools supported by the provider.
  3. Infrastructure as Service (IaaS): the capability provided to the consumer is to provision processing, storage, networks, and other fundamental computing resources where the consumer is able to deploy and run arbitrary software, which can include operating systems and applications.
- With regard to RQ2 (C6: Quality aspects considered in the migration), we consider the quality characteristics from the ISO/IEC 25010 standard SQuaRE [24].
- With regard to RQ3 (C7: Type of support used in the migration), we consider the following answers:

1. Automated: if it presents a tool that automatically performs the entire migration or a large portion of the migration.
2. Semi-automated: if it presents a partially migration using a software tool.
3. Manual: if it presents an approach that is performed manually, signifying that the migration can be computer-aided but that the main tasks need to be performed by a human.

Finally, with regard to RQ4 (Addressing of migration), we consider the following C8–C12 extraction criteria:

– C8: Phase(s) in which the studies are based: one or more ISO/IEC 12207 [25] high-level processes:
   1. Requirements: if the artifacts that are used as input for the migration include high-level specifications of the application (e.g., task models, uses cases, usage scenarios).
   2. Design: if the migration is conducted on the intermediate artifacts that are created during the development process (e.g., navigational models, abstract user interface models, dialog models).
   3. Implementation: if the migration is conducted at the final user interface or once the application is completed.
– C9: Artifacts involved:
   1. Models/Transformations: the artifacts used for the migration include models or transformations (e.g., uses cases, class diagrams, transformations).
   2. Source code: the artifacts used for the migration include any collection of computer instructions.
   3. Others: the artifacts used for the migration include elements not mentioned above (e.g., components, tasks, VMs images, databases).
– C10: Type of validation: types of validations [26]:
   1. Survey: if it provides an investigation performed in retrospect.
   2. Case study: if it provides an observational study in which data is collected during real/simulated environments.
   3. Experiment controlled: if it provides a formal, rigorous, and controlled investigation that is based on verifying hypotheses. (d) Others: if it provides others forms not mentioned above (e.g., examples).
– C11: Usage scope: the context in which the migration strategy has been defined or used (industrial and/or academic).
– C12: Environment of use: the environment in which the migration strategy has been defined or used (mobile application, Web application, Ubiquitous, Extension).

Synthesis method. We applied both quantitative and qualitative synthesis methods. The quantitative synthesis was based on:

– Counting the primary studies that are classified in each answer from our research sub-questions.
– Counting the number of papers found in each bibliographic source per year.

The qualitative synthesis is based on including several representative studies for each criterion by considering the results from the quality assessment.

3.2 Conducting Stage

The application of the review protocol yielded the following preliminary results (see Table 2): A total of 105 research papers were therefore selected in accordance with the inclusion criteria.

Table 2. Results of conducting stage.

Source	Potential studies	Selected studies
Automated search		
IEEEXplore (IEEE)	1686	82
ACM DL (ACM)	35	8
Science Direct (SD)	431	7
Springer Link (SL)	629	3
Total	2781	100
Manual search		
CLOUD COMPUTING	8	1
IEEE CLOUD	7	4
Total	15	5
Overall results from both searches	2796	105

4 Results

The overall results, which are based on counting the primary studies that are classified in each of the answers to our research sub-questions, are presented in Table 3. The included papers which are cited in this section as [SXX] are referred to Appendix A.

Migration strategies. The results for criteria C1 (migration strategies) revealed around 93% of the papers reviewed presented conventional strategy (e.g., Babar et al. [S04], and Tran et al. [S30]). The remaining 7% of the studies reported the use of MDD strategy. MDD approaches rely on models as a means of abstracting the development process from the peculiarities of each cloud platform. These results may indicate that there are few studies that used this strategy to migrate existing system to cloud computing environment (e.g., Guillen et al. [S14], and Mohagheghi et al. [S25]).

Migration approaches. The results for criteria C2 (migration approaches) revealed that the most frequently used migration way is *rehost*, with around 72% of the papers reviewed (e.g., Li et al. [S22], and Zhou et al. [S33]). *Refactor* account for around 17% of the papers reviewed (e.g., Beserra et al. [S05], and Chee et al. [S09]). *Rebuild* account for around 11% of the papers reviewed (e.g., Cai et al. [S06], and Song et al. [S28]).

Table 3. Results of conducting stage.

Research Sub-questions	Criteria	Possible answers		# Studies	Percentage (%)
	C1: Migration strategies	Conventional		98	93
		MDD approach		7	7
	C2: Migration ways	Rehost		75	72
		Refactor		18	17
RQ1: Which strategies are used to migrate Service-Oriented Architecture applications to Cloud Computing environments?		Revise		-	-
		Rebuild		12	11
	C3: Migration types	Replace		-	-
		Partially migrate		12	12
		Migrate the whole software stack		60	57
		Cloudify		33	31
		Private		24	23
	C4: Model deployments	Community		-	-
		Public		18	17
		Hybrid		63	60
	C5: Service deployments	SaaS		31	30
		PaaS		26	25
		IaaS		48	46
RQ2: Which are the consequences of the migration on the product quality?	C6: Quality aspects	Performance efficiency		28	27
		Compatibility		7	7
		Reliability		18	17
		Security		23	22
		Maintainability		12	11
		Portability		17	16
RQ3: Which type of support is used to migrating SOA applications to Cloud Computing environments?	C7: Type of support employed	Automated	Conv.	26	25
			MDD	2	2
		Semi-Automated	Conv.	54	51
			MDD	6	6
		Manual	Conv.	17	16
			MDD	-	-
	C8: Phase(s) in which the studies are based	Analysis		9	9
		Design		6	6
		Implementation		90	86
RQ4: How is addressed the migration of SOA applications to Cloud Computing environments?	C9: Artifacts used	Models/Transformations		7	7
		Source code		47	45
		Others		51	48
	C10: Type of Validation	Survey		2	2
		Case Study		34	33
		Experiment		56	53
		Others		13	12
	C11: Approach scope	Industry		18	17
		Academy		87	83
	C12: Environment of use	Mobile Application		8	8
		Web Application		79	75
		Others (Ubiquitous)		7	7
		Extension		11	10

Migration types. The results for criteria C3 (migration types) revealed around 57% of the papers reviewed presented *Migrate the whole software stack* (e.g., Suen et al. [S29]). On the other hand, *cloudify* account for around 31% of the papers reviewed (e.g., Lamberti et al. [S21]). Lastly, *partially migrate* account for around 12% (e.g., Gerhards et al. [S12]).

Deployment models. The results for criteria C4 (deployment models) revealed around 23% of the papers reviewed select *private*. On the other hand, around 17% present *public* (e.g., Khajeh-Hosseini et al. [S20]). Finally, *hybrid* account for around 60% of the papers reviewed (e.g., Fan et al. [S11], and Hajjat et al. [S15]).

Service models. The results for criteria C5 (service deployments) revealed around 46% of the papers reviewed presented *Infrastructure as a Service* (e.g., Khajeh-Hosseini et al. [S19], and Lloyd et al. [S23]). *Platform as a Service (PaaS)* account for around 25% (e.g., Menzel et al. [S24]). Finally, *Software as a Service (SaaS)* account for around 30% of the papers reviewed (e.g., Azeemi et al. [S03]).

Quality aspects. The results for criteria C6 (quality aspects) revealed the most frequently quality aspects were *performance/efficiency* and *security* with around 27% and 22% respectively. The rationale is because of the elasticity property of applications where quick and secure deployment is typically required. Others quality aspects as *maintainability* and *compatibility* account for around 11% and 7% respectively. This is in line with some claims stated by other researchers such as "Quality aspects such as maintainability to play a minor role because the cloud providers is responsible of this part their platforms". We found following example for these aspects in Guillen et al. [S13]. On the other hand, *reliability* and *portability* account with 17% and 16% respectively received less considerations (e.g., Babar et al. [S04]).

Type of support employed. The results for criteria C7 (type of support) revealed around 6% of the papers reviewed considered *semi-automated MDD* (e.g., Guillen et al. [S14], Mohagheghi et al. [S25]) used Model-Driven Development to implement the cloud migration. On the other hand, around 16% present *manual conventional*. The findings is because they did not use any tool to carry out the cloud migration. Finally, the most addressed types of support were *semi-automated* and *automated* fulfilled in *conventional* strategy with 51% and 25% respectively. The rationale is because the majority of studies used tool that let the cloud migration with intervention of developers, or only the tool implemented the cloud migration (e.g., Juan-Verdejo et al. [S17], Kempf et al. [S18], and Khajeh-Hosseini et al. [S20]).

Phase(s) in which the studies are based. The results for criteria C8 (Phase in which the studies are based) indicated the less addressed phases were *analysis* and *design* with 9% and 6% respectively of the papers reviewed (e.g., Andrikopoulos et al. [S02], and Qiu et al. [S27]). Finally, the majority of the studies reviewed are based at *implementation*. We identified a representative example in Chen et al. [S10].

Artifacts involved. The results for criteria C9 (artifacts involved) revealed the most frequently artifacts involved was others (e.g., architecture, components, VMs, service) account for around 51 (48%) of the studies reviewed (e.g., Beserra et al. [S05]). On the other hand, *models/transformation* account for around 7% of the papers reviewed considered (e.g., Mohagheghi et al. [S25]). Lastly, around 45% of the papers reviewed implicated at *source code* (e.g., Chauhan et al. [S07]).

Type of validation. The results for criteria C10 (type of validation) revealed around 33% of the papers reviewed presented *case studies*, in order to validate their approaches. This is an encouraged result since it improves the situation described in a systematic review presented in [27] which stated a lack of rigorous empirical studies for Web Engineering research (e.g., Vu et al. [S32]). However, *others* (e.g., examples) account for around 12% (e.g., Venugopal et al. [S31]). Beside, *experiments* account for around 53%. Experiments should be more employed since they provide a high level of control and are useful for evaluating approaches in a more rigorous way (e.g., Lamberti et al. [S21]). Finally, *surveys* are the less preferred study accounting for 2%.

Approach usage. The results for criteria C11 (Approach usage) revealed the majority of the studies have been performed from the *academic* research viewpoint account for around 83% (e.g., Hao et al. [S16]). However, it is also important to note that a worthy 17% of the studies were performed from the *industry* research viewpoint (e.g., Pfitzmann et al. [S26]).

Environment of use. The results for criteria C12 (Environment of use) revealed around 75% of the papers reviewed have been performed in *web applications* (e.g., Chauhan et al. [S07]). On the other hand, around 8% of the papers reviewed have been implemented *mobile applications* (e.g., Amoretti et al. [S01]). Amoretti et al. illustrated an approach based on *service mobility*, which allows systems to cope with highly dynamic environmental conditions. *Others* (e.g., Ubiquitous) account for around 7%, and finally, the 10% of the studies have been fulfilled to *extension* (e.g., Suen et al. [S29]).

It is worthy to mention that the analysis of the number of research studies on cloud migration showed that there has been a growth of interest on this topic since 2009. Figure 1 shows the number of selected publications by year and source. We believe that this growing interest supports the relevance of conducting evidence-based studies in this area.

The criteria were combined to establish a mapping with the aim of providing an overview of migration strategies. This mapping allows us to obtain more information about how the results from each criterion are related to the others, and what the possible research gaps are. Due to space reasons, Fig. 2 only shows one of the bubble plots which is related to the comparison of criterion C1 "migration strategies" against the C2 "migration types", C9 "artifacts" and C10 "type of validation". Other bubble plots are available at http://www.win.tue.nl/~mbottoto/resources/citi2017.

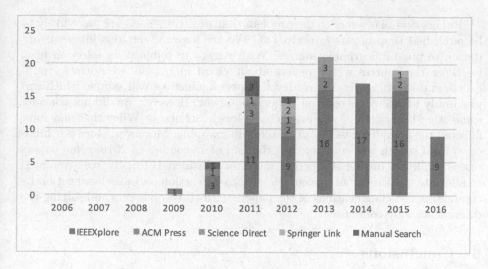

Fig. 1. Number of publications by year and source.

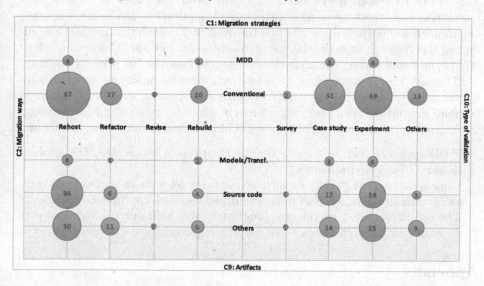

Fig. 2. Mapping results obtained from the combination of C1 against C2, C9 and C10.

5 Threats to Validity

The main limitations of this study are the scope of our research questions, publication and selection bias, inaccuracy in data extraction, and misclassification.

The scope of our research question was limited to the migration SOA applications to cloud computing environment. However, we realized during the conduction of this mapping that migration using model-driven development paradigm is an interesting extension which will be explored as further work.

Publication bias refers to the problem that positive results are more likely to be published than negative results [20]. We are aware about this inherent limitation to our bibliographic sources. With regard to publication selection bias, we chose the sources where papers about cloud migration are normally published, and we compared the retrieved papers against a small sample which was previously identified as relevant papers to appear. However, we did not consider some other bibliographic sources such as Google Scholar or Wiley that may have affected the completeness of our systematic mapping. Moreover, since our bibliographical search was conducted at the end of December of 2016, some papers not yet indexed in this last period were not considered. Finally, we attempted to alleviate the threats of inaccuracy in data extraction and misclassification by conducting the classifications of the papers with three reviewers and solving the discrepancies by consensus.

6   Conclusions

This study presented a systematic mapping study in order to address how researchers and practitioners migrate their SOA applications to Cloud Computing environments and which is the effect on the quality. Through that method we conducted this research investigating the state-of-the-art in Cloud Computing, clarifying open issues through an analysis of evidences found in 105 primary studies.

Through the answers found in a research question and four research subquestions, it was possible to identify evidence that point applications migration to cloud computing as an emerging approach, which proposes a shift of paradigm in the context of Information Technology. The principal findings of our study are:

- MDD approach had been rarely used in the process to migrate SOA applications to Cloud environments.
- Some quality characteristics which we consider relevant in applications (reliability, maintainability, portability) had not received appropriate coverage.
- The results achieved by this mapping study will help our research group to develop new research fronts about cloud computing.

Appendix

A   Excerpt of the Papers Selected

Complete list available at: http://www.win.tue.nl/~mbottoto/resources/citi2017.

S01. Amoretti M, Laghi MC, Tassoni F, Zanichelli F. Service migration within the cloud: Code mobility in SP2A, in 2010 International Conference on High Performance Computing & Simulation, 2010, 196202.

S02 Andrikopoulos V, Binz T, Leymann F, Strauch S. How to adapt applications for the Cloud environment. Computing 2012; 95: 493535.

S03. Azeemi IK, Lewis M, Tryfonas T. Migrating To The Cloud: Lessons And Limitations Of Traditional IS Success Models. Procedia Comput. Sci. 2013; 16: 737746.

S04. Babar MA, Chauhan MA. A tale of migration to cloud computing for sharing experiences and observations, in Proceeding of the 2nd international workshop on Software engineering for cloud computing - SECLOUD 11, 2011, 50.

S05. Beserra P V., Camara A, Ximenes R, Albuquerque AB, Mendonca NC. Cloudstep: A step-by-step decision process to support legacy application mi-gration to the cloud, in 2012 IEEE 6th International Workshop on the Maintenance and Evolution of Service-Oriented and Cloud-Based Systems (MESOCA), 2012, 716.

S06. Cai B, Xu F, Ye F, Zhou W. Research and application of migrating legacy systems to the private cloud platform with cloudstack. Autom. Logist. (ICAL), 2012; 400404.

S07. Chauhan MA, Babar MA. Migrating Service-Oriented System to Cloud Computing: An Experience Report. 2011 IEEE 4th Int. Conf. Cloud Comput. 2011; 404411.

S08. Chauhan MA, Babar MA. Towards Process Support for Migrating Applications to Cloud Computing, in 2012 International Conference on Cloud and Service Computing, 2012, 8087.

S09. Chee Y-M, Zhou N, Meng FJ, Bagheri S, Zhong P. A Pattern-Based Approach to Cloud Transformation, in 2011 IEEE 4th International Conference on Cloud Computing, 2011, 388395.

S10. Chen Y, Shen Q, Sun P, Li Y, Chen Z, Qing S. Reliable Migration Module in Trusted Cloud Based on Security Level - Design and Implementation, in 2012 IEEE 26th International Parallel and Distributed Processing Symposi-um Workshops & PhD Forum, 2012, 22302236.

S11. Fan C-T, Wang W-J, Chang Y-S. Agent-Based Service Migration Framework in Hybrid Cloud, in 2011 IEEE International Conference on High Perfor-mance Computing and Communications, 2011, 887892.

S12. Gerhards M, Sander V, Belloum A. About the flexible Migration of Workflow Tasks to Clouds Combining on- and off-premise Executions of Applications, in CLOUD COMPUTING 2012, The Third International Conference on Cloud Computing, GRIDs, and Virtualization, 2012, 8287.

References

1. Coombe, B.: Cloud computing-overview, advantages, and challenges for enterprise deployment. Bechtel Technol. J. **2**(1), 1–11 (2009)
2. Mell, P., Grance, T., et al.: The NIST definition of cloud computing (2011)
3. Mohagheghi, P., Sæther, T.: Software engineering challenges for migration to the service cloud paradigm: Ongoing work in the REMICS project. In: 2011 IEEE World Congress on Services, pp. 507–514. IEEE (2011)
4. Pace, E., Betts, D., Densmore, S., Dunn, R., Narumoto, M., Woloski, M.: Moving Applications to the Cloud on the Microsoft Azure Platform. Microsoft Press, Redmond (2010)

5. Yunus, M.: Understanding enterprise-to-cloud migration costs and risks. EbizQ Journal **11**, 143–152 (2010)
6. Louridas, P.: Up in the air: moving your applications to the cloud. IEEE software **27**(4), 6–11 (2010)
7. Rimal, B.P., Choi, E., Lumb, I.: A taxonomy and survey of cloud computing systems, pp. 44–51. IMS and IDC, INC (2009)
8. Khajeh-Hosseini, A., Greenwood, D., Sommerville, I.: Cloud migration: a case study of migrating an enterprise IT system to IaaS. In: 2010 IEEE 3rd International Conference on Cloud Computing, pp. 450–457. IEEE (2010)
9. Kothari, C., Arumugam, A.: Cloud application migration. Cloud. Comput. J. **5**(4), 175–189 (2010)
10. Sattaluri, R.: Application migration considerations for cloud computing. Cloud Comput. J. **77**, 0975–8887 (2011)
11. Mossburg, G.: 4 keys to success in the cloud. Gov. Comput. News Journalernment Comput. News J. **4**, 341–344 (2011)
12. Microsoft: Tips for Migrating Your Applications to the Cloud. MSDN Magazine (2010)
13. Varia, J.: Migrating your existing applications to the AWS cloud. A Phase-driven Approach to Cloud Migration (2010)
14. System, C.: Planning the Migration of Enterprise Applications to the Cloud, pp. 1–9. White Paper (2010)
15. Tran, V., Keung, J., Liu, A., Fekete, A.: Application migration to cloud: a taxonomy of critical factors. In: Proceedings of the 2nd International Workshop on Software Engineering for Cloud Computing, pp. 22–28. ACM (2011)
16. Andrikopoulos, V., Binz, T., Leymann, F., Strauch, S.: How to adapt applications for the cloud environment. Computing **95**(6), 493–535 (2013)
17. Botto, M., González-Huerta, J., Insfran, E.: Are model-driven techniques used as a means to migrate SOA applications to cloud computing? In: WEBIST (1), pp. 208–213 (2014)
18. Budgen, D., Turner, M., Brereton, P., Kitchenham, B.: Using mapping studies in software engineering. In: Proceedings of PPIG, vol. 8, pp. 195–204. Lancaster University (2008)
19. Petersen, K., Feldt, R., Mujtaba, S., Mattsson, M.: Systematic mapping studies in software engineering. EASE **8**, 68–77 (2008)
20. Kitchenham, B., Charters, S.: Guidelines for Performing Systematic Literature Reviews in Software Engineering. Technical Report, Keele University and Durham University Joint Report (2007)
21. Amazon Web Services: What is Cloud Computing by Amazon Web Services
22. Tankovic, N.: Model driven development approaches: comparison and opportunities
23. Watson, R.: How to migrate applications to the cloud (2012)
24. International Organization for Standardization: ISO/IEC 25010: Systems and Software Engineering—Systems and software Quality Requirements and Evaluation (SQuaRE)—System and Software Quality Models (2011)
25. International Organization for Standardization: ISO/IEC 12207: Standard for Information Technology—Software Lifecycle Processes (1998)
26. Fenton, N.E., Pfleeger, S.L.: Software Metrics: A Rigorous and Practical Approach, 2nd edn. PWS Publishing Co., Boston (1998)
27. Mendes, E.: A systematic review of web engineering research. In: 2005 International Symposium on Empirical Software Engineering, p. 10. IEEE (2005)

Analysis of Mobile Applications for Self-healthcare of Panamanian Patients with Hepatitis

Denis Cedeño-Moreno[1](✉) , Miguel Vargas-Lombardo[1](✉) ,
María Pilar Salas-Zárate[2] , Mario Andrés Paredes-Valverde[2] ,
and Rafael Valencia-García[2]

[1] Grupo de Investigación en Salud Electrónica y Supercomputación,
Universidad Tecnológica de Panamá, Panama City, Panama
denis.cedeno@utp.ac.com, miguel.vargas@utp.ac.pa
[2] Facultad de Informática, Universidad de Murcia,
Campus de Espinardo, 30100 Murcia, Spain
{mariapilar.salas,marioandres.paredes,valencia}@um.es

Abstract. Hepatitis B infection and liver disease are the leading causes
of cirrhosis and liver cancer in the world. The use of computer solutions
applied to the medicine is increasing every day. Scientific research in
areas of health, as well as the development of new technologies involving smartphones and sensors, is making possible self-management of
health. In this context, interest in mobile health (mHealth) applications
for self-management of diseases is growing. Hence, this research aims
to analyze this kind of applications, specifically, those ones focused on
hepatitis B. Furthermore, an ontological model for the effective management of knowledge of the hepatitis B domain is proposed in this research.

Keywords: Ontology · Hepatitis B · Mobile applications ·
Self-healthcare

1 Introduction

Hepatitis is a viral infection that causes acute and chronic disease, and sometimes death. Several types of virus have been classified: hepatitis A (HAV) and
hepatitis B (HBV), hepatitis C (HCV), hepatitis D (HDV), hepatitis E (HEV),
hepatitis G (HGV) [1].

Hepatitis B is the most common liver infection in the world. It causes hepatitis B virus (HBV) [2], which attacks the liver and injures it. The hepatitis is
passed through the blood, unprotected sex, needles shared or reused, and from
the infected mother to the newborn baby during childbirth. Most infected adults
can get rid of the hepatitis B virus without any problem, but some adults and
most infected infants and children cannot get rid of the virus which causes chronic
infections.

© Springer International Publishing AG 2017
R. Valencia-García et al. (Eds.): CITI 2017, CCIS 749, pp. 17–28, 2017.
DOI: 10.1007/978-3-319-67283-0_2

When this disease attacks the liver, it blocks the passage of bile by breaking down fat, disrupting its function of removing toxins from the blood, producing various important substances and storing and distributing glucose, vitamins and minerals. According to the World Health Organization (WHO), the hepatitis B virus infects 10 to 30 million people worldwide every year, most of them children and adolescents [3]. About 2 billion people have been exposed to the hepatitis B virus through contact with blood or infected organic fluids [4]. The infections can occur during labor, sharing infected needles, or transfusions of infected blood [5]. Symptoms of hepatitis B may not appear for up to 6 months after the time of infection. The early symptoms include: lack of appetite, fatigue, body weakness, low fever, nausea, vomiting, dyspepsia, abdominal discomfort, bleeding tendency, swelling, abdominal edema, yellow skin, turbid urine and jaundice.

The symptoms will disappear in a few weeks to months if the body is capable of combating the infection. Some people never get rid of HBV; this is known as chronic hepatitis B. People with chronic hepatitis may not have symptoms and not know they are infected. Some people may submit symptoms of chronic liver damage and cirrhosis of the liver.

In addition, hepatitis B can cause psychosocial problems, such as anxiety and withdrawal of interpersonal relationships. Such physical, psychological problems, and socio-economic problems constantly affect activities and quality of life of patients [6].

If this disease is not treated properly, it can result in death due to its many complications [7] in most developing countries (sub-Saharan Africa, for example) chronic hepatitis B represents between 8% and 15% of the population. In these countries, liver cancer associated with the hepatitis B virus is the third leading cause of cancer death.

In Panama, the incidence of hepatitis B virus reported annually is relatively low, compared to other chronic degenerative diseases, but has had a variable behavior in the last six years and it is important for health organizations to maintain a balance of the patients who have the disease in order to monitor them and stop spreading [8]. Next, Table 1 shows a balance of the number of deaths due to the hepatitis B virus, in the last 6 years in Panama.

Hepatitis B is the most common virus in Panama, 14 cases of cellular hepatic cancer were diagnosed in 2014, according to statistics from the Ministry of Health (MINSA-Panama).

Nowadays, the convergence of several areas of knowledge [9] has led to the design and implementation of computer systems using tools such as tablets, mobile phones, Internet, wireless networks [10], sensors attached to the body [11] and other devices that allow to perform monitoring [11] of various factors such as medication intake, blood pressure, and blood glucose, among others.

The management of ontological models that can shape the knowledge of domain experts, especially those of hepatitis B, is of utmost importance. Based on this understanding, we propose an ontology in order to semantically describe relations between concepts in hepatitis B domain. Ontologies allow static knowledge representation and enable knowledge sharing and reuse, thus reducing

Table 1. Number of death in Panama attributable to hepatitis B.

Year	Quantity of deaths
2009	250
2010	480
2011	279
2012	365
2013	268
2014	214

the effort needed to implement expert systems. Ontologies are currently being applied in several different domains, such as sentiment analysis [12], recommendation systems [13], natural language interfaces [14], or bioinformatics [15].

The use of these information technology solutions applied to health is increasing and there are many applications focused on the user, these applications are known as mobile health [16] or mHealth [17]. The main objective of these applications is that through any smart device it can be downloaded, installed and used, with the advantage that most of them are free. Also, mHealth applications bring useful tools for health care and for a better quality of life, such as monitor the heart rate, consult the vaccination schedule, take control of chronic diseases such as hepatitis B, and remember taking a drug and even triggering it quickly in the face of an emergency [18].

By the year 2020, 6.1 billion people, or about 70% of the world's population, will use smartphones, and at least 50% of smartphone users will use health-related mobile applications [19].

Therefore, we present an in-depth analysis of the features of Hepatitis B mobile applications. In addition, we contrast the requirements derived from evidence-based recommendations with the functions available in existing interventions.

2   Background

Nowadays, the main causes of death in Panama are mostly chronic degenerative diseases: cancer, cardiovascular disease, diabetes mellitus and hepatitis B. The WHO estimates that 46% of global disease is due to chronic diseases [20].

Panama started in the Telemedicine area in 1999, when the Documentation and Medical Information Center was created in the Faculty of Medicine of the University of Panama (UP).

In MINSA-Panama, there is a system of teleradiology, which has been operating for almost 10 years, the purpose of this project is to make teleconsultations through e-mails, queries that are sent from different regions of the interior of the country. Nowadays, Panama has a National Telemedicine and Telehealth Program, of the MINSA, where teleradiology is developed more than anything else.

There is a lack of studies in the self-management [21] of the health of patients with the virus of the hepatitis B. Although they exist in other specialties like diabetes.

When a patient with the hepatitis B virus becomes ill, clinical symptoms often do not manifest clearly in their entirety until the liver damage has progressed. In this situation, many patients do not take the disease self-management seriously, they do not inform themselves about the causes, or possible procedures, as well as they lose follow-up appointments with their specialists or they do not follow the treatment adequately due to a lack of knowledge of the disease [6].

Panama is the fourth country in the world that has the highest penetration of cellular telephony, based on the Global Index of Information Technology. The country is located below Honkong, Arabia Saudi and Montenegro. According to sources from the Ministry of Economy and Finance of Panama (MEF) and the National Institute of Census Statistics, 83.9% of households had at least one telephone cell phone.

Table 2 shows the proportion of households with cellular telephony, according to provinces and indigenous districts (data obtained from the 2010 Census).

Table 2. Proportion of households with smartphones.

Provinces and indigenous regions	Proportion of households with smartphones (%)
Total provinces	**83.9**
Bocas del Toro	72.7
Cocle	279
Colon	365
Chiriqui	85.6
Darien	71.7
Herrera	81.8
Los Santos	80.5
Panama	90.8
Varaguas	70.9
Indigenous regions	
Kuna Yala	46.5
Embera	37.3
Ngöbe Bugle	26.9

With these high percentages, the strong dependence of Panamanian households on cellular technology was sustained. On average 83 per 100 households or 8 per 10 had a smartphone.

Even in the Indian regions, where the cultural aspect is very discriminatory when deciding which technology to use, due to bias or myths, the demand for mobile telephony service was very high.

Therefore, it is important that patients with the hepatitis B virus perform self-care in order to manage their own health and well-being. Self-care is an extended concept that includes activities related to the prevention and treatment of chronic diseases, rehabilitation and health.

Adequate and active self-care of patients [22] can positively improve prognosis. Reports have indicated that knowledge of a disease [23] and self-efficacy are the main factors that can improve the self-care of patients.

However, studies have revealed low levels of knowledge of the disease in patients with hepatitis B virus, or negligence of self-care in these patients, as well as in the transmission of hepatitis virus B [24].

3   Method

3.1   Search Strategy

The search was based on online stores for mobile applications, using the search terms related to Hepatitis B to ensure that all relevant applications were detected. We chose the following keywords related to the hepatitis B virus: hepatitis B, hepatology, HBV and HCV.

This review was focused on the operating system Android. Therefore, the analysis was carried out using the Google Play Store for Android applications.

3.2   Selection Criteria

The main inclusion criteria were quantity of downloads, last update, rating, number of opinions, functionality, usability, and price. Also, We excluded applications not centered on the specific condition, based on others language different that Spanish, or those included in the category of games, entertainment, or music.

3.3   Evaluation and Assessment of Application Functionalities

Next, each one of the selected functionalities for the analysis are presented.

1. Sending reports to the doctor. This refers to the ability of the application to collect certain information and issue reports to the doctor or the person in charge of the patient's treatment.
2. Drug database. It includes commonly used reference drugs in hepatology, with emphasis on practical advice and common complications.
3. Analysis of formulas and equations. The applications present information calculations, risks or projections about diseases related to hepatitis.
4. Reminder of medication intake. This feature allows the application to send reminders of the medication to be taken by the patient according to the doctor's prescription.
5. Data storage and processing. This feature allows to store information directly in certain storage services of the phone and then perform some analysis.

6. Social networks. This functionality establishes a connection with social networks such as Facebook or chat rooms in order to communicate with other patients, send messages related with the progress achieved through the treatment followed.
7. Alerts for testing. This allows scheduling the days on which the patient should do medical examinations.
8. Reminder visits to the specialist doctor. This functionality allows the patient to receive reminders about visits to the specialist.
9. Health tips. This refers to the ability of the application to provide preventive health advice, decision-making and general information on the treated disease.
10. Access to teaching materials. Applications have access to medical journals.

4   Results

This section presents a comparative analysis of the mobile applications oriented to the management of hepatitis B. The main objective of this analysis is to know the characteristics and functionalities provided by the most popular applications in the virtual stores, and determine the main Advantages and disadvantages of these.

The applications studied are summarized in Table 3. As can be seen, iLiver is the applications more download and more popular with 50000 downloads and 150 opinions. On the other hand, the application with the highest ranking was VitalTalk Tips with a score of 5. All these applications analyzed have a score of 3 to 5 in rating. Regarding to the price, applications can be purchased from 2.33 to 56.20 dollars.

Table 3. Selected applications.

Apps	Type of mobile device	Cost	Download	Rating	No. Opinions
EASL LiverTree	Android 4.1 (and higher)	free	1000	4.5	10
GIT & Hepatology News	Android 4.0 (and higher)	free	5000	4.1	14
Healthy B	Android 2.2 (and higher)	free	5000	3.5	8
Hepatitis B Disease	Android 2.2 (and higher)	free	10000	3.9	15
HepB Story	Android 4.0 (and higher)	free	500	3	2
iLiver	Android 2.2 (and higher)	free	50000	4.4	154
iLiver Tablet	5000	free	1000	4.5	20
inPractice Hepatology	Android 4.0 (and higher)	free	500	5	3
LiverCalc	Android 2.2 (and higher)	free	10000	4.2	44
Liverpool HEP iChart	Android 4.0 (and higher)	free	10000	4.6	65
ScaleHBV	Android 4.1 (and higher)	free	50	4	1
STD Info, Symptoms & Testing	Android 2.3.3 (and higher)	free	5000	3.4	7
The Journal of Hepatology	Android 4.4 (and higher)	free	1000	4.8	6
Understanding Hepatitis B	Android 2.3.3 (and higher)	2,33	5000	4.1	12
VitalTalk Tips	Android 4.2 (and higher)	free	500	5	7

Table 4 shows the results from the analysis of the functionalities that were studied in each application selected.

Table 4. Features analysis of selected apps.

App's	Features									
	1	2	3	4	5	6	7	8	9	10
EASL LiverTree										x
GIT & Hepatology News			x	x			x	x	x	x
Healthy B			x	x			x	x	x	x
Hepatitis B Disease										x
HepB Story - Menzies									x	x
iLiver			x						x	x
iLiver Tablet			x							x
inPractice Hepatology		x							x	x
LiverCalc			x		x				x	x
Liverpool HEP iChart		x							x	x
ScaleHBV										x
STD Info, Symptoms & Testing									x	x
The Journal of Hepatology									x	x
Understanding Hepatitis B	x		x	x	x	x	x	x	x	x
VitalTalk Tips öbe Bugle									x	x

4.1 Classification of the Application

There is a very important issue in this context of health self-management applications [25] and it is the reliability of health information on the Internet addressed to non-professional users, this is a relevant topic and widely debated by professionals and patients themselves.

We have proceeded to classify the mobile applications [26] according to a series of criteria that generalize basic elements that constitute them and for these applications to be accepted by the users in general, which are: use, interest and confidence. This study classified several applications into different categories as explained below.

Self Care. The performance of self-care includes the daily activities that a patient performs to maintain his/her health. In order to measure the performance of self-care, we reviewed of different applications, especially those containing elements or modules related medical instructions, medication, manage symptoms and complications, follow up appointments, record and analyze liver function tests (ALB Albumin, ALT Alanine Transaminase). The applications that have elements that can be identified in this category and are: iLiver, Understanding Hepatitis B, LiverCalc and Healthy B Handbook.

The Understanding Hepatitis B application contains many of the elements identified for self-care of the patient, allows to register certain analyzes of patients with hepatitis (ALB, AST etc.) and send them to the patient for review. Schedule the examinations that the patient should perform, as well as reminder of appointments and taking medications.

The Healthy B Handbook application contains some elements within this category of self-care. For example, a module that calculates the "liver cancer risk forecast", records the levels of ALT and other antigens and projects the probability of having liver cancer. Also, it has module of reminder of exams to be realized, visits to the specialist and taking of medicines.

The LiverCalc application includes the formulas and equations used in the daily evaluations of patients with liver disease, such as cirrhosis, hepatitis, and liver transplantation. This innovative calculator allows calculating 17 hepatic parameters in a single panel, ensuring convenience and accuracy. LiverCalc facilitates the organization and processing of patient data. It is an application intuitive and very easy to use.

Drug Database. In hepatitis therapy, patients take more than one drug at the same time and other drugs to treat coexisting conditions. Many of the drug combinations have the potential to interact and this can affect patient safety or treatment efficacy. Two of the applications analyzed, inPractice Hepatology and Liverpool HEP iChart, fall into this category.

With regards to inPractice Hepatology, it is a complete database of drugs. The physician specifies the drug and the application brings the required information. It was approved by the Food and Drug Administration (FDA). Also, this application has access to summaries of PubMed which is a database with information and clinical trials.

Liverpool HEP iChart contains a database of drugs, where the patient or doctor selects the medicines to be evaluated and through a dashboard shows with color the results after of analyzing them, which determine if there are opposite reactions between them. The results are presented as a system of "Traffic light" (red, yellow, green) to indicate the recommendation.

Knowledge of the Disease. To be aware of his/her treatment and self-management of the disease, the patient must have access to information that allows him/her to know everything related to his/her disease. Most of the applications analyzed fall into this category, approximately 95% are focused on teaching and/or training.

The Hepatitis B Disease application gives the patient complete information about the disease, such as symptoms, causes, diagnoses, treatments and prevention.

Understanding Hepatitis B is an informational application about hepatitis B disease and has a FAQ section.

STD is an application that is approved by the FDA and allows a patient anonymously through a series of questionnaires to determine what type of sexually transmitted disease can have, including hepatitis B.

HepB Story provides information on how the virus. Also, it provides information about stages of illness, symptoms, as well as details on immunization and treatment. There is also a section with information for women dealing with mother-to-child transmission of the virus and ways to prevent it.

SCALE HBV provides counseling guidance to address patients' questions and concerns about the prevention, testing, and treatment of hepatitis B.

The Journal of Hepatology application publishes original papers, reviews, case reports and letters to the Editor concerned with clinical and basic research in the field of hepatology. We also find the iLiver application that is for professional use that provides immediate medical information and clinical recommendations for medical experts. This application contains information specifically related to liver disease.

It is important to note that of the applications analized, only two of them have access to PubMed that allows access to bibliographic databases such as MEDLINE, these applications are GIT & Hepatology News and inPractice Hepatology.

Applications for Doctors. This category consists of applications that can provide useful information to the medical specialist such as reports and statistics. This information allows to the specialist to carry out monitoring of patients with diabetes. SCALE B is an application that provides clinicians with an easy way to link patients with local HBV specialists based on zip code, city or state of patients.

The main objective of InPractice Hepatology is intended to meet the needs of medical specialists, hepatologists, gastroenterologists, infectious disease clinicians and others who treat patients with viral hepatitis, including HBV and HCV. The iLiver application provides immediate medical information and clinical recommendations for medical experts.

Social Forums/Blogs. This category consists of applications that allow interaction between people with hepatitis B, aiming to share information and experiences. An example of this application is "Understanding Hepatitis B".

5   Ontological Model

In this work, we present a model based on the construction of an ontology for the hepatitis B domain. This ontology represent a detail every facet of the Hepatitis disease. Among the main aspects included are types of patients depending on the level of reagent obtained in the tests: Anti-HBc, Anti-HBs and HBsAg; the phenotypes of the disease describe both the causes as well as the symptoms of the disease; and treatments administered to a patient in a chronic condition, either antiviral or injectable. This ontology is described using the second version of the Web Ontology Language (OWL2). The ontology defines 37 classes, 3 data type properties, 8 object properties, 8 individuals and 183 axioms. An excerpt of the ontology is shown in Fig. 1.

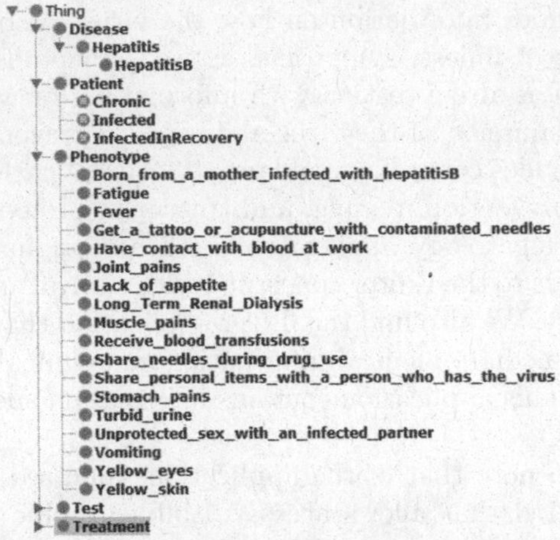

Fig. 1. Extract the ontology of the hepatitis B domain.

In the model, we can see, the Phenotype hierarchy represents observable characteristics of the Hepatitis B disease, such as symptoms or causes. For example, some of the symptoms of the Hepatitis B disease are Fatigue, Fever or Muscle-Pains. On the other hand some of the causes are Share-Needles-During-Drug-Use, Receive-Blood-Transfusion or Long-Term-Renal-Dialysis. All these classes are related to the Hepatitis B class by means of the isSymptompsOf and isCauseOf object property.

The Test hierarchy represents the kind of tests that are done to a patient with Hepatitis B (i.e. Anti-HBs, Anti-HBc and HBsAg). The values of these test determine the level of the disease into Chronic, Infected or InfectedInRecovery that are equivalent classes. For example, if all the tests are positive for a particular patient then the level of her/his disease is Chronic.

It is important to mention the relationship isTreatmentOf that represents the type of treatment that should be recommended to patients with Hepatitis B. There are different treatments, such as, Antiviral, Injectable or Oral.

Finally, the ontology includes some axioms to inferred new knowledge such as the kind of recommended treatments from the state or level of the disease.

6 Conclusion

Although the Central America region is under development, Panama country has important technological and communications infrastructure that allows it to advance and adapt new services based on mobile devices, as well as Internet services.

There is also high demand for public health services and the number of patients at different levels of hospital care is growing rapidly, especially those with chronic degenerative diseases such as hepatitis B.

The use of health technologies, e-health and m-health can play an important role in the health strategies of the country. A strategy should be definitively established to regulate and propose appropriate methodologies for the use of health technologies, taking care of the patient's intimacy with potential chronic diseases such as diabetes.

It is also necessary to establish an evaluation agency in health technology and to adequately promote services that allow the Panamanian population to be educated in the adoption of new health care services.

Acknowledgement. This work has been developed under the ERASMUS-Cruz del Sur grant. Also, this work has been supported by the Spanish National Research Agency (AEI) and the European Regional Development Fund (FEDER/ERDF) through project KBS4FIA (TIN2016-76323-R). María del Pilar Salas-Zárate and Mario Andrés Paredes Valverde are supported by the National Council of Science and Technology (CONACYT), the Secretariat of Public Education (SEP) and the Mexican government. Likewise, we are grateful for the support provided by the National Secretariat of Science and Technology of Panama (SENACYT), through the National Research System (SNI), to the GISES-CIDITIC Research Group.

References

1. Hadler, S.C., Fay, O.H., Pinheiro, F.P., Maynard, J.: La hepatitis en las Américas: informe del grupo colaborador de la OPS. Bol. Oficina Sanit. Panam. (OSP) **103**(3), 185–209 (1987)
2. Shepard, C.W., Simard, E.P., Finelli, L., Fiore, A.E., Bell, B.P.: Hepatitis B virus infection: epidemiology and vaccination. Epidemiol. Rev. **28**(1), 112–125 (2006)
3. PKIDs: Diseases, Hepatitis B en Niños
4. Pyrsopoulos, N.T.: Reactivation of hepatitis B. Hepatology **49**(S5), S156–S165 (2009)
5. Tseng, T., Liu, C., Yang, H., Su, T., Wang, C., Chen, C., Kuo, S.F., Liu, C., Chen, P., Chen, D., Kao, J.: High levels of hepatitis B surface antigen increase risk of hepatocellular carcinoma in patients with low HBV load. Gastroenterology **142**(5), 1140–1149 (2012)
6. Che, Y.H., You, J., Chongsuvivatwong, V., Li, L., Sriplung, H., Yan, Y.Z., Ma, S.J., Zhang, X., Shen, T., Chen, H.M., Rao, S.F., Zhang, R.Y.: Dynamics and liver disease specific aspects of quality of life among patients with chronic liver disease in Yunnan, China. Asian Pac. J. Cancer Prev. APJCP **15**(12), 4765–71 (2014)
7. Cantudo-Cuenca, M.R., Robustillo-Cortés, M.A., Cantudo-Cuenca, M.D., Morillo-Verdugo, R.: A better regulation is required in viral hepatitis smartphone applications. Farmacia Hospitalaria: Organo Oficial de Expresion Cientifica de la Sociedad Espanola de Farmacia Hospitalaria **38**(2), 112–117 (2014)
8. Panama Ministry of Health: indicadores de salud bÁsicos. Panamá **2014**, 1–26 (2014)

9. Maier, R.: Knowledge Management Systems: Information and Communication Technologies for Knowledge Management. Springer, New York (2007)

10. Davies, E., Davies, E., Sanjay, K.: A survey on wireless body area network. Int. J. Sci. Res. Publ. **4**(3), 1–7 (2014)

11. Movassaghi, S., Abolhasan, M., Lipman, J., Smith, D., Jamalipour, A.: Wireless body area networks: a survey. IEEE Commun. Surv. Tutorials **16**(3), 1658–1686 (2014)

12. Salas-Zárate, M.D.P., Valencia-García, R., Ruiz-Martínez, A., Colomo-Palacios, R.: Feature-based opinion mining in financial news: an ontology-driven approach. J. Inf. Sci. **1**, 016555151664552 (2016)

13. Carrer-Neto, W., Hernández-Alcaraz, M.L., Valencia-García, R., García-Sánchez, F.: Social knowledge-based recommender system. Application to the movies domain. Expert Syst. Appl. **39**(12), 10990–11000 (2012)

14. Paredes-Valverde, M.A., Ángel Rodríguez-García, M., Ruiz-Martínez, A., Valencia-García, R., Alor-Hernández, G.: ONLI: an ontology-based system for querying DBpedia using natural language paradigm. Expert Syst. Appl. **42**(12), 5163–5176 (2015)

15. Mayor, C., Robinson, L.: Ontological realism, concepts and classification in molecular biology. J. Documentation **70**(1), 173–193 (2014)

16. Jeon, J.H.: Evaluation of a smartphone application for self-care performance of patients with chronic hepatitis B: a randomized controlled trial. Appl. Nurs. Res. **32**, 182–189 (2016)

17. Gallagher, J., ODonoghue, J., Car, J.: Managing immune diseases in the smartphone era: how have apps impacted disease management and their future? Expert Rev. Clin. Immunol. **11**(4), 431–433 (2015)

18. Jeon, J.H., Kim, K.: Development of mobile app for self-management performance of patients with CHB. Adv. Sci. Technol. Lett. Mech. Eng. **129**, 229–233 (2016)

19. Miller, A.S., Cafazzo, J.A., Seto, E.: A game plan: gamification design principles in mHealth applications for chronic disease management. Health Inf. J. **22**(2), 184–193 (2016)

20. Bengmark, S.: Curcumin: an atoxic antioxidant and natural NF-~B, Cyclooxygenase-2, lipooxygenase, and inducible nitric oxide synthase inhibitor: a shield against acute and chronic diseases. Am. Soc. Parenter. Enteral Nutr. **30**(1), 1–7 (2006)

21. Krishna, S., Boren, S.A., Balas, E.A.: Healthcare via cell phones: a systematic review. Telemedicine e-Health **15**(3), 231–240 (2009)

22. Wagner, E.H., Austin, B.T., Korff, M.V.: Organizing care for patients with chronic illness. Milbank Q. **74**(4), 511 (1996)

23. Kennedy, A., Rogers, A., Bower, P.: Support for self care for patients with chronic disease. BMJ (Clinical research ed.) **335**(7627), 968–970 (2007)

24. Dahlström, E., Funegård Viberg, E.: Knowledge about hepatitis B virus infection and attitudes towards hepatitis B virus vaccination among Vietnamese university students in Ho Chi Minh City : - A quantitative study. Uppsala Universitet 1–39 (2013)

25. Demidowich, A.P., Lu, K., Tamler, R., Bloomgarden, Z.: An evaluation of diabetes self-management applications for Android smartphones. J. Telemedicine Telecare **18**(4), 235–238 (2012)

26. Lorig, K., Ritter, P.L., Pifer, C., Werner, P.: Effectiveness of the chronic disease self-management program for persons with a serious mental illness: a translation study. Commun. Ment. Health J. **50**(1), 96–103 (2014)

Intelligent Agents and Semantic Web Services: Friends or Foes?

Francisco García-Sánchez[1](✉) 🆔
and Héctor Hiram Guedea-Noriega[2] 🆔

[1] DIS, Faculty of Computer Science, University of Murcia, 30100 Murcia, Spain
frgarcia@um.es
[2] Escuela Internacional de Doctorado, University of Murcia,
30100 Murcia, Spain
hector.guedea@um.es

Abstract. Some controversial approaches have derived from the discussion about the scope of the well-established Multiagent Systems technology, and the functionality expected from the ever-evolving Web Services technology. While some authors in the field of intelligent agents state that Semantic Web Services can be also viewed as services provided by agents distributed all over the Internet using semantic mark-up, others believe that the agent functionality can be integrated in the core of intelligent Web Services. A converging trend claims that the next generation Web will be integrated by both agents and Web services working seamlessly. In this work, we establish a set of parameters within three different dimensions, namely, general issues, matureness level, and applicability, by means of which these technologies can be evaluated and compared. From the results of this study we conclude that both technologies are completely inter-operable and the strength of their union depends on the way it is achieved.

Keywords: Multiagent systems · Internet of Services · Semantic Web

1 Introduction

The Intelligent Agents (IAs) field has been broadly studied over the last 40 years and nowadays the topic under question is being revisited thanks to its relation to the Semantic Web (SW) and the potential benefits that can be reached from their potential integration [1, 2]. IAs emerged due to the promising benefits of having applications with a technology that allows applications to decide for themselves what they need to do in order to satisfy their design objectives. IAs are mainly characterized by four properties [3]: autonomy, social ability, reactivity, and proactiveness. Furthermore, agents hardly ever operate isolated but they exist in environments that contain other agents, so constituting multiagent systems (MASs). There exist several application fields where agents can be applied [4], including systems and networks management, mobile access and management, mail and messaging, information access and management, collaboration, workflow and administrative management, electronic commerce, and adaptive user interfaces. Nevertheless, agents face the problems derived from the lack of structure in the information published on the current Web.

© Springer International Publishing AG 2017
R. Valencia-García et al. (Eds.): CITI 2017, CCIS 749, pp. 29–43, 2017.
DOI: 10.1007/978-3-319-67283-0_3

On the other hand, Web Services (WS) have arisen as the best solution for remote execution of functionality [5]. This is due to some promising properties such as operating systems and programming languages independence, interoperability, ubiquity, loosely coupled applications, etc. However, as the Web grows in size and diversity, there is an increased need to automate aspects of WS such as their discovery, execution, selection, composition and interoperation. The problem is that current technology around WS (e.g. UDDI, WSDL, and SOAP) provides limited support for all what has been pointed out before [6].

The emergence of the SW [7] involved the overcome of the mentioned drawbacks for both IAs [8] and WS [6]. SW technology aims at adding semantics to the data published on the Web (i.e., it attempts to establish the meaning of the data), so that machines are able to process these data in a similar way a human can do. Therefore, IAs can exploit the semantics to perform their assigned tasks in a better way. On the other hand, WS capability descriptions can be semantically annotated so that automatic discovery, composition, and invocation can be achieved. One might think that the next obvious step towards more powerful Web applications should be the mixture of IA and Semantic Web Service (SWS) technologies, which by working together can make the Next Generation Web become real [9]. However, some controversial approaches have appeared at this point. While some researchers claim that services can be part of agents' functionalities [10, 11], others state that WS can include all kinds of behaviors [12].

The aim of this document is to clarify as much as possible whether IAs and SWS are compatible or not. With this goal in mind, a comparison framework has been designed to evaluate both technologies. The framework contemplates three different dimensions: general issues, matureness level, and applicability. A wide study of each of these dimensions has been done. From the results obtained in our research, the feasibility and appropriateness of integrating together these two technologies can be concluded.

The rest of the paper is organized as follows. Section 2 offers a brief description of IA and SWS technologies. In Sect. 3, a comparison framework is established with the purpose of determining the pros and cons of both technologies and whether they are compatible or not. A broad study is presented and a summary with the main results is given. Finally, in Sect. 4 the feasibility and advantage of integrating IA and SWS technologies are discussed, some related work is presented and future work is briefly explained.

2   State of the Art

2.1   IAs

A common accepted definition of the term 'Agent' determines that an agent is a computer system placed in some environment and capable of autonomous action in this environment in order to meet its design objectives [3]. Wooldridge also highlights that an agent has to fulfil some properties in order to become intelligent: reactivity (the ability to perceive its environment and respond to changes in it in a timely fashion), pro-activeness (the ability to exhibit goal-directed behavior by taking the initiative), and social ability (the ability to interact with other agents). Agents can be useful as stand-alone entities that are delegated particular tasks on behalf of a user. However, in most cases agents exist in environments that contain other agents, constituting MASs. A MAS can be seen as a system consisting of a group of agents that can potentially interact with each other [13]. These agents can either cooperate (if they have the same global objective) or compete (they have different yet conflictive objectives). In this latter case, a negotiation mechanism, such as auctions or argumentation-based nego-tiation, becomes necessary [14]. Some design methodologies have been proposed to facilitate the development process of MASs [15].

The research in this field is following several paths. A standardization process related to all the concepts pertaining to the Multiagent field is under consideration. FIPA (The Foundation for Intelligent Physical Agents) [16], currently an IEEE Computer Society standards organization, seeks to standardize several aspects of the agent-based technology. FIPA offers architectural guidelines and specifications for constructing agents and agent platforms. It also defines open standard interfaces for accessing agent management services, the human agent interaction part of an agent system, security management and facilities for securing interagent communication, software agent mobility, and some other issues. FIPA aims at enabling the interoperation of hetero-geneous software agents, and has developed some specifications with a group of nor-mative rules that permit an agent society to operate among themselves. These rules include some necessary agent's roles for the platform and agent management.

Agents negotiation is another very active research field [14, 17]. Negotiation becomes essential when a group of individual agents who have different yet conflictive objectives form a MAS. It can be defined as the process by means of which several agents communicate and commit themselves to reach a mutually beneficial agreement. Other interesting issues under scrutiny in this context are security [18] and commu-nication protocols [19]. Although MASs security has been arduously treated, several additional factors need to be addressed for agents autonomously acting on behalf of their owner, especially in open agent systems. Ensuring user confidence and trust in this kind of applications is a basic requirement. On the other hand, after reaching an agreement over the use of agent protocols and languages (likely, public libraries of alternative protocols), and of standard, agent-specific design methodologies in open agent systems in specific domains, truly-open and fully-scalable MASs across domains will probably be more popular.

2.2 SWS

A WS can be defined in a simple way as a service located at some location on the Internet that can be accessed through a standard protocol. The key to WS is on-the-fly software creation through the use of loosely coupled, reusable software components in such a way that software can be delivered and paid for as fluid streams of services [20]. WS tech-nology is not an innovative idea, since techniques such as DCOM, RMI and CORBA have been previously applied for remote execution of functionality. Although they work properly on local networks, they fail when transposed to a web environment. The difference between WS and other pre-existing remote procedure call (RPC) methods is that, by using SOAP, XML messages are passed over plain HTTP (also SMTP), thus avoiding firewall problems and allowing for "RPC over the Web" [20].

The continuous evolution of the services landscape, from SOAP services to REST services through cloud services and mobile services, has given rise to the so called 'Internet of Services' [21]. The European Commission defines the Internet of Services as *"a vision of the Internet of the Future where everything that is needed to use software applications is available as a service on the Internet, such as the software itself, the tools to develop the software, the platform (servers, storage and communication) to run the software...Anybody who wants to develop applications can use the resources in the Internet of Services to develop them. Advantages of the "Internet of Services" include the little investments needed upfront to develop an application and the possibility to build upon other people's efforts. The risk involved in pursuing new business ideas is diminished, and might lead to more innovative ideas being tried out in practice"* [22].

With all, WS try to transform the Web into a global infrastructure for distributed computation, application integration and business process automation. However, as the Web grows in size and diversity, there is an increased need to automate aspects of WS such as automatic discovery, execution, selection, composition and interoperation. The problem is that the syntactic nature of WS underpinning technologies provide limited support for all that [20]. The SW [7] aims at adding machine-processable semantic content to the data published on the Web so that computers can 'understand' and process the information in a similar way to that done by a human. Several different approaches have been conceived to add semantics to service descriptions [23–25]. The joint application of SW and WS to create intelligent WS is referred as SWS [26]. The main formalisms to semantically annotate WS are the Web Ontology Language for Services (OWL-S), the Web Service Modelling Ontology (WSMO) and the Semantic Annotations for the Web Services Description Language (SAWSDL).

3   Agents Versus Services

There are different opinions among the researchers about what WS and what IAs are, and whether they are compatible or not. Many researchers coming from the WS community think that all software components can be seen as a WS, which can incorporate all kinds of behaviors [12]. Unlike this opinion, part of the agent community considers that WS can be viewed as (a part of) an agent [10, 11]. In this section, we propose an evaluation framework by means of which we can compare and contrast both technologies.

3.1   Comparison Framework

To establish an objective framework with which to compare the above referred fields, a number of relevant criteria can be specified. Three dimensions (see Table 1) can thus be defined. First, we propose a general dimension, which refers to the most common aspects of the technologies. This dimension refers to information about the knowledge a programmer, designer or modeler must possess prior to being capable of effectively

Table 1. A comparison of IAs and SWS

Comparison framework
1. General
a. Epistemological assumptions
b. Key enabling technology
c. Autonomy degree
d. Flexibility
e. Interactivity
2. Matureness level
a. Supporting infrastructure
b. Languages
c. Development methodologies
d. Platforms
e. Security
f. Degree of standardization
g. Global matureness
3. Applicability
a. Task types
b. Application areas
c. Application level in industry
d. Successful tools implemented

using the technology (epistemological assumptions), these one's autonomy degree regarding user interaction, the flexibility or adaptation possibilities, and the key enabling technology.

The second dimension, the matureness level, refers to the state of the art found for these technologies, regarding aspects such as the languages, platforms, and methodologies developed for the technology under question to implement effective real applications. This dimension also accounts for technology security issues and standardization degree. This dimension is summarized by depicting an overall view of the global matureness for each above-mentioned aspect.

The last dimension is that of applicability. It refers to the impact of MAS and SWS technologies on the real world. This dimension provides information about application areas where these technologies are being applied, tasks they are suited to (e.g., planning, search, diagnosis, etc.), their (successful) implantation in industry, and the tools that have been developed by making use of them.

We do not pretend to present a broad study nor being exhaustive about each of these issues but to depict the main points related to these innovative fields.

3.2 IAs Analysis

General

Epistemological assumptions. IA research has been influenced by work done in a number of fields including Artificial Intelligence (e.g., reasoning theory and artificial life), Software Engineering (e.g., object-oriented programming and distributed processing), and Human-Computer Interaction (e.g., user modelling and cognitive engineering). Therefore, it is needed for the designer or modeler of IAs to possess knowledge about techniques such as case-based reasoning and neural networks, object and role-oriented programming, and user profiling among others.

Key enabling technology. Since the IAs field is related to several others, it is difficult to determine a single key enabling technology. Instead, many different technologies form the core of agents systems: ontologies for the establishment of a common vocabulary, protocols for remote execution of functionality, languages for the communication and the negotiation among agents, knowledge management and learning procedures for the achievement of intelligent tasks. Recently, WS have been included in the list of the agents supporting infrastructure.

Autonomy degree. A major ability of agents is autonomy, which implies that an agent takes initiative and grips the control of its own actions. The autonomy is achieved by means of several characteristics such as goal-oriented behavior (the agent accepts high-level request indicating what a person wants and is responsible for deciding how and where to satisfy the requests), collaborative actions (it can modify request or even refuse them – if it thinks it is not worth to do it), and flexibility (it can dynamically choose which actions to invoke by taking into account the state of its external environment). Therefore, the maximum autonomy degree is achieved by IAs. It is quite logical if we consider that one of the main goals assumed by their creators was that users do not have to worry about tedious and repetitive tasks.

Flexibility and Interactivity. Both individual agents and MASs are flexible. IAs are called 'intelligent' mainly because they can learn, so that they show a dynamic behavior dependent on the situation as it has been mentioned above. In the same way, when a set of IAs join forming a MAS, they show a global, flexible and dynamic behavior. A goal can be achieved in several ways and, depending on the knowledge each agent possesses, the goal will be performed in one way or another. Besides, IAs interact with other agents apart from interacting with the users they act on behalf of. The interactivity with other agents is very important as in most situations an individual agent is not able to perform a task by itself. It is because an agent hardly ever has a complete knowledge of its environment. In such a situation, the cooperation with other agents becomes necessary to achieve a goal.

Matureness Level

Platforms, languages, and degree of standardization. MASs are a sub-field of computer science that have been studied since about 1980. This field has only gained widespread recognition since about the mid-1990s. Since then, the interest in the field has grown rapidly. This rapid evolution has been reflected in some standardization initiatives. Much of the agent standardization effort has fallen into the Foundation for Intelligent Physical Agents (FIPA) and the Object Management Group (OMG). In terms of languages, the most widespread are the Knowledge Query and Manipulation Language (KQML) proposed by the US-based DARPA-funded Knowledge Sharing Effort (KSE), and

FIPA-ACL (FIPA Agent Communication Language). Some FIPA-compliant agent platforms have been released such as, for example, JADE, ZEUS and FIPA-OS.

Supporting infrastructure. A major obstacle for the adoption of agent technologies has been the lack of infrastructure able to support the creation of dynamic and heterogeneous networks of devices and services that is central to the support of significant agent-based systems. In the last few years, several technologies have emerged that can facilitate agent-based systems development. Among them, WS are the most promising because they provide for a platform- and programming language-independent solution that can deal with messages exchange, services description and their publication and discovery. All these capabilities are necessary for any agent-based architecture. Other important contributions in this sense are internet technologies (e.g., XML, RDF, and lately the SW), remote procedure call (RPC) (e.g., RMI, CORBA), and distributed object technologies. All these technological developments are responding to some of the underlying infrastructural needs for agent-based systems.

Development methodologies. Another fundamental obstacle to the acceptance of agent technology is the lack of mature software development methodologies for agent-based systems. Based on principles of software and knowledge engineering, augmented to suit the differing demands of this new paradigm, several methodologies have been proposed. The most employed are MAS-CommonKADS (an extension of CommonKADS), MaSE (Multi-agent systems Software Engineering), ZEUS (Belief-Desire-Intention agents), GAIA (a set of entities that execute interactions), and INGENIAS (an evolution of MESSAGE), but there is no common accepted one (they need to maturate).

Security. Security is a central issue for MASs as they are characterized by an intrinsic openness, heterogeneity and because of the autonomous and potentially self-interested nature of the agents therein. So far, the main focus of the work with the FIPA agent platform has been related to specification, development, and testing of this platform, while little effort has been made on investigating security issues. Although currently deployed agent applications often provide good means of security, several additional factors need to be addressed. Security issues such as the problem of agents authentication, securing communication, and preventing unauthorized activity from hackers or malevolent agents among others should be studied.

Global matureness. To summarize, although the agent field has been studied over the last 30 years, more effort should be made in order to standardize all the issues concerning agent technologies. Special care should be taken in security issues, as this is a key factor for the migration of the technology to the industry in real applications.

Applicability

Task types. The current applications of agents are rather experimental and ad hoc ones. IAs aim to solve problems that require the application of knowledge, that is, intelligence. Examples of knowledge-intensive tasks are classification, assessment, diagnosis, monitoring, prediction, design, modelling, planning, scheduling and assignment. Methods to solve these kinds of tasks may be included in the core of IAs' design.

It is also usual to find agents acting autonomously on behalf of a user. These users try to save their time by delegating repetitive tasks to software agents that should achieve them with minimum interaction of users.

Application areas. In [3], the author divides the possible application of agents into two main groups: distributed systems and personal software assistants. Systems and network management is one of the earliest application areas to be enhanced using IAs technology. Agents can help filter and take automatic actions at a higher level of abstraction, and can even be used to detect and react to patterns in systems behavior. Another area where agents can act is mobile access and management. In this environment, IAs, which reside in the network rather than on the users' personal computers, can address the needs of such an unstable environment by persistently carrying out user requests despite network disturbances. Mail and messaging applications, information access and management, electronic commerce, etc., are some other application areas.

Industrial applications. The three industry sectors most likely to have the greatest impact from the application of agent systems are telecommunications and networks, manufacturing, and transport. Currently, IAs are being applied in industries such as: telecommunications, manufacturing, finance, air traffic management, aerospace, eCommerce, customer management, defense simulation and decision support, government services, education, and product support /helpdesk.

Successful tools implemented. Several IA applications have been developed in health care. IAs have been also applied extensively for network management. Another broad application field for IAs is eCommerce. A list of tools implemented by using agent technologies can be found in the AgentLink Web site [27].

3.3   SWS Analysis

General

Epistemological assumptions and Key enabling technologies. SWS come from the mixture of SW and WS technologies. Thus, many of their properties are derived from those ground technologies. The key enabling technologies for SWS are ontologies and WS. Ontologies, which are the backbone of the SW, are used to add semantics to the data published on the Internet. On the other hand, WS transform the Web from a distributed source of information to a distributed source of functionality. WS capabilities are described by means of ontologies in the world of SWS. Hence, the epistemological assumptions for SWS can be deduced from those of both, SW and WS. While people within the SW field should have a broad background on the area of knowledge representation and, in particular, ontologies, those related to the WS field should know the basis for remote procedure calls (RPCs) and have clear ideas about component-based programming and distributed computing.

Autonomy degree. The autonomy degree here is lesser than for IAs. However, the necessity of a payment in order to get a WS to perform a task can be seen in some way as an autonomy act. Furthermore, once the execution of a WS has started it is likely that the user interaction becomes unnecessary. Nonetheless, with semantics added to WS the degree of autonomy raises up since it is possible to automatically discover, compose, invoke and monitor WS.

Flexibility. If we consider SWS as a whole, we can observe a dynamic behavior. A SWS framework can adapt itself according to changes in its environment. However, this is not the case for WS as individuals. Globally, depending on the services available in a specific period of time, the execution of a high-level task can be performed in different ways and it is possible to obtain different results. On the other hand, if WS are considered as individual entities then we find out that their behavior is not adaptable, and they are not able to learn: a WS executes the same actions once and again each time the service is required.

Interactivity. Finally, we can point out that SWS are fully interactive. Actions may be initiated by either the user (by means of agents) or other WS. In a common environment, we can find users asking their agents for the execution of different tasks. Then, these agents will request WS for the services they advertise. At the end, WS interact among themselves for services execution.

Matureness Level

Infrastructure. The supporting infrastructure for SWS is the one inherited from WS (software components that should be published somehow and can interact with each other) and SW (language for incorporating semantics into web content). Besides, most of the researchers in this field claim that an ontology for describing WS is needed. Two ontology models have been proposed for this purpose [26]: OWL-S and WSMO. Another possibility is to extend WSDL with semantic annotations as established in the SAWSDL proposal [26].

Languages. For SWS to become a reality, a markup language is needed to describe WS capabilities. That language must be descriptive enough so that a computer can automatically determine its meaning. The goal is to facilitate the automatic discovery, composition, invocation, and monitoring of WS. A language with these characteristics can be taken from the SW. The most extended ones are OWL and WSML.

Development methodologies. There are not methodologies either for SWS or for WS development. However, some efforts are being made in the field of Service Oriented Architecture (SOA) to obtain a methodology from the patterns already devised. A methodology for development and deployment of applications using SW technology should be the result of combining standard software development methodologies with those for knowledge-based applications adapted to SW technologies' particularities.

Platforms. SWS infrastructures can be characterized along three dimensions: usage activities (functional requirements that a framework should support), architecture (components needed for accomplishing the activities), and service ontology (ontology for describing WS capabilities). So far, some approaches such as WSMX and IRS-II present a complete infrastructure that (intend to) include most of the required functionalities (i.e., discovery, composition, invocation) within one platform [26].

Security. Security consists of maintaining confidentiality, integrity and availability of software, hardware and data. A key enabler of the development and future deployment of SWS is the creation and adoption of an effective security model for the current generation of WS. Despite being a major inhibitor for implementing WS, little effort has been made on security issues. So far, the main focus of the work with this technology has been related to the specification and development of ontologies for WS capabilities description. However, it is likely that effective security models for WS be extended to be applied to the SWS field. The conclusion is that to ensure the future success of SWS, it is important to develop a flexible and expandable security architecture for the current generation of WS.

Standardization degree. The standardization process of this technology is almost non-existent. The ontology for describing the WS capabilities, which is the most basic element to be established, is not a standard yet. OWL-S, WSMO and SAWSDL are the most promising approaches [26], but SAWSDL is the only W3C recommendation. Certainly, no other standards have been defined in this field, although it is expected that solutions obtained in the two sub-fields the SWS come from will be inherited and adapted.

Global matureness. The matureness of SWS is tightly related to the development of its two base technologies, that is, WS and the SW. While WS have been studied deeply over the last few years and its core is based on well-established concepts such as RPC and distributed computing, the SW was firstly envisioned in 2001. To sum up, SWS need a long way to become steady. Hard work is needed in areas such as security and development methodologies. We believe that after a global approach (i.e., OWL-S, WSMO, SAWSDL) is chosen, the remainder standardization process will be easier.

Applicability

Task types. The tasks which a software developed by using SWS best fits do not require any knowledge/intelligence. The behavior of the service is established at design time and no adaptive actions dependent on the environment are implemented. The services are intended to interact with the business process of a company. While IAs were conceived to act proactively without user interaction, a WS cannot decide what to do by itself. Thus, we will refer to the tasks carried out in SWS frameworks as 'systematic tasks' given that they follow a strict and previously planned method.

Application areas. As we pointed out before, among the application areas on which SWS applications are expected to impact more we find Knowledge Management, Enterprise Application Integration, and eCommerce. Other application areas include e-contracting, supply chain management, retailing, auctions, insurance, international aspects of eCommerce, security authorization policies, reputation systems, dispute resolution, computer games, advertising, bioinformatics [28, 29] and those that are intended to provide information such as financial services [30], news or travel agency [31], etc.

Successful tools implemented. Most of the tools implemented in this field aim to enable the technology itself. Tools for WS annotation and infrastructures for WS automatic

Table 2. Comparison summary table

Criterion		MAS	SWS
Generalities	*Epistemological assumptions*	Yes (Artificial Intelligence, Software Engineering, Human-Computer Interaction, ...)	Yes (Knowledge management (Ontologies), RPCs, component-based programming)
	Key enabling technology	Yes (Ontologies, remote execution protocols, communication/negotiation languages, knowledge-related procedures)	Yes (Ontologies SW & WS)
	Autonomy degree	Yes (almost total)	No (but increasing)
	Flexibility	Yes (dynamic behavior)	Not as individuals but possible as a whole – a set of services that can be composed
Matureness level	*Supporting infrastructure*	Yes (Internet technologies, remote procedure call, distributed object technologies)	Yes (SW – in development –, WS, Ontologies (WSMO, OWL-S))
	Languages available	Yes (FIPA-ACL, KQML)	Yes (OWL, WSML)
	Development methodologies	Yes (INGENIAS, ZEUS, MaSE, GAIA, MAS-CommonKADS)	No (import from SOA? WS patterns?)
	Platforms	Yes (FIPA-OS, JADE, ZEUS)	Yes (WSMX, IRS-II)
	Security level	Low (Little FIPA effort, infrastructure-dependent)	Low (to extend WS security models, a flexible and expandable security architecture is needed)
	Standardization	Yes (Base infrastructure)	No
	Global matureness	Medium	Low
Applicability	*Task orientedness*	Yes (Knowledge-based tasks)	Yes (Systematic tasks)
	Application areas	Yes (Social simulation, eCommerce, Human-Computer interfaces, ...)	Yes (Knowledge management, Enterprise Application integration, eCommerce)
	Industrial applications	Yes (Telecommunications, manufacturing, finance, air traffic management, ...)	No (this technology is still immature)
	Successful tools implemented	Yes (Health care, network management, eCommerce, human assistant,...)	Yes (Technology-enablers)

discovery, composition, and invocation are being implemented. The purpose of all the referred tools is to facilitate the creation of applications using SWS and to show the viability of this new technology. SWS require that each service be annotated with semantic metadata.

Adoption by industry. Although the technology under question has not been transferred into industry yet, some applications of the referred technology are expected in domains such as entertainment, health care, manufacturing, law enforcement, education, defense, and science. Several tools have been developed using WS (several examples can be found in http://www.webservices.org) or the SW (http://www.semanticweb.org) as the subjacent technologies. By examining these tools, it is possible to realize about the potential applicability of this mixed technology. The main idea behind all this technological development is to improve WS applications by adding semantics to WS capability descriptions.

Table 3. General conclusions

	SWS	MAS	SWS & MAS
Promising aspects	Distributed source of functionality + Machine interpretable information → intelligent access to distributed functionality.	Task delegation. Automatic achievement of reiterative processes. Aggregation and coherent representation of distributed content. Execution of distributed functions	Intelligent and powerful applications: total integration of the supply chain linking B2B and B2C sides.
Current limitations	Manual annotation of content is not scalable. Interoperability among different sources (e.g., ontology mapping). Security.	Need clearly defined representation. User profiles are still poor from the business point of view. Security.	SWS matureness. Security issues.
Challenge	Mediation. Security, trust, reputation. Automatic annotation. Choreography and Orchestration.	Exploit the functionality of SWS and the content of the SW.	Standardization (basic). Communication: languages (ontologies, ontology mappings), protocols (security)

4 Conclusions and Future Work

Nowadays, with the emergence of the SW, which provides the infrastructure for the semantic interoperability of WS, and the evolution of the IA field some controversial viewpoints have appeared. While some researchers coming from the WS community think that all can be seen as a WS (they can provide all kinds of behaviors), others coming from the agent community claim that WS can be viewed as (a part of) an agent. It is the aim of this paper to determine whether IAs and SWS technologies are compatible or not.

In Table 2, we present a brief summary of the issues studied above in order to compare the two technologies. From the information contained in that table is possible to conclude that MASs are a much more mature technology but there is great effort in the research community to make SWS (technically) feasible.

From the results obtained in our study, we conclude that both technologies can go together and cooperate to develop fully-fledged applications and reach the Next Generation Web. A clear example of the likely synergies is the supporting infrastructure, where WS can be seen as a technology perfectly suited for implementing MAS environments. By examining the section related to applicability, it becomes clear that while WS are involved in low level tasks (related to the business model), IAs can act at a higher level, thus allowing these ones to work cooperatively. Our point of view is that agents can be considered as intelligent entities that work to achieve or maintain goals on behalf of their corresponding users. Agents incorporate functionality or perform knowledge-intensive tasks showing an intelligent behavior and interacting with WS to accomplish these tasks. On the other hand, WS are the computational entities in charge of interacting with the business model of the companies that offer these services. This idea is supported by the fact that the main aim of the SW envisioned by Tim Berners-Lee was to add semantics to the Web content in order for agents or other software entities to be able to process it. Therefore, WS semantically annotated can be accessed by IAs performing high level, abstract user requests. Table 3 summarizes the promising aspects, the current problems and the main challenges that the referred technologies face. It also describes the advantages that can be obtained if they work cooperatively.

To sum up, we may say that agents can act on behalf of service providers, managing access to services, and ensuring that contracts are fulfilled. On the other hand, they can act on behalf of service consumers as well, locating services, agreeing contracts, and receiving and presenting results. Finally, agents will also be crucial for the interaction with Web users, achieving the goals their users establish. For this, different kinds of agents will have to communicate and negotiate with one another and several (semantic) WS will likely be invoked. Several studies have addressed the integration of agents and (semantic) WS for different purposes successfully [9, 28, 31–33].

Acknowledgements. This work has been supported by the Spanish National Research Agency (AEI) and the European Regional Development Fund (FEDER /ERDF) through project KBS4FIA (TIN2016-76323-R).

References

1. Garrido, P., Barrachina, J., Martinez, F.J., Serón, F.J.: Smart tourist information points by combining agents, semantics and AI techniques. Comput. Sci. Inf. Syst. **14**(1), 1–23 (2017)
2. Kravari, K., Bassiliades, N., Governatori, G.: A policy-based B2C e-Contract management workflow methodology using semantic web agents. Artif. Intell. Law **24**(2), 93–131 (2016)
3. Wooldridge, M.: An Introduction to MultiAgent Systems, 2 edn. John Wiley & Sons Ltd, New York (2002)
4. Byrski, A., Kisiel-Dorohinicki, M.: Evolutionary multi-agent systems—from inspirations to applications. In: Studies in Computational Intelligence, vol. 680. Springer, New York (2017)
5. Miller, J.A., Zhu, H., Zhang, J.: Guest editorial: advances in web services research. IEEE Trans. Serv. Comput. **10**(1), 5–8 (2017)
6. Maleshkova, M.: Towards Open Services on the Web—A Semantic Approach. PhD Thesis. The Open University, UK (2015)
7. Bernstein, A., Hendler, J.A., Noy, N.F.: A new look at the semantic web. Commun. ACM **59**(9), 35–37 (2016)
8. Pai, F., Hsu, I., Chung, Y.: Semantic web technology for agent interoperability: a proposed infrastructure. Appl. Intell. **44**(1), 1–16 (2016)
9. García-Sánchez, F., Valencia-García, R., Martínez-Bejar, R., Fernández-Breis, J.T.: An ontology, intelligent agent-based framework for the provision of semantic web services. Expert Syst. Appl. **36**(2), 3167–3187 (2009)
10. Buhler, P.A., Vidal, J.M.: Semantic web services as agent behaviors. In: Burg, B., Dale, J. (eds.) Agentcities: challenges in open agent environments, LNCS/LNAI, pp. 25–31. Springer, New York (2003)
11. Paolucci, M., Sycara, K.: Autonomous semantic web services. IEEE Internet Comput. **7**(5), 34–41 (2003)
12. Blacoe, I., Portabella, D.: Guidelines for the integration of agent-based services and web-based services. Deliverable D2.4.4 (WP2.4), Knowledge Web project (2005)
13. Ye, D., Zhang, M., Vasilakos, A.V.: A survey of self-organization mechanisms in multiagent systems. IEEE Trans. Syst. Man Cybern.: Syst. **47**(3), 441–461 (2017)
14. Berndt, J.O.: Self-organizing multiagent negotiations: cooperation and competition of concurrently acting agents with limited knowledge. Ph. D. thesis, University of Bremen, Germany (2015)
15. Abdelaziz, T., Elammari, M., Unland, R.: Branki. C.: MASD: multi-agent systems development methodology. Multiagent Grid Syst. **6**(1), 71–101 (2010)
16. The Foundation for Intelligent Physical Agents. http://www.fipa.org/. Accessed 04 May 2017
17. Syed, T.Q., Khan, B., Shams, F., Khan, M.F., Behlim, S.I., Khatoon, H., Shaikh, Z.: A robust strategy for automated negotiations. Multiagent Grid Syst. **13**(1), 1–17 (2017)
18. Venkateshwaran, K., Malviya, A., Dikshit, U., Venkatesan, S.: Security framework for agent-based cloud computing. Int. J. Interact. Multimedia Artif. Intell. **3**(3), 35–42 (2015)
19. Meng, X., Xie, L., Soh, Y.C.: Communication protocol design in event-triggered control of multi-agent systems. In: 14th International Conference on Control, Automation, Robotics and Vision, pp. 1–6. Phuket, Thailand (2016)
20. Fensel, D., Bussler, C.: The web service modeling framework WSMF. Electron. Commer. Res. Appl. **1**(2), 113–137 (2002)
21. Liu, L.: Services computing: from cloud services, mobile services to internet of services. IEEE Trans. Serv. Comput. **9**(5), 661–663 (2016)

22. Software & Service Architectures and Infrastructures, CORDIS, European Commission. http://cordis.europa.eu/fp7/ict/ssai/. Accessed 05 May 2017

23. Rodríguez-García, M.A., Valencia-García, R., García-Sánchez, F., Samper, J.J.: Creating a semantically-enhanced cloud services environment through ontology evolution. Future Gener. Comput. Syst. **32**, 295–306 (2014)

24. Rodríguez-García, M.A., Valencia-García, R., García-Sánchez, F., Samper, J.J.: Ontology-based annotation and retrieval of services in the cloud. Knowl.-Based Syst. **56**, 15–25 (2014)

25. Blakowski, S., Brune, P.: May the Ontologies Be with You! Towards a user-friendly web-based editor for semantic web service description. In: 2016 IEEE Symposium on Service-Oriented System Engineering, pp. 203–210. IEEE Computer Society (2016)

26. Wang, H.H., Gibbins, N., Payne, T.R., Patelli, Al., Wang, Y.: A survey of Semantic Web Services formalisms. Concurrency Comput.: Pract. Experience **27**(15), 4053–4072 (2015)

27. AgenLink, European Co-ordination Action for Agent-based Computing. http://www.agentlink.org/. Accessed 05 May 2017

28. García-Sánchez, F., Fernández-Breis, J.T., Valencia-García, R., Gómez, J.M., Martínez-Bejar, R.: Combining Semantic Web Technologies with Multi-Agent Systems for integrated access to biological resources. J. Biomed. Inform. **41**(5), 848–859 (2008)

29. Sernadela, P., González-Castro, L., Oliveira, J.L.: SCALEUS: Semantic Web Services integration for biomedical applications. J. Med. Syst. **41**(4), 54:1–54:11 (2017)

30. Esteban-Gil, A., García-Sánchez, F., Valencia-García, R., Fernández-Breis, J.T.: Social-BROKER: a collaborative social space for gathering semantically-enhanced financial information. Expert Syst. Appl. **39**(10), 9712–9715 (2012)

31. Rico, M., García-Sánchez, F., Gómez, J.M., Valencia-García, R., Fernández-Breis, J.T.: Enabling intelligent service discovery with GGODO. J. Inf. Sci. Eng. **26**(4), 1161–1180 (2010)

32. Vidoni, R., García-Sánchez, F., Gasparetto, A., Martínez-Bejar, R.: An intelligent framework to manage robotic autonomous agents. Expert Syst. Appl. **38**(6), 7430–7439 (2011)

33. García-Sánchez, F., Álvarez-Sabucedo, L., Martínez-Bejar, R., Anido-Rifón, L.E., Valencia-García, R., Gómez, J.M.: Applying intelligent agents and semantic web services in eGovernment environments. Expert Syst. **28**(5), 416–436 (2011)

Knowledge Based and Expert Systems

An Ontology-Based Decision Support System for the Management of Home Gardens

Vanessa Vergara-Lozano[1](✉) ⓘ, José Medina-Moreira[1,3] ⓘ,
Christian Rochina[2] ⓘ, Mayra Garzón-Goya[1] ⓘ,
Andrea Sinche-Guzmán[1] ⓘ, and Martha Bucaram-Leverone[1] ⓘ

[1] Universidad Agraria del Ecuador, Avenida 25 de Julio, Guayaquil, Ecuador
{vvergara, jmedina, mgarzon, asinche,
mbucaram}@uagraria.edu.ec
[2] Universidad Internacional del Ecuador,
Avenida Juan Tanca Marengo, Guayaquil, Ecuador
chrochinaga@internacional.edu.ec
[3] Universidad de Guayaquil, Av. Delta, Guayaquil, Ecuador
jose.medinamo@ug.edu.ec

Abstract. Home gardens or family gardens are the oldest cultivation systems used in the world. The home garden has different goals which gone from leisure and recreation to self-consumption, healthy production, family savings and community integration. Home garden management has become a knowledge problem since the community needs to know what vegetables can be planted as well as the activities that must be performed according to different parameters such as illumination, harvest time, irrigation time, among others. In this sense, there is a clear need for new mechanisms in which experts' knowledge are integrated to support decision making in the context of the home garden. In this work, we present a DSS focused on the management of home gardens. This system takes advantages of semantic technologies, more specifically ontologies, to model the main activities related to the home garden management such as creation, irrigation, transplanting and harvesting. The DSS proposed was evaluated in the context of medicinal plants and vegetables obtaining encouraging results.

Keywords: Home garden · Ontologies · Support system · Agriculture

1 Introduction

Home gardens or family gardens are the oldest cultivation systems used in the world. In Latin America, there is a growing interest for this kind of systems because of the boom achieved by the agroforestry systems and the efforts of many international organizations [1]. The home garden has different goals which gone from leisure and recreation to self-consumption, healthy production, family savings and community integration.

According to the latest results of poverty, inequality and labor market from INEC, in Ecuador the 28.6% of population live in urban-rural areas where they have food, social and economic problems. This value is due to the migration of people from the countryside to the city. Due to this phenomenon, the use of home garden has increased

R. Valencia-García et al. (Eds.): CITI 2017, CCIS 749, pp. 47–59, 2017.
DOI: 10.1007/978-3-319-67283-0_4

significantly, thus creating a new concept of agriculture known as urban agriculture. Furthermore, according to the AEISA [2], 5 out of 10 Ecuadorians prefer the production of 100% organic products.

According to the FAO [3], it is estimated that up to 15% of world's food is produced through urban agriculture and 70% of urban households in developing countries participate in agricultural activities.

In Guayaquil, people living in the marginal urban area represent the 18% of the total population. Therefore, there have been several social assistance programs by government authorities and NGOs such as ZUMAR. This last organization is focused on the generation of family gardens through the Funding Agreement between the European Union and Guayaquil government.

All home garden programs that have been created are oriented to mitigate community problems such as malnutrition, lack of family incomes and savings, as well as to enjoy organic food and establish a relationship with nature. These efforts are disappearing due to the lack of follow-up given to the orchards after these ones have been implemented. This follow-up includes the construction of orchards, community training and technical advice.

Home garden management has become a knowledge problem since the community need to know what vegetables can be planted and the activities that must be performed according to different parameters considering the place of implementation, i.e., community need to be supported from home garden construction to the harvest time. In this sense, there is a clear need for new mechanisms in which scientific knowledge, in this case, the knowledge of management of home gardens, be integrated to support agricultural decision making [4]. Examples of this kind of tools are the decision support systems (DSS) which have been widely used in agricultural processes such as precision agriculture, climate risk analysis [5], among others. Summarizing, DSSs can support people in charge of home gardens by means of experts' knowledge.

The Semantic Web has emerged as a new approach whose main goal is to provide the information with a well-defined meaning and make it understandable not only by humans but also by computers [6]. Thanks to the Semantic Web, computers can automate, integrate and reuse high-quality information from distributed data sources. One of the pillars of the Semantic Web are the ontologies, which are defined as a formal and explicit specification of a shared conceptualization [7]. Ontologies have been successfully applied in different fields such as finances [8], cloud computing [9], and question and answering systems [10], among others.

According to the above discussed, communities interested in the implementation of home gardens need to know all tasks and criteria that must be considered for the correct management of a home garden. In this work, we present a DSS focused on the management of home gardens. This system takes advantage of semantic technologies, more specifically ontologies, to model the main activities related to the home garden management such as creation, irrigation, transplanting and harvesting. This system is based on the expertise of domain experts. In this way, when users want to create a home garden, they must provide a set of parameters through which the system suggests which activities must be performed. For this purpose, the system uses the knowledge stored in the semantic repository and a rule-based engine to infer the activities and recommendations according to the parameters provided by the users.

The rest of this paper is structured as follows. Section 2 describes research works that implement the technologies involved in this work. Section 3 describes the sociodemographic features of Guayaquil as well as its planting preferences. Section 4 presents the general architecture of the system and its components. Section 5 describes a case study for evaluating the effectiveness of the proposed method. Finally, conclusions and future work are presented.

2 Related Works

Home gardens are very important for community because they improve que quality of life of citizens who own it, either economically (saving, additional income), social (human-nature relation and community relation) and food (consumption of healthy and organic vegetables) [11]. To implement home gardens in cities, it is necessary to have the knowledge for managing home gardens. An innovative way to perform this task is the use of DSS's whose main goal is to provide users with tools for improving the decision-making process, thus obtaining more informed decisions [12]. DSS's have been implemented in different areas such as medical care [13] for dosing, diagnosis, preventive care and quality assurance as well as for sharing information and decisions about patients' management. In the contexts of Big Data and Cloud computing, Haluk Demirkan and Dursun Delen [14] define a list of requirements for DSS's oriented to services. Also, they propose a conceptual framework through which opportunities and challenges of service-oriented engineering are established. In the political field, Vicki L. Sauter [15] provides several examples of DSS's used in this field. For instance, the Neighbor-to-Neighbor system that helped the Obama campaign in 2008. This system includes the names and addresses of all undecided voters and the specific topics of interest for this group of citizens. By means of this tool, it is possible to identify and convince these people to vote for Obama. In the agricultural field, there are different systems for supporting different processes. For example, the DSS Vite.Net [16] is a system composed of two main parts namely, an integrated system for real-time monitoring of the components of the vineyard, and a Web-based tool for analyzing the data collected by means of advanced modeling techniques. Furthermore, DSS has also been used in the diagnosis of plant diseases. For example, in [17] authors present an Ontology-based DSS that promotes the experts' knowledge for diagnosing plant diseases.

In the context of agriculture, ontologies are used to solve interoperability and integration problems of heterogeneous data sources [18]. Several ontological models have been developed for agricultural processes such as citrus fruit production [19]. This ontology defines three decision services: fertilization, nutrient imbalance, and irrigation/drainage. In the context of plant diseases, in [20], the authors describe an expert system that diagnoses plant diseases based on a multicriteria approach. In [21], authors present and intelligent irrigation system that considers weather conditions collected by several IoT-based devices distributed along area. In the biorefinery context [22], a DSS for assessing the sustainability of biorefinery systems. Finally, in [23], the authors propose an extensible and self-adaptive DSS for the management of heterogenous data sources.

The research works above-analyzed propose DSS -based solutions to many problems from different domains. Most of them use ontologies for representing the knowledge of experts related to disease diagnosis and citrus fruit production. However, none of them is focused on the management of home gardens and family gardens. This work aims to provide a DSS for helping non-expert people interested in owning a home garden. This system has been designed to use the experience and knowledge from experts in the creation and management of home garden. All this knowledge is formalized by means of an ontology that guides processes related to the provision of place, planting of vegetables, irrigation, transplant, and harvest, based on a set of premises provided by the users. The following sections describe in detail the design of the architecture and the functionality of each of its components.

3 Socio-Demographic Characteristics of Guayaquil and Its Planting Preferences in Organic Orchards

According to the latest Population Census conducted in 2010 [24], 2,291,158 people are living in the urban area of Guayaquil. This fact makes of Guayaquil the most populated city in Ecuador. With a territorial extension of 2,493.86 Km2, Guayaquil has an urban population density of 919 inhabitants per kilometer square, 54.4% more than its population density in 2001. This increase is mainly due to the migration of Ecuadorians from the countryside to the city. These people look for better opportunities in economically attractive cities like Guayaquil.

One of the positive aspects of this migration is that now a part of the inhabitants has acquired the knowledge about a specific activity such as agriculture. Sometimes this knowledge remains latent for its use in activities of similar characteristics such as gardening, parks, among others [25].

Considering the fact above presented, the promotion of home gardens development is an important task to be considered. Unlike commercial crops that require a large area of land and a large investment in both seeds and fertilizers for their care, a home garden does not demand a large piece of land or an expensive investment for the care of the farm since they use organic natural products.

The Provincial Council of Guayas and the M.I. Municipality of Guayaquil have focused their efforts on the development of home gardens. Even, this project has obtained very positive results which are reflected in a better nutrition of the members of the family, economic saving as they produce their own food, and a better use of the leisure time in home [25].

Regarding the preferences of people from Guayaquil to implement a home garden, there are market research that aims to know the importance that people give to the home gardens and the benefits of their use. Figure 1 shows the results obtained from a market research about planting preferences in urban homes from Guayaquil. As can be seen in Fig. 1, 9 out of 10 homes are interested in implementing an organic orchard. With respect to their planting preferences, 6 out of 10 homes prefer planting the tomato. Other vegetables that people want to plant are radish, artichoke, pepper, red onion, chamomile, and anise.

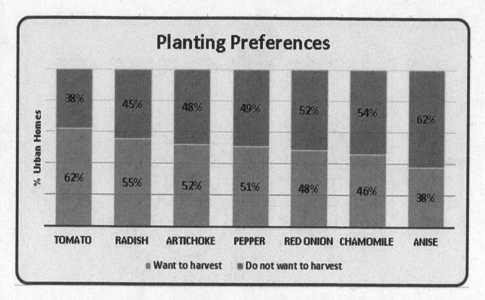

Fig. 1. Planting preferences in urban homes from Guayaquil.

Finally, it is important to emphasize the increasing availability of information technology for the benefit of the world population. In the case of Guayaquil, in 8 out of 10 homes at least one of its members has a mobile phone. On the other hand, in Guayas, 6 out of 10 people use a computer, and 6 out of 10 people have access to the Internet.

4   An Ontology-Based Decision Support System

The system proposed in this work generates recommendations about plantations in home gardens from the Coastal Region of Ecuador, based on a set of parameters provided by the user. This system is configurated for the tomato, radish, artichoke, pepper, red onion, chamomile and anise. The recommendations depend on the crop selected and the set of parameters provided. Figure 2 shows the architecture of the proposed system which consists of two main parts, a rule-based engine and the home garden ontology.

The DSS here proposed, in conjunction with the home garden ontology, aims to generate recommendations based on the experts' knowledge. In a nutshell, the system works as follows: (1) the user selects the seed to cultivate and provide a set of parameters such as quantity and space. This information is provided through a mobile application; (2) once the information has been provided, the system generates a set of recommendations based on a set of rules; (3) the system shows the user the set of recommendations which consider the soil conditions, climatic conditions, humidity, and appropriate harvest time. The next section describes the home garden ontology, which is one of the pillar of the system here proposed.

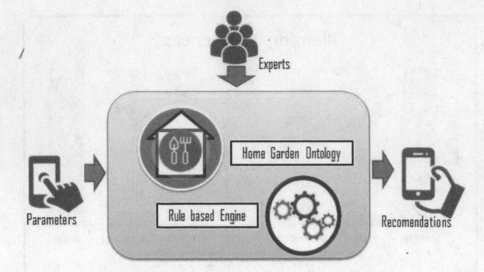

Fig. 2. Overall architecture guided by ontologies.

4.1 Home Garden Ontology

As has been mentioned, the system here proposed is based on an ontology that describes the home garden domain through concepts such as irrigation, pesticides, climatic conditions, among others. Figure 3 shows an extract of the ontology proposed in this work. This ontology has been created by using OWL and Protégé 4.3.

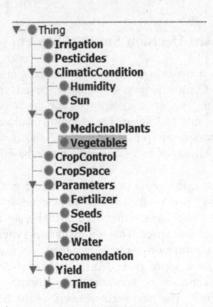

Fig. 3. Home Garden Ontology.

Types

The home garden ontology defines nine types namely, irrigation, pesticide, climatic condition, crop, crop control, crop space, parameter, recommendation and harvest time. All these types are defined as disjoint types; however, the types recommendation, climatic conditions and parameter share criteria of several entities or instances. This ontology has been created based on the cultivate preferences of a group of users. However, this ontology can evolve by including more types of crops such as vegetables, fruits and medicinal plants.

The types defined by the ontology allow classifying the preferred crops for home gardens implementation. In this way, the class *Crop* has two subtypes, *MedicinalPlant* and *Vegetables*. The first subclass represents crops such as anis and chamomile. Meanwhile, the second subclass represents crops such as tomato, radish, artichoke, pepper and onion.

Regarding the class *parameter*, it refers to those parameters provided by the user such as seed and quantity. The class *recommendation* covers all those recommendations about crop control, pesticide control, harvest time and crop recommendations. Also, it is important to consider the climatic conditions such as humidity, sun, and water, among others.

Finally, it must be remarked that the home garden ontology describes such domain based on the knowledge and expertise of domain experts, to provide user appropriate recommendations.

Properties

The home garden ontology defines a set of properties that allow the system to generate a set of recommendations about care and control crop according to the parameters provided by the user. These properties represent the existing relationship between the domain types. All types are related to the Crop class due to factors such as irrigation, pesticides, climatic conditions, crop control, crop space, parameters, recommendations and harvest time depend on the crop the user want to plant. The properties described by the home garden ontology are presented in Fig. 4.

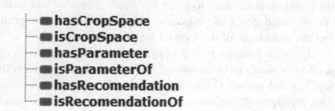

Fig. 4. Properties of the Home Garden Ontology.

- *isParameterOf*. It defines the input parameters such as crop and quantity. For instance, for the Tomato, it must be provided the amount of seed and the area (square meter) on which will be cultivated.
- *isCropSpaceOf*. It is used to define the recommended area of cultivation according to the chosen crop. For example, the cultivation of radish or pepper requires an area of one square meter.

- *hasRecommendation*. It uses a set of relations among the types defined by the ontology since the recommendations depends on the irrigation, pesticides, climatic conditions and the way crops are controlled.

The properties above have their corresponding inverse properties that allow establishing relations among entities. In this way, the property *isParameterOf* is the inverse property of *hasParameter*, the property *isCropSpaceOf* is the inverse property of *hasCropSpace*, and *hasRecommendation* is the inverse property of *isRecommendationOf*.

Individuals

The home garden ontology defines the types MedicinalPlants and Vegetables to classify the cultivation preferences of people from the Coastal Region of Ecuador. The type MedicinalPlants groups crops such as anise and chamomile. Meanwhile, the class Vegetables groups crops such as tomato, radish, artichoke, pepper and red onion. Furthermore, climatic conditions such as humidity and sunlight have been considered by this ontology. Finally, each crop has a set of recommendations about the crops control and harvest time. These recommendations are related to the crop by means of the properties described in the previous section.

Finally, it is worth mentioning that a semantic knowledge base based on descriptive logic has two fundamental elements clearly defined: TBox (terminological axioms) which contains the schema that defines the domain through concepts, relations and constraints; and the ABox (assertions) which contains all instances of the domain.

4.2   Rule-Based Engine

The rules definition process involved the participation of domain experts who were asked to express their knowledge and experiences regarding the parameters to be considered during home garden implementation, as well as the recommendations to follow for controlling and harvesting home gardens.

The recommendations provided by the experts were analyzed according to the space and distance used to plant the seeds, the way and frequency of irrigation, the recommended doses of pesticides, crop control, the appropriate harvest time and the climatic conditions of the Coastal Region of Ecuador.

The input parameters that must be provided by the user are the product to grow, quantity of seeds to be cultivated, the space (square meters) that he/she owns for the crop, and the season (winter or summer). Based on such parameters, the system provides recommendations about the distance between seeds, harvest time, the yield to be obtained from the crop, frequency of irrigation, time of exposure to the sun and amount of nutrients to add to the crop.

Once this information was obtained, a set of inference rules were established. For this purpose, the SWRL [26] language was used. The set of rules created from the experts' knowledge are used to obtain recommendations according to the type of crop. The inference process emphasizes the type of crop (vegetables or medicinal plants) because they share some recommendation criteria.

Table 1 presents a set of recommendations provided by the system. For example, when the user provides the input parameters Tomato, as seed, and 3 m^2, as the space to be cultivated, the system generates next recommendations: a distance between seeds of 1 m, a yield of 8–10 tomatoes, and that the harvest time must be every 90 days.

Table 1. Home Garden recommendations

Input data		Recommendations		
Seed	Space	Distance between seeds	Yield	Harvest time
Tomato	3 m^2	1 m	8–10	90 days
Onion	3 m^2	1 m	4–6	Only one
Radish	3 m^2	1 m	2–3	Only one

5 Evaluation

5.1 Method

We perform an evaluation process to validate the coherence and correctness of the recommendations provided by the system. This process required the participation of 50 urban farmers from Guayaquil. These people are immersed in a program of home gardening promoted by the Municipality of Guayaquil. Table 2 shows the type of crops considered by this program. These farmers cultivated medicinal plants such as chamomile and anise, and vegetables such as tomatoes, radishes, artichokes, peppers and red onions. Each participant provided different sets of conditions and parameters concerning their home garden. Some of these parameters are the type of crop, seed quantity, area for cultivation, and climatic conditions.

Table 2. Types of plants grown by urban farmers

Plant	Total of home gardens
Medicinal plant	30
Vegetables	53
Total	83

For the purposes of this evaluation, the type of plants grown by urban farmers was divided into two main groups:

- Medicinal plants. These plants are used for health problems. They offer economic benefits since they do not need a large area and do not require a big investment. The medicinal plants considered in this evaluation were chamomile and anise.
- Vegetables. These plants are used for a balanced diet. This evaluation considers vegetables from the Coast Region of Ecuador namely tomatoes, radishes, artichokes, peppers, and red onions.

Once all sets of parameters were provided by the farmers, these were provided as input to the system proposed. Then, the DSS generates a set of recommendations for the maintenance of the home garden as well as about the harvest time and yield of the harvest. The recommendations provided by the system were compared to the maintenance tasks, harvest time and yield previously known. Finally, the results were evaluated by using the metrics of precision, recall, and their harmonic mean F-measure whose formulas are shown below.

$$recall = \frac{TP}{TP+FN} \tag{1}$$

$$precision = \frac{TP}{TP+FP} \tag{2}$$

$$F1 = 2 * \frac{precision * recall}{precision + recall} \tag{3}$$

The TP (True Positives) refers to those recommendations provided by the system that match those ones established by the experts. The FP (False Positives) are the set of recommendations obtained by the system but they do not match with those ones established by the experts. Finally, FN (False Negatives) are the set of recommendations provided by the system that were related to another type of planting, that is, those sets of recommendation that was not related to the correct plant. The F1 metric corresponds to the weighted average of the precision and recall obtained by the system. Next section discusses the results of this evaluation.

5.2 Discussion

The evaluation results obtained by the system for medicinal plants cultivation are shown in Table 3. The system obtained an average precision score of 0.7965, and average recall score of 0.9183, and an average F-measure score of 0.8474. The system obtained the best results when recommendations about illumination that need the plants are provided. Meanwhile, the aspect with the lowest precision (0.6316) is the distance that must exist between the plants cultivated.

Table 3. Evaluation results for medicinal plants

	TP	FN	FP	Precision	Recall	F-measure
Distance	12	5	7	0,631578947	0,705882353	0,666667
Irrigation time	13	2	2	0,866666667	0,866666667	0,866667
Illumination	26	0	0	1	1	1
Nutrients	15	1	2	0,882352941	0,9375	0,909091
Performance	12	0	7	0,631578947	1	0,774194
Harvest time	23	0	7	0,766666667	1	0,867925
Average				0,796474028	0,918341503	0,84742

The evaluation results obtained by the system for vegetable cultivation are shown in Table 4. In this case, the system obtained better results than with medicinal plants. More specifically, the system obtained scores of 0.8598, 0.9716 and 0.90988 for the precision, recall, and F-measure, respectively. In this context, the aspect for which better results were obtained is the irrigation time with a score of 0.9167. Meanwhile, the lowest score was obtained for the aspect of illumination with a score of 0.8301.

Table 4. Evaluation results

Plant	TP	FN	FP	Precision	Recall	F-measure
Distance	33	0	0	1	1	1
Irrigation time	44	3	4	0,916666667	0,936170213	0,926316
Illumination	44	0	9	0,830188679	1	0,907216
Nutrients	40	3	6	0,869565217	0,930232558	0,898876
Performance	26	1	7	0,787878788	0,962962963	0,866667
Harvest time	40	0	13	0,754716981	1	0,860215
Average				0,859836055	0,971560956	0,90988

The evaluation results obtained by the system are good for both medicinal plants and vegetables. In Tables 3 and 4 we can observe that there is no a big difference among the results obtained in both scenarios. We attribute these differences to two main facts: (1) some plants were cultivated in winter, and the climate in this season varies widely, hence, urban farmers make certain changes in the cultivation process; and (2) some medicinal plants and vegetables share several parameters; therefore, it was difficult to provide the specific recommendation when more than 3 parameters were the same for a medicinal plant and a vegetable.

Sometimes, urban farmers provided parameter related to the season (winter or summer), e.g., they provide the parameter rainy, very rainy or wet. These values are not considered by the system. Hence, it is necessary to extend the ontology by adding new parameters as well as jargon used in the domain of home gardens. Furthermore, it would be important to integrate a broader set of properties that allow the system to provide the correct recommendations when two or more parameters are common between different plants. Finally, it is necessary to generate more rules to improve the effectiveness of the system.

6 Conclusions and Future Work

In response to the requirements of food, leisure and social welfare in big cities, the creation of home gardens is proposed. To help this task, in this work we present a DSS that aims to provide urban farmers support for decision making. Thanks to this system, these farmers have access to experts' knowledge in the form of recommendations about the general implementation process of a home garden including harvest time and yield. In this system, ontologies and semantic reasoning play a fundamental role.

The main goal of this project is to make this type of technology accessible to urban farmers to reduce the rate of premature abandonment of their home garden project. The system here proposed obtained encouraging results with an average F-measure of 0.8787 for the cultivation of medicinal plants and vegetables.

As future work, authors plan to generate new rules and recommendations, as well as to extend the knowledge described by the ontology. Furthermore, the authors are considering the possibility of covering a new set of crops such as fruits. The ontology proposed in this work could be extended by including new seeds that can be planted in home gardens. Furthermore, it will be necessary to include information concerning their harvest time, yield and distance between seeds. For this purpose, a bigger group of experts will be involved. Also, it is important to integrate a mechanism that allows users to share information and experiences through a social network or a messaging service, thus improving the teamwork for solving specific problems. Finally, authors plan to extend the ontology by integrating the knowledge concerning control of pests and insects that affect home gardens.

References

1. Lork, R.: Huertos caseros tradicionales de América Central: características, beneficios e importancia, desde un enfoque multidisciplinario (1998)
2. AEISA: AEISA | Asociación Ecuatoriana de Ingeniería Sanitaria y Ambiental. http://aeisa.com.ec/
3. Organización de las Naciones Unidas para la Alimentación y la Agricultura. http://www.fao.org/home/es/
4. Jakku, E., Thorburn, P.J.: A conceptual framework for guiding the participatory development of agricultural decision support systems. Agric. Syst. **103**, 675–682 (2010)
5. Churri, A.J., Mlozi, M., Mahoo, H., Tumbo, S., Casmir, R.: A decision support system for enhancing crop productivity of smallholder farmers in semi-arid agriculture. Int. J. Inf. Commun. Technol. Res. **3**, 1079–1081 (2013)
6. Berners-Lee, T., Hendler, J., Lassila, O.: The semantic web. Sci. Am. **284**, 34–35 (2001)
7. Studer, R., Benjamins, V.R., Fensel, D.: Knowledge engineering: principles and methods. Data Knowl. Eng. **25**, 161–197 (1998)
8. Salas-Zárate, M.P., Valencia-García, R., Ruiz-Martínez, A., Colomo-Palacios, R.: Feature-based opinion mining in financial news: an ontology-driven approach. J. Inf. Sci. 16555151664552 (2016)
9. Rodríguez-García, M.Á., Valencia-García, R., García-Sánchez, F., Samper-Zapater, J.J.: Ontology-based annotation and retrieval of services in the cloud. Knowl.-Based Syst. **56**, 15–25 (2014)
10. Paredes-Valverde, M.A., Rodríguez-García, M.Á., Ruiz-Martínez, A., Valencia-García, R., Alor-Hernández, G.: ONLI: an ontology-based system for querying DBpedia using natural language paradigm. Expert Syst. Appl. **42**, 5163–5176 (2015)
11. Varras, G., Andreopoulou, Z., Koliouska, C., Tasoulas, E., Myriounis, C.: A web-based DSS for sustainability in Urban Green Zones. | BibSonomy. Int. Conf. Inf. Commun. Technol. Agric. Food Environ. **1498**, 263–269 (2015)
12. Shibl, R., Lawley, M., Debuse, J.: Factors influencing decision support system acceptance. Decis. Support Syst. **54**, 953–961 (2013)

13. Delaney, B.C., Fitzmaurice, D.A., Riaz, A., Hobbs, F.D.: Can computerised decision support systems deliver improved quality in primary care? Interview Abi Berger. BMJ. **319**, 1281 (1999)
14. Demirkan, H., Delen, D.: Leveraging the capabilities of service-oriented decision support systems: Putting analytics and big data in cloud. Decis. Support Syst. **55**, 412–421 (2013)
15. Sauter, V.L., Sauter, V.L.: Wiley InterScience (Online service): decision support systems for business intelligence. Wiley, Hoboken (2010)
16. Rossi, V., Salinari, F., Poni, S., Caffi, T., Bettati, T.: Addressing the implementation problem in agricultural decision support systems: the example of vite.net®. Comput. Electron. Agric. **100**, 88–99 (2014)
17. Lagos-Ortíz, K., Medina-Moreira, J., Paredes-Valverde, M.A., Valencia-García, R.: An ontology-based decision support system for the diagnosis of plant diseases. J. Inf. Technol. Res. **6**, 3 (2017)
18. Roussey, C., Soulignac, V., Champomier, J.C., Chanet, J.-P.: Ontologies in Agriculture. Int. Conf. Agric. Eng. **103**, 463–477 (2010)
19. Wang, Y., Wang, Y., Wang, J., Yuan, Y., Zhang, Z.: An ontology-based approach to integration of hilly citrus production knowledge. Comput. Electron. Agric. **113**, 24–43 (2015)
20. Goodridge, W., Bernard, M., Jordan, R., Rampersad, R.: Intelligent diagnosis of diseases in plants using a hybrid Multi-Criteria decision making technique. Comput. Electron. Agric. **133**, 80–87 (2017)
21. Navarro-Hellín, H., Martínez-del-Rincon, J., Domingo-Miguel, R., Soto-Valles, F., Torres-Sánchez, R.: A decision support system for managing irrigation in agriculture. Comput. Electron. Agric. **124**, 121–131 (2016)
22. Lousteau-Cazalet, C., Barakat, A., Belaud, J.-P., Buche, P., Busset, G., Charnomordic, B., Dervaux, S., Destercke, S., Dibie, J., Sablayrolles, C., Vialle, C.: A decision support system for eco-efficient biorefinery process comparison using a semantic approach. Comput. Electron. Agric. **127**, 351–367 (2016)
23. Noia, T.D., Mongiello, M., Nocera, F., Sciascio, E.D.: Ontology-based Reflective IoT Middleware-Enabled Agriculture Decision Support System. SWAT4LS (2016)
24. Guerrero, J.: Instituto Nacional de Estadística y Censos. http://inec.gob.ec/estadisticas/index.php?option=com_remository&Itemid=0&func=select&id=109&orderby=5&page=1&lang=es
25. Betancourt Vargas, G.V., Orlando Montesdeoca, R.D.: Evaluación de diversos prototipos de huertos familiares en zonas urbanas de la ciudad de Guayaquil (2015)
26. Horrocks, I., Patel-Schneider, P., Boley, H.: SWRL: a semantic web rule language combining OWL and RuleML. W3C Memb (2004)

A Collaborative Filtering Based Recommender System for Disease Self-management

José Medina-Moreira[1](✉) ⓘ, Oscar Apolinario[1], Harry Luna-Aveiga[1],
Katty Lagos-Ortiz[1] ⓘ, Mario Andrés Paredes-Valverde[2] ⓘ,
and Rafael Valencia-García[2] ⓘ

[1] Universidad de Guayaquil. Cdla. Universitaria Salvador Allende,
Guayaquil, Ecuador
{jose.medinamo, oscar.apolinarioa, harry.lunaa,
katty.lagoso}@ug.edu.ec
[2] Facultad de Informática. Universidad de Murcia. Campus de Espinardo,
30100 Murcia, Spain
{marioandres.paredes, valencia}@um.es

Abstract. Diabetes is a chronic disease that is diagnosed by observing raised levels of glucose in the blood. High levels of glucose in the blood damage many tissues in the body, thus bringing life-threating and disabling health complications. According to the World Health Organization, the number of people with diabetes is around 422 million, and the diabetes prevalence has been raising more rapidly in middle and low-income countries. People with diabetes must have periodic contact with healthcare professionals. However, it is necessary for them to have the skills, attitude, and support for self-management. In other words, people with diabetes should be active participants in the treatment. In this work, we present a system for diabetes self-management. This system deals with different subjects related to the control and management of glucose levels in the blood, such as diet, physical activity, mood, medication, and treatment. Furthermore, this system implements the collaborative filtering recommendation algorithm for generating health recommendations. This module was evaluated to measure its effectiveness providing such recommendations obtaining encouraging results. This evaluation involved the participation of real patients with diabetes and healthcare professionals.

Keywords: Diabetes self-management · Collaborative filtering · Cloud computing

1 Introduction

The WHO (World Health Organization) defines diabetes as a chronic disease that occurs either when the pancreas does not produce enough insulin or when the body cannot effectively use the insulin it produces [1]. Diabetes is diagnosed by observing raised levels of glucose in the blood. In this sense, high levels of glucose in the blood damage many tissues in the body, thus bringing life-threatening and disabling health complications [2].

© Springer International Publishing AG 2017
R. Valencia-García et al. (Eds.): CITI 2017, CCIS 749, pp. 60–71, 2017.
DOI: 10.1007/978-3-319-67283-0_5

According to the Global Report on Diabetes [3] performed by the WHO in April 2016, the number of people with diabetes was around 422 million in 2014. Furthermore, the global prevalence of diabetes among adults (over 18 years of age) was 8.5% in 2014. It must be emphasized that the number of diabetic people has been rising more rapidly in middle and low-income countries.

People with diabetes must have periodic contact with healthcare professionals. However, it is necessary for them to have the skills, attitude, and support for self-management of their condition [4]. In other words, people with diabetes should be active participants in the treatment.

Diabetes has an effect not only on patients but also on their families, the healthcare system and the society. Therefore, diabetes self-management education (DSME) is a critical element of care for all people with diabetes and is necessary to improve patients' outcomes [5]. DSME is the process of providing the person with diabetes with the necessary knowledge and skills to perform self-care, manage crises, and make lifestyle changes required to successfully manage this disease [6].

Recommender systems are software tools and techniques which provide suggestions for items to be of use to a user [7]. This kind of systems offer filtered information from many elements, i.e., those recommendations are intended to provide elements of interest to users. Recommender systems have been successfully applied in different contexts such as movie show times [8], passengers and vacant taxis [9], digital libraries [10], and Web services [11], among others.

In this work, we present a system for diabetes self-management. This system provides a mobile application for monitoring different subjects related to the control and management of glucose levels in the blood, such as diet, physical activity, mood, medication, and treatment. Furthermore, this mobile application aims to improve the relationship between patients and healthcare professionals, because healthcare professionals can obtain real-time information about the health status of the patient, as well as a detailed description of the patients' treatments.

In addition to the features above mentioned, the system provides a set of health recommendations based on the collaborative filtering (CF) recommendation algorithm, which bases its predictions and recommendations on the ratings or behavior of the users in the system [12]. Thanks to this algorithm, the system can recommend the active user (patient with diabetes) the items (food, exercise, treatments) that other patients with similar tastes liked in the past.

The rest of this paper is structured as follows. Section 2 describes the most relevant research efforts regarding diabetes self-management. Section 3 presents the architecture of the system here presented, as well as of all modules that compose it. Furthermore, this section provides a detailed description of the recommender module which is based on collaborative filtering. Section 4 describes the evaluation process that was performed to evaluate the effectiveness of the recommendations provided by the system. Finally, conclusions and future work are presented.

2 State of the Art

There are many works in the literature that deal with different activities related to the self-management of diseases. For instance, in [13], the authors present WEALTHY, a wearable health care system for vital signs monitoring. This system integrates smart sensors, computing techniques, portable devices, and decision support system. The simultaneous recording of vital signs allows generating alert messages and a synoptic patient table. On other hand, the CARE (Collaborative Assessment and Recommendation Engine) system [14] implements a novel collaborative filtering method that captures patients' similarities and produces personalized disease risk profiles for individuals. In [15], the authors present a recommender system for constructing nursing care plans. This system uses correlations among nursing diagnosis, outcomes and interventions. Furthermore, this system provides a ranked list of suggested care plan items based on previously-entered items.

Regarding mobile application for diabetes management, in [16] the authors present an study about the effectiveness of available smartphone applications combined with text-message feedback from a certified diabetes educator. The evaluation results show an improvement in the glycemic control of the patients. On the other hand, in [17] a systematic review of mobile applications for diabetes self-management is performed. This study aimed to determine whether diabetes applications have been helping patients with type 1 and type 2 diabetes. The authors conclude that application usage is associated with improved attitudes favorable to diabetes self-management. In the context of systematic reviews, in [18] the authors present an analysis of the features and contents of Chinese diabetes mobile applications in terms of their suitability for use by older adults with diabetes. The authors conclude that the features of most mobile applications failed to include areas of known which were important for managing diabetes in older adults. Another work focused on the development of mobile application for diabetes self-management is the presented in [19], which describes a systematic approach to the design and development of a diabetes self-management mobile application. The resulting application provides a set of features to the self-monitoring of blood glucose, physical activity, diet and weight, the identification of glycemic patterns in relation to the patient's lifestyle and a remedial decision making.

Our approach is different from existing works in that it tries to provide a tool for diabetes self-management that considers the daily routine of patients to generate tips and recommendations that help them to manage and control their disease. Furthermore, this system allows patients with diabetes to register information about their daily routine including information about food intakes, insulin intakes, physical activities performance, as well as their mood. All this information can be accessed by healthcare professionals to determine a new treatment or improve the current one. The next section describes the functional architecture of the system here proposed. Also, all its functionalities are described in detail.

3 A Collaborative Filtering Based Recommender System for Diabetes Self-management

This work describes a system that aims to help people with diabetes to control and manage their disease. This application allows patients to keep a record of their daily routine including activities related to their physical activity, diet, mood, medication and treatment. Furthermore, it aims to improve communication between patients and healthcare professionals since it offers healthcare professionals a general perspective of the daily routine of their patients. This information, represented in form of charts, allows healthcare professionals to detect the problems related to the treatment, diet or physical activity, as well as to establish new routes for improving the health status of their patients.

Figure 1 shows the functional architecture of the system for diabetes self-management. This architecture is decomposed into three main modules namely Web application, mobile application and the collaborative filtering based recommender module.

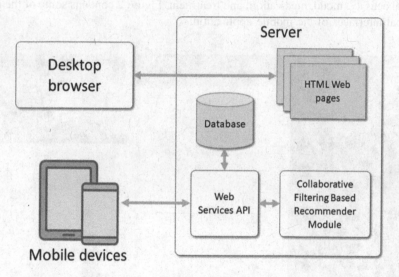

Fig. 1. Functional architecture.

In a nutshell, the system for diabetes self-management works as follows. Both, patients with diabetes and healthcare professionals have access to the system via Web or through the mobile application. The mobile application allows patients to register their daily routine including information about the levels of glucose in the blood, physical activity, food intakes, mood, insulin intakes, and intakes of medication. All this information is stored in the database, which is accessed via REST-based Web services. The data collected through the mobile application is presented to the healthcare professionals by means of charts, which provide an easy to understand graphical representation, which shows, in a straightforward way, a summary of all subjects above mentioned. This summary aims to facilitate healthcare professionals to detect the weak points in the treatment of the patients, i.e., thanks to this information, the healthcare professionals can determine if the patients need to do more exercise, include more high carbohydrate food, or increase the insulin intakes, among other facts. Furthermore, this information can be exported to pdf files or can be shared via email.

The system has been developed by using SCRUM [20], an agile development method for developing flexible software systems, i.e. it allows managing software development when business conditions are changing. Regarding the mobile application, it works on Android devices.

Next sections provide a description in detail of the two main components of the present system namely, the mobile application for diabetes self-management, and the collaborative filtering based recommender module.

3.1 Mobile Application for Diabetes Self-management

As was previously mentioned, the mobile application presented in this work provides support for diabetes self-management activities such as vital sign monitoring, diet, physical activity, mood, medication, and treatment. Figure 2 contains some of the main graphical interfaces of the mobile application.

Fig. 2. User interfaces of the mobile application.

The left-side interface represents a list menu that contains all functionalities provided by the mobile application such as the registration of physical activity, food intakes, medical notifications, and reports generation. The interface of the middle refers to the registration of the mood as well as a short description of it. Finally, the right-side interface provides a view of the reports generated by the application. In this case, the interface presents a summary of the insulin intakes from a specific period.

The following sections provide a description in detail of each of the functionalities provided by the mobile application.

Vital Signs Monitoring

Vital signs are measurements of the body's functions, more specifically, the most basic functions namely body temperature, pulse rate, respiration rate (rate of breathing) and blood pressure (the blood pressure is often measured along with the vital signs; however, it is not considered a vital sign). Due to the fact that the vital signs are useful in detecting and monitoring health problems, the mobile application allows patients to keep a record of their vital signs. From this information, the system provides a set of recommendations and tips that allow them to manage their disease in a better way.

Diet

People with diabetes must take extra care to make sure that their food is balanced with their levels of glucose in blood, insulin, and oral medication (if they take it), as well as to the type of diabetes that they suffer. In this sense, it is well known that there is not a perfect diet for people with diabetes. However, including a variety of food and watching portion sizes is a key factor to a healthy diet. Furthermore, this diet must be rich in vegetables, whole grains, fruits, non-fat dairy products, beans, lean meat, poultry, and fish, among other foods.

To help patients to control their levels of glucose in the blood, the present system provides a module that allows users to register information concerning the food intakes, emphasizing the quantities of carbohydrates, calories, fat, and proteins. The information collected is used by the system to recommend diets from 1800–2400 calories per day.

Physical activity

Diabetes is associated with the increased risk of cardiovascular disease and premature mortality [21, 22]. According to [23], the most proximal behavioral cause of insulin resistance is physical inactivity. Considering these facts, the mobile application helps patients to record their physical activities at the same time that provides them with tips and recommendations about exercise routines that can help them to improve their health status.

Mood

The mood is a key element to be considered within diabetes self-management be-cause mood changes are a common to people with type 2 or type 1 diabetes. These changes can be attributed to several factors such as stress, depression, and rapid changes in blood sugars, among others. Hence, the mobile application provides the patients with the opportunity to record their mood in such a way that healthcare professionals can establish ways to address the problem related to this subject.

Medication

To achieve a good control over diabetes patients must follow a series of corrective measures such as the ingestion of hypoglycemic pills or the injection of insulin. For this purpose, this system allows patients to register all insulin intakes as well as the intake of medication. In this context, it must be mentioned that the system has a wide drug database which can be extended by the users, more specifically by healthcare professionals.

Treatment
There are several treatments to help people manage and control their diabetes. Each patient is different, so the treatments vary depending on individual needs. For instance, people with Type 1 diabetes may need to treat their condition with insulin. Meanwhile, people with Type 2 diabetes may be able to manage their condition with exercise and diet. In this sense, the mobile application allows patients to record all information related to the food intakes, physical activity, and insulin intakes. These data will allow healthcare professionals to determine the main reasons for the success or failure of the treatment established, and assign a new treatment when it is necessary.

Communication between patient and healthcare professional
People with diabetes have periodic contact with healthcare professionals. In these meetings, healthcare professionals need for information that help them to determine what is the health status of the patient and, when the health status is not positive, to determine the main factors that caused this status. To help healthcare professionals to perform such diagnosis, the mobile application provides a summary of the insulin takes, the level of glucose in the blood, heart rate, blood pressure, weight, intake of medication, mood and food intakes. This information is provided through charts, which can be customized by selecting a specific period. Furthermore, these charts can be exported to pdf files or can be sent via e-mail.

Alerts and Recommendations
The system here presented generates a set of tips and health recommendations based on two main facts: (1) the current health status of the patient, which is determined by the glucose levels in the blood registered by the users; and (2) the data provided by the users regarding their diet, mood, and physical activity.

The recommendations were established in conjunction with a group of healthcare professionals from the Valdivia IESS (Ecuadorian Social Security Institute) Ambulatory Hospital. A detailed description of this functionality is provided in the next section.

3.2   Collaborative Filtering Based Recommender Module

One of the most important components of the system for health monitoring is the recommender module. This module implements a CF (Collaborative Filtering) method that captures patients' similarities and provides health recommendations concerning food, exercise and treatments.

CF-based systems work by collecting the user's feedback in the form of rating for items in a specific domain. Furthermore, this kind of systems exploits differences among profiles of several users in determining how to recommend and item [24].

In a nutshell, the recommender module works as follows. Firstly, the system stores (database) the patients' profiles which contain information such as age, weight, type of diabetes, as well as information concerning the treatment he/she follows, e.g., food intakes, physical activity, and insulin or medication used. Also, this database stores the patients' interest in items, in this case, in food, physical exercises, etc.

The next step consists in implementing a mechanism that compares a particular patient's profile to the profiles of other patients to determine similarity.

For this purpose, the K-means algorithm was implemented. More specifically, this module uses the MSD (Mean Squared Difference). MSD (see Eq. 1) measures the mean squared difference between two vectors.

$$sim(x, y) = 1 - \frac{1}{\#B_{x,y}} \sum_{i \in I_u} \left(\frac{r_{x,i} - r_{y,i}}{max - min} \right)^2 \epsilon [0, 1] \tag{1}$$

Where $\#B_{x,y}$ is the number of items that both patients have rated; $r_{x,i}$ and $r_{y,i}$ are the rates provided by the patients x and y respectively.

Based on the similarity computation, the most similar patients to the patient under consideration are selected. The patients selected are those whose similarity score is close to 1. Once the group of patients is selected, the module predicts how the patient under consideration would rate items that have not been evaluated. For this purpose, the weighted average is used. In the final phase, the module considers the n items that were rated with the highest values. This group of items is recommended to the target patient [25].

4 Evaluation and Results

4.1 Method

As has been described in this work, the system presented in this work provides a set of recommendations based on the similarities between patients. Therefore, to measure the performance of the system here proposed, i.e. to evaluate the efficacy and effectiveness of the system to provide the correct recommendations, the precision, recall and f-measure metrics [26] were used. These metrics have traditionally been used for evaluating information retrieval systems [27]. However, they have been more recently applied to recommender systems because this kind of systems is usually considered a particular case of personalized information retrieval system [28]. The formulas of precision, recall, and f-measure are shown below.

$$recall = \frac{correctly\ recommended\ items}{relevant\ items} \tag{2}$$

$$precision = \frac{correclty\ recommended\ items}{total\ recommended\ items} \tag{3}$$

$$F1 = 2 * \frac{precision * recall}{precision + recall} \tag{4}$$

In this evaluation, precision (see Eq. 3) is interpreted as the system's ability to recommend as many relevant items as possible. Therefore, *correctly recommended items* represents the number of items classified as relevant by the patient that are recommended by the system. Meanwhile, *total recommended items* is the total number of items recommended by the system. Regarding the recall metric, it is interpreted as the ability of the system to recommend as few non-relevant items as possible.

From Eq. 2, *relevant items* is the number of items classified as relevant by the patient. Finally, the f-measure score is calculated by using the Eq. 4.

This evaluation was conducted in a real-life scenario. More specifically, this evaluation involved the participation of 10 patients of diabetes and healthcare professionals from the Valdivia IESS (Ecuadorian Social Security Institute) Ambulatory Hospital. These patients were asked to interact with the mobile application. The corresponding patients' profiles were generated based on the information provided by the patients. The participants were directly asked about their food and physical activity preferences. The information provided by the patients was compared with the recommendations provided automatically by the system. The results obtained by the system are presented in the next section.

4.2 Results

Table 1 presents the evaluation results obtained by the system here presented. As can be seen, this system obtained and average rate of 0.799 for the precision metric, 0.812 for the recall metric, and 0.803 for the f-measure metric. Taking into account the results obtained by each patient, patient 4 (P4) obtained the highest F-measure rate (0.889). Meanwhile, patient 3 (P3) and patient 6 (P6) obtained the lowest F-measure score (0.727).

Table 1. Evaluation results.

Patient	Total	Relevant	Correct	Precision	Recall	F-measure
P1	7	6	5	0.714	0.833	0.769
P2	7	8	6	0.857	0.750	0.800
P3	6	5	4	0.667	0.800	0.727
P4	9	9	8	0.889	0.889	0.889
P5	7	7	6	0.857	0.857	0.857
P6	5	6	4	0.800	0.667	0.727
P7	5	5	4	0.800	0.800	0.800
P8	7	6	5	0.714	0.833	0.769
P9	7	7	6	0.857	0.857	0.857
P10	6	6	5	0.833	0.833	0.833
Average				0.799	0.812	0.803

Considering the results obtained by the system presented in this work, it can be concluded that this system provides good recommendations based on the similarities between patients. However, as can be seen from Table 1, there is not a big difference between the results obtained by the patients. For instance, for patient 4 (P4) the system could correctly provide 8 out of 9 items (food or physical activities) labelled as relevant by the patient. In the case of patient 3 (P3) and patient 6 (P6), the system could correctly provide just 4 out of 5 and 4 out of 6 items labelled as relevant by the users, respectively.

5   Conclusions and Future Work

In this paper, a system for diabetes self-management was presented. This application offers a set of recommendations related to the food and physical activity that patients with diabetes can perform. These recommendations aim to improve the health status of the patient. Some experiments were performed to evaluate the effectiveness of the system to provide the correct recommendations. The system obtained encouraging results, with a precision of 0.799, a recall of 0.812 and an F-measure of 0.803.

As future work, we plan to extend the system to other degenerative diseases such as hepatitis and arterial hypertension. For this purpose, it will also be necessary to analyze the treatments recommended for people with the diseases to be involved, for example the recommendations presented in [29]. On the other hand, we plan to integrate wearable healthcare devices [30] that allow the system to automatically collect data about vital signs such as body temperature, pulse rate, respiration rate, blood pressure, and weight, among others, as well as the levels of glucose in the blood. This kind of devices has been applied for monitoring other diseases such as Parkinson [31]. This goal will be achieved thanks to the proliferation of such type of devices in the market, some of which do not represent high investment costs. However, an analysis of the health devices available on the market will be performed to ensure the correct performance of the application with the smallest investment. This fact will allow the application to be accessible for most people.

Acknowledgments. This work has been funded by the Universidad de Guayaquil (Ecuador) through the project entitled "Tecnologías inteligentes para la autogestión de la salud". Finally, this work has been also partially supported by the Spanish National Research Agency (AEI) and the European Regional Development Fund (FEDER / ERDF) through project KBS4FIA (TIN2016-76323-R).

References

1. WHO | Diabetes. World Heal. Organ (2016)
2. Ren, L., Han, W., Yang, H., Sun, F., Xu, S., Hu, S., Zhang, M., He, X., Hua, J., Peng, S.: Autophagy stimulated proliferation of porcine PSCs might be regulated by the canonical Wnt signaling pathway. Biochem. Biophys. Res. Commun. **479**, 537–543 (2016)
3. World Health Organization: Global report on diabetes. World Health Organization (2016)
4. Salas-Zárate, M.P., Medina-Moreira, J., Lagos-Ortiz, K., Luna-Aveiga, H., Rodríguez-García, M.Á., Valencia-García, R.: Sentiment analysis on tweets about diabetes: an aspect-level approach. Comput. Math. Methods Med. **2017**, 1–9 (2017)
5. Funnell, M.M., Brown, T.L., Childs, B.P., Haas, L.B., Hosey, G.M., Jensen, B., Maryniuk, M., Peyrot, M., Piette, J.D., Reader, D., Siminerio, L.M., Weinger, K., Weiss, M.A.: National standards for diabetes self-management education. Diabetes Care **33**(Suppl 1), S89–S96 (2010)
6. Clement, S.: Diabetes self-management education. Diabetes Care **18**, 1204–1214 (1995)
7. Ricci, F., Rokach, L., Shapira, B.: Introduction to recommender systems handbook. In: Recommender Systems Handbook, pp. 1–35. Springer, Boston (2011)

8. Colombo-Mendoza, L.O., Valencia-García, R., Rodríguez-González, A., Alor-Hernández, G., Samper-Zapater, J.J.: RecomMetz: A context-aware knowledge-based mobile recommender system for movie showtimes. Expert Syst. Appl. **42**, 1202–1222 (2015)
9. Yuan, N.J., Zheng, Y., Zhang, L., Xie, X.: T-Finder: a recommender system for finding passengers and Vacant Taxis. IEEE Trans. Knowl. Data Eng. **25**, 2390–2403 (2013)
10. Tejeda-Lorente, Á., Porcel, C., Peis, E., Sanz, R., Herrera-Viedma, E.: A quality based recommender system to disseminate information in a university digital library. Inf. Sci. (Ny) **261**, 52–69 (2014)
11. Zheng, Z., Ma, H., Lyu, M.R., King, I.: WSRec: a collaborative filtering based web service recommender system. In: 2009 IEEE International Conference on Web Services, pp. 437–444. IEEE (2009)
12. Ekstrand, M.D., Riedl, J.T., Konstan, J.A.: Collaborative filtering recommender systems. Found. Trends Hum. Comput. Interact. **4**, 81–173 (2011)
13. Paradiso, R.: Wearable health care system for vital signs monitoring. In: 4th International IEEE EMBS Special Topic Conference on Information Technology Applications in Biomedicine, pp. 283–286. IEEE (2003)
14. Chawla, N.V., Davis, D.A.: Bringing big data to personalized healthcare: a patient-centered framework. J. Gen. Intern. Med. **28**, 660–665 (2013)
15. Duan, L., Street, W.N., Xu, E.: Healthcare information systems: data mining methods in the creation of a clinical recommender system. Enterp. Inf. Syst. **5**, 169–181 (2011)
16. Kirwan, M., Vandelanotte, C., Fenning, A., Duncan, M.J.: Diabetes self-management smartphone application for adults with type 1 diabetes: randomized controlled trial. J. Med. Internet Res. **15**, e235 (2013)
17. El-Gayar, O., Timsina, P., Nawar, N., Eid, W.: Mobile applications for diabetes self-management: status and potential. J. Diabetes Sci. Technol. **7**, 247–262 (2013)
18. Gao, C., Zhou, L., Liu, Z., Wang, H., Bowers, B.: Mobile application for diabetes self-management in China: do they fit for older adults? Int. J. Med. Inform. **101**, 68–74 (2017)
19. Goyal, S., Morita, P., Lewis, G.F., Yu, C., Seto, E., Cafazzo, J.A.: The systematic design of a behavioural mobile health application for the self-management of type 2 diabetes. Can. J. Diabetes **40**, 95–104 (2016)
20. Schwaber, K., Beedle, M.: Agile software development with Scrum. Prentice Hall, Upper Saddle River (2002)
21. Colberg, S.R., Sigal, R.J., Yardley, J.E., Riddell, M.C., Dunstan, D.W., Dempsey, P.C., Horton, E.S., Castorino, K., Tate, D.F.: Physical activity/exercise and diabetes: a position statement of the American Diabetes Association. Diabetes Care **39**, 2065–2079 (2016)
22. Colberg, S.R., Sigal, R.J., Fernhall, B., Regensteiner, J.G., Blissmer, B.J., Rubin, R.R., Chasan-Taber, L., Albright, A.L., Braun, B.: American College of Sports Medicine, American Diabetes Association: exercise and type 2 diabetes: the American College of Sports Medicine and the American Diabetes Association: joint position statement. Diabetes Care **33**, e147–e167 (2010)
23. LaMonte, M.J., Blair, S.N., Church, T.S.: Physical activity and diabetes prevention. J. Appl. Physiol. **99**, 1205–1213 (2005)
24. Melville, P., Mooney, R.J., Nagarajan, R.: Content-boosted collaborative filtering for improved recommendations. Eighteenth Natl. Conf. Artif. Intell. **1034**, 187–192 (2002)
25. Shardanand, U., Maes, P.: Social information filtering: algorithms for automating "word of mouth." In: Proceedings of the SIGCHI conference on Human factors in computing systems —CHI 1995, pp. 210–217. ACM Press, New York (1995)
26. Salton, G., McGill, M.J.: Introduction to Modern Information Retrieval. McGraw-Hill, New York (1983)

27. Raghavan, V., Bollmann, P., Jung, G.S.: A critical investigation of recall and precision as measures of retrieval system performance. ACM Trans. Inf. Syst. **7**, 205–229 (1989)
28. Fang, B., Liao, S., Xu, K., Cheng, H., Zhu, C., Chen, H.: A novel mobile recommender system for indoor shopping. Expert Syst. Appl. **39**, 11992–12000 (2012)
29. European Association for the Study of the Liver: Electronic address: easloffice@easloffice. eu: EASL Recommendations on Treatment of Hepatitis C 2016. J. Hepatol. **66**, 153–194 (2017)
30. Badreddin, O., Castillo, R., Lessard, L., Albanese, M.: Towards improved performance and compliance in healthcare using wearables and bluetooth technologies (2015). http://dl.acm. org/citation.cfm?id=2886482
31. Klucken, J.: Mobile Healthcare Technologies—"Wearables" for objective measures of motor symptoms in Parkinson's disease. Basal Ganglia **8**, 119–121 (2017)

Analysis of a Network Fault Detection System to Support Decision Making

Mitchell Vásquez-Bermúdez[1,2] (iD), Jorge Hidalgo[1] (iD),
María del Pilar Avilés-Vera[1(✉)] (iD), José Sánchez-Cercado[1] (iD),
and Christian Roberto Antón-Cedeño[2] (iD)

[1] Escuela de Ingeniería en Computación e Informática,
Facultad de Ciencias Agrarias, Universidad Agraria del Ecuador,
Av. 25 de Julio y Pio Jaramillo, Guayaquil, Ecuador
{mitchell.vasquezb, jhidalgo,
maviles}@uagraria.edu.ec, joseph.saenz91@gmail.com
[2] Universidad de Guayaquil. Cdla. Universitaria Salvador Allende,
Guayaquil, Ecuador
{mitchell.vasquezb, christian.antonc}@ug.edu.ec

Abstract. When a network fault occurs, administrators spend a lot of time finding the causes as well as solving the problem. Network fault localization is a process that aims to find the exact source of the fault. This process consists of a diagnosis process that considers the symptoms ranging from end-to-end connectivity fault to more sophisticated symptoms such as SLA violations. To solve network faults, it is necessary a great amount of information that allows network administrators to analyze and determine symptoms, and then reduce the number of possible solutions. Considering the above discussed, it is necessary a decision support system that allows network administrators to diagnose a network fault and solve it. In this work, we present a fault detection system for LAN networks. This system is based on a set of rules that allows determining the specific problem as well as to obtain possible solutions to them. The rules were defined based on the data collected from network monitoring process as well as the expertise of network administrators. The system was evaluated to measure its effectiveness regarding network fault detection, obtaining encouraging results.

Keywords: Network fault detection · Decision making

1 Introduction

One of the main problems that LANs (Local Area Network) administrators face is the lack of a network monitoring and management system that monitors the computer network for detecting faults and that notifies them. When a network fault occurs, administrators spend a lot of time finding the causes as well as solving the problem.

Network fault localization is a process that aims to find the exact source of the fault [1]. This process is performed in several layers of the network protocol stack. Furthermore, it diagnoses the symptoms ranging from end-to-end connectivity fault to more sophisticated symptoms such as SLA (Service-Level Agreement) violations [2].

© Springer International Publishing AG 2017
R. Valencia-García et al. (Eds.): CITI 2017, CCIS 749, pp. 72–83, 2017.
DOI: 10.1007/978-3-319-67283-0_6

Most problems that reduce the performance of LANs are related to the physical layer of the OSI model, which includes wiring, NIC (Network Interface Card), routers and switches. Network connectivity faults represent a permanent or intermittent inability of communication with a network or performing tasks related to it. There are multiple causes of this kind of problems, for example, a cable with incorrect splicing, incorrect NICs, and faults in routing devices. These kinds of problems are difficult to diagnose, isolate and solve [3]. On the other hand, there are no tools that provide solutions to problems such as the logic fault identification that can occur in a network.

To solve network faults, it is necessary a great amount of information that allows us to analyze and determine symptoms that reduce the number of possible solutions. The network management solution must be easy to deploy and cost effective. In this sense, it must have a graphical user interface that can be implemented in an easy and fast way [4].

Network monitoring processes are complicated because of the lot of available network management system [5], which makes it difficult to find a solution for the problems. To achieve a correct network management, administrators must know the real-time operation of the network and find security threats and faults as soon as possible. To perform the analysis and diagnosis of problems, it is necessary to locate the network fault and then give a quick response and solution to the problem [6].

Considering the above discussed, it is necessary a 24/7 network monitoring system. For instance, when the network administrator receives a call from a user who has a problem accessing to a website, he/she doesn't have a specific information about the problem. Such information could be provided by a 24/7 network monitoring system [7].

In this work, a system for detecting faults presented in LAN networks is presented. This system allows detecting faults based on a set of rules. Once the fault is detected, the system provides a possible solution to the problem. Thanks to this information, network administrator saves time and effort for solving the problem.

The system proposed was evaluated to know its effectiveness detecting networks faults. For this purpose, the metrics precision, recall and F-measure were used.

The rest of this paper is structured as follows. Section 2 provides a description of the most relevant works regarding network monitoring. Section 3 presents the architecture of the system proposed. Evaluation and results are described in Sect. 4. Finally, conclusions and feature work are presented.

2   Related Works

In the context of communication networks, fault localization is an important fact that must be considered because this kind of problems cannot be avoided. Hence, its fast detection is a task that must be addressed. Fault detection and localization are tasks of great significance because they allow to protect and restore the network performance [8]. Furthermore, the detection of link faults, as well as their location, can be present in different layers of the protocol stack. Therefore, it is desired that these faults can be identified and corrected in the physical layer before they spread to higher layers.

Usually, fault management in computer networks has four main phases: detection, localization, repair and testing. The most important phase is the localization phase [9]. There are approaches focused on the fault treatment. These approaches use different techniques according to the number of nodes. These techniques combine active and passive measurements to localize faults in networks.

The end-to-end approach uses passive measurements to localize faults in networks [10]. This approach considers fault location as an optimization problem. Therefore, it uses the GA-FL (Genetic Algorithm Fault Location) applied to a small set of components, and then it uses the rest of nodes. Also, the end-to-end can be implemented with heuristic algorithms [11, 12], which retrieve scattered information through the network to detect and repair faulty components. This algorithm selects a sequence of routers for performing tests. When a router is considered as faulty, it is repaired by reconfiguring the topology and wrong routes. Simulation results show that this algorithm requires a very small set of network components to detect and repair all faults in the network.

Classic tools for network fault detection use passive methods, which monitor the operational state of the network and detect the presence of faults. These faults are located based on the information collected from the nodes that were damaged. In this context, there is an active method [13], which works in a network with several nodes and a polling station. This method assumes that all components work fine. Furthermore, this method consumes bandwidth resources. Many researchers have tried to address this drawback through programming methods and describing algorithms as a set of problems and simulation results [14]. The experiments performed demonstrate a reduction of network traffic and fault diagnosis time.

3   Architecture of the System for Network Fault Detection

This section describes the main components of the system for network fault detection proposed in this work. As can be shown in Fig. 1, the system architecture is composed of four modules, namely: (1) monitoring module, (2) fault detection module, (3) fault history module, and (4) new knowledge module. Also, it can be noted that client applications interact with the server to detect faults that can occur.

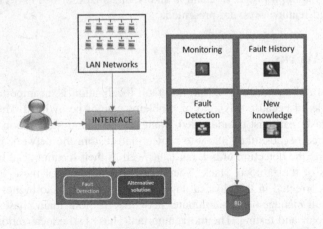

Fig. 1. Architecture of the system for network fault detection.

The fault detection system for LAN networks is based on rules. Thanks to this feature, new knowledge can be added to support decision making of networks administrators.

The system constantly monitors all host devices of the network to obtain information that helps to verify the parameters received. The response of each host device is analyzed and verified by means of a set of rules that help to identify the possible problem. This information is stored as an unknown parameter for the knowledge base.

Common problems in LAN networks are:

1. Host disconnection. The host cannot connect to the network due to a malfunction of the network card, a damaged UTP cable, among other problems.
2. Host without Internet access. The host has no access to Internet due to a bad configuration or a damaged modem.
3. Unconfigured host. It occurs when users or network administrators make a bad network/host configuration.
4. Communication between hosts. This problem refers to the case when the host cannot be seen or accessed by other computers despite it has access to the Internet and it has an active state within the network.

3.1   Monitoring Module

This module shows the information of all host devices of the network such as connected hosts, IP direction, host name, and its state.

This module constantly monitors the input and output of network packages. Monitoring module obtains information about the network traffic as well as the data necessary to verify the correct operation of the network. This information allows the system to determine the possible cause of the problem.

To perform the tasks above mentioned, this module uses the SNMP (Simple Network Management Protocol) protocol [15], which in turn uses the following ports:

- 161/UDP to get the value of an object.
- 162/UDP to receive SNMP traps.

The process carried out by this module can be summarized as follows:

- The monitoring module sends a GetRequest message to the managed host to get the state of it. For example, for the message "OID_sysUpTime = 1.3.6.1.2.1.1.3.0", the module obtains the active time of a network interface, in this case, all managed hosts.
- The system captures the flow obtained from both the SNMP and ICMP requests, which are done to the host. The responses obtained are analyzed by the fault detection module, which relates the request values with one of the rules defined by the system.

3.2   Fault Detection Module

This module identifies and localizes the faults that occur in the network [16]. This process validates each parameter obtained by the monitoring module.

As was previously mentioned, the fault detection module is based on a set of rules which were defined by using the Clips [17] library. This tool allows executing and validating the knowledge base by means of rules.

The rules used by the module were established based on information about common problems detected during network monitoring process. In this way, each rule defines a response to each problem that can occur in the network. All rules are contained in a text file to allow Clips software to select the correct rule. Figure 2 depicts the fault detection process.

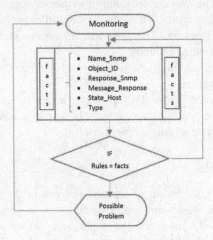

Fig. 2. Rule workflow.

The main component of fault detection module is the facts collected from the monitoring process. Based on this information, rules are established by means of six main parameters:

- Nombre_Snmp: It represents the name of the ObjectID, i.e. it stores the name of the SNMP parameter received by the network monitoring module, e.g., OID: sysUpTime.
- Object_ID. It refers to the identifier value of the Object ID. It is obtained by the network monitoring module. An example of this value is "OID: 1.3.6.1.2.1.1.3.0."
- Response_Snmp: It represents the response given by the SNMP. It stores the response obtained by the network monitoring module when a SNMP request to the hosts managed is performed.
- Mensaje_Respuesta. It is the value obtained from the ICMP request. It stores the value obtained when a SNMP request is performed and it receives a response from the hosts managed.
- Estado Host. It refers to the state of the host (Active or Inactive). This value is obtained through the ICMP request from the network monitoring module.
- Tipo. It represents the value of the kind of request performed, e.g. communication network request.

Each rule contains all information necessary to perform the retract process. This process is carried out by the CLIPs to identify the problem. This response is assigned to a variable of type "Tipo", which is read by the system to show the identified problem.

As was previously mentioned, all rules are defined in a text file. Figure 3. shows an extract of this text file, where it can be noted that each rule is composed of its name, the known facts, and the response. A detailed description of this rule is provided below.

The *defrule* function allows assigning the name of the rule. The *hecho* elements are represented by means of a template which contains all variables. Each *hecho* element contains the variables to be evaluated to detect the problem. On the other hand, the *retract* function is used to eliminate *hecho* elements when new variables are provided. When the rule matches the variables provided, the name of the problem is stored in a template called *resultado_diagnostico_problema*. Finally, this information is provided to the user.

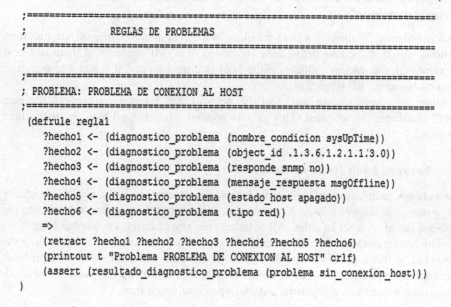

```
;========================================================================
;                REGLAS DE PROBLEMAS
;========================================================================


;========================================================================
; PROBLEMA: PROBLEMA DE CONEXION AL HOST
;========================================================================
  (defrule regla1
     ?hecho1 <- (diagnostico_problema (nombre_condicion sysUpTime))
     ?hecho2 <- (diagnostico_problema (object_id .1.3.6.1.2.1.1.3.0))
     ?hecho3 <- (diagnostico_problema (responde_snmp no))
     ?hecho4 <- (diagnostico_problema (mensaje_respuesta msgOffline))
     ?hecho5 <- (diagnostico_problema (estado_host apagado))
     ?hecho6 <- (diagnostico_problema (tipo red))
     =>
     (retract ?hecho1 ?hecho2 ?hecho3 ?hecho4 ?hecho5 ?hecho6)
     (printout t "Problema PROBLEMA DE CONEXION AL HOST" crlf)
     (assert (resultado_diagnostico_problema (problema sin_conexion_host)))
  )
```

Fig. 3. Rule structure.

The problem detection is performed through the validation of all parameterized rules. Some of the problems covered by these rules are described below.

Host disconnection. It occurs when it is not possible to establish communication with the remote host. In this case, the system compares the parameters provided, specifically the state of the host (Active or Inactive). Considering this information, the system performs a request using ICMO packages. If these parameters are met and the response is "Inactive", the problem detected is identified as "Host disconnection".

Communication problems between hosts. When communication cannot be established between hosts of the network, the system validates if the state of the host is not "inactive", and the request by means of ICMP packages is not "Active".

Considering the above-described data, the system determines that the problem is due to the fact that there is no communication between hosts of the network.

IP duplication. When an IP duplication problem occurs, Windows hosts detect the problem and exclude the network host until a valid IP is assigned. The system here proposed validates, through rules, if there is a response to the request performed by means of ICMP packages, and if there is a connection with the host. If both conditions are met the problem detected is IP duplication.

Printer connection problems. The rule that was established for printer connection problems, validates the state of the network interface through a Trap. If this state is "Link down", and the host type is "Printer", then the problem detected is "Printer Connection problem".

DNS problems. To identify a DNS problem in the host managed, the system monitors all hosts stored in the knowledge base by means of SNMP requests. If there is a host disconnected, the system validates if the host is turned on and if it has a response to requests based on ICMP packages.

When all conditions are met, and the network has Internet connection, the rule "DNS problems" is activated. This rule is applied when the problem is in the host managed.

3.3   Network Fault History Module

The network fault history module provides users a description of the faults detected by the system. To achieve this goal, this module determines the possible solutions to the problem based on a set of rules. All solutions are stored in the knowledge base.

The results obtained by this module are provided to the users in a format like the presented in Table 1, where the ID, description, date and hour when the problem occurred are presented. Thanks to the information provided by this module, network administrators can solve problems without spending much time.

3.4   New Knowledge Module

This module allows establishing new rules to deal with problems arisen from SNMP requests. These rules are established based on the information stored in the knowledge base and information about the new problem detected by the network monitoring module.

The new knowledge module uses the CLIPs file which describes all rules of the system. This module uses the SNMO protocol, which receives the Trap [18], and obtains the OID (Unique Identifiers). When the system detects a network fault, it provides the network administrator with the corresponding information that helps them to establish a new rule, and to add information related to possible solutions.

Table 1. Network fault history.

ID	Example	Description	Date	Hour
75	DNS problem	The host has an IP address. However, it does not have Internet access.	02/08/2016	1:19:14
76	Host connection problem	The host cannot be found on the network. The host has been disconnected.	24/08/2016	13:59:32
77	Bandwidth problem	High bandwidth consumption.	14/09/2016	14:00:25
78	DNS problem	The host has an IP address. However, it does not have Internet access.	04/09/2016	22:04:12
79	Bandwidth problem	High bandwidth consumption.	14/09/2016	14:00:25

For instance, to obtain a new fault, a new IP configuration is performed in the router. Then, the SNMO agent sends trap alerts when the problem occurs, and the system receives a description of the fault such as "v2 public host 1192.193.194.195" 1.11.12.12.15.15 "IP change". The message selected by the application is saved as new knowledge. Finally, the network administrator must define a new rule, assigning a name to the Trap received.

4   Evaluation and Results

To evaluate the effectiveness of the system detecting failures in a LAN network, the recall, precision, and F-measure evaluation metrics were used. Recall (1) is the proportion of actual positive cases that were correctly predicted as such. On the other hand, precision (2) represents the proportion of predicted positive cases that are real positives. Finally, F-measure (3) is the harmonic mean of precision and recall [19].

$$recall = \frac{TP}{TP + FN} \tag{1}$$

$$precision = \frac{TP}{TP + FP} \tag{2}$$

$$F1 = 2 * \frac{precision * recall}{precision + recall} \tag{3}$$

Where TP is the number of true positives, FN is the number of false negatives, and FP is the number of false positives.

Specifically, the variables used to measure the effectiveness of the system are:

- True positives. The items that were correctly identified as network faults.
- False positives. The items that were identified as network faults, but they are not network faults.

- False negatives. The items that were not identified as errors, but they are network faults.

The experiments were performed in a LAN network (Fig. 4) with access to Internet, IP directions ranging from 192.168.1.1 to 192.168.4.14. A network fault detection system was installed in the administrator host. This system monitored all hosts including PC's and printers.

To simulate network faults, several network faults were generated, which were detected by the system installed in the administrator host. Once all network faults were generated and detected, these ones were provided to the system proposed in this work. Then, the evaluation metrics above were used to measure the effectiveness of this system.

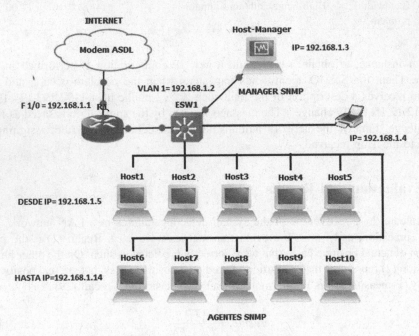

Fig. 4. Network topology simulation

4.1 Fault Detection

As was previously mentioned, the effectiveness of the system proposed in this work was evaluated over the LAN topology presented in Fig. 4. The evaluation results are shown in Table 2. Five hundred network faults were generated, which were divided into 20 groups. Some of the network faults generated are cable disconnection, IP duplication, host shutdown, SNMP port deactivation, printer disconnected, DNS problem, Internet access blocked by antivirus, as well as other networks faults that were not considered by the system. Most common network problems were "communication problems between hosts" and "DNS problems". The main cause of these problems was an unstable Internet connection. Table 2 presents the precision, recall and f-measure

Table 2. Evaluation results of the fault detection system

Test	P	R	F	Test	P	R	F
1	0,	0,7	0,6	11	0,8	0,6	0,7
2	0,8	0,7	0,9	12	0,7	0,7	0,8
3	0,7	0,7	0,6	13	0,8	0,7	0,6
4	0,8	0,8	0,7	14	0,9	0,8	0,6
5	0,9	0,9	0,7	15	0,6	0,8	0,6
6	0,8	0,6	0,8	16	0,7	0,9	0,7
7	0,7	0,7	0,7	17	0,8	0,9	0,7
8	0,8	0,7	0,8	18	0,6	0,6	0,8
9	0,9	0,8	0,9	19	0,6	0,8	0,9
10	0,6	0,9	0,6	20	0,7	0,8	0,7
AVG	0,76	0,75	0,73	AVG	0,72	0,76	0,71

scores obtained for each group of network failures. As can be seen in Table 2, the system got encouraging results regarding network fault detection, with values of 0.74, 0.76 and 0.72 for precision, recall, and F-measure, respectively.

5 Conclusions and Future Work

This work presents the analysis of a network fault detection system that provides network administrators with possible solutions to the network problems detected in a LAN network. The general performance of this system is based on the information collected from network monitoring process. Furthermore, the solutions were established based on the expertise of network administrators. The system was evaluated to measure its effectiveness regarding network fault detection. The results obtained are encouraging.

Despite all advantages and features provided by the system, it has several limitations that must be addressed in future work. For example, the system depends on a knowledge base about network faults, which must be fed by network administrators. In this sense, it is important to explore new mechanisms that allow the system to learn and generate new rules through solutions based on expert systems [20].

On the other hand, the experiments were performed in a simulated environment, which is not enough to obtain a wide perspective of all failures that can occur in real-world scenarios. Therefore, we plan to implement the system in LAN networks from the Ecuadorian universities.

Finally, the system here presented is focused on LAN networks, which limits its use to a narrow set of scenarios. Hence, it is important to perform new experiments in wireless networks that integrate mechanisms based on expert systems [21]. Furthermore, it will be very interesting to carry out experiments with WiMAX technology, by using algorithms that reduce the delay of transmissions [22].

References

1. Steinder, M.ł., Sethi, A.S.: A survey of fault localization techniques in computer networks. Sci. Comput. Program. **53**, 165–194 (2004)
2. Natu, M., Sethi, A.S.: Active probing approach for fault localization in computer networks. In: 2006 4th IEEE/IFIP Workshop on End-to-End Monitoring Techniques and Services, pp. 25–33. IEEE (2006)
3. Falahati, B., Fu, Y.: Faults and failures in cyber-power interdependent networks. In: 2014 IEEE PES T&D Conference and Exposition, pp. 1–5. IEEE (2014)
4. Hendrawan, T., Rachmana, N., Iskandar, M.U.: Network management system (NMS) using local collector mediation devices. In: 2016 10th International Conference on Telecommunication Systems Services and Applications, pp. 1–4. IEEE (2016)
5. Hedström, T., Lundahl, S.: Evaluation of monitoring systems and processes (2016)
6. Fei, H., Yu, B.: Performance evaluation of wireless mesh networks with self-similar traffic. In: 2007 International Conference on Wireless Communications, Networking and Mobile Computing, pp. 1697–1700. IEEE (2007)
7. Sonawane, V.R., Singh, L.L., Nunse, P.R., Nalage, S.D.: Visual monitoring system using simple network management protocol. In: 2015 International Conference on Computational Intelligence and Communication Networks, pp. 197–200. IEEE (2015)
8. Wang, R., Wu, D., Li, Y., Yu, X., Hui, Z., Long, K.: Knight's tour-based fast fault localization mechanism in mesh optical communication networks. Photonic Netw. Commun. **23**, 123–129 (2012)
9. Garshasbi, M.S.: Fault localization based on combines active and passive measurements in computer networks by ant colony optimization. Reliab. Eng. Syst. Saf. **152**, 205–212 (2016)
10. Jamali, S., Garshasbi, M.S.: Fault localization algorithm in computer networks by employing a genetic algorithm. J. Exp. Theor. Artif. Intell. **29**, 157–174 (2017)
11. Garshasbi, M.S., Jamali, S.: A new fault detection method using end-to-end data and sequential testing for computer networks. Int. J. Inf. Technol. Comput. Sci. **6**, 93–100 (2014)
12. Zhang, X., Zhou, Z., Hasker, G., Perrig, A., Gligor, V.: Network fault localization with small TCB. In: 2011 19th IEEE International Conference on Network Protocols, pp. 143–154. IEEE (2011)
13. Lu, L., Xu, Z., Wang, W., Sun, Y.: A new fault detection method for computer networks. Reliab. Eng. Syst. Saf. **114**, 45–51 (2013)
14. McCloghrie, K., Rose, M.T.: Management information base for network management of TCP/IP-based internets: MIB-II (1991). http://dl.acm.org/citation.cfm?id=RFC1213
15. Lee, S., Levanti, K., Kim, H.S.: Network monitoring: present and future. Comput. Netw. **65**, 84–98 (2014)
16. Wu, C.-C., Lai, L.-F., Chang, Y.-S.: Parallelizing CLIPS-based expert systems by the permutation feature of pattern matching. In: 2010 Second International Conference on Computer Engineering and Applications, pp. 214–218. IEEE (2010)
17. Rose, M.T.: IETF Tools. https://tools.ietf.org/
18. Salas-Zárate, M.P., Valencia-García, R., Ruiz-Martínez, A., Colomo-Palacios, R.: Feature-based opinion mining in financial news: an ontology-driven approach. J. Inf. Sci. 16555151664552 (2016)
19. Khalid, R., Jassim, R.: Expert diagnosis systems for network connection problems. In: 2014 2nd International Conference on Artificial Intelligence, Modelling and Simulation, pp. 15–18. IEEE (2014)
20. Frantti, T., Majanen, M.: An expert system for real-time traffic management in wireless local area networks. Expert Syst. Appl. **41**, 4996–5008 (2014)

21. Hesselfelt, H.F.J., Dekker, J.H., Boes, G.: Handoff Delay Optimization in IEEE 802.16e (Mobile WiMAX) using Fuzzy Expert System. Agon Elsevier, Amsterdam (1962)
22. Dong, C., Dulay, N.: Argumentation-based fault diagnosis for home networks. In: Proceedings of the 2nd ACM SIGCOMM workshop on Home networks—HomeNets 2011, p. 37. ACM Press, New York (2011)

Knowledge-Based Expert System for Control of Corn Crops

Karen Mite-Baidal$^{(\boxtimes)}$ iD, Carlota Delgado-Vera iD,
Evelyn Solís-Avilés iD, Manuel Jiménez-Icaza iD, Wilmer Baque iD,
and Mónica Patricia Santos-Chico iD

Computer Science Department, Faculty of Agricultural Sciences,
Agrarian University of Ecuador, Av. 25 de Julio y Pio Jaramillo,
P.O. BOX 09-04-100, Guayaquil, Ecuador
{kmite, cdelgado, esolis, mjimenez, wbaque,
msantos}@uagraria.edu.ec

Abstract. Information and communication technology in agriculture has emerged for the enhancement of agricultural and rural development through improved information and communication processes. In this context, this paper presents the design and development of a knowledge-based expert system to the control and monitoring of corn crop. The main objective of this work is to obtain a knowledge base from experts' information that helps to determine the factors (soil, diseases and pests) that should be considered for generating recommendations. The system provides a recommendation according to the problem detected and the attributes established. For this purpose, the system used a set of inference rules. The use of this system would allow farmers to obtain important benefits such as increasing the yield and productivity of their orchards, supporting inexperienced users in crop management, increasing quality in the decision making process, and reliable results.

Keywords: Expert systems · Inference rules · Knowledge-based system

1 Introduction

In recent years, microcomputers have become instruments that facilitate the development of systems to make decisions. The intelligent systems are the way to manage information that allows making decisions about problems of specific fields [1].

These expert systems have two main objectives: (1) obtain the criteria of the experts and make them more accessible and (2) improve the information about the control of the crop. Experts systems can be used when experts' knowledge about a specific problem is needed. In addition, this knowledge will be always available when requested. Furthermore, a criterion could be provided without the presence of an expert or the bibliographic material.

The aim of this study is to develop an expert system able to generate recommendations about the control of corn crops. The recommendations are based on rules for the control and monitoring of corn. This field was selected since, in Ecuador, corn crops are some of the main sources of the economy.

© Springer International Publishing AG 2017
R. Valencia-García et al. (Eds.): CITI 2017, CCIS 749, pp. 84–95, 2017.
DOI: 10.1007/978-3-319-67283-0_7

Several expert systems have been developed to help farmers to make decisions on control of crops. These systems are oriented to different stages of corn growth such as soil preparation, planting or germination, vegetative growth, flowering, and fertilization, among others [2].

In Ecuador, maize agriculture is an important economic activity. According to a study conducted by the Ministry of Agriculture, Livestock, Aquaculture, and Fisheries from the year 2000 to 2012, the production of soft corn increased by 68.43%. This result is mainly due to two reasons (1) the growing demand for this product and (2) corn has been considered as a staple food in the diet of the population. In the 2000 census was reported a production of 43 thousand tons, whereas in the 2012 survey (ESPAC-INEC) it increased to 73 thousand tons, which indicates an average annual growth rate of 6.93% [3].

For the development of the application proposed in this work, we consider a rule-based expert system able to generate recommendations. Therefore, two knowledge bases of the corn crop control domain were generated. The first one represents input and output variables. The second one represents the rules to be used [4].

In the domain of expert systems, several rules are activated for the same configuration of input parameters, and an output is generated for each one of the rules. These outputs cause a change in the knowledge thus activating other rules. This process is known as chaining rules. There are two specific chaining rules: forward and backward [5].

The rest of this paper is organized as follows. Section 2 presents a review of the literature concerning agriculture. Section 3 presents a knowledge-based expert system for control of corn crops. A case study is described in Sect. 4. Finally, our conclusions and future work are presented in Sect. 5.

2 Related Works

Maize is known in different ways depending on the country and culture. In America, it is known as "corn", "choclo", "elote", "jojoto", "sara" or "zara".

The growth of maize is classified into five stages: (1) germination and emergence, (2) initial vegetation, (3) vegetative growth, (4) flowering, and (5) grain filling and maturity [6].

The agricultural sector constantly undergoes changes with respect to the nutrients of the land due to climatic changes and other factors [7]. In this sense, it is important to identify the type of crop to plant according to the area and climate, among other factors. The technology plays an important role in identifying these aspects. For example, Antonopoulou et al. [8] proposed a support system for farmers to select alternative crops specifically maize, soybean, sorghum, rapeseed, and thistle.

The importance of the design of computer models based on rules is a mechanism to obtain a technical decision that considers the necessary conditions and parameters. For instance, Debaeke et al. [9] proposed a set of rules based on agronomic principles (density of plants).

Several works distinguish recommendation techniques into following four classes (1) collaborative-filtering, (2) demographic filtering, (3) knowledge-based filtering, and (4) content-based filtering [10]. Furthermore, there are different ways to infer knowledge stored in the system, such as decision trees, clustering, and rule-based. The last one is the method selected in this work [11].

Gordon [12] mentioned that rules can be stored and updated as needed. These rules are converted into a knowledge file rather than an information file since the rules would be used as the automated reasoning. A rule-based system consists of three components: (1) working memory, (2) the rule base, and (3) the inference engine. The rule base and working memory are data structures that the system uses, and the inference engine is the basic program. The advantage of this framework is the clear separation between data (knowledge about the domain) and control (how knowledge should be used) [13].

Sarma et al. [14] presented a logical programming approach where the system integrates a structured knowledge base that contains remedies of diseases about the rice plant. Also, this database is integrated with images related to the symptoms of the disease and an interface that contains rules-based decision-making algorithms, which are validated by experts.

On the other hand, Marwaha [15] proposed the use of knowledge-based systems based on ontologies. The authors claim that these systems help to farmers to improve efficiency, crop yield, and productivity with respect to the identification of diseases, insects or pests.

In [16], the authors propose a robust and dynamic nutrient management known as SSNM (Site-specific Nutrient Management) which aims to increase yields and optimize profits while maintaining the productivity of cropping systems.

Finally, in [17], the authors present AGRIdaksh, a tool for building online experts systems. This tool enables domain experts to build agricultural expert systems for crop management with the minimal intervention of knowledge engineers and programmers.

3 Knowledge-Based Expert System for Control of Corn Crops

3.1 Modules of the Expert System

The knowledge-based expert system proposed in this work has as purpose to guide students in the best practices of control of the maize crop from the preparation of the soil to the harvest [18]. The mobile application is composed of four modules: (1) soil preparation, (2) planting or germination, (3) vegetative growth, and (4) flowering.

Figure 1 shows a scheme of the system dependent relationships [12], and the variables needed by each module to generate the recommendations. These relationships allow organizing the structure of the rules. These rules are based on the work presented in [19].

Soil Preparation. The main variables verified at this stage are (1) texture of the land, (2) date of the crop, and (3) the place to carry out the sowing. With respect to the first one it can be sandy, clayey and loamy-loamy. The system will show the features of each kind of soil to allow user to determine the correct one. Regarding the second one, the January to May months are not suitable for the crop. Finally, in the case study, it was applied in the Coast region.

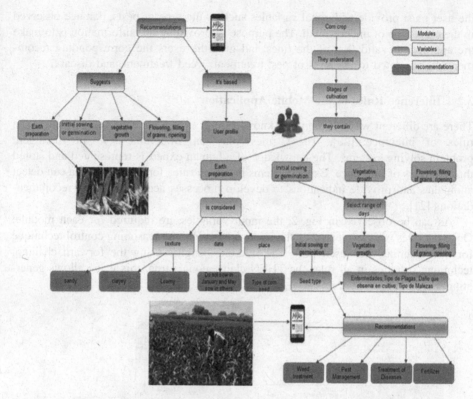

Fig. 1. Modules of the expert system for the control of corn crops.

Planting or Germination. The system at this stage requests that the user selects between the ranges from 0 to 1 (sowing period), and from 2 to 6 (germination period). In addition, the user must enter additional variables such as seed type, type of pests, type of disease, and type of weed, among others. Regarding pests, the system will provide information about different types of pests and diseases commonly presented in the seed type. The purpose of providing this information is to make the appropriate validation of the rules and give the users the corresponding recommendations. With regards to the weeds, the system will provide a set of images to allow users to identify the correct one.

Vegetative Growth. The system at this stage requests the user to choose between the range of 7 to 48 days called the period of vegetative development. Furthermore, the user must provide additional variables such as the type of pests, damage observed in the crop, type of undergrowth, among others. The purpose of providing this information is to make the appropriate validation of the rules and give the users the corresponding recommendations related to the level of pest treatment, weed treatment, and disease.

Flowering. The system at this stage requires the user to choose between the range of 49 to 52 days, 53 to 67 days, 68 to 110 days called the development period. In addition, the user must provide additional variables such as the type of pests, damage observed in the crop, type of undergrowth. The purpose of providing this information is to make the appropriate validation of the rules and give the users the corresponding recommendations related to the level of pest treatment, weed treatment, and disease.

3.2 Inference Rules of the Mobile Application

There are different ways to represent knowledge in expert systems, one of them is the rules of inference [20]. These rules play an important role in intelligent problem-solving systems. The knowledge of a human expert is represented and stored through rules of inference. Expert systems based on rules for a specific area can detect anomalies and provide indications to develop processes according to the recommendations [21].

As can be observed in Fig. 2, the input variables are required for each module. Once the rules were evaluated by the inference engine, the reasoning control technique forward chaining was used [22]. The inference engine using the forward chaining technique searches in all rules the THEN clause equals true, this value allows generating a recommendation.

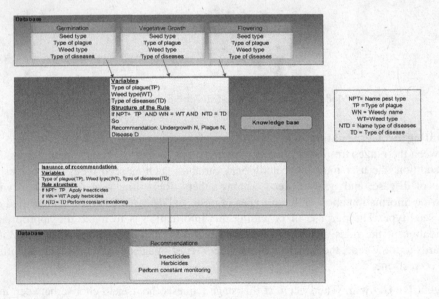

Fig. 2. Internal processing of app modules.

Table 1 shows an extract of the recommendations with respect to the different variables provided by the users according to each stage of maize cultivation.

Table 1. Recommendations for the module of vegetative growth and flowering.

Days	Seed	Pest	Undergrowth	Disease	Recommendation
2–6	Hybrid or variety	Cutting worms	jointed grass	Curvular spot	Recommendation 6, 9 and 10
7–48	Hybrid or variety	screwworm	Ipomoea	Rust	Recommendation 6, 9 and 10
49–110	Hybrid or variety	fall armyworm	Purple nutsedge	Red ribbon	Recommendation 6, 9 and 10

The description of the recommendations that the system provides for the user are the following:

- Recommendation 6.
  - Apply Insecticides.
  - Perform constant monitoring in the crop to identify damages in the crop.
  - Perform trapping to know stages and populations of the plague.
- Recommendation 7.
  - Pest detected: Diatraea spp.
  - Apply Insecticides bait.
  - Perform constant monitoring in the crop to identify damages in the crop.
  - Perform trapping to know stages and populations of the plague.
- Recommendation 8.
  - Pest detected: Spodoptera frugiperda
  - Apply Insecticides to foliage.
  - Perform constant monitoring in the crop to identify damages in the crop.
  - Perform trapping to know stages and populations of the plague.
- Recommendation 9.
  - Weed detected: Cyperus Rotundus
  - Apply herbicide.
  - The type and dose of the herbicides used will depend on the age of the crop and population of the undergrowth.
- Recommendation 10.
  - Disease detected: Spiroplasma, Phytoplasma and virus.
  - Perform constant monitoring in the crop to identify early symptoms of diseases to be able to perform an efficient control.
  - Use certified seed.
  - Use resistant hybrids.
  - Control insect vectors.

3.3 Architecture

Figure 3 shows the architecture of the mobile application presented in this paper. The storage layer is composed of the knowledge base which contains the structure of the rules and the database which stores the information to be provided to the users. The application layer is composed of an inference engine which interacts with the

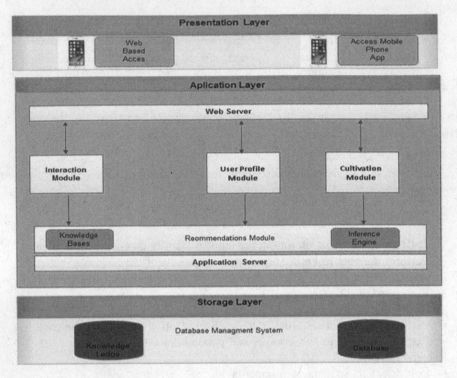

Fig. 3. Architecture of the mobile expert system

knowledge base to provide the recommendations. Finally, the presentation layer is responsible for delivering and formatting of information to the application layer for further processing or display.

4   Case Study: Mobile Application for the Control of Maize Crop

Thanks to the increasing use of the Internet in the agriculture domain, it has been possible to develop a mobile application focused on corn crops management. This application aims to be used for helping farmers to increase the yield of the crop. The present case study was carried out at the Regional Program of Teaching Naranjal of the Agrarian University of Ecuador, whose coordinates are latitude 2°40′25″ S, longitude 79°37′05″ O, and altitude of 25 m. In this place, several plots were installed to perform the different processes related to the crop management. Furthermore, to test the use of the mobile application during maize growth, the application generates a set of recommendations [23] about such agricultural processes. The recommendations provided by the application aim to help farmers to make decisions based on parameters related to each phase of the crop.

Figure 4 presents the graphical user interface of the mobile application presented in this work. To access to all functionalities provided by this application, users must perform the authentication process by using their corresponding username and password. The main interface of the applications shows a list of all phases of the crop, from which users can select one. These phases are surface preparation, planting, crop growth and flowering. Once a phase is selected, users must select the specific parameters. Finally, the system generates a set of recommendations considering the parameters selected by the users.

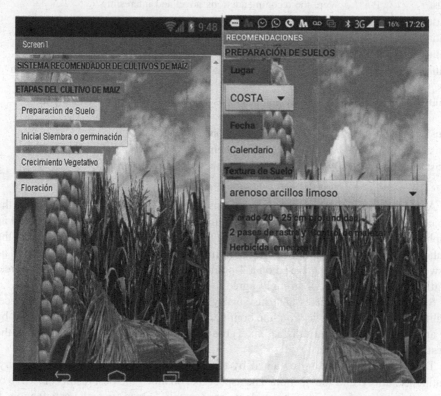

Fig. 4. Stages of corn crops. Preparation module soil with a recommendation.

4.1 Results

Once the mobile application presented in this work was used by the students from the Agricultural University of Ecuador, they were asked to answer a set of questions related to their experience using the application. Table 2 presents the questions that were used in this process.

The aspects of the system that were evaluated are: (1) quality, which refers to the objectivity of the recommendations provided by the system, (2) trust, which refers to the novelty of the recommendations, (3) utility, which refers to the reliability and effectiveness of the recommendations, and (4) satisfaction, which evaluates the users' satisfaction about the recommendations provided by the system.

Table 2. Satisfaction survey questions

Variable	Item	Question
Quality	P.1	Does the recommender system provide clear explanations of the recommendations?
Quality	P.2	Is the recommender system easy to use?
Quality	P.3	Is the system interface attractive, clear and adequate?
Trust	P.4	Did the recommendations correspond with your needs?
Trust	P.5	Were the recommendations novel and interesting?
Trust	P.6	Were the recommendations out of context?
Utility	P.7	Do you agree with the recommendations received from the system?
Utility	P.8	Are the recommendations sometimes confused?
Utility	P.9	Did the recommendations help you to improve the effective-ness in the crop?
Utility	P.10	Did the recommendations help you increasing productivity in the crop?
Satisfaction	P.11	Were the recommendations satisfactory?
Satisfaction	P.12	Would you use the system again?
Satisfaction	P.13	Would you recommend the system to farmers?

As can be seen, a total of thirteen questions were asked to the students. Some of the subjects to be evaluated through this survey are the ease of use of the application and its graphical interface. Furthermore, this survey aims to collect information about the confidence that users have about the recommendations provided by the system. The answer to the questions was based on a 4-point Likert scale where 1 indicates disagree, 2 little agree, 3 agree and 4 strongly agree.

Summarizing, the aspects that this survey aims to evaluate are the user inter-face, quality/novelty of the application, the confidence of the recommendations provided by the application, utility, and satisfaction. Table 2 presents the main subject to which the question aims to evaluate.

Table 3 shows the rating obtained by the four aspects evaluated namely, quality, confidence, utility, and satisfaction. The aspect that obtained the best results (17.67% of students agree and 57.00% of the students are strongly agreed) was the satisfaction. It means that most students have a feeling of fulfillment of de-sires and expectations about the mobile application. Regarding quality of the application, 72% of the users (30.67% - agree and 41.33% - strongly agree) think that the application is very useful for corn cultivation activities. Furthermore, the application obtained a high level of confidence about the recommendations provided by the application (15.75% - agree and 48.75 - strongly agree). With regards to the utility of the application, 64.50% of the students (15.75% - agree and 48.75% - strongly agree) think that the system provides efficient recommendations about corn crops.

The tabulation of the survey data was expressed as a central tendency (mode). The mode is the value that occurs most often in the distribution of data. The mode was used to determine the scores corresponding to each category. The mode of this survey is presented in Table 4.

Table 3. Evaluation results of the recommender system.

	Disagree	%	Little agree	%	Agree	%	Strongly agree	%	Total
Quality	1,33	0,02	1,67	0,02	30,67	0,41	41,33	0,55	75
Trust	12,67	0,17	3,00	0,04	21,67	0,29	37,67	0,50	75
Utility	7,75	0,10	2,75	0,04	15,75	0,21	48,75	0,65	75
Satisfaction	0,00	0,00	0,33	0,00	17,67	0,24	57,00	0,76	75
Average	5,43	0,07	1,93	0,02	21,44	0,28	46,18	0,61	75

Table 4. Results obtained in the user evaluation

Category	Score (mode)
Quality	4.0
Trust	4.0
Utility	4.0
Satisfaction	4.0
General	4.0

For the confidence category, the same number of scores was obtained with a value of 4. Therefore, a score of 4 was assigned to this category. This score corresponds to the arithmetic mean of the three values. This score demonstrates that the level of confidence of users correspond to strongly agree.

The scores assigned by the users who completed the survey cover a range of 1 to 4 point to express: strongly agree (4), agree (3), little agree (2) and disagree (1). Considering this scale, the scores of 1 and 2 can be considered as negative scores and the scores of 3 and 4 as positive scores.

An analysis of the results obtained by the survey shows that users have a high degree of satisfaction (4.0 points) about the application. Furthermore, these users are highly agreed (4.0 points) with the utility and quality of the recommendations provide by the system.

Regarding the confidence that the users shown about the recommendations provided by the system, it obtained a score of 4.0.

With regards to the quality, utility, and satisfaction about the application and the recommendations provided by it, the users shown to highly agree with these subjects.

A combined analysis of the scores assigned by the users to the different sub-jects places the recommendation system with an average score of 4 points, ac-cording to the histogram of mode corresponding to the general evaluation.

5 Conclusions and Future Work

The knowledge-based expert system proposed in this work was used by students from the Agricultural University of Ecuador during the whole course of cultivation. More specifically, they used this system for the control of corn crops. To store and represent the experts' knowledge, several rules were implemented. These rules allowed generating recommendations for the different phases of corn cultivation.

The interaction between rules as well as the relative independence of the different pieces of knowledge are some advantages of the rule-based approach followed in this work. In many systems, it cannot be assumed that rules do not inter-act among them, because when this interaction is ignored it could lead to unexpected results that would undermine system recommendations.

Some tasks that can be easily defined in terms of procedural representations are not very easy to define by means of rules. The rule-based approach is very useful because it provides a thorough analysis about the solution of human problems. However, there are systems where the use of rules is tedious.

The system here proposed was designed to generate recommendations oriented to the different phases of corn cultivation, using the rules. More specifically, these recommendations are oriented to students for corn cultivation and for determining the problems that affect their crops.

There are no methodologies for implementing rule-based systems. These systems are implemented based on intuition, experience, trial and errors. Our system has been implemented following the expertise and knowledge of experts on crop control and management. Furthermore, this system is based on pictures taken on crop from the Cantón Naranjal, Ecuador. Despite the features provided by our proposal, it has a main disadvantage, which refers to the fact that it is mainly oriented to corn crops management. In this sense, as future work we plan to include new types of crops in order to allow a bigger group of farmers to take advantage of this technology.

The students involved in this work are satisfied with the use of the system. Also, they consider that the system can be qualified as a tool that contributes to decision-making in the corn cultivation processes. The system here proposed represents a technological tool that allows people to learn about the monitorization of crops as well as the pests and weeds that affect them.

The inference process performed by this system is based on first-order logic, where each variable takes values within limited intervals which are defined by facts. In this sense, the authors plan to implement fuzzy sets [22]. This approach has been applied in Asthma as well as different processes in medicine. The authors think that this approach must be applied in agriculture as an efficient mechanism for the control and management of maize crops and other short-cycle and perennial crops.

The simplicity of the rules used in this system leads to the disadvantage that all they have the same level. Therefore, it is necessary to have rules at different levels, working with a hierarchy. However, this change will demand the system to be consistent with this hierarchy. It is worth mentioning that the needs of farmers can change continuously, and users have long-term information needs. Therefore, instead of providing a query, users could directly collect information from weather stations.

References

1. Davis, R., Buchanan, B., Shortliffe, E.: Production rules as a representation for a knowledge-based consultation program. Artif. Intell. **8**, 15–45 (1977)
2. Jin, Z., Prasad, R., Shriver, J., Zhuang, Q.: Crop model- and satellite imagery-based recommendation tool for variable rate N fertilizer application for the US Corn system. Precis. Agric. 1–22 (2016). doi:10.1007/s11119-016-9488-z

3. Ministerio de Agricultura, Ganadería, A. y P.: Maíz Suave Choclo (2012)
4. Palm, T.: Semantic tags: evaluating the functioning of rules in a knowledge based system (2005)
5. Richards, D.: Knowledge-based system explanation: the ripple-down rules alternative. Knowl. Inf. Syst. **5**, 2–25 (2003)
6. Belfield, S., Brown, C.: Field Crop Manual: Maize–A Guide to Upland Production in Cambodia. NSW Department of Primary Industries, Orange (2008)
7. Goll, D.S., Brovkin, V., Parida, B.R., Reick, C.H., Kattge, J., Reich, P.B., van Bodegom, P. M., Niinemets, Ü.: Nutrient limitation reduces land carbon uptake in simulations with a model of combined carbon, nitrogen and phosphorus cycling. Biogeosciences **9**, 3547–3569 (2012)
8. Antonopoulou, E., Karetsos, S.T., Maliappis, M., Sideridis, A.B.: Web and mobile technologies in a prototype DSS for major field crops. Comput. Electron. Agric. **70**, 292–301 (2010)
9. Debaeke, P., Nolot, J.-M., Raffaillac, D.: A rule-based method for the development of crop management systems applied to grain sorghum in south-western France. Agric. Syst. **90**, 180–201 (2006)
10. Porcel, C., del Castillo, J.M.M., Cobo, M.J., Ruız, A.A., Herrera-Viedma, E.: An improved recommender system to avoid the persistent information overload in a university digital library. Control Cybern. **39**, 899–923 (2010)
11. Shortliffe, E.H.: Computer-based Medical Consultations: MYCIN. Elsevier, Amsterdam (1976)
12. Gordon, J.: Creating knowledge maps by exploiting dependent relationships. Knowl. Based Syst. **13**, 71–79 (2000)
13. Sasikumar, M., Ramani, S., Raman, S.M., Anjaneyulu, K.S.R., Chandrasekar, R.: A Practical Introduction to Rule Based Expert Systems. New Delhi Narosa Publishing House, New Delhi (2007)
14. Sarma, S.K., Singh, K.R., Singh, A.: An expert system for diagnosis of diseases in Rice Plant. Int. J. Artif. Intell. **1**, 26–31 (2010)
15. Marwaha, S.: Ontology based Expert System. (2016)
16. Pampolino, M.F., Witt, C., Pasuquin, J.M., Johnston, A., Fisher, M.J.: Development approach and evaluation of the Nutrient Expert software for nutrient management in cereal crops. Comput. Electron. Agric. **88**, 103–110 (2012)
17. Marwaha, S.: Agridaksh—a tool for developing online expert system - semantic scholar. In: Proceedings of AIPA 2012 (2012)
18. Tripathi, K.P.: A review on knowledge-based expert system: concept and architecture. Artif. Intell. Tech. Nov. Approaches Pract. Appl. **4**, 19–23 (2011)
19. Lai, J., Ming, B., Li, S., Wang, K., Xie, R., Gao, S.: An image-based diagnostic expert system for corn diseases. Agric. Sci. China **9**, 1221–1229 (2010)
20. Abraham, A.: Rule-based expert systems. In: Sydenham, P.H., Thorn, R. (eds.) Handbook of Measuring System Design. Wiley, Chichester (2005)
21. Roy, J.: Rule-based expert system for maritime anomaly detection. In: Carapezza, E.M. (ed.) Proceedings of the SPIE, vol. 7666, p. 76662N (2010)
22. Sharma, T., Tiwari, N., Kelkar, D.: Study of difference between forward and backward reasoning. Int. J. Emerg. Technol. Adv. Eng. **2**, 271–273 (2012)
23. Shishehchi, S., Banihashem, S.Y., Zin, N.A.M.: A proposed semantic recommendation system for e-learning: a rule and ontology based e-learning recommendation system. In: 2010 International Symposium on Information Technology, pp. 1–5. IEEE (2010)

Applying a Software Estimation Method to the Human Resources Management Based on PMBOK

Nemury Silega[1], Gilberto Fernando Castro[2,4(✉)], Danaysa Macías[1],
Mitchell Vasquez-Bermúdez[3,4] (iD), Walter Eduardo Paredes[2,4],
Néstor Vera-Lucio[3] (iD), and Jessenia Chalén[2,5]

[1] University of Informatics Sciences, Habana, Cuba
{nsilega,dmacias}@uci.cu
[2] Catholic University of Santiago de Guayaquil, Guayaquil, Ecuador
{gilberto.castro,walter.paredes}@cu.ucsg.edu.ec
[3] Agricultural University of Ecuador, Guayaquil, Ecuador
{mvasquez,nvera}@ugraria.edu.ec
[4] University of Guayaquil, Guayaquil, Ecuador
{gilberto.castroa,mitchell.vasquezb,
walter.paredesm}@ug.edu.ec
[5] Universidad Politécnica Salesiana del Ecuador, Guayaquil, Ecuador
jchalen@ups.edu.ec

Abstract. The component based software development (CBSD) allows developing components independently and integrating them in a system. However it is not easy to manage the human resources during a project based on CBSD, usually some important tasks are not executed successfully, such as selection of the right human resources, tasks assigning and incentive to the workers according to their performance. PMBOK is a methodology for the project management. One of its areas is the human resources management. This paper argues about the impact for the human resources management at applying a method to calculate the absolute value of work in the component based software development. Therefore, how this method supports the activities for the human resources management proposed by PMBOK is illustrated in this paper.

Keywords: Human resources management · Component based software development on (CBSD) · PMBOK

1 Introduction

The companies in the industry for the software development have the mission to obtain software with high quality and make it efficiently. Therefore, nowadays the community of software development uses new paradigms in order to build software more efficiently. For instance, the component based software development (CBSD) receives the attention of both, the research and the industrial community.

It is possible to find numerous evidences of the benefits of applying CBSD in the literature. In spite of these benefits, it is not easy to find proposals with a

R. Valencia-García et al. (Eds.): CITI 2017, CCIS 749, pp. 96–112, 2017.
DOI: 10.1007/978-3-319-67283-0_8

methodological orientation that help to manage the human resources in a project based on CBSD. Hence, some problems with the human resources management arise, such as inefficient selection of the developers and the wrong assignation of tasks according to the skills of the workers. The human resources management in a software project is essential to achieve a successful conclusion. In this regard, it is crucial to follow an appropriate project management methodology which guides and controls the software development activities and the human resources management.

PMBOK is a project management methodology. The integration of DSBC and PMBOK methodology synergistically may ensure the implementation of best practices in software development. The aim of this paper is to demonstrate the benefits of applying a method to calculate the absolute value of work in the software development. Specifically, we provide evidences of the positive influence of the method for the human resources management, in especial, we demonstrate how this method supports the activities for the human resources management defined by PMBOK.

The structure of the paper is as follows: Sect. 2 describes the related work. Next, in Sect. 3, a discussion about some common problems in the human resources management is presented. In Sect. 4, a method to calculate the absolute value of work in the development of a component is described. Section 5 describes how the method supports the activities for the human resources management which are proposed by PMBOK. In the last section conclusions and future work are presented.

2 Related Work

In this section we present related work from existing literature about estimation methods. We identified some limitations of these approaches.

2.1 Function Points

This method is intended to measure the software from the logical design of the system [1]. The method was proposed by Albrecht in 1970. It allows quantifying the size of a system by independent units of the programming language, methodologies, platforms as well as used technologies, called Function points. Function points allow estimating the size of a software from its requirements. During the initial stage of the lifecycle of the project, actors and use cases of the system are identified as well as the functionalities which are documented through a brief description. By applying Function points to use cases, a preliminary estimate of size can be obtained [2]. This estimation is inexact because the information about software is not enough at the beginning of a project, but it provides an idea about the size of the system.

2.2 Use-Case Points Analysis

This method helps to estimate the time of a project by assigning "weights" to a number of factors that affect it. The steps to calculate the variables were presented by Nageswaran [3–5]. In step 1, calculation of unadjusted use-case points is made, in step 2 Calculation of Adjusted Use Case points is made and in step 3 calculation of required effort is made.

This method allows estimating effort considering only the development of the functionalities specified by means of use cases. This effort corresponds to the implementation stage of the project and represents 40% of the total time. To estimate the overall duration of the project, the estimated effort from other related activities in the software development must be included, such as: analysis with 10% of the total time, design with 20% of the total time, test with 15% of the total time and other activities with 15% of the total time.

2.3   COCOMO II

This is a method for estimating the effort proposed by the Software Engineering Institute (SEI). It is based on mathematical equations that allow calculating the effort from metrics of estimated size, such as the Function point analysis and Source Lines of Code (SLOC). These equations are weighed by cost factors that influence the effort required for software development. COCOMO II has two variants: one variant for the beginning of the project called preliminary design and the other variant to apply after the definition of the architecture system called post architecture [6, 7].

After the review of these three important estimation methods in the software development some conclusions can be presented:

- The estimation with adjusted function points and conversion factors is difficult to apply if there does not exist an historical database with information of the projects to obtain the converting coefficients.
- The estimation with COCOMO II with unadjusted function points as input is very useful to estimate a project in a global way when there is a set of use cases with little level of detail.
- The estimation with use-case points is very effective to estimate the required effort to develop the first use cases of a system following an iterative approach. These use cases are classified as critical and represent a key part of the architecture.

The studied methods have a high dependence of development software methodology, especially those that are based on use cases. These methods cannot adjust favorably to the development of components, because all components not necessarily respond to a functionality or may have features that are present in several components. Hence, an estimation method to the component based software development is necessary.

In addition to the analysis of these three methods, we examined other proposals to have a better perception of the state of the art about the estimation. In the work of Dapozo et al. [8] remark the relevance of the estimation in the early stages of the project because it represents a crucial factor to anticipate solutions to potential problems and reduce the cost for the identification and solution of changes in the final stages. Nevertheless, they do not make a concrete proposal. They identified some research lines about estimation methods as well as tools to support thes methods [9, 10].

Salazar [11] describes a methodology to estimate software projects. However, the methodology is based on Albrecht technique; we already argued about this technique.

Bohem and Humphrey propose two of the most important theories for the estimation of software projects. Ruís and Cordero [12] apply these techniques in a practical case. But to adopt this proposal, it is required to know the number of code lines, sometimes, it is not possible to have this data in early stages of the project.

Robiolo et al. [13] demonstrated the precision of the methods based on experts judgment for the estimation. In spite of benefits of this kind of methods, they have to be complemented with formal methods which provide quantitative measures.

Pow-Sang and Imbert [14] describe an approach to estimate the effort in software projects which make use of use cases. They make the estimation with COCOMO and Function points. These techniques were already analyzed.

These works are usually based on Function points, use-case point analysis and COCOMO II. We discussed previously some limitation of these three techniques. To make a deep study of the estimation method is not in the scope of this work. With this purpose some works can be consulted [15–17]. The lacks of the estimation methods usually have a negative effect in the human resources management. Therefore, in the next section we discuss about these facts.

In Sect. 4, an estimation method is described. This method is focused to be applied in the based component software development and does not dependent on use cases like most of the studied methods. After describing the method, we discuss how it supports the activities for the human resources management.

3 Problems for the Human Resources Management in Software Projects

This section describes some of the most common deficiencies related to the human resources management in the software projects, such as:

- *The incorrect delineation of the responsibilities for each role*: this situation is caused because in the development of a component usually workers with different roles take part and it is difficult to differentiate the responsibilities for each role, for example, an user-interface developer is often the same that carries out the required functions in the business logic, it means that user-interface developer is making extra tasks but usually he does not receive any additional compensation.
- *Wrong task plan*: Usually, the metrics are not used to make the plan. Therefore the plan is often wrong and its consequences are very negative for the project. For example, if a developer has the task to make a trigger function in the database, but the defined time is based on subjective elements and not on quantitative metrics, some negative effects could appear such as delays to accomplish the tasks, non-conformity of the developers, among other negative consequences.
- *Performance evaluation of the project members*: The evaluation is usually carried out considering only the task names or other subjective elements. This kind of evaluation does not allow taking into account the particularities or the complexity of the components, for example, if the developers A and B work in the components C1 and C2 respectively, both could have a task named *"develop the user interfaces"*, but to make a proper evaluation, checking the complexity of the components C1 and C2 is required to because maybe C1 is more complex than C2 since developer A should have a better evaluation than developer B. Nevertheless, usually both

receive the same evaluation. This situation could be compared with the traditional industries; for example, it is very easy to evaluate the barbers in a barber shop, simply by knowing how many people they give a service to in a period of time.

- *Stimulation to the project members*: In a software project based on CBSD the components usually are be developed by independent teams, for example if team A and team B develop the components C1 and C2 respectively. How could the best developer in the area of database design be identified? To answer this question could be a bit complicated if there are not metrics that support this selection. On the contrary, if no metrics have been applied in this selection, the result could be wrong and stimulate the incorrect person. This situation could generate dissatisfaction on the affected workers and reduce their performance in the project.

The elements described above, are negative effects in software projects when metrics have not been used properly. Metrics are mechanisms which help to assign and assess the work in a project. Especially in projects based on CBSD, where sometimes the activities proposed for this purpose in traditional methods cannot be applied properly. These facts motivated the creation of a method to estimate the absolute value of work in a software project based on CBSD. The next section describes this method.

4   Estimation Method to Calculate the Absolute Value of Work

This method has been called MCAVW (Method to calculate the absolute value of work). The authors have been members of several software development projects. Therefore some specifications of the method are based on this empirical experience. The method deals with four areas which are common to most components, although some components may have more impact in some of them. The areas are: User Interface, Business Logic, Data and Integration. The components may have some of these areas, only one area or all of them. After applying the method, a value for each area expressed in Work Unit (WU) is obtained.

4.1   Calculation in Data Area

In this area the calculation of work would be performed with the following equation:

$$ED = CT * \left(\sum ET_i + \sum ED_j + \sum EF_k \right) \tag{1}$$

Where:

- CT is the complexity of the technology used in the area concerned, it receives a value from 1 to 10 and 1 is the lowest complexity.

- ET_i is the required work to develop each table that the component has.

$$ET_i = cc + cr + clf \tag{2}$$

cc: number of fields
cr: number of restrictions
clf: number of foreign keys

- ED_j is the required work to develop each Trigger that the component has.

$$ED_j = cg * (ct + cp) \tag{3}$$

cg: complexity of the trigger
ct: number of associated tables
cp: number of fields updated

- EF_k is the work to develop each function that the component in the database has.

$$EF_k = cf * (ct + cp) \tag{4}$$

cf: complexity of the function
ct: number of associated tables
cp: number of fields updated

4.2   Calculation in Business Logic Area

This area connects all the intermediate elements between the user interface and database, remarking that investigating about different architectural styles is out of the scope of this article. It has only been recognized that any component independently of architectural style has these common elements. One element to consider is that actions in one component can be divided into four main groups: actions to insert, delete, update and display data. Hence the calculation in this area is defined as described below:

$$EL = cmt * \left(\sum EFI_i + \sum EFE_j + \sum EFA_k + \sum EFM_l \right) + EAD \tag{5}$$

Where:

- cmt is the complexity of the framework used to develop the software. It receives a value from 1 to 10 and 1 is the lowest complexity.

- EFI$_i$ is the value of the work needed to develop each function used to insert data.

$$EFI_i = cna * (cp + cc + co + cpc + cpoc) \tag{6}$$

cna: complexity of insert functions. This constant is defined for this type of function.
cp: number of parameters
cc: number of cycles
co: number of objects that are instantiated in the function
cpc: number of preconditions
cpoc: number of postconditions

- EFE$_j$ is the work required to develop each function used for deleting data.

$$EFE_j = cnd * (cp + cc + co + cpc + cpoc) \tag{7}$$

cnd: complexity of delete functions. This constant is defined for this type of function.
cp: number of parameters
cc: number of cycles
co: number of objects that are instantiated in the function
cpc: number of preconditions
cpoc: number of postconditions

- EFA$_k$ is the work required to develop each function used for updating data.

$$EFA_k = cnu * (cp + cc + co + cpc + cpoc) \tag{8}$$

cnu: complexity of update functions. This constant is defined for this type of function
cp: number of parameters
cc: number of cycles
co: number of objects that are instantiated in the function
cpc: number of preconditions
cpoc: number of postconditions

- EFM$_l$ is the work required to develop each function used for extracting data.

$$EFM_l = cn * (cp + cc + ca + co + cpc) \tag{9}$$

cn: complexity of the function
cp: number of parameters
cc: number of cycles
ca: number of display attributes
co: number of objects that are instantiated in the function
cpc: number of preconditions

- EAD is the required work to develop data access operations. This represents the data access work taking into account the technology to be used. For example: Hibernate, Doctrine, among others. In this article a way to calculate this element is not defined due to variation in the available tools. For example, using Hibernate is easy to get the result, while with other technology could be more complex.

4.3   Calculation in User Interface Area

This area is responsible for interaction with the user. The elements proposed for this area are influenced by the experience of the authors and have particularities of management systems in general. Here we take into account common and traditional components in management applications.

$$EIU = CT * \left(\sum EL_i + \sum ECID_j + \sum EE_l \right) \tag{10}$$

Where:

- CT is the complexity of the technology to be used in the area. It receives a value from 1 to 10 and 1 is the lowest complexity.
- EL_i is the required work to create each component that lists elements (table, grid).

$$EL_i = c * ca + \sum Ec_i \tag{11}$$

c: complexity of the current component, it receives a value in the range of 1 to 10 and 1 is the lowest complexity.
ca: number of attributes to display.
Ec_i: complexity assigned to each internal component of the current component. A value from 1 to 10 must be assigned to each visual component.

- $ECID_j$ is the required work to develop each component to insert data.

$$ECID_j = ccv + \sum Ec_i \tag{12}$$

ccv: complexity of the visual component. It receives a value in the range of 1 to 10 and 1 is the lowest complexity.

Ec_i: is the complexity to develop each internal component of the current component. A value in the range from 1 to 10 should be assigned to each visual component.

- EE_l is the required work to develop each event running on the interface (e.g. during the on click of a button or in a row on a table)

$$EE_l = ce * (cva + cc + cf + CI * cp) \tag{13}$$

ce: complexity of the event
cva: number of visual components affected
cc: number of cycles on the event
cf: number of functions called in the event
CI: complexity of the integration with the bottom layer
cp: number of requests to the bottom layer in the event

4.4   Calculation in Integration Area

This area is responsible for the integration of the components. The integrations can be among the components of the own system or with components of an external system. Hence there is a high dependence on the policies defined in the project for the integration as well as the complexity of the implementation.

$$EI = CT * \left(\sum SC_i + \sum SO_j \right) \tag{14}$$

Where:

- CT is the complexity of the technology to be used in this area. It receives a value in the range of 1 to 10 and 1 is the lowest complexity.
- SC_i is the work to develop each service that the component consumes.

$$SC_i = cs * (cc + cp + co) \tag{15}$$

cs: complexity of the service
cc: number of cycles on the service
cp: number of parameters
co: number of objects instantiated to implement the service

- SO_j is the work to develop each service that the component offers.

$$SO_j = cs * (cc + cp + co) \tag{16}$$

cs: complexity of the service
cc: number of cycles on the service
cp: number of parameters
co: number of objects instantiated to implement the service

4.5   Calculation of Performance and Time

The following equation links Total Work, Performance and Time:

$$\text{Total Work} = \text{Performance} * \text{Time} \tag{17}$$

With the estimation of Total Work for each area, it is possible to fix (assign a value according to the characteristics of the project) a variable with the objective to obtain the value of the other variable, according to formula 18. For example, if the time is fixed, then the performance can be calculated. This value is expressed in WU/h and can be used to calculate the human resources required to develop a project, taking into account that the sum of the individual performances of workers must be equal to the value of performance obtained after applying Eq. 17. The performance of each worker should be established at the beginning of the project taking into account their performance in previous projects. To illustrate the results of applying the method, we describe two examples. In Example 1, we calculated the Total Work required to develop one of the areas of a project; then the required performance for the project, if the time was already defined is needed to know. In Example 2, the Total work and the performance are known; then we want to know the overall time to achieve the project.

Example 1: Calculate the required Total Work in the user interface area using the formulas explained in the previous section. The technology that will be used has a low complexity. The interfaces from Figs. 1 and 2 will be used to exemplify the calculation. The maximum time for the implementation of this area is 20 h, so we need to know: What human resources could be required to develop with these conditions?

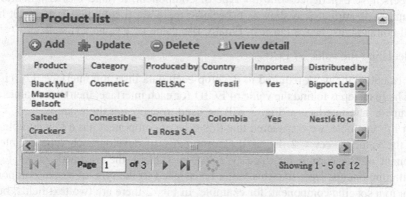

Fig. 1. User interface – product list.

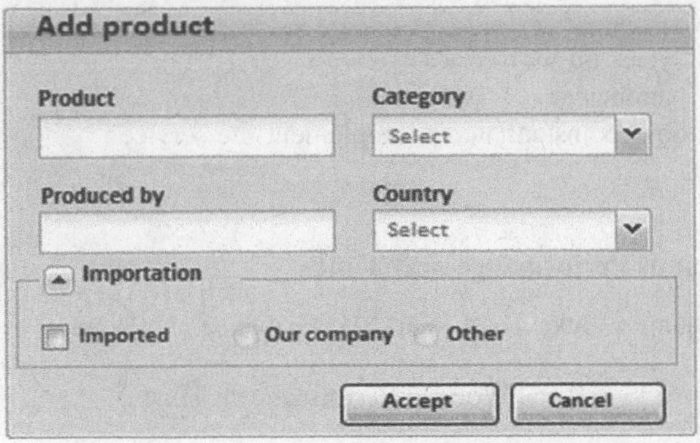

Fig. 2. User interface – add product.

Solution:
Time = 20 h
EIU = ?
Performance = ?

To estimate the work for developing the user interface, Eq. (10) is applied:

- Assigning a value to CT (Complexity Technology):

CT receives a value in the range from 1 to 10. In this case, the technology has a low complexity; hence value 1 is assigned to CT.

CT = 1

- Calculating the value of EL_i

To calculate the work to develop each component of listing elements, Eq. (11) is used. The first step is to find the value of El_i for each component; then these values will be added. The interface of Fig. 1 will be used to carry out the example.

In this example, there is one component that lists elements (T_1). Supposing that developers have experience with this type of component, a value 1 is assigned to **ca**. The number of attributes to show is 6 because there are 6 columns. T does not have internal components; hence $Eci = 0$. Finally the value of EL_i is: $EL_i = 6$.

- Calculating the value of $ECID_j$

To calculate the work required to develop each data insertion interface, Eq. (12) is used. The first step is to find the value of ECID for each interface; then these values will be summed. The interface of Fig. 2 will be used to carry out the example.

For this example, we considered that this type of component has a low complexity, hence the value of **ccv** = 2. Ec_i is the complexity to develop each type of internal component of the current interface. We list in Table 1 the assigned values to the internal components. Note that this value is assigned to the type of visual component and not to a specific component; for example, in Fig. 2 there are two text fields, but in Table 1, we only consider one, because both fields have the same type.

Table 1. Complexity of internal components

Component type	Value
Textfield	1
Combobox	2
Checkbox	1
Radiobutton	1

The sum of the values of the development complexity assigned to each internal component is Eci = 5. Finally the value of ECID is: ECID = 7

- Calculating the value of EEl

To calculate the work required to develop each event that is executed in the interface, Eq. (13) is used. The first step is to find the value of EEl for each event; then these values will be summed. The interface of Fig. 1 will be used to carry out the example.

Table 1 shows the events of the interface of the Fig. 1. In order to make the calculation easier, we stated that the complexity of each event is **ce = 1**. The value of **cc** in every case is 0 because the events do not require cycles to be executed. The value of **cf = 1** since each event calls only one function.

Considering that developers have good experience with the technology of the project we stated that complexity of the integration with the bottom layer is **CI = 2**. The values of **cp** depend on the numbers of requests made in the event to the bottom layer; e.g., the event onclick_btnadd has a value of **cp = 4** because it makes 4 requests: to obtain the list of categories, to obtain the list of countries, to save the introduced data in the form and to update the list of products showed on the table. Table 2 shows the values of the variables for each event.

Table 2. Values of the varibles for each event.

Event	ce	cva	cc	cf	CI	cp	EE$_l$
onclick_btnadd	1	2	0	1	2	4	11
onclick_btnupd	1	3	0	1	2	5	14
onclick_btndelete	1	2	0	1	2	2	7
onclick_btndetail	1	3	0	1	2	1	6
onrowclick_table	1	6	0	1	2	0	7
onrowmouseover_table	1	2	0	1	2	0	3

Finally, the sum of the required work to develop the events executed in the interface is **EE$_l$ = 48**.

- Substituting the values obtained above for EE, ECID and EL into Eq. (10) to find the value of EIU then:

$$EIU = 1 * (6 + 7 + 48)$$
$$EIU = 61\,WU$$

With the value of EIU and knowing that the maximum time for the implementation of these interfaces is 20 h then the performance is:

$$Performance = \frac{EIU}{Time} = \frac{61\,WU}{20\,h} = 3.05\,WU/h$$

The value obtained was EIU = 61 WU. With this value, different variants of selection of human capital could be analyzed, taking into account that the sum of the selected workers performance must be equal to 3.05 WU/h. In this case, one worker could be selected with a minimum performance of 3.05 WU/h.

Example 2: After calculating (in the previous example) the Total Work in the user interface area, the value obtained was EIU = 61 WU. Now, if we have one developer whose performance is 5 WU/h. What is the required time to develop the project with these conditions?

Solution:
EIU = 61 WU
Performance = 5 WU/h
Time = ?

Applying Eq. (17) we have to:

$$Time = \frac{TotalWork}{Performance} = \frac{61\,WU}{5\,WU/h} = 12.2\,h$$

After carrying out the corresponding calculations we can conclude that with the established conditions the time required to develop the project is 12.2 h.

5   Applying MCAVW to Support the Processes for Managing Human Resources Defined in the PMBOK

In Sect. 2, some of the common problems in software development projects related with the human resources management were analyzed. While in the previous section a method to calculate the absolute value of work in a component based software development was introduced. In this section, we will discuss how this method could help to tackle some of the aforementioned problems related with the human resources management. Here we will explain how the use of MCAVW supports the development of processes for managing human resources defined in the PMBOK which is a methodology for the project management. First of all, the processes for the human resources management proposed by PMBOK are presented. Then we provide an explanation about the way that MCAVC supports the execution of these processes.

5.1 Develop the Plan of the Human Resources

In this process, the roles and responsibilities for the members of a project are determined. It develops the project organization chart with the graphical representation of the project members and their relationships. Furthermore, the personnel management plan is elaborated. This plan includes the requirements for the human resources and other specifications, such as the steps for acquisition of staff, definition of work system, needs of training as well as strategies of payments and recompenses (PMI, Project Management Institute, 2008).

This process may take advantage of applying MCAVC. First of all, after the design phase, MCAVC will let know to the project management the absolute work required to develop the components that will compose the system. With the work absolute value for each component and depending on the first variable set in (18), the project management has a quantitative value to take important decisions about the project. For example, if the human resources are predetermined, then it is necessary to calculate the time required to develop each component with these workers, taking into account their coefficients of performance that already must be known by the managers. While if the default variable is the time, then the project management should calculate the performance coefficients of the workers required to develop the project in the time contracted with the client.

The foregoing would give quantitative elements to acquire or hire the required personnel. Besides, the working hours of each worker should be established according to their performance in order to achieve the activities. If the workers hired do not have all the desired knowledge, then training strategies must be drawn up that contribute to the perfection of their knowledge, and thus to the improvement of their performance.

Recognition and recompenses are key elements for the human resources management. With the use of MCAVC, the project management can determine the work absolute values that deserve some stimulation. The explicit definition of this value will reduce the impact of subjective indicators and could increase the performance of the developers because they know what they have to do in order to obtain recompense. For example, if the standard for a UI developer is that an interface with specific characteristics should be developed in two days and this developer made the interface in a day, then this worker is worthy of some recognition.

5.2 Acquire the Team of the Project

The aim of this process is to obtain the necessary human resources to complete the project. The documentation related to the availability of human resources and the time periods where each project team member can work is made. Besides, the staff management plan is updated (PMI, Project Management Institute, 2008).

In this process, the people who will work on the project will be defined according to the performance required for the project. Hence, MCAVC may represent a useful tool to know the performance coefficients for each candidate. It is important to know the performance coefficient of the members of the project to make the plan as well as to evaluate workers during the execution phase.

5.3   Develop the Project Team

In this process, the skills and interactions of team members are improved in order to increase and evaluate the project performance. Hence some activities are executed to increase the feelings of trust and cohesiveness among the team members in order to increase productivity through greater teamwork (PMI, 2008).

MCAVC could be a useful tool to support this process since this method provides objective elements to analyze how the performance of the team and of each individual evolves. This information can be recorded in evaluation reports where the effectiveness of the project team is included. Therefore, the project manager could recognize what decisions helped to improve or worsen the collective and individual performance. These insights may be useful to make training strategies, among other options to improve the performance.

With the specialization of personnel by areas of development, it will be easier to evaluate the performance of each worker, according to the capabilities demonstrated during the execution of the assigned activities. These elements may improve the team work and increase the project productivity.

5.4   Manage the Project Team

The primary goal of this process is to track the performance of team members, provide feedback, resolve polemics, and coordinate changes to improve project performance. The project management observes team behavior, manages conflicts, resolves polemics, and evaluates the performance of its members. As a result of managing the project team, the personnel management plan is updated, change requests are submitted, disputes are resolved and some inputs are provided for the evaluations of organization performance (PMI, Project Management Institute, 2008).

Similarly to the previous process, the MCAVC may be an effective help to analyze the performance of the project members. This approach may contribute to homogenize the work of the project members. Since MCAVC is focused in the component-based software development, the manager will have the possibility of objectively comparing the work of several people who have the same role, but who work in different components. So; for example, it is possible to identify the member of the database area who has the most outstanding performance in a given period or who is the one that has the better progress with respect to the preceding period. The possibility to have a quantitative measure to evaluate the performance of the workers allows to make some analyzes similar to other fields; for example, in soccer, the best forward in a championship is the one who scored more goals. With these analyzes, it is possible to reduce the utilization of methods based on subjective elements to evaluate the workers. This type of method can generate incorrect assessments and produce discontent on the workers.

On the other hand, the project manager must update the indexes of workers performance and improve the implementation of the MCAVC to turn it in an aid tool which provides feedback to the management team. These indexes could be used in future projects as inputs to apply the MCAVC.

6 Conclusions

In this paper the benefits of applying the method to calculate the absolute value of work for managing human resources were presented. We illustrated how this approach supports the success execution of the processes defined in PMBOK for managing human resources, in special in a context of component based software development. The method provides quantitative values that can help the organization towards optimization of resources, time and production costs. It also helps companies to make decisions about staff hires, to create strategies for monitoring the evolution of individual and group performance, to plan courses for specific roles as well as to compensate the most outstanding workers. In order to make the adoption of this method easier, we are working in the development of an automated tool which will reduce considerably the manual work.

References

1. The International Function Point Users Group IFPUG: Function Point Counting Practices. Manual-Release 4.1 USA (1999)
2. Longstreet, D.: Use case and function points. http://www.softwaremetrics.com. Accessed 10 May 2016
3. Anda, B., Dreiem, H., Sjøberg, Dag I.K., Jørgensen, M.: Estimating software development effort based on use cases — experiences from industry. In: Gogolla, M., Kobryn, C. (eds.) UML 2001. LNCS, vol. 2185, pp. 487–502. Springer, Heidelberg (2001). doi:10.1007/3-540-45441-1_35
4. Carmen, G.M., Garzás, J.: Método de Estimación de Puntos de Caso de Uso. Kybele Consulting.   http://www.kybeleconsulting.com/recursos/articulos/estimacion-puntos-caso-de-uso/. Accessed 12 May 2016
5. Nageswaran, S.: Test effort estimation using use case points (2001). http://www.cts-corp. com/cogcommunity/presentations/Test%20Effort%20Estimation%20Using%20Use% 20Case%20Points.pdf
6. Chris Abts, A., et al.: Software Cost Estimation with COCOMO II. Prentice-Hall, Englewood Cliffs (2000)
7. Center for Systems and Software Engineering: COCOMO II. http://sunset.usc.edu/csse/ research/COCOMOII/cocomo_main.html/. Accessed 15 May 2016
8. Dapozo, G.G., Cristina, L.G., Ferraro, M., Medina, Y., Petrazzini, G.P., Lencina, B.: Medición y estimación del software: métodos y herramientas para mejorar la calidad del software. In: WICC 2014 XVI Workshop de Investigadores en Ciencias de la Computación, Argentina (2014)
9. Dragicevic, S., Celar, S., Novak, L.: Use of method for elicitation documentation and validation of software user requirements (MEDoV) in agile software development projects. In: Sixth International Conference on Computational Intelligence Communication Systems and Networks (CICSyN), pp. 65–70 (2014)

10. Genero, M., Piattini, M., Calero, C.: Early measures For UML class diagrams. L'objet **6**(4), 489–505 (2000)
11. Salazar, G.: Estimación de proyectos de software: un caso práctico. Ingeniería y Ciencia **5** (9), 123–143 (2009)
12. Constanten, Y.R., Morales, D.C.: Estimación en proyectos de software integrando los métodos de Boehm y Humphrey. Revista Cubana de Ciencias Informáticas **7**(3), 23–36 (2013)
13. Robiolo, G., et al.: Es posible superar la precisión basada en el juicio de expertos de la estimación de esfuerzo de productos de software? In: CIbSE 2013 X Workshop Latinoamericano Ingeniería de Software Experimental, Montevideo Uruguay (2013)
14. Pow-Sang, J.A., Imbert, R.: Estimación y planificación de proyectos software con ciclo de vida iterativo-incremental y empleo de casos de uso. In: Memorias de 7° Workshop Iberoamericano de Ingeniería de Requisitos y Ambientes Software IDEAS, Paraguay (2004)
15. Dapozo, G., et al.: Análisis comparativo de métodos de estimación basados en puntos de función para proyectos web. In: XX Congreso Argentino de Ciencias de la Computación, Buenos Aires Argentina (2014)
16. Páez, I.D.: Estudio Empírico del estado actual de la estimación de software en pymes de colombia. In: Departamento de Informática y Sistemas, Universidad EAFIT (2012)
17. Piattini, M.G., García, F.O., Garzas, J., Genero, B., Marcela, F.: Medición y estimación del software. técnicas y métodos para mejorar la calidad y la productividad, 1st edn. RA-MA EDITORIAL, Mexico (2008)

Evaluation of Vulnerability and Seismic Risk Parameters Through a Fuzzy Logic Approach

Lorenzo J. Cevallos-Torres[✉], Alfonso Guijarro-Rodriguez,
Nelly Valencia-Martínez, Jorge Tapia-Celi,
and Wilmer Naranjo-Rosales

Faculty of Mathematical and Physical Sciences, University of Guayaquil,
Guayaquil, Guayas, Ecuador
{lorenzo.cevallost,Alfonso.guijarror}@ug.edu.ec

Abstract. Due to the geographical location of the Pacific fire belt, Ecuador is the scenery of natural phenomena such as earthquakes, which might be the main threat source on national territory and their intensity is likely to cause disasters, to facilitate the identification process of the risk level these disaster cause, we apply techniques of fuzzy logic, because related studies in this area have given more accurate results when working directly with the qualitative values of the data, allowing to deal with the uncertainty of the information on physical and social damages in a given area. For this study, the information was classified considering loss and immediate response scenarios, obtaining variables to which the Analytic Hierarchy Process (AHP) model and the fuzzy set theory were applied using the software "Matlab" for the evaluation of the results.

Keywords: Earthquakes · Uncertainty · Decision making · Risk · Fuzzy logic · Fuzzy sets · AHP

1 Introduction

Natural disasters, in the case of earthquakes, have been over the last years a very broad discussion topic as these events unleashed great negative effects, especially in those urban regions constituting the basic poles of a city system and densely populated [1]. Because of these continuous telluric movements due to the sliding of the tectonic plates, a high level of uncertainty is induced, followed by great social, environmental, infrastructure consequences, as well as a destabilization in the economy and finally human losses; these factors depend on the intensity of the natural phenomenon [2–4]. Few works have been carried out regarding seismic disasters, amongst which we can find a study carried out by the Geophysical Institute of the National Polytechnic School of Ecuador. It is important to indicate that these works were carried out in an empirical way since prevention methods were used rather than prediction ones to minimize any damage from seismic hazard, which means an accurate seismic risk assessment cannot be achieved. Fuzzy logic yet offers significant advantages over such approaches thanks to its ability to represent qualitative aspects of examination data in a natural way and to apply flexible inference rules [5].

© Springer International Publishing AG 2017
R. Valencia-García et al. (Eds.): CITI 2017, CCIS 749, pp. 113–130, 2017.
DOI: 10.1007/978-3-319-67283-0_9

One of the main tools for computational intelligence is fuzzy logic, which is why this tool has been very helpful in the field of seismic engineering, allowing dealing with uncertainty due to imprecision of data, achieving favorable results and providing a wide knowledge. For instance, there are many uncertainties in the assessment of seismic hazard during calculation phases, such as the definition of seismic sources and wave attenuation models that present a greater degree of imprecision in the data, unlike other phases, while these data are more relevant in their result, as shown in [6–9]. Therefore, it has been considered in this paper to use a fuzzy approach with fuzzy sets to evaluate earthquakes and to use it to study the earthquake registered in Ecuador on April 16, 2016, having a magnitude of 7.8 degrees on the Richter scale. [1, 10–12].

2 Fuzzy Logic Techniques

Fuzzy logic techniques, initiated by [13], are used to define processes that are imprecise and ambiguous. Fuzzy sets are used to define the membership of data that don't belong to a particular group, but are rather part of a set. An important point within fuzzy logic and specifically fuzzy sets is the so-called membership function of a set, i.e. determining the fact of "belonging to a set" or "not belonging to a set" in a gradual way, where a membership function of a set A on a universe X is defined as follows: μA: $X \rightarrow [0,1]$ where $\mu A (x) = r$ if r is the degree to which x belongs to A, whose characteristic will have values whose set is $\{0,1\}$, whereas, if it is fuzzy, it will have them in the closed interval of $[0,1]$. If $\mu A (x) = 0$ the element does not belong to the set, otherwise if $\mu A (x) = 1$ the element does belong completely to the set [14].

Fuzzy logic allows transferring sophisticated precepts from the natural language to a mathematical formulation, which means they give flexibility to modeling using linguistic expressions such as "much", "little", "severe", "scarce", and so on. As an example, we can determine that fuzzy sets are used to define magnitudes observed when an earthquake occurs and that can be considered as "mild", "moderate" or "serious"; otherwise when distances from the epicenter where the earthquake originates, which are "near field", "intermediate field" and "far field". The degree of membership of a set describes the level by which the data belong to that particular group. As for instance, the distance from the source where the earthquake occurs. [15], is given by.

$$r_{close}(x) \in [0, 1] \tag{1}$$

Where $r_{close}(x)$ is the degree of membership that X has in the fuzzy site set "near the source of the earthquake" and x is the distance between the site and the epicenter (3). The fuzzy set of the distance from the source is shown on Fig. 1

Determining seismic sources is very important because of the vagueness degree of the information, since spatial locations of earthquakes can be grouped by fuzzy grouping analysis, making it possible to specify the extent of each seismic source [14, 16].

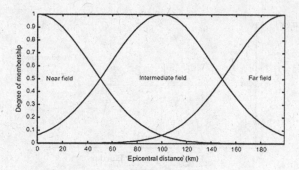

Fig. 1. Distance fuzzy sets

2.1 Fuzzy Sets

Fuzzy sets are collections of elements whose characteristics are defined by linguistic values having a degree of membership between {0, 1} within a discourse universe. The notation defined for fuzzy sets is the one established by Lofti Zadeh, which combines the concepts of logic and the Lukasiewicz set by means of the degree of relationship [13]

$$A = \{(x, u_A(x))/x \in \cup\} \tag{2}$$

Where A is the ordered pairs of x and the result of the membership function $u_A(x)$ for every element x of the discourse universe U.

2.2 Fuzzy Sets Operations

The basic operations in fuzzy logic and fuzzy sets are Intersection, Union and Complement; these operations are performed in the membership function of the fuzzy sets [17]. The operations of fuzzy sets are used for the following properties (Table 1 and Fig. 2):

Table 1. Fuzzy sets properties

Properties	Definition
Associative	$A \cup (B \cap C) = (A \cup B) \cap C \; A \cup (B \cup C) = (A \cup B) \cup C$
Commutative	$A \cap B = B \cap A \; A \cup B = B \cup A$
Involution	$\bar{\bar{A}} = A$
Identity	$A \cap X = A \; A \cup \emptyset = A$
Morgan law	$A \cap B = \overline{A \cup B} = \bar{A} \cup \bar{B}$

2.3 Membership Functions Characteristics

$$\text{Core}(A) = \{x \in X/u_A(x) = 1\} \tag{3}$$

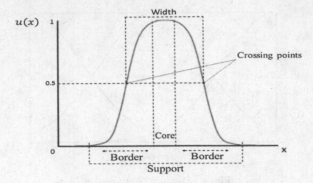

Fig. 2. Membership functions characteristics

$$\text{Border}(A) = \{x \in X / 0 < u_A(x) < 1\} \tag{4}$$

$$\text{Support}(A) = \{x \in X / u_A(x) > 1\} \tag{5}$$

$$\text{Crossing}(A) = \{x \in X / u_A(x) = 0.5\} \tag{6}$$

$$\text{Width}(A) = |x_2 - x_1| \tag{7}$$

2.4   Integration of AHP with Fuzzy Sets

In order to justify the relationship and the support of the AHP model to the theory of fuzzy sets, we can indicate that a fuzzy inference model, which allowed us to incorporate AHP, to obtain a value of membership with regard to set variables used. Using this methodology, we give account altering the process established by the model of fuzzy inference, i.e. AHP change the numbers employed in the scale of assessment of Saaty (Table 2) by fuzzy numbers, since this usually gets the value of membership by

Table 2. Saaty's evaluation scale.

Saaty scale	
9	A is extremely better than B
7	A is markedly better than B
5	A is better than B
3	A is slightly better than B
1	A is equal to B
1/3	B is slightly better than A
1/5	B is better than A
1/7	B is markedly better than A
1/9	B is extremely better than A
2, 4, 6, 8	**Intermediate values - used in case of evaluation with different judgments**

the cut of the function in the calculation of abscissas While the model AHP does so by its evaluation, allowing that the fuzzy inference only gets a level of risk.

3 Study of the Seismic Case Through the Analytic Hierarchy Process (AHP)

For this research study, we chose the cantons of Manabí that were affected by the earthquake in April 2016, whose epicenter was located in the city of Pedernales. The seismic risk will be assessed from a physical and social damage approach since the degree of seismic threat in those areas is high; in addition, the information obtained from the reports of the SGR (Secretariat for Risk Management) and the INEC (National Institute of Statistics and Censuses), both for damages and for resources used to solve the emergency, are available. It is important to emphasize that during the process to determine the exact number of casualties situation reports were generated by the risk management Secretariat, in his web page (http://www.gestionderiesgos.gob.ec/informes-de-situacion-actual-terremoto-magnitud-7-8/), from the number 1 status report until the number 71, in order to be able to clearly demonstrate the official results of the most relevant variables, which caused inconsistencies during the analysis of weights of importance. The results obtained will help us identify areas of greater risk and thus contribute to the decision making helping to mitigate the seismic threat (Fig. 3).

Fig. 3. Seismic intensities registered in the Ecuadorian coastline

The technique to make decisions using the ranking proposed by Saaty (Table 2), it is in essence the reduction of the complexity of the evaluation of multiple attributes, replacing it with a series of comparisons by pairs, which are grouped into a matrix reciprocal positive.

The values in the array will be numeric and the method to guarantee the results imposed by a couple of logical constraints: (i) when you compare an alternative against itself, you are given "equal importance", and (ii) if option A is assigned a number x to compare it with the B option, then when it is compared against the option B option value that will be assigned to this comparison is 1, in our case study when comparing the variable A variable B, for a certain period of time, the variable A, was "more important". In any case this value may vary when analyzing another period of time.

During the process of evaluating seismic risk, the use of fuzzy sets by weighting the input variables through the Analytic Hierarchy Process (AHP) allows us to identify the level of risk in a geographic area with respect to a level of physical risk caused by the telluric event and a level of social aggravation [18]. Fuzzy inference systems help to interpret human knowledge through a set of rules helping the decision making and as an alternative to determine the digital processing of seismic signals, and in this study we decided to use the programming language of "MATLAB", a mathematical calculation platform; it shall allow us to develop fuzzy systems that streamline the process of estimating the total risk of a given area.

The Analytic Hierarchy Process (AHP) is a basic analysis model for decision making allowing to represent a problem through a hierarchical structure in order to establish the criteria importance of a level with respect to a higher level and thus to select the best alternative [19]. The steps to follow are:

3.1   Structuring the Problem

This step is the most important one because the problem must be broken down into components that are relevant to it. The basic hierarchy is established by a goal or objective, criteria and alternatives. The Fig. 4 shows the variables of physical risk and social aggravation used in the total risk calculation process.

X_{RF1}	Affected buildings	W_{RF1}						
X_{RF2}	Deceased	W_{RF2}						
X_{RF3}	Wounded	W_{RF3}						
X_{RF4}	Injured	W_{F4}	RF	Physical risk				
X_{RF5}	Damage to drinking water service	W_{RF5}						
X_{RF6}	Damage to electrical service	W_{RF6}						
X_{RF7}	Damage to the telecommunications system	W_{RF7}						
X_{RF8}	Damage to the productive sector	W_{RF8}						
						RT	Total risk	
X_{FS1}	Poverty rate	W_{FS1}						
X_{FS2}	Mortality rate	W_{FS2}						
X_{FS3}	Population Density	W_{FS3}						
X_{FR1}	Food Kits	W_{FR1}	F	Social Aggravation				
X_{FR2}	Hostels and Shelters	W_{FR2}						
X_{FR3}	Rescue Staff	W_{FR3}						
X_{FR4}	Water supply	W_{FR4}						

Fig. 4. Calculation of total risk, variables of physical risk and aggravation factors (social fragility and lack of resilience) with their respective weights.

3.2   Construction of the Comparison Matrix

Once the criteria and alternatives have been defined, they are hierarchized through the design of a square matrix called peer comparison matrix that is based on a relative importance where the paired comparison is made between the criteria and alternatives established.

$$A = \begin{bmatrix} a_{1,1} & \cdots & a_{1,n} \\ \vdots & \ddots & \vdots \\ a_{n,1} & \cdots & a_{n,n} \end{bmatrix} \tag{8}$$

To calculate the priority level between the paired comparisons we use a scale of proportions or intensities denominated by Saaty, shown in Table 2. This numerical scale is used effectively for qualitative interpretation in many applications requiring a weighting of its elements through their homogeneous comparison [19]. In addition, a type of comparison must be considered. The existing ones are:

- Importance: Appropriate when comparing criteria with each other.
- Preference: Appropriate when comparing alternatives.
- Most likely: Used when you compare the probability of the results, either with criteria or alternatives.

3.3   Estimation of Relative Weights

It is being done using the eigenvalues method where weights are assigned amongst n alternatives, to do so, one only needs to perform n-1 estimates.

Once the values of the comparison matrix are calculated, the columns are normalized to 1 by dividing each element by the total sum of the columns. The eigenvector is obtained by calculating the average of each row of the normalized matrix.

$$p = \begin{pmatrix} \frac{1}{n}\sum_1^n a_{1j} \\ \frac{1}{n}\sum_1^n a_{2j} \\ \cdots \\ \frac{1}{n}\sum_1^n a_{nj} \end{pmatrix} \tag{9}$$

Vector of criteria priorities is obtained as shown in 10

$$p = \begin{pmatrix} p_{c11} \\ p_{c12} \\ \cdots \\ p_{c1n} \end{pmatrix} \tag{10}$$

3.4   Results Analysis

The AHP method allows measuring the non-consistency and sensitivity of the judgments by calculating the consistency ratio, to this extent the consistency index must first be obtained.

Calculation of the consistency index.
It is the index measuring the consistency of the comparison matrix, its formula is the following:

$$CI = \frac{\lambda_{max} - n}{n - 1} \tag{11}$$

Where n is the size of the matrix and λ_{max} is the eigenvalue, which is obtained through the multiplication of matrices between the elements of the eigenvector and the original matrix, thus obtaining a quotient for each element that we must add and then divide for n elements.

Calculation of the consistency ratio.
It is obtained by dividing the consistency index for an already established random value that depends on n elements used, it is recommended not to use more than nine elements so that the method can maintain consistent (Table 3).

$$CR = \frac{IC}{ICA} \tag{12}$$

According to Saaty, a good accuracy of the consistency value is recommended, with CR less than 0.1, however, values ranging up to 0.2 are mentioned; if the condition is not met, the whole process must be re-run from the comparison matrix until it can have an acceptable consistency.

Table 3. Random consistency according to the number of criteria

	3	4	5	6	7	8	9	10	11	12	13	14	15
ICA	0.525	0.882	1.115	1.252	1.341	1.404	1.1452	1.1484	1.1513	1.1535	1.555	1.570	1.583

In this case several tests for the evaluation, in order to obtain a better accuracy of the values corresponding to each of the variables using the AHP model, with respect to the weights that were used for the evaluation by fuzzy sets, these will indicate the degree of membership of each variable were considering their level of risk. The method gives us an analysis of consistency, which if it is greater than 0.1, will indicate that the evaluation is inconsistent.

Regarding the seismic risk assessment, this methodology will help us obtain the weights of the input variables belonging to the risk factors for physical damage and social aggravation, they will be used in the application of fuzzy sets during the estimation process. Below are shown the tables of the analytic hierarchy process for the weighting of each group of factors $(F_{RFk}, F_{FSk,}, F_{FRk,})$ shown before on Table 4 (Tables 5, 6, 7, 8 and 9).

Table 4. Comparison matrix of physical risk.

	F_{RF1}	F_{RF2}	F_{RF3}	F_{RF4}	F_{RF5}	F_{RF6}	F_{RF7}	F_{RF8}
F_{RF1}	1	3	3	3	5	5	7	5
F_{RF2}	0,33	1	1	1	3	3	5	3
F_{RF3}	0,33	1,00	1	1	3	3	5	4
F_{RF4}	0,33	1,00	1,00	1	4	4	5	3
F_{RF5}	0,20	0,33	0,33	0,25	1	3	5	3
F_{RF6}	0,20	0,33	0,33	0,25	0,33	1	5	3
F_{RF7}	0,14	0,20	0,20	0,20	0,20	0,20	1	1/2
F_{RF8}	0,20	0,33	0,25	0,33	0,33	0,33	2,00	1

Table 5. Normalized matrix of physical risk.

	F_{RF1}	F_{RF2}	F_{RF3}	F_{RF4}	F_{RF5}	F_{RF6}	F_{RF7}	F_{RF8}
F_{RF1}	0,3646	0,4167	0,4215	0,4265	0,2964	0,2560	0,2000	0,2222
F_{RF2}	0,1215	0,1389	0,1405	0,1422	0,1779	0,1536	0,1429	0,1333
F_{RF3}	0,1215	0,1389	0,1405	0,1422	0,1779	0,1536	0,1429	0,1778
F_{RF4}	0,1215	0,1389	0,1405	0,1422	0,2372	0,2048	0,1429	0,1333
F_{RF5}	0,0729	0,0463	0,0468	0,0355	0,0593	0,1536	0,1429	0,1333
F_{RF6}	0,0729	0,0463	0,0468	0,0355	0,0198	0,0512	0,1429	0,1333
F_{RF7}	0,0521	0,0278	0,0281	0,0284	0,0119	0,0102	0,0286	0,0222
F_{RF8}	0,0729	0,0463	0,0351	0,0474	0,0198	0,0171	0,0571	0,0444

Table 6. Priority Vector and Weight Allocation

Factor	Variables	Weights	Priority vector
F_{RF1}	Affected buildings	W_{RF1}	0,33
F_{RF2}	Deceased	W_{RF2}	0,14
F_{RF3}	Attended people	W_{RF3}	0,15
F_{RF4}	Injured	W_{RF4}	0,16
F_{RF5}	Effect on drinking water service	W_{RF5}	0,09
F_{RF6}	Effect on electric system	W_{RF6}	0,07
F_{RF7}	Effect on telecommunications system	W_{RF7}	0,03
F_{RF8}	Effect on productive sector	W_{RF8}	0,04

Eigenvalue = 8,6185
CI = 0,0884
CR = 0,0629

Table 7. Comparison matrix of social aggravation.

	F_{FS1}	F_{FS2}	F_{FS3}	F_{FR1}	F_{FR2}	F_{FR3}	F_{FR4}
F_{FS1}	1	3	4	1/3	1	1	1/2
F_{FS2}	0,33	1	3	1/5	1/5	1/5	1/3
F_{FS3}	0,25	0,33	1	1/3	1	1/3	1/2
F_{FR1}	3,00	5,00	3,00	1	1	2	2
F_{FR2}	1,00	5,00	1,00	1,00	1	2	1
F_{FR3}	1,00	5,00	3,00	0,50	0,50	1	1
F_{FR4}	2,00	3,00	2,00	0,50	1,00	1,00	1

Table 8. Normalized matrix of social aggravation.

	F_{FS1}	F_{FS2}	F_{FS3}	F_{FR1}	F_{FR2}	F_{FR3}	F_{FR4}
F_{FS1}	0,1165	0,1343	0,2353	0,0862	0,1754	0,1327	0,0789
F_{FS2}	0,0388	0,0448	0,1765	0,0517	0,0351	0,0265	0,0526
F_{FS3}	0,0291	0,0149	0,0588	0,0862	0,1754	0,0442	0,0739
F_{FR1}	0,3495	0,2239	0,1765	0,2586	0,1754	0,2655	0,3158
F_{FR2}	0,1165	0,2239	0,0588	0,2586	0,1754	0,2655	0,1579
F_{FR3}	0,1165	0,2239	0,1765	0,1293	0,0877	0,1327	0,1579
F_{FR4}	0,2330	0,1343	0,1176	0,1293	0,1754	0,1327	0,1579

Table 9. Priority vector and weight allocation

Factor	Variables	Weights	Priority vector
F_{FS1}	Poverty rate	W_{FS1}	0,14
F_{FS2}	Mortality rate	W_{FS2}	0,06
F_{FS3}	Population density	W_{FS3}	0,07
F_{FR1}	Food Kits	W_{FR1}	0,25
F_{FR2}	Hostels and Shelters	W_{FR2}	0,18
F_{FR3}	Rescue staff	W_{FR3}	0,15
F_{FR4}	Water supply	W_{FR4}	0,15

Eigenvalue = 7,78
CI = 0,1307
CR = 0,0975

4   Seismic Risk Assessment - Set Method

For the case study, the theory of fuzzy sets was applied in order to identify the level of seismic risk of a given geographical area, considering risk variables for physical damage and social aggravation extracted from a database provided by the INEC (http://www.ecuadorencifras.gob.ec/institucional/home/) and the Secretariat for Risk Management (http://www.gestionderiesgos.gob.ec/).

Once the variables are established, we proceed to obtain their weights (W_{RFk}, W_{FSi}, W_{FRj}) corresponding to the variables of physical risk and social aggravation (social fragility and lack of resilience) (X_{RFk}, X_{FSi}, X_{FRj}) through the AHP (Analytic Hierarchy Process) method applied in Sect. 4.

With this method, the problem will be structured, i.e. the physical risk factor F_{RFk} and aggravation factor F_{FSk}, then a matrix will be designed for each factor; and then values will be assigned through the Saaty comparison scale.

It is important to define the linguistic values for the calculation of the total risk. For this study five linguistic values will be used (very low, low, medium, high, very high) and using fuzzy sets, one obtains the membership functions of each variable; in this process, it is necessary to define the range of the abscissa next to their grades corresponding to the degree of membership as shown in Table 10.

Next are presented the following nomenclatures:

- L_{RFi} Physical risk level.
- L_{Fj} Aggravation level.
- $u(x)$ Membership function.
- u_{LRF} Membership function of physical risk.
- u_{LF} Membership function of aggravation.

It is essential to establish the membership functions well because the fact of having a good estimate of the total seismic risk depends on them; the variables input values for the evaluation process can be considered of good quality since the fuzzy logic deals with this imprecision in the data. Once the incoming information is established, it is compared with the values of the abscissas previously defined in the membership functions in order to obtain a level of physical risk or aggravation for each variable. This process is called fuzzification and it is used in the methods of inference to obtain a fuzzy value from said comparison.

Following the sequence of the fuzzy inference model, a new output fuzzy set must be generated using the implication where a cut is made, choosing the minimum membership degree between the fuzzy value obtained and the fuzzy set of the output variable. Table 11 shows the membership functions of the variable outputs of physical risk and aggravation.

By using the fuzzy output sets we perform the aggregation through the union operation of the membership functions and then with the centroid method we defuzzify, in order to generate an index and linguistic value of physical risk or aggravation. For these two processes, the following formulas are defined:

Physical Risk

Union

$$u_{RF}(X_{RF}) = \max(W_{RF1}u_{LRF1}(L_{RF1}), \ldots, W_{RFk}u_{LRFk}(L_{RFk})) \tag{1}$$

It is the union (max) of the output sets relative to the physical risk input membership functions, weighted with their weights and risk level of each variable.

124   L.J. Cevallos-Torres et al.

Table 10. Code developed on Matlab for the design of membership functions for deceased, poverty rate and hostels/shelter

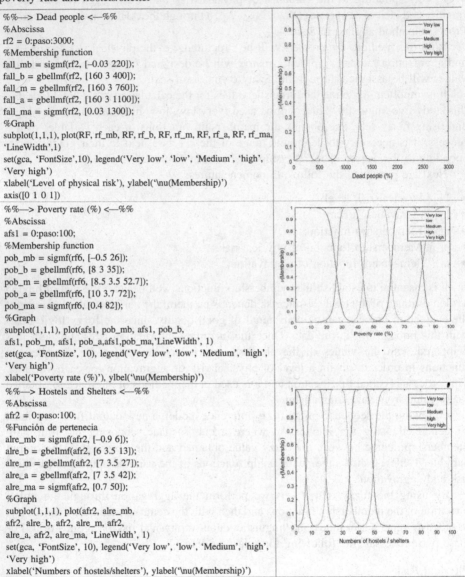

```
%%—> Dead people <—%%
%Abscissa
rf2 = 0:paso:3000;
%Membership function
fall_mb = sigmf(rf2, [−0.03 220]);
fall_b = gbellmf(rf2, [160 3 400]);
fall_m = gbellmf(rf2, [160 3 760]);
fall_a = gbellmf(rf2, [160 3 1100]);
fall_ma = sigmf(rf2, [0.03 1300]);
%Graph
subplot(1,1,1), plot(RF, rf_mb, RF, rf_b, RF, rf_m, RF, rf_a, RF, rf_ma,
'LineWidth',1)
set(gca, 'FontSize',10), legend('Very low', 'low', 'Medium', 'high',
'Very high')
xlabel('Level of physical risk'), ylabel('\nu(Membership)')
axis([0 1 0 1])
```

```
%%—> Poverty rate (%) <—%%
%Abscissa
afs1 = 0:paso:100;
%Membership function
pob_mb = sigmf(rf6, [−0.5 26]);
pob_b = gbellmf(rf6, [8 3 35]);
pob_m = gbellmf(rf6, [8.5 3.5 52.7]);
pob_a = gbellmf(rf6, [10 3.7 72]);
pob_ma = sigmf(rf6, [0.4 82]);
%Graph
subplot(1,1,1), plot(afs1, pob_mb, afs1, pob_b,
afs1, pob_m, afs1, pob_a,afs1,pob_ma,'LineWidth', 1)
set(gca, 'FontSize', 10), legend('Very low', 'low', 'Medium', 'high',
'Very high')
xlabel('Poverty rate (%)'), ylbel('\nu(Membership)')
```

```
%%—> Hostels and Shelters <—%%
%Abscissa
afr2 = 0:paso:100;
%Función de pertenecia
alre_mb = sigmf(afr2, [−0.9 6]);
alre_b = gbellmf(afr2, [6 3.5 13]);
alre_m = gbellmf(afr2, [7 3.5 27]);
alre_a = gbellmf(afr2, [7 3.5 42]);
alre_ma = sigmf(afr2, [0.7 50]);
%Graph
subplot(1,1,1), plot(afr2, alre_mb,
afr2, alre_b, afr2, alre_m, afr2,
alre_a, afr2, alre_ma, 'LineWidth', 1)
set(gca, 'FontSize', 10), legend('Very low', 'low', 'Medium', 'high',
'Very high')
xlabel('Numbers of hostels/shelters'), ylabel('\nu(Membership)')
```

Defuzzification

$$.R_F = [\max(W_{RF1}u_{LRF1}(L_{RF1}), \ldots, W_{RFk}u_{LRFk}(L_{RFk}))]_{centroid} \qquad (2)$$

It is the center calculation of the area under the union curve of the membership functions of the physical risk R_F.

Table 11. Code developed on Matlab for the design of membership output functions, physical risk and social aggravation.

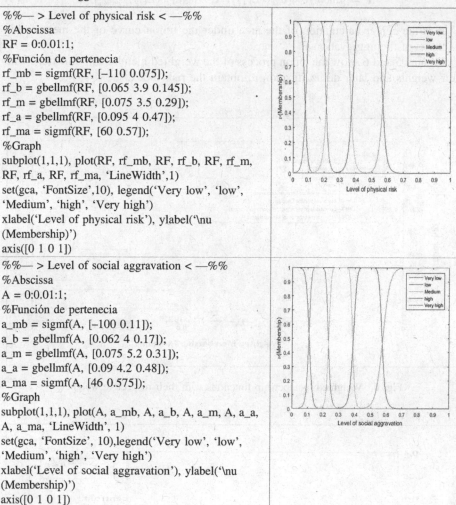

```
%%— > Level of physical risk < —%%
%Abscissa
RF = 0:0.01:1;
%Función de pertenecia
rf_mb = sigmf(RF, [–110 0.075]);
rf_b = gbellmf(RF, [0.065 3.9 0.145]);
rf_m = gbellmf(RF, [0.075 3.5 0.29]);
rf_a = gbellmf(RF, [0.095 4 0.47]);
rf_ma = sigmf(RF, [60 0.57]);
%Graph
subplot(1,1,1), plot(RF, rf_mb, RF, rf_b, RF, rf_m,
RF, rf_a, RF, rf_ma, 'LineWidth',1)
set(gca, 'FontSize',10), legend('Very low', 'low',
'Medium', 'high', 'Very high')
xlabel('Level of physical risk'), ylabel('\nu
(Membership)')
axis([0 1 0 1])
```

```
%%— > Level of social aggravation < —%%
%Abscissa
A = 0:0.01:1;
%Función de pertenecia
a_mb = sigmf(A, [–100 0.11]);
a_b = gbellmf(A, [0.062 4 0.17]);
a_m = gbellmf(A, [0.075 5.2 0.31]);
a_a = gbellmf(A, [0.09 4.2 0.48]);
a_ma = sigmf(A, [46 0.575]);
%Graph
subplot(1,1,1), plot(A, a_mb, A, a_b, A, a_m, A, a_a,
A, a_ma, 'LineWidth', 1)
set(gca, 'FontSize', 10),legend('Very low', 'low',
'Medium', 'high', 'Very high')
xlabel('Level of social aggravation'), ylabel('\nu
(Membership)')
axis([0 1 0 1])
```

Aggravation

Union

$$u_F(X_{FS}, X_{FR}) = \max\left(W_{FS1}u_{LF1}(L_{F1}), \ldots, W_{FRj}u_{LFj}(L_{Fj})\right) \tag{3}$$

It is the union (max) of the output sets relative to the social fragility and lack of resiliency input membership functions, weighted with their weights and aggravation level of each variable.

Defuzzification

$$.F = [\max(W_{FS1}u_{LF1}(L_{F1}), \ldots, W_{FRi}u_{LFi}(L_{Fi}))]_{centroid} \qquad (4)$$

It is the center calculation of the area under the union curve of the membership functions of the aggravation F.

Figures 5 and 6 show the union process of the weighted membership functions with their weights and later defuzzification to obtain the risk index.

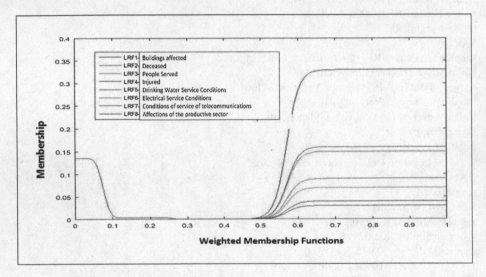

Fig. 5. Weighted membership functions with their respective weights

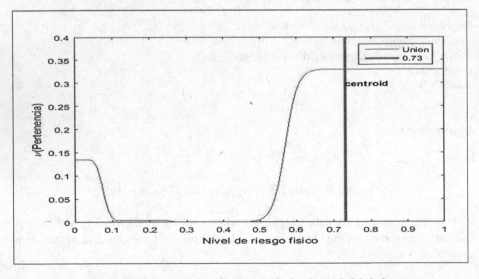

Fig. 6. Union and defuzzification to obtain physical risk index

Once the physical risk and the aggravation indexes have been calculated, we assign a level to each factor using the linguistic values defined in the membership functions and the comparison of the input values with their respective abscissas. For the final calculation of the total risk assessment, we compare the levels of each factor with the fuzzy rules established in Table 12.

Table 12. Fuzzy rules to estimate total risk.

Physical risk	Aggravation				
	Low	Medium Low	Medium high	High	Very high
Low	Low	Low	Medium Low	Medium Low	Medium Low
Medium Low	Medium Low	Medium Low	Medium high	Medium high	Medium high
Medium high	Medium high	Medium high	High	High	Very high
High	High	High	Very high	Very high	Very high
Very high	Very high	Very high	Very high	Very high	Very high

4.1 Fuzzy Logic Toolbox - Matlab

Matlab is a mathematical calculation development platform that facilitates the analysis, design and visualization of results. For this study, we used the fuzzy logic toolbox using inference modeling functions, it facilitates the design and simulation of fuzzy systems.

In the estimation of the total seismic risk it shall help us model the membership functions of each variable, as well as execute the inference process (fuzzification, implication, aggregation and defuzzification) allowing us to obtain the resulting indexes. In Fig. 7, we can see that the greatest physical risk are in the cities of Puerto Lopez, Portoviejo, Jama, El Carmen, and the greatest social aggravation is in the cities of Puerto Lopez, El Carmen, Jama, Portoviejo.

Table 13 shows the qualitative value of the total risk obtained through the fuzzy rules established.

Table 13 shows the qualitative value of the total risk obtained through the fuzzy rules. The case in the proposed study, the total risk level is "very high" in almost all of the variables, when comparing the abscissas of the crisp output value from Fig. 6, (which indicates that the rate of physical risk of the canton Portoviejo is 0.73) and Fig. 7 (both physical risk levels as social aggravation of 22 cantons) This indicates the index of the level of risk that will be used in the diffuse tables (Table 12), and in this case it is to us that it is "very high", this same procedure is done for all other situations, where the level of overall risk resulting in "high"; It is worth highlighting that the design of the membership function of fuzzy sets, were analyzed on the basis of reports published on the website of the Secretariat of management of risk, however other potential extension of the proposal is to allow opinions without interaction of several experts and working on a method previously established consensus-based comparisons of experts within the framework of fuzzy systems.

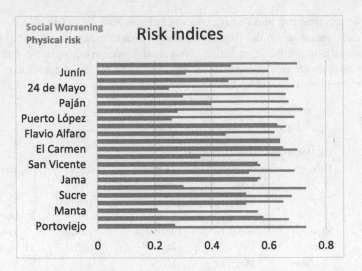

Fig. 7. Indices of the physical risk level and aggravation of the cantons of the province of Manabí.

Table 13. Total risk level of the Manabí province cantons

Canton	Total risk level
Portoviejo	Very high
Chone	Very high
Manta	Medium
Montecristi	Very high
Sucre	Very high
Pedernales	Very high
Jama	High
Jaramijo	Very high
San Vicente	High
Bolivar	Very high
El Carmen	Very high
Rocafuerte	Very high
Flavio Alfaro	Very high
Tosagua	Very high
Puerto Lopez	Very high
Santa Ana	Very high
Pajan	Very high
Jipijapa	Very high
24 de Mayo	Very high
Olmedo	Very high
Junin	Very high
Pichincha	Very high

5   Conclusions

The study focused on the 22 cantons of the province of Manabí, where data of the potential losses suffered by these areas during the earthquake of April 2016 were obtained. The information was classified for physical risk and social aggravation scenarios, the fuzzy sets theory was applied to it, in order to identify the risk levels of each zone.

The physical risk and social aggravation indices of each canton; according to the results shown in Fig. 7, all of the cantons of Manabí were severely affected: with respect to physical damages, the most affected ones were Pedernales, El Carmen and Portoviejo, while the one with the smallest damage is 24 de Mayo. With respect to the aggravation, the biggest situation was seen in Santa Ana, and the smallest was Manta.

Total risk was assessed using fuzzy rules with the risk levels assigned by the calculation of their indices, and just like in the previous analysis, we observed that the situation in the affected areas was of high gravity. The context of material losses was the most influent one for social impact, as it is the case in the Pedernales canton which was totally destroyed, leaving its population in extreme poverty. Others were impacted by the scarcity of resources and basic services that led the inhabitants to stay in shelters until they found a way to recover in a socio-economic way.

Fuzzy set generations allow obtain high quality pattern easily understood. In future research, it is expected to improve the results by delving deeper in the study of data sets.

References

1. Parra, H., Benito, M.B., Gaspar-Escribano, J.M.: Seismic hazard assessment in continental Ecuador. Bull. Earthq. Eng. **14**(8), 2129–2159 (2016)
2. Saaty, T., Vargas, L.: Models, Methods, Concepts and Applications of the Analytic Hierarchy Process, vol. 175, 2nd edn., p. 5. Springer (2012)
3. Martínez, F.M., Sánchez Meca, J., Lopez, J.: The meta-analysis in the field of Health Sciences: an indispensable methodology for the efficient accumulation of knowledge. Physiotherapy **31**(3), 107–114 (2009)
4. Höhle, U., Rodabaugh, S.E.: Mathematics of Fuzzy Sets: Logic, Topology, and Measure Theory, vol. 3. Springer, Heidelberg (2012)
5. Cardona, O.D.: Indicators of Disaster Risk and Risk Management: Program for Latin America and the Caribbean. Summary Report. Inter-American Development Bank (2005)
6. Laasri, E., Akhouayri, E.S., Agliz, D., Zonta, D., Atmani, A.: A fuzzy expert system for automatic seismic signal classification. Expert Syst. Appl. **42**(3), 1013–1027 (2015)
7. Ahumada, A., Altunkaynak, A., Ayoub, A.: Fuzzy logic-based attenuation relationships of strong motion earthquake records. Expert Syst. Appl. **42**(3), 1287–1297 (2015). doi:10.1016/j.eswa.2014.09.035
8. Carreño, M., Barbat, A., Cardona, O.: Numerical method for the holistic evaluation of the seismic risk using the set theory Diffuses. In: Numerical Methods for Calculation and Design in Engineering (2013)

9. Messick, M.A.: Natural disasters in Latin America: The role of disaster type and productive sector on the urban-rural income gap and rural to urban migration. The University of Southern Mississippi (2016)
10. Toya, H., Skidmore, M.: Economic development and the impacts of natural disasters. Econ. Lett. **94**(1), 20–25 (2007)
11. Espinilla, M., Liu, J., Martínez, L.: An extended hierarchical linguistic model for decisionmaking problems. Comput. Intell **27**(3), 489–512 (2011)
12. Sharma, M.L.: Attenuation relationship for estimation of peak ground horizontal acceleration using data from strong-motion arrays in India. Bull. Seismol. Soc. Am. **88**(4), 1063–1069 (1998)
13. Po-Shen, L., Chyi-Tyi, L.: Ground-motion attenuation relationships for subduction-zone earthquakes in Northeastern Taiwan. Bull. Seismol. Soc. Am. **98**(1), 220–240 (2008)
14. Ambrasseys, N., Douglas, J.: Near field horizontal and vertical earthquake ground motions. Soil Dyn. Earthq. Eng. **23**, 1–18 (2003)
15. Wadia-Fascetti, S., Gunes, B.: Earthquake response spectra models incorporating fuzzy logic with statistics Computer-Aided. Civil Infrastruct. Eng. **15**, 134–146 (2000)
16. Coburn, A., Spence, R., Pomonis, A.: Factors determining human casualty levels in earthquakes: Mortality prediction in building collapse. In: Proceedings of the Tenth, World Conference on Earthquakes Engineering (1992)
17. Maldonado, E., Casas, J., Canas, J.: Use of fuzzy sets in seismic vulnerability models. Monograph CIMNE IS-39 (2000a)
18. Maldonado, E., Casas, J., Canas, J.: Models of seismic vulnerability of bridges based on "Fuzzy sets". Monograph CIMNE IS-39 (2000b)
19. Maldonado, E., Casas, J., Canas, J.: Application of fuzzy sets in the evaluation of the parameters of the seismic vulnerability of bridges. International Journal of Numerical Methods for Calculation and Design in Engineering **18**(2), 209–226 (2000)

Applications in Healthcare and Wellness

An IoT-Based Architecture to Develop a Healthcare Smart Platform

Isaac Machorro-Cano[1](✉), Uriel Ramos-Deonati[1],
Giner Alor-Hernández[1], José Luis Sánchez-Cervantes[2],
Cuauhtémoc Sánchez-Ramírez[1], Lisbeth Rodríguez-Mazahua[1],
and Mónica Guadalupe Segura-Ozuna[3]

[1] Division of Research and Postgraduate Studies,
Instituto Tecnológico de Orizaba, Av. Oriente 9,
852. Col. Emiliano Zapata, 94320 Orizaba, Veracruz, Mexico
imachorro@gmail.com, uramos.dvc@gmail.com,
{galor, csanchez, lrodriguez}@itorizaba.edu.mx
[2] CONACYT - Instituto Tecnológico de Orizaba, Av. Oriente 9,
852. Col. Emiliano Zapata, 94320 Orizaba, Veracruz, Mexico
jlsanchez@conacyt.mx
[3] Universidad del Papaloapan (UNPA),
Circuito Central #200. Col. Parque Industrial, 68301 Tuxtepec, Oaxaca, Mexico
msegura@unpa.edu.mx

Abstract. Nowadays, obesity and hypertension are two global health problems that affect the quality of life of people and thus their work life. The Internet of Things (IoT) is a paradigm in which everyday objects are equipped with identification, detection, interconnection, and processing capabilities that allow them to communicate with one another and with other devices and services through the Internet to achieve some goal. The IoT great opportunities for monitoring, analyzing, diagnosing, controlling and providing treatment recommendations for chronic-degenerative diseases, such as obesity and hypertension. In this work, we design a smart healthcare platform architecture based on the IoT paradigm; the paper also discusses important literature associating obesity, hypertension, and other chronic-degenerative diseases with the applications of the IoT paradigm. Finally, to validate our architecture, we present the case study of an elderly patient suffering from overweight and hypertension.

Keywords: Monitoring · Obesity and hypertension · IoT

1 Introduction

Obesity is a pathological state characterized by excessive accumulation of body fat. Since 1980, global obesity has more than doubled. In 2014, more than 1.9 billion adults, aged 18 and over, around the world that is, 39% were overweight, over 600 million that is, 13% were obese, and 41 million children under the age of 5 were either overweight or obese [1]. In fact, most of the world's population lives in countries where overweight and obesity kills more people than underweight. As for Arterial Hypertension (AH), it is a common condition characterized by high blood pressure,

© Springer International Publishing AG 2017
R. Valencia-García et al. (Eds.): CITI 2017, CCIS 749, pp. 133–145, 2017.
DOI: 10.1007/978-3-319-67283-0_10

which is the force of blood pushing against the artery walls. Hypertension is a highly prevalent cardiovascular risk factor worldwide because of the increasing longevity and prevalence of contributing factors such as obesity. Whereas the treatment of hypertension has been shown to prevent cardiovascular diseases and to extend and enhance life, hypertension remains inadequately managed everywhere [2]. In other words, both obesity and hypertension are two health problems that affect the quality of the people, especially at work.

Healthcare is a popular and important application area of the IoT, since the IoT is adapted to improve service quality and reduce costs. Various medical sensors or devices are used to monitor medical parameters, such as body temperature, blood glucose level and blood pressure. Recent advances in sensors, wireless communication, and processing technologies are the driving force behind the application of the IoT in healthcare systems. Lately, portable body sensors, better known as wearables, are being developed to continuously monitor patient activities or parameters in real time. In this context, the IoT offers healthcare systems an interconnection of the diverse heterogeneous devices to obtain fast, complete, and accurate information of health parameters [3].

Assisted living environments facilitate the daily lives of people with disabilities and chronic medical conditions. Thanks to the sensors' capability to efficiently manage data, it is possible to provide patients with real time assisted living services. Using the IoT in healthcare contributes to innovative services, such as the collection of vital patient data through a network of sensors connected to medical devices. It also contributes to, delivering data to the cloud of a medical center for their storage and processing, and ensures ubiquitous access or sharing of medical data (e.g. health records) [4]. Similarly, the challenges of the healthcare sector are an opportunity to develop and implement the IoT and thus contribute to the improvement of healthcare services.

In this paper, we propose smart healthcare platform architecture. The architecture relies on the IoT paradigm in such a way that it citizen participation in and responsibility for self-care. Maximizing citizen involvement in self-care can reduce the number of patients suffering from obesity and hypertension and thus minimize social cost incurred to prevent and care for patients suffering from these diseases.

This research is structured as follows: Sect. 2 discusses works related to obesity, hypertension, and IoT, whereas Sect. 3, explains the design methodology adopted to create the IoT-based architecture. Section 4, presents the case study of an elderly patient suffering from both obesity and hypertension. Finally, Sect. 5, presents the research conclusions and a plan for future work.

2   Related Works

The IoT is a paradigm in which everyday objects are equipped with identification, detection, interconnection and processing capabilities that allow them to communicate with each other and with one another and other devices and services through the Internet to achieve some goal. The IoT assumes that any single object is a real-time data source. This principle is transforming the lifestyle of millions of people, particularly in the healthcare domain [5]. One, of the many applications of the IoT includes disease prevention and control, especially hypertension [6]. Additionally, the IoT provides great opportunities for monitoring, analyzing, diagnosing, controlling, and providing treatment recommendations for obesity and others chronic-degenerative diseases. The IoT has thus become the source of great interest in the scientific community. Below, we present some works exploring the impact of the IoT paradigm on the treatment of obesity, hypertension and other chronic-degenerative diseases.

2.1 Obesity in the IoT Paradigm

Vasquez et al. [7] proposed (mhealth, a mobile health) platform whose aim is to increase children's health awareness by tracking their food intake and sending proper notifications and messages based on their food choices. On the other hand, Vilallonga et al. [8] presented a follow-up study of obese patients after surgery. Patients considered the time saving as very valuable and concluded that visualizing their progress charts on a constant basis was very motivating for them. Similarly, Lee and Ouyang [9] presented a study enabled for UHD (Ubiquitous-Healthcare Device) based on the IoT to recognize the relationships between and risk factors of mutual diseases. In turn, Zaragozá et al. [10] described a monitoring platform intended to establish a sensor network for obese children under clinical treatment.

Lee and Ouyang [11] proposed an intelligent service model for healthcare that gives effective feedback to an individual. The authors introduced the collaboration protocol that transfers risk factors among IoT personal health devices and proposed an intellectualized service application algorithm to be operated in the personal health device. Likewise, Hiremath et al. [12] tried to conceptualize Wearable IoT (WIoT) in terms of their design, function, and applications. The authors discussed the building blocks of WIoT including wearable sensors, internet-connected gateways, and cloud and big data support which are a key to its future success in healthcare related applications. Finally, the authors also proposed a new system science for WIoT that suggests future directions, encompassing operational and clinical aspects.

Vazquez et al. [13] presented a mobile health architecture intended to prevent childhood obesity by promoting good health behaviors with a set of mHealth applications. The applications also provide notifications and messages from adults to improve results. Kim et al. [14] presented the design and usage of iN Touch, a mobile self-management application for tracking observations of daily living (ODLs) in a health coaching program for low-income, urban, minority youth with overweight/obesity. Also, Alloghani et al. [15] proposed a mobile health application intended to increase the awareness levels of parents and children about the risks of obesity and help them sustain a balanced and healthy eating lifestyle.

Wibisono and Astawa [16] presented a Website and mobile applications for a weight loss program with machine-to-machine (M2M) technology using a special weight scale to upload data to the server. From a different perspective, Dobbins et al. [17] evaluated the performance of the classifiers, which are able to distinguish physical activity from personal life logs and they designed a method to collect streams of life logging data from wearable accelerometer and heart rate devices. Finally, Shin et al. [18] defined the new concept of IoT-learning by integrating the IoT technologies and

Ubiquitous-learning and proposed a personalized personal training program using IoT-learning for weight management.

2.2 Hypertension in the IoT Paradigm

Krawczyk and Wozniak [6] presented the experimental evaluation of a set of compound classifiers for highly imbalanced multi-class classification task. The task was related to the crucial problem of hypertension type diagnosis, which is recognized as one of the main serious social diseases. Similarly, Antonovici et al. [19] proposed an Android application that aims at recording the systolic blood pressure, the diastolic blood pressure, and heart rate, obtained from the electronic sphygmomanometer. The application offers transmitting medical data via mobile or wireless internet. The data are compared with standard values and if they are not in the normal range, the patient is alerted, but also the family physician, or in the worst case the emergency service. Similarly, authors Akutekwe and Seker [20] presented a hybrid Dynamic Bayesian Network approach to modeling and inferencing made up of five feature selection methods and Dynamic Bayesian Network. The approach was successfully applied to the discovery of possible key biomarkers for hypertension.

Deen [21] proposed several low-cost, noninvasive, user-friendly sensing and actuating systems using information and communication technologies. These systems can be used to create engineering solutions to some of the pressing healthcare problems in our society, especially as it pertains to the elderly. Jeong et al. [22] presented blueprints of iotHEALTHCARE, a smart healthcare system, and its logical architecture. In this work, medical data are collected by sensors, then they are processed via a mobile and intelligent network. Then, after the data goes to cloud computing to be analyzed with complex algorithms, and medical professionals make diagnoses and treatment recommendations in a smart healthcare system, such as iotHEALTHCARE. On the other hand, authors Gupta et al. [23] proposed an architecture based on the embedded sensors of the equipment, rather than using wearable sensors or Smartphone sensors, to store the value of basic health-related parameters.

Chen et al. [24] presented Smart Clothing as an innovative health monitoring system that incorporates the new textile manufacturing techniques to overcome shortcomings of traditional wearable devices in health monitoring applications, such as low comfort level, low accuracy, complex operation, and inappropriate long-term monitoring. Also Jung [25] proposed a framework for personal disease diagnosis with IoT contexts. The framework depends is on observations of trajectory information of measurements for a period of time for personal healthcare application. From a different perspective, Lake et al. [26] presented an architecture and framework to development and supports solutions. The authors identified core standards and industry bodies where eHealth-M2M-IoT standardization was in progress. Finally, Zhang et al. [27] provided a comprehensive survey of recent advancement in Wireless Sensor Networks-based healthcare, thus exploiting the potential of ubiquitous sensing for healthcare (USH) service.

2.3   Chronic-Degenerative Diseases in the IoT Paradigm

Santos et al. [28] proposed a novel IoT-based mobile gateway solution for mobile health (m-Health) scenarios. This gateway autonomously collects information about the user/patient location, heart rate, and possible fall detection. Also, Hossain and Muhammad [29] presented a Healthcare Industrial IoT (HealthIIoT), a monitoring framework where healthcare data are collected by mobile devices and sensors, and they are securely sent to the cloud for seamless access by healthcare professionals. Then, authors Jara et al. [30] proposed a personal device to assist and consider more factors in the insulin therapy dosage calculation for patients with diabetes in ambient assisted living (AAL). Whereas Paschou et al. [31] presented novel metrics and methods in an attempt to maximize the capabilities of IoT and widen its acceptance/usage. Without losing its generality, the method of Paschou et al. was experimentally evaluated the healthcare domain.

Authors similar Gia et al. [32] proposed an IoT-based architecture and system for healthcare applications. The presented IoT-based system provides a cost-effective and easy way to analyze and monitor, either remotely or on the spot, real-time health data such as Electrocardiogram (ECG) and Electromyography (EMG) data. On the other hand, Jung et al. [33] developed a mobile healthcare application for Android OS to provide self-diabetes management. The application has five functions: diabetes management, weight management, brain attack risk evaluation, stress and depression evaluation and exercise management. Likewise, Hu et al. [34] investigated and proposed a scalable RFID-based architecture that was deployed cost-effectively and at the same time supported the delivery of accurate and timely healthcare to all patients. On the other hand, Kumar [35] discussed the concept of Internet of Fitness Things (IoFT) wearable devices and how the sensors inside these devices interact with the user and the cloud. A new methodology to help patients with Obstructive Sleep Apnea (OSA) and similar life-threatening diseases based on the IoFT was proposed in this work.

Ganzha et al. [36] presented a study develop methods and tools to support semantic interoperability in the INTER-IoT project, taking advantage of ontologies and semantic data processing to facilitate interoperability through the IoT landscape. The INTER-IoT project is driven by two use cases originating from, the (E/m) health and transportation and logistics. Similarly, Raza et al. [37] presented an overview of the telehealth, then they addressesed the possible telehealth technologies and applications that could be applied to improve the healthcare service performance in developing countries. Also, Camara [38] discussed several technological trends in wireless communications toward 5G networks. The author highlights the influence of e-health and IoT applications. On the other hand, Ifrim et al. [39] presented the current status of IoT evolution, trends, and research in e-Health, highlighting from a research perspective the performance and limitations of existing healthcare architectures, services, and applications.

As can be observed, some IoT-based methods or techniques have been developed to decrease the rate of obesity, while others diagnose hypertension. Others methods rely on mobile devices and wearable devices to collect, store, and analyze information that can be useful to a person's health status.

In the following section, we present the design of our IoT-based architecture that integrates components, services for data detection and collection, protocols, and data communications and data mining technologies.

3 Architecture of the Healthcare Smart Platform

A fundamental requirement in IoT is that things on the network must be interconnected, so the IoT architecture guarantees the proper functioning of things and serves as a bridge between the physical world and the virtual world. Designing architectures for IoT involves considering many factors, such as networking, communication, security, business models and processes. Additionally, it is important to take into account the extensibility, scalability, and interoperability between heterogeneous devices and their business models. Because things in the IoT move geographically and need to interact with other things in real time, an IoT architecture is adaptable to make the devices interact with other things dynamically and helps achieve unequivocal communication of the events. Moreover, the IoT is decentralized and heterogeneous [40]. In this work, we propose an approach that integrates different Information and Communication Technologies (ICTs) and the discuss the development of new artificial intelligence algorithms that identify critical variables based on the monitoring of vital signs extracted from sensors and devices to the prediction of obesity, and hypertension, and their possible complications. Also, the architecture can generate medical recommendations to treat obesity and hypertension. In this sense, Fig. 1 depicts our proposed IoT-based architecture of a smart healthcare platform. The architecture is composed of five layers:

1. **Presentation layer.** It integrates with available wearables, sensors, and devices with Internet connection to send and receive data or events. The presentation layer holds direct communication with the user.
2. **Integration layer.** This layer is integrated by the wearable or sensor provider, the query selector component and the response formulator. All of them, collaborate together to receive data and queries from the user, and formulate the corresponding answers.
3. **Layer of services in the IoT.** This layer includes the service caller, the search service selector, the services in the IoT, and the dynamic search and storage component. This layer is responsible for linking, invocating, selecting, and confirming the services in the IoT.
4. **Analytical data layer.** This layer includes the critical variable identification service and the medical recommendation system. It is responsible for identifying critical variables and medical recommendations.
5. **Data layer.** It contains all the data useful to the Healthcare Smart Platform and is integrated by data or events in real time, critical variables, medical recommendations, the IoT services repository, and the clinical history of patients.

The following nine steps explain the workflow between the components that integrate each layer, as well as their relationships with the components of other layers.

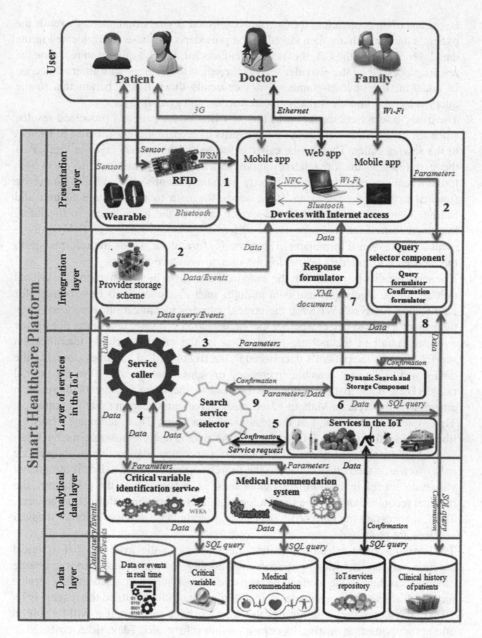

Fig. 1. Architecture of the healthcare smart platform

1. In the presentation layer, the wearable sensor or wearable detects and collects a patient's physical state (temperature, heart rate, blood pressure) and physical activity (burned calories, movements, number of steps) parameters, among others. The monitored parameters are then sent to one or more devices with an Internet connection (smartphone, laptop, tablet).

2. By means of an application, the Internet-connected device simultaneously sends the patient's data, which are then stored in the provider's database (DB), located in the data layer. Through the DB, the user (patient, doctor, family) queries in real time the results processed by the provider and displayed on the devices with Internet access. In addition, the Internet-connected device sends the patient's parameters to the query selector component that is located in the integration layer.

3. The query selector component asks the provider for the patient's processed results, since the query formulator needs such results to prepare the information to be sent to the service caller. The service caller is located in the service layer in the IoT. If the user (patient, doctor, relative) about patient's clinical history, the query formulator requests the information directly from the patient's clinical history database (located in the data layer) and then sends the data to the DynamicSearch and Storage Component (located in the service layer in the IoT), where in the information is formulated and sent via an eXtensible Markup Language (XML) document to the response formulator. The response formulator, sends the information to the devices with Internet access for the user to visualize them.

4. The service caller interacts with the analytical data layer by first invoking the critical ugh automatic algorithms and data mining, such as the Waikato Environment for Knowledge Analysis (WEKA), the critical variable identification service analyzes the patient's data to detect whether the values blood pressure, heart rate, obesity, or overweight fall in the normal range. That is, the critical variable identification service consults the patient's data stored in the BD of critical variables (found in the data layer) to detect a possible emergency or values that do not fall in the normal range. Then if the patient values do not fall in the normal range or there is an emergency, the Apache-Mahout-based medical recommendation system is invoked. This system, is also found in the analytical data layer. Then, automated learning libraries, identify in their DB (located in the data layer) the possible medical recommendation and, notify caller about such a recommendation. Then, the service caller forwards the patient's data to the search service selector. Also, if the patient values do not fall in the normal range or these is an emergency, the parameters, the medical recommendation, the patient location, and the patient information are sent. Then, if necessary, an emergency service (e.g. ambulance service) or other medical services are requested.

5. The search service selector identifies the services in the available IoT (clinical analysis service, nutrition, physical conditioning, or ambulance service, among others) according to the medical recommendations issued and performs the service request. Each service consults its availability and capacity to attend the request in its DB (in the data layer) and, notifies the search service selector, if it will be able to attend the request, indicating its corresponding information (day, time, costs, etc.). If a service cannot attend the request. The search service selector sends the data to the Dynamic Search and Storage Component, also located in the service layer in the IoT.

6. The Dynamic Search and Storage Component first sends the data to a DB to be stored in the intelligent platform containing the patient's medical history located in the data layer. Then, the component performs a query requesting a history of possible problems or emergencies similar to those detected. Afterward, it sends the

data to the response formulator, located in the integration layer, via an XML-based document.

7. The response formulator sends the analyzed data to the devices with Internet access, and it also sends the values that do not fall in the normal range or the emergency. The medical recommendation, the patient's location, and the requested and recommended emergency service information are sent to notify the patient, the doctor, and the relative.

8. If there is a requests for one or more services (clinical analysis, nutrition, or physical conditioning service, among others), the patient consults each service's information, regarding its availability (day, time, costs) to choose the service options that suits him/her better. Then, the patient selects a recommended service provider on the Internet-connected device. Afterward, the connected device located in the presentation layer sends the patient's specifications to the confirmation formulator subcomponent, which is integrated in the query selector component. The confirmation formulator then sends the confirmation to the Dynamic Search and Storage component (found in the service layer in the IoT), where it sends the confirmation data to the search service selector located in the same layer and to the backup in the patient's clinical history found in the data layer.

9. Finally, the search service selector sends the patient confirmation to the service provider in the IoT to confirm the service reservation, considering the patient's specifications (day, time, cost).

4   Case Study: An Elderly Patient with Overweight and Hypertension

This section presents a case study to validate our IoT-based smart healthcare platform architecture. The study addresses the situation of an elderly patient that suffers from both overweight and hypertension. The case study scenario is as follows:

• An elderly patient with overweight and high blood pressure needs to monitor how many calories he burns and his daily physical activity. Also, this person needs to constantly monitor his blood pressure to keep it stable and controlled. All the monitored data must be sent to a relative and the patient's doctor.

Figure 2 depicts the scenario of an elderly patient with overweight and hypertension. The patient's parameters (burnt calories, physical activity, and hypertension values) are collected by a wearable device that is synchronized with a smart phone.

Through an application, the patient, the family, and the physician can access the smart healthcare platform, which requests the patient's data to the wearable provider. The application analyzes and processes such data to monitor the patient's weight loss progress and his blood pressure and makes such information available in real time to the patient's relative and physician. If the patient exceeds the amount of weight to be lost or exceeds the goals set, the smart healthcare platform invokes a clinical analysis service to verify the patient's health and issues a recommendation. On the other hand, if the patient does not meet the goals set for weight loss the platform invokes the nutrition

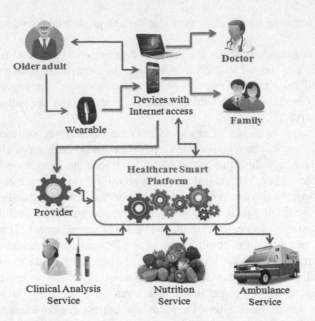

Fig. 2. Scenario of an elderly patient with overweight and hypertension

service to make appropriate modifications to the patient's diet. Also, the platform may recommend or not increasing the physical activity that helps the patient lose weight.

Detects values that do not fall in the normal range in a given period, it will invoke a clinical analysis service to verify the patient´s health status. If the platform detects abnormally high values of systolic blood pressure or abnormally low values of diastolic blood pressure, it immediately invokes an ambulance service, sending the service provider the patient's medical parameters as well as his exact location. Also, platform immediately informs the family and the doctor of the emergency.

5   Conclusions and Future Work

Obesity and hypertension are transverse health problems that impact on the quality of life of people, including their work life. In this sense, the IoT provides great opportunities for monitoring, analyzing, diagnosing, controlling, and providing treatment recommendations for chronic-degenerative diseases, such as obesity and hypertension. In this work, we propose smart healthcare platform architecture that relies on the IoT paradigm to monitor overweight, obesity, and hypertension condition. Similarly, we discuss how, through various research works, the IoT has contributed to diagnosing and treating chronic-degenerative diseases.

To validate our architecture, we propose the case study of an elderly patient that suffers from both overweight and hypertension. The architecture considers factors such as networks, communication, business models, and processes, among others. Also, the architecture takes into account the extensibility, scalability, and interoperability between different heterogeneous devices and their business models. In addition, the architecture is adaptable, so that the devices interact dynamically with other objects to reach unequivocal communication.

Regarding our plan for future work, we look forward to performing a comparative analysis of the most relevant works that address the role of the IoT in preventing, controlling, treating, and tackling obesity, hypertension, and other chronic-degenerative diseases. Additionally, we will seek to validate our IoT-based smart healthcare platform architecture in other healthcare scenarios and to actually construct the IoT-based smart healthcare platform to prevent, monitor and treat obesity and hypertension.

Acknowledgments. This work was supported by Tecnológico Nacional de México (TecNM) and sponsored by the National Council of Science and Technology (CONACYT), the Secretariat of Public Education (SEP) through PRODEP (Programa para el Desarrollo Profesional Docente) and the Sistema de Universidades Estatales de Oaxaca (SUNEO).

References

1. World Health Organization. Obesity and overweight (2017). http://www.who.int/mediacentre/factsheets/fs311/en/
2. World Health Organization. WHO/ISH Hypertension guidelines (2017). http://www.who.int/cardiovascular_diseases/guidelines/hypertension/en/
3. Li, L., Li, S., Zhao, S.: QoS-aware scheduling of services-oriented Internet of Things. IEEE Trans. Ind. Inf. **10**, 1497–1505 (2014). doi:10.1109/TII.2014.2306782
4. Xu, L.D., He, W., Li, S.: Internet of Things in industries: a survey. IEEE Trans. Ind. Inf. **10**, 2233–2243 (2014). doi:10.1109/TII.2014.2300753
5. Bhatt, Y., Bhatt, C.: Internet of Things in HealthCare. In: Bhatt, C., Dey, N., Ashour, A.S. (eds.) Internet of Things and Big Data Technologies for Next Generation Healthcare. SBD, vol. 23, pp. 13–33. Springer, Cham (2017). doi:10.1007/978-3-319-49736-5_2
6. Krawczyk, B., Woźniak, M.: Hypertension type classification using hierarchical ensemble of one-class classifiers for imbalanced data. In: Bogdanova, A.M., Gjorgjevikj, D. (eds.) ICT Innovations 2014. AISC, vol. 311, pp. 341–349. Springer, Cham (2015). doi:10.1007/978-3-319-09879-1_34
7. Vazquez-Briseno, M., Navarro-Cota, C., Nieto-Hipolito,J.I., Jimenez-Garcia, E., Sanchez-Lopez, J.D.: A proposal for using the Internet of Things concept to increase children's health awareness. In: 2012 22nd International Conference on Electrical Communications and Computers (CONIELECOMP), pp. 168–172 (2012). doi:10.1109/CONIELECOMP.2012.6189903
8. Vilollonga, R., Lecube, A., Fort, J.M., Boleko, M.A., Hidalgo, M., Armengol, M.: Internet of Things and bariatric surgery follow-up: comparative study of standard and IoT follow-up. Minim. Invasive Ther. Inf. Healthcare **22**, 304–311 (2013). doi:10.3109/13645706.2013.779282
9. Mun Lee, B., Ouyang, J.: Application protocol adapted to health awareness for smart healthcare service. Adv. Sci. Technol. Lett. **43**, 101–104 (2013). doi:10.14257/astl.2013.43.21
10. Zaragozá, I., Guixeres, J., Alcañiz, M., Cebolla, A., Saiz, J., Álvarez, J.: Ubiquitous monitoring and assessment of childhood obesity. Pers. Ubiquit. Comput. **17**, 1147–1157 (2013). doi:10.1007/s00779-012-0562-x

11. Mun Lee, B., Ouyang, J.: Intelligent healthcare service by using collaborations between IoT personal health devices. Int. J. Bio-Science Bio-Technology **6**, 155–164 (2014). doi:10. 14257/ijbsbt.2014.6.1.17

12. Hiremath, S., Yang, G., Mankodiya, K.: Wearable Internet of Things: concept, architectural components and promises for person-centered healthcare. In: 2014 EAI 4th International Conference on Wireless Mobile Communication and Healthcare (Mobihealth), pp. 304–307 (2014). doi:10.4108/icst.mobihealth.2014.257440

13. Vazquez, M., Jimenez, E., Nieto, J.I., Sanchez, J.D.D., Garcia, A., Torres, J.P.: Development of a mobile health architecture to prevent childhood obesity. IEEE Lat. Am. Trans. **13**, 1520–1527 (2015). doi:10.1109/TLA.2015.7112010

14. Kim, K.K., Logan, H.C., Young, E., Sabee, C.M.: Youth-centered design and usage results of the iN Touch mobile self-management program for overweight/obesity. Pers. Ubiquit. Comput. **19**, 59–68 (2015). doi:10.1007/s00779-014-0808-x

15. Alloghani, M., Hussain, A., Al-Jumeily, D., Fergus, P., Abuelma'atti, O., Hamden, H.: A Mobile Health Monitoring Application for Obesity Management and Control Using the Internet-of-Things, pp. 19–24. IEEE (2016). doi:10.1109/ICDIPC.2016.7470785

16. Wibisono, G., Astawa, I.G.B.: Designing Machine-to-Machine (M2M) prototype system for weight loss program for obesity and overweight patients. In: 7th International Conference on Intelligent Systems, Modelling and Simulation, pp. 138–143 (2016). doi:10.1109/ISMS. 2016.52

17. Dobbins, C., Rawassizadeh, R., Momeni, E.: Detecting physical activity within lifelogs towards preventing obesity and aiding ambient assisted living. Neurocomputing **230**, 1–23 (2016). doi:10.1016/j.neucom.2016.02.088

18. Shin, S.-A., Lee, N.-Y., Park, J.-H.: Empirical study of the IoT-learning for obese patients that require personal training. In: Park, J.J.(Jong Hyuk), Pan, Y., Yi, G., Loia, V. (eds.) Advances in Computer Science and Ubiquitous Computing. LNEE, vol. 421, pp. 1005–1012. Springer, Singapore (2017). doi:10.1007/978-981-10-3023-9_156

19. Antonovici, D.A., Chiuachisan, I., Geman, O., Tomegea, A.: Acquisition and management of biomedical data using Internet of Things concepts. In: IEEE - 2014 International Symposium on Fundamentals of Electrical Engineering, pp. 1–4 (2014). doi:10.1109/ISFEE. 2014.7050625

20. Akutekwe, A., Seker, H.: A hybrid dynamic Bayesian network approach for modeling temporal associations of gene expressions for hypertension diagnosis. In: 36th Annual International Conference of the IEEE Engineering in Medicine and Biology Society (EMBC), pp. 804–807 (2014). doi:10.1109/EMBC.2014.6943713

21. Deen, M.J.: Information and communications technologies for elderly ubiquitous healthcare in a smart home. Pers. Ubiquit. Comput. **19**, 573–599 (2015). doi:10.1007/s00779-015-0856-x

22. Jeong, J.S., Han, O., You, Y.Y.: A design characteristics of smart healthcare system as the IoT application. Indian J. Sci. Technol. **9**, 1–8 (2016). doi:10.17485/ijst/2016/v9i37/102547

23. Gupta, P.K., Maharaj, B.T., Malekian, R.: A novel and secure IoT based cloud centric architecture to perform predictive analysis of users activities in sustainable health centres. Multimedia Tools Appl. **76**, 1–24 (2016). doi:10.1007/s11042-016-4050-6

24. Chen, M., Ma, Y., Song, J., Lai, C.F., Hu, B.: Smart clothing: connecting human with clouds and big data for sustainable health monitoring. Mob. Netw. Appl. **21**, 825–845 (2016). doi:10.1007/s11036-016-0745-1

25. Jung, H.: A conceptual framework for trajectory-based medical analytics with IoT contexts. J. Comput. Syst. Sci. **82**, 610–626 (2016). doi:10.1016/j.jcss.2015.10.007

26. Lake, D., Milito, R., Morrow, M., Vargheese, R.: Internet of Things: architectural framework for eHealth security. J. ICT, **3** & **4**, 301–328 (2014). doi:10.13052/jicts2245-800X.133

27. Zhang, H., Song, H.: Ubiquitous WSN for healthcare: recent advances and future prospects. IEEE IoT J. **4**, 311–318 (2014). doi:10.1109/JIOT.2014.2329462
28. Santos, J., Rodrigues, J.P.C., Silva, B., Casal, J., Saleem, K., Denisov, V.: An IoT-based mobile gateway for intelligent personal assistants on mobile health environments. J. Netw. Comput. Appl. **71**, 194–204 (2016). doi:10.1016/j.jnca.2016.03.014
29. Hossain, M.S., Muhammad, G.: Cloud-assisted industrial Internet of Things (IIoT) – enabled framework for health monitoring. Comput. Netw. **101**, 192–202 (2016). doi:10.1016/j.comnet.2016.01.009
30. Jara, A.J., Zamora, M.A., Skarmeta, A.F.G.: An Internet of Things–based personal device for diabetes therapy management in ambient assisted living (AAL). Pers. Ubiquit. Comput. **15**, 431–440 (2011). doi:10.1007/s00779-010-0353-1
31. Paschou, M., Sakkopoulos, E., Sourla, E., Tsakalidis, A.: Health Internet of Things: metrics and methods for efficient data transfer. Simul. Model. Pract. Theor. **34**, 186–199 (2013). doi:10.1016/j.simpat.2012.08.002
32. Gia, T.N., Thanigaivelan, N.K., Rahmani, A.M., Westerlund, T., Liljeberg, P., Tenhunen, H.: Customizing 6lowpan networks towards internet-of-things based ubiquitous healthcare systems. In: NORCHIP, pp. 1–6. IEEE (2014). doi:10.1109/NORCHIP.2014.7004716
33. Jung, E.Y., Kim, J., Chung, K.Y., Park, D.K.: Mobile healthcare application with EMR interoperability for diabetes patients. Cluster Comput. **17**, 871–880 (2013). doi:10.1007/s10586-013-0315-2
34. Hu, L., Ong, D.M., Zhu, X., Liu, Q., Song, E.: Enabling RFID technology for healthcare: application, architecture, and challenges. Telecommun. Syst. **58**, 259–271 (2015). doi:10.1007/s11235-014-9871-x
35. Kumar, K.M.C.: Internet of fitness things – a move towards quantified health: concept, sensor-cloud network, protocols and a new methodology for OSA patients. In: 2015 IEEE Recent Advances in Intelligent Computational Systems (RAICS), pp. 364–369 (2015). doi:10.1109/RAICS.2015.7488443
36. Ganzha, M., Paprzycki, M., Pawłowski, W., Szmeja, P., Wasielewska, K.: Semantic interoperability in the Internet of Things: an overview from the INTER-IoT perspective. J. Netw. Comput. Appl. **81**, 1–23 (2016). doi:10.1016/j.jnca.2016.08.007
37. Raza, M., Hoa Le, M., Aslam, N., Hieu Le, C., Tam Le, N., Ly Le, T.: Telehealth Technology: Potentials, Challenges and Research Directions for Developing Countries. IFMBE Proceedings, pp. 233–236. Springer (2016)
38. Camara-Brito, J.M.: Trends in wireless communications towards 5G networks – the influence of e-health and IoT applications. In: International Multidisciplinary Conference on Computer and Energy Science (SpliTech), pp. 1–7 IEEE (2016). doi:10.1109/SpliTech.2016.7555949
39. Ifrim, C., Pintilie, A.-M., Apostol, E., Dobre, C., Pop, F.: The art of advanced healthcare applications in big data and IoT systems. In: Mavromoustakis, C.X., Mastorakis, G., Dobre, C. (eds.) Advances in Mobile Cloud Computing and Big Data in the 5G Era. SBD, vol. 22, pp. 133–149. Springer, Cham (2017). doi:10.1007/978-3-319-45145-9_6
40. Li, S., Xu, L.D., Zhao, S.: The Internet of Things: a survey. Inf. Syst. Front. **17**, 243–259 (2015). doi:10.1007/s10796-014-9492-7

A Development Model of an Embedded System for Improving the Mobility of People with Physical Disabilities

Maritza Aguirre-Munizaga$^{(\boxtimes)}$ ⓘ, Vanessa Vergara-Lozano ⓘ,
Carlota Delgado-Vera ⓘ, Jorge Hidalgo ⓘ,
and Rosa González-Villalta ⓘ

Facultad de Ciencias Agrarias, Escuela de Ingeniería en Computación e
Informática, Universidad Agraria del Ecuador,
Avenue 25 de Julio y Pio Jaramillo, P.O. Box 09-04-100, Guayaquil, Ecuador
{maguirre, vvergara, cdelgado,
jhidalgo, rgonzalez}@uagraria.edu.ec

Abstract. Worldwide there is a high amount of people with disabilities. For instance, according to the National Council for the Equalization of People with Disabilities, there are approximately 418,001 people with disabilities in Ecuador. On the other hand, nowadays there are a lot of electronic devices that allow people to perform everyday activities in a fast and easy way. Considering these premises, the automated control of electronic devices through mobile devices has emerged as a new challenge, whose main goal is to improve the quality of life of people. In this work, we present HomeR, a system that allows people, including people with disabilities, to manage smart home appliances through a mobile application. This system uses the Arduino and Raspberry Pi technologies to provide a low-cost solution that can be used by people independently of their status and abilities. HomeR was evaluated in terms of its implementation cost and accessibility. The results show that HomeR can be implemented in real environments with a low investment compared to already available solutions in Ecuador.

Keywords: Arduino · Raspberry Pi · Home automation · Paraplegia

1 Introduction

Nowadays, there are a lot of electronic devices that allow people to perform everyday activities in a fast and easy way, thus improving the quality of life of users. Due to this phenomenon, automated control of electronic devices through mobile devices has emerged as a new challenge in which Human Computer Interaction (HCI) plays an important role [1]. For instance, in [2], authors present an ontology-based natural language interface that allows users to interact with different home appliances through instant messaging services.

On the other hand, paraplegia refers to impairment or loss of motor and/or sensory function related to the thoracic, lumbar, or sacral spinal cord segments [3]. People with

© Springer International Publishing AG 2017
R. Valencia-García et al. (Eds.): CITI 2017, CCIS 749, pp. 146–157, 2017.
DOI: 10.1007/978-3-319-67283-0_11

paraplegia are unable to walk hence they must use wheelchair or assistance devices for mobility. Therefore, there is a need for automation and control processes focused on providing safety for people with paraplegia. In this sense, there are several works that aim to solve mobility problems of paraplegic people. Even Artificial Intelligence has been used for this purpose [4].

According to the National Council for the Equalization of People with Disabilities [5], there are approximately 418,001 disable people in Ecuador, of which 196,758 people have a physical disability. Regarding this group, 148,487 people do not have a job and lack economic income. With this regard, Government grants them a monthly monetary bonus, as well as specialized medical assistance through the Ministry of Social Inclusion.

According to the Ecuadorian Institute of Statistics and Censuses, 9 out of each 10 Ecuadorians have a cell phone, of which 53.9% are smartphones. Also, 36% of the households have access to the Internet. Hence, it is necessary to take advantage of these devices, to develop a system that can be embedded in them to improve the life quality of people with paraplegia.

In this work, we present a system that aims to improve the life quality of people with disabilities, including paraplegia. This system uses already available technology, and it is supported by embedded systems [6], which are composed of hardware and control software. Furthermore, it aims to provide a low-cost solution since not all people have the economic resources to implement this system in their home or office.

In order to carry out this work, people with paraplegia who attend the Ecuadorian Society Pro-Rehabilitation of Crippled [7] were asked to collect information about relevant and important activities that they perform within their home or environment. Some of these activities are: controlling ventilation, lighting control, wheelchair movement, and controlling the room temperature. Based on such information, we established their automation needs.

The technological solution suggested allows people with paraplegia to perform all activities above mentioned. This application was developed by using smart home automation devices. A prototype of this system was installed considering the performance of the intelligent home network model [8].

The rest of this work is structured as follows. Section 2 describes a set of related works. Section 3 describes the architecture of the proposed solution. Section 4 analyses the results obtained from a survey performed to Ecuadorians from different social status. Finally, conclusions and future work are presented.

2 Related Works

In the literature, there are different works that aim to provide solutions for people with paraplegia. For instance, UbiTrak [9] is a location application that combines indoor and outdoor information. This application has proven to be accurate, and feasible to be used in real-world scenarios.

In [10], a home automation system is presented. This system allows controlling different home appliances, thus contributing to the safety of elderly people or people with disabilities [11].

Some of the current solutions integrate technologies such as Cloud computing. For example, in [12] authors evaluate the use of a Cloud-based robotics system to provide assistance services for the promotion of the active and healthy ageing. Despite the fact that the system obtained good results, authors suggest deeper investigation about the reliability of the communication technologies adopted by this system.

On the other hand, in [13] authors present a low-cost system that allows remotely controlling and monitoring home appliances and several sensors in the home by means of an Android application.

In the last years, several approaches based on WiFi connectivity have been proposed [14–17]. Although this kind of solutions has been applied at a commercial level, their implementation requires great investment.

It is important to design computer models based on embedded systems that allow communication between users and machines. In this sense, the present work takes as reference the work presented in [18], at the same time that most current solutions use embedded systems to integrate hardware and software focused on the users' needs [19].

The research efforts presented in this section are clear examples of the successful use of embedded systems for implementing home automation systems that benefit people from different domains e.g. older adults and people with disabilities. Hence, it is important to contribute to the improvement of this kind of technology to generate low-cost solutions.

3   Design and Implementation

This section describes the design and implementation details about HomeR, an embedded system that allows people to manage smart home appliances through a mobile application. HomeR represents a low-cost solution thanks to which several housework activities that require much time and effort were automated.

3.1   HomeR Architecture

A sensor network consists of a set of intelligent sensors that are connected among them through wire or wireless mechanisms. In the context of networks, each network component that has a module is known as node [20].

HomeR architecture is composed of two main elements, namely: a hardware-software component and a user interface. HomeR uses the Arduino platform as it offers a high compatibility with several sensors and it is easy-to-use technology regarding its development environment, programming languages, and the Arduino boards. Furthermore, this technology is multiplatform, i.e., it can work on different operating systems such as Linux, Windows, MacOS, among others.

The HomeR architecture takes as reference the work presented in [21], which aims to provide a system that uses low-cost hardware to obtain data in real time, as well as to show this data to the users. Next section describes the main components that have been used as the basis for the development of the prototype.

- **Arduino Uno.** This component [22] consists of an MCU (Micro Controller Unit) based on RISC (Reduced Instruction Set Computer) which works at a clock speed of up to 8/16 MHz. This hardware has a flash memory module of 32 kB (0.5 kB are used by the boot loader) and a SRAM (Static Random-Access Memory) module of 2 kB. Furthermore, this board has 11 digital pins that can be configured as input or output. These pins have been used for the HomeR implementation since it is through them that the Internet connection is established. Another important feature of the Arduino platform is the Bootloader that runs on the microcontroller. This component can be reprogrammed through an USB converter, which makes it easy the configuration of the sensors used in the project. Finally, it should be mentioned that in the Arduino platform [23] all computing and communication processes (except Ethernet) are handled by the microcontroller. This fact allows the project to be extended in future work.

- **Raspberry Pi3 with SD camera and charger (raspberry pi kit).** Raspberry Pi [24] solves the problem of remote communications [25] that is present in Arduino, thus allowing to take advantage of all features of an open connectivity. In this work, Raspberry [26] works as a Web Server [27] that helps monitoring all sensors and collects data from them. This information is stored in a small database.

- **Gas sensor.** The gas sensor [28] ensures a safety level within home. When it detects a high level of gas, it sends an alert to the user. Therefore, it is important for this element to have high sensitivity and fast response time.

- **Relay.** It is managed by the Arduino electronic board and allows turning on/off the lights.

- **Servo motor.** (Metal Servo Motor) It is a small motor that can move in different directions and angles [29] without losing stability. This element helps moving the wheelchair from the mobile application [30].

- **Cables (jumper male to male, female to female).**

- **Others.** Also, this project uses an ethernet cable, a USB camera, LEDs and a power supply.

The HomeR's architecture is presented in Fig. 1.

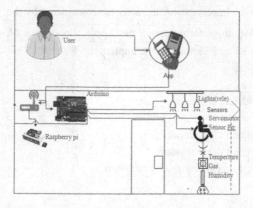

Fig. 1. HomeR architecture.

The HomeR's architecture was implemented through a set of iterations, where each of them involved analysis, design and implementation tasks. The result of the first iteration was a basic architecture which was incrementally refined. In a nutshell, the HomeR work as follows: the user interacts with the lights, wheelchair and other sensors through a mobile application. This application receives all data collected by the Arduino microcontroller and the Raspberry Pi card.

3.2   Methodology

The methodology used for the development of HomeR involved to carry out a survey on a sample of 120 people with paraplegia from the SERLI (Ecuadorian Pro-Rehabilitation of Crippled) [7]. This survey aimed to know the people requirements according to their daily activities and the demographic and socioeconomic characteristics of all of them.

The survey results are shown in Table 1, where it can be noted that 98% of people think that a mobile application for people with paraplegia is needed. Furthermore, the intended use of this kind of application is of 82%.

Table 1. Variables analyzed in a survey to patients with paraplegia.

Variable	Frequency	%
Cell phone	120	100%
Cell phone usage frequency	88	73%
Apps usage	90	75%
Need for Apps for people with paraplegia	117	98%
Intended use of Apps for people with paraplegia	98	82%
Average	102.6	86%

Also, people involved were asked to sort a set of activities according to the importance they have in their daily life. The results obtained are shown in Table 2.

Table 2. Importance of the activities considered by the App.

Activity to perform through the App	Importance (Avg.)
Turn-on and Turn-off home appliances	8
Ventilation	7
Lights	6
Wheelchair movement	5
Gas system	4
Open and close doors	3
Open and close windows	2
Security regarding fire or intrusion	1

In Table 2, it can be noted that most people see security regarding fire or intrusion as the most important fact to be considered by the application. Meanwhile, the turning on/off home appliances is the least important task.

Also, the survey provided relevant information related to the number of people that are benefited from a human development bonus. Based on all the information obtained from the survey, the requirements and the budget were established.

The system here presented was developed by using the Android operating system, particularly the Ice Cream Sandwich version. Also, Putty was used as an SSH client (Secure SHeel) to manage the Raspberry card from the mobile application. The Python language was used since it provides a graphical user interface to access and controlling several home appliances.

Figure 2 depicts the main functionalities of the system, which are: (a) turning on/off the lights, (b) ventilation, (c) gas sensors, (d) humidity of the environment. It should be mentioned that the system provides a remote connection between the smartphone and the sensors distributed in the house. Also, it allows obtaining the location of the user.

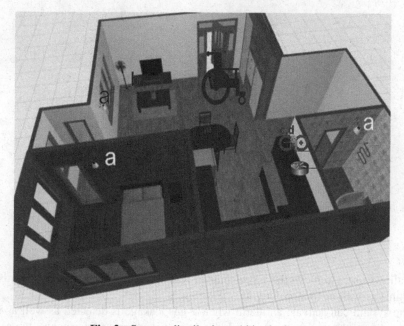

Fig. 2. Sensors distribution within the house.

Figure 3 presents the general model of the remote monitoring process, where it can be noted that the system allows users to manage all components at home by using the mobile application. For this purpose, users need to log into the system. Then, the system shows them all available devices that they can manage.

Figure 4 presents a set of interfaces of the mobile application: (a) it allows users to log into the system, (b) it provides a perspective of all devices that users can manage, (c) it shows data collected by the sensors such as temperature, humidity, and gas, and

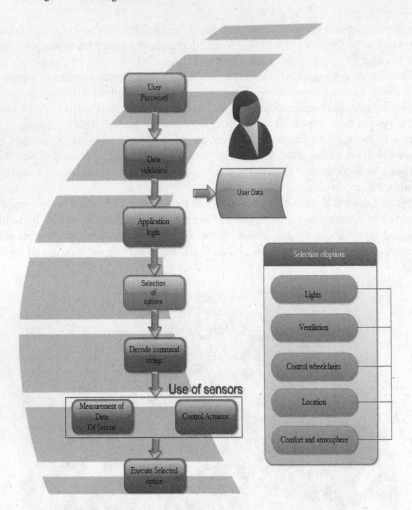

Fig. 3. Remote monitoring process.

(d) it allows users to move the wheelchair in four directions (forward, backwards, left and right) as well as to stop moving.

The system can activate an alarm when a gas leakage is detected as well as when the humidity of the environment is high. To ensure its correct performance, the sensors must be correctly installed. When the temperature is too high or low, users can control the ventilation. Regarding the GPS location [31], it is stored in a text file which is sent via email. In this sense, it is worth mentioning that the GPS location is estimated by using the Wi-Fi signal.

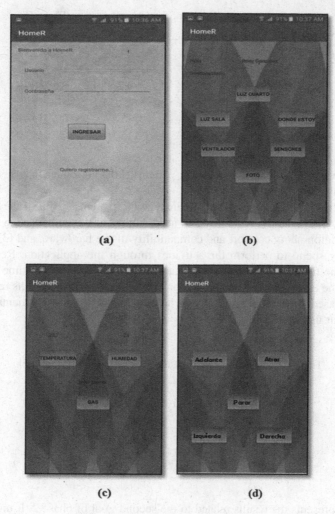

Fig. 4. User interfaces of HomeR.

4 Results

To know the people's point of view and their expectations about HomeR, the system was evaluated inside SERLI facilities. For this purpose, the people sample population that was involved in the requirements specification were asked to collaborate again. This validation consisted of two phases which are described below.

In phase 1, people were asked to install the mobile application and to analyze all functionalities provided. Then they were asked to answer a survey about complexity of installation, implementation, aesthetic, download time and intuitiveness. Table 3 presents the evaluation results of the first phase. According to these results, 76.7% of patients consider that the installation process was very easy, and the aesthetic of the

Table 3. Evaluation results of the HomeR system (Phase 1).

Variable	None	Low	Medium	High	Higher
Complexity of installation	0.8%	3.3%	19.2%	34.2%	42.5%
Implementation	0.8%	3.3%	16.7%	33.3%	45.8%
Aesthetic	2.5%	4.2%	9.2%	37.5%	46.7%
Download time	0.8%	3.3%	15.0%	31.7%	49.2%
Intuitiveness	0.8%	3.3%	15.8%	30.0%	50.0%
Average	1.2%	3.5%	15.2%	0.8%	46.8%

application was very pleasant. Also, most patients (80%) consider that the application is very intuitive.

Phase 2 had three main goals: (1) to analyze the patients' point of view regarding the usability, functionality, reliability and accessibility of the embedded system, (2) to know the opinion about comfort and compatibility of the hardware, and (3) to analyze the time they spend to perform the activities through the application. Regarding the third goal, the time spent with the application was compared to the time they spend performing the tasks without the application. Table 4 presents the results related to the first goal. Based on these results, it can be concluded that most patients feel comfortable about using the application.

Table 4. Evaluation results of the HomeR software (Phase 2).

Variable	None	Low	Medium	High	Higher
Usability	0.0%	0.8%	20.8%	36.7%	41.7%
Functionality	0.0%	1.7%	15.0%	37.5%	45.8%
Reliability	0.0%	0.8%	12.5%	31.7%	55.0%
Accessibility	0.0%	0.8%	8.3%	33.3%	57.5%
Average	0.0%	1.0%	14.2%	34.8%	50.0%

Table 5 presents the results related to the second goal of phase 2. It must be noted that 98.3% of patients think that HomeR allows controlling home devices in an easy and intuitive way. Furthermore, the compatibility of the system with several sensors was successful.

Another aspect that was considered by this evaluation is the implementation cost regarding hardware. Table 6 shows a comparative among the average cost of hardware used in HomeR and the real cost of it. As it can be noted from Table 6, there is a big difference between the costs, which amounts to $ 585.79.

Table 5. Evaluation results of the HomeR hardware (Phase 2).

Variable	Yes	No
Comfort	99.2%	0.8%
Compatibility	97.5%	2.5%
Average	98.3%	1.7%

Table 6. Hardware costs of HomeR in phase 2.

Functionalities	Average cost	Implementation cost	Difference	%
Location	$ 56.23	$ 27.00	$ −29.23	51.98%
Turn on/off lights	$ 105.85	$ 23.96	$ −81.89	77.36%
Ventilation	$ 41.22	$ 25.68	$ −15.54	37.70%
Wheelchair movement	$ 581.96	$ 241.89	$ −340.07	58.44%
Gas sensor	$ 91.58	$ 15.00	$ −76.85	83.67%
Humidity of the environment	$ 56.21	$ 14.0	$ −42.21	75.09%
Total	$ 933.32	$ 347.53	$ −585.79	62.76%

Finally, the time patients spend performing the activities by means of HomeR was compared to the time they spend performing the tasks without this application. As can be noted from Table 7, there is a big difference between these values.

Table 7. Usage time of HomeR.

Functionalities	With HomeR	Without HomeR	Difference	%
Location	3	1.26	−1.74	58.00%
Turn on/off lights	5.2	1.15	−4.05	77.88%
Ventilation	5.4	1.2	−4.2	77.78%
Wheelchair movement	10.5	4.3	−6.2	59.05%
Gas sensor	14.8	2.1	−12.7	85.81%
Humidity of the environment	15.6	2.3	−13.3	85.26%
Average	9.08	2.052	−7.032	77.41%

Usually, people with disabilities need help to perform their daily life activities. Therefore, based on the results obtained, HomeR is an application that must be considered by patients with paraplegia because it helps them to carry out this kind of activities in an autonomous way. Furthermore, HomeR have proven to be effective regarding detection of gas leaks, which makes the system reliable in terms of security.

5 Conclusions and Future Work

This work presents HomeR, a system that aims to improve the life quality of people with physical disabilities including people with paraplegia. This solution is based on free hardware and software. HomeR was evaluated in terms of its implementation cost and accessibility. The results show that HomeR can be implemented in real environments with low investment compared to already available solutions in Ecuador.

As future work, authors plan to implement a larger scale project that allows implementing home automation of at least 50% of people with paraplegia who receive the human development bonus in the city of Guayaquil. This project aims to have high social impact by establishing links between people and advanced technologies. In this sense, the graphical user interface of HomeR must include new mechanisms that improve the human-computer interaction. For this purpose, we plan to integrate natural language mechanisms that allow people to interact with their home devices in an easier and more intuitive way, regardless their status and abilities.

Acknowledgements. Special thanks are given to the SERLI (Ecuadorian Society Pro-Rehabilitation of Crippled), which has allowed authors to conduct tests at its facilities.

References

1. Gomes Sakamoto, S., de Miranda, L.C., Hornung, H.: Home Control via Mobile Devices: State of the Art and HCI Challenges under the Perspective of Diversity (2014)
2. Noguera-Arnaldos, J.Á., Rodriguez-García, M.Á., Ochoa, J.L., Paredes-Valverde, M.A., Alcaraz-Mármol, G., Valencia-García, R.: Ontology-Driven Instant Messaging-Based Dialogue System for Device Control (2015)
3. Baker, J.S., et al.: Paraplegia. In: Encyclopedia of Exercise Medicine in Health and Disease, p. 690. Springer, Heidelberg (2012)
4. Zhang, X.: Intelligent Assistive and Robotics Development in China (2012)
5. Consejo Nacional para la Igualdad de Discapacitados (CONADIS): Información estadística de personas con discapacidad. http://www.consejodiscapacidades.gob.ec/estadistica/index.html
6. Coelho, C.J.N., Silva, D.C.D., Fernandes, A.O.: Hardware-software codesign of embedded systems. In: Proceedings of XI Brazilian Symposium on Integrated Circuit Design (Cat. No. 98EX216), pp. 2–8. IEEE Computer Society
7. SERLI - Sociedad Ecuatoriana Pro Rehabilitacion de Lisiados. http://www.serli.org.ec/
8. Kevin, K.M., Kogeda, O.P., Lall, M.: Performance optimization of intelligent home networks. In: Mahmood, Z. (ed.) Computer Communications and Networks, pp. 209–234. Springer, Heidelberg (2016)
9. Chen, K.-Y., Harniss, M., Patel, S., Johnson, K.: Implementing technology-based embedded assessment in the home and community life of individuals aging with disabilities: a participatory research and development study. Disabil. Rehabil. Assist. Technol. **9**, 112–120 (2014)
10. Javale, D., Mohsin, M., Nandanwar, S.: Home automation and security system using Android ADK. Int. J. Electron. Commun. Comput. Technol. **13**, 382–385 (2013)
11. Baladrón, C., Aguiar, J.M., Gobernado, J., Carro, B., Sánchez, A.: User-driven context aware creation and execution of home care applications. Ann. Telecommun. - Ann. des Télécommunications **65**, 545–556 (2010)
12. Bonaccorsi, M., Fiorini, L., Cavallo, F., Saffiotti, A., Dario, P.: A cloud robotics solution to improve social assistive robots for active and healthy aging. Int. J. Soc. Robot. **8**, 393–408 (2016)
13. Piyare, R.: Internet of things: ubiquitous home control and monitoring system using android based smart phone. Int. J. Internet Things **2**, 5–11 (2013)
14. ElShafee, A., Hamed, K.: Design and implementation of a WIFI based home automation system. World Acad. Sci. Eng. Technol. **68**, 2177–2180 (2012)
15. Caytiles, R.D., Park, B.: Mobile IP-Based Architecture for Smart Homes. Int. J. Smart Home. 6, 29–36
16. Santoso, F.K., Vun, N.C.H.: Securing IoT for smart home system. In: 2015 International Symposium on Consumer Electronics (ISCE), pp. 1–2. IEEE (2015)

17. Rathnayaka, A.J.D., Potdar, V.M., Kuruppu, S.J.: Evaluation of wireless home automation technologies. In: 5th IEEE International Conference on Digital Ecosystems and Technologies (IEEE DEST 2011), pp. 76–81. IEEE (2011)
18. Lancheros-Cuesta, D.J., Marin, M.P., Saenz, Y.V.: Intelligent system (HCI) for people with motor misabilities. In: 2015 10th Iberian Conference on Information Systems and Technologies (CISTI), pp. 1–6. IEEE (2015)
19. Mulfari, D., Celesti, A., Fazio, M., Villari, M., Puliafito, A.: Using embedded systems to spread assistive technology on multiple devices in smart environments. In: 2014 IEEE International Conference on Bioinformatics and Biomedicine (BIBM), pp. 5–11. IEEE (2014)
20. McGrath, M.J., Scanaill, C.N.: Sensor network topologies and design considerations. In: Sensor Technologies, pp. 79–95. Apress, Berkeley (2013)
21. Klemenjak, C., Egarter, D., Elmenreich, W.: YoMo: the Arduino-based smart metering board. Comput. Sci. Res. Dev. **31**, 97–103 (2016)
22. Guerreiro, J., Lourenço, A., Silva, H., Fred, A.: Performance comparison of low-cost hardware platforms targeting physiological computing applications. Procedia Technol. **17**, 399–406 (2014)
23. Bajer, L., Krejcar, O.: Design and realization of low cost control for greenhouse environment with remote control. IFAC-PapersOnLine **48**, 368–373 (2015)
24. Goodwin, S.: Smart home automation with Linux and Raspberry Pi
25. Reguera, P., García, D., Domínguez, M., Prada, M.A., Alonso, S.: A low-cost open source hardware in control education. IFAC-PapersOnLine **48**, 117–122 (2015)
26. Llanos, D.R.: Teaching "Embedded Operating Systems" using Raspberry Pi and virtual machines, **4** (2014). http://digibug.ugr.es/bitstream/10481/32196/1/T3_N4_Revista_EAIC_2014.pdf
27. Vujović, V., Maksimović, M.: Raspberry Pi as a sensor web node for home automation. Comput. Electr. Eng. **44**, 153–171 (2015)
28. Maier, K., Helwig, A., Müller, G.: Room-temperature dosimeter-type gas sensors with periodic reset. Sens. Actuators B Chem. **244**, 701–708 (2017)
29. Soriano, A., Marín, L., Vallés, M., Valera, A., Albertos, P.: Low cost platform for automatic control education based on open hardware. IFAC Proc. **47**, 9044–9050 (2014)
30. Futaba: Futaba Digital Servos. http://www.futabarc.com/servos/digital.html
31. Timmis, H.: Robot integration engineering a GPS module with the Arduino. In: Practical Arduino Engineering, pp. 97–131. Apress, Berkeley (2011)

A Decision Support Visualization Tool for Infection Management Based on BMPN and DMN

Bernardo Cánovas-Segura[1]([⊠]), Francesca Zerbato[2], Barbara Oliboni[2],
Carlo Combi[2], Manuel Campos[1], Antonio Morales[1], Jose M. Juarez[1],
Francisco Palacios[3], and Roque Marín[1]

[1] Computer Science Faculty, University of Murcia, Murcia, Spain
{bernardocs,manuelcampos,morales,jmjuarez,roquemm}@um.es
[2] Computer Science Faculty, University of Verona, Verona, Italy
{francesca.zerbato,barbara.oliboni,carlo.combi}@univr.it
[3] University Hospital of Getafe, Getafe, Spain
franciscodepaula@gmail.com

Abstract. The interdisciplinary team of an Antimicrobial Stewardship Program is indispensable to preserve the antibiotic utility and avoid resistance in a hospital. One key duty of this team is the administration behaviour surveillance, which is a complex and tedious issue.

In this work we present a tool to support this supervision by visualising some essential elements of the antimicrobial therapy: patient record, guidelines and key decision actions. The tool uses standardized models of industry (BPMN, DMN) to ease its maintenance in the long term and its interopreability.

1 Introduction

There is an increasing concern worldwide about the loss of efficacy of antibiotics in bacterial infection [12,13,21]. Antimicrobial Stewardship Program teams (ASPs) are the hospital response to global antibiotic resistance, composed of multidisciplinary members. They are aimed to achieve a rational use of antibiotics, improving the collaboration between the hospital departments [3,16]. Data integration, visualization, and clinical decision support systems based on Clinical Practice Guidelines (CPGs) can be helpful tools for ASPs to manage the overwhelming information produced in hospitals [2]. However, most clinicians admit that they do not make an intensive use of CPGs in their daily practice. During the last decades, there are different proposals of automatization and representation in the literature, such as Asbru, GLARE, PROforma and GLIF, among others [17]. Some recent studies have focused on the use of available business process standards, such as the Business Process Model and Notation (BPMN 2.0) or conformance checking [22]. Other improvements to business process technologies might be also useful in medical scenarios, such as the Decision Model Notation (DMN 1.1) [15], a new standard specifically designed for the modelling of decisions.

© Springer International Publishing AG 2017
R. Valencia-García et al. (Eds.): CITI 2017, CCIS 749, pp. 158–168, 2017.
DOI: 10.1007/978-3-319-67288-0_12

In this work, we present a visualization tool to support decisions for ASP teams, according to the needs identified in a previous work [2]. This proposal lies on the use of standardized models of industry to show the current state of the patient, the context of a potential CPG (BPMN) in use and specific medical actions (DMN).

The remainder of this paper is structured as follows: in Sect. 3 we introduce the tool architecture and the details of its implementation. Section 4 describes the results of implementing a specific case of Vancomycin management. Finally, in Sect. 5 we present our conclusions and future work.

2 Related Work

Visualization is a key aspect for clinical decision support systems [5]. The purpose of using visual analysis of data is to exploit human perception as well as to help in the understanding and communication of data and concepts.

The National Research Council of the National Academies [14] diagnosed that the extra time required to introduce data into review systems for decision making is largely owing to the lack of adequate cognitive support when interacting with clinicians. In fact, in 2012, the US Institute of Medicine recommended solving this problem through the use of visualisation models with scenarios of interdisciplinary clinical practice [8].

Visualisation models in the clinical context are mainly focused on two aspects: the custom visualisation of a single patient health record and the visualisation of groups of patients [20].

For example, the goal of IPBC [4] was to improve the therapeutic adjustment in haemodialysis using a three-dimensional visualization. KHOSPAD [18] was designed to identify temporal relationships between primary care doctors, the patient and hospital stays. The objective of KNAVE-II [23] is to visualise oncological treatment information, while the VISITORS system [10] combines intelligent temporal analysis and information visualisation techniques in order to integrate, process and visualise information concerning multiple patients and information sources.

With regard to the visualisation of groups of patients and their characteristics, we can highlight sequence visualisation models such as lifeLines2 [24] and viscareTrails [11], along with techniques based on a single temporal axis like IPBC [4] and InfoZoom [1].

Nevertheless, little attention has been explicitly paid to clinical decision support systems for healthcare associated infection, and very few specific works on the visualisation of epidemiology statistics [7] have been used to detect the outbreak of infections. In [6], a visualization tool is proposed to assist clinicians in the prescription of empiric treatment.

In this work, we propose the use of visualisation techniques combining standard industry models (BPMN and DMN) to guide physicians according to a given guideline.

3   Decision Support Tool

We propose a visualization tool designed to support decisions for antibiotic and infection management embedded in a general platform to support antimicrobial management teams called WASPSS. Our proposal is based on the following aspects:

1. patients: visualization of relevant information of the patient record, using an interactive timeline representation;
2. processes: visualization of the process of potential CPG in use, using standard process models and indicating the current status. We propose the use of BPMN;
3. actions: decision making of specific clinical actions using standard decision models such as using the new DMN model.

Figure 1a shows the general architecture of the tool. The rest of the section describes the components and their implementation in detail.

3.1   WASPSS Platform

The Wise Antimicrobial Stewardship Program Support System (WASPSS) [16] is a technological platform that comprises the integration of hospital departments databases (laboratory, pharmacy, etc.) and the Health Information System (HIS) to support the ASP team activity and to improve the collaboration between the hospital departments. WASPSS also provides basic alerts on administration of antibiotic therapy (prescription and therapeutic limits). Current version of WASPSS is running at the University Hospital of Getafe, Spain. The visualization tool presented is an extension of the current version.

3.2   EHR Interactive Timeline

The linearly organised flow of a timeline provides a great communicative power to easily summarise the current state of the patient record.

The WASPSS system already has a simple timeline chart of several events in a patient's clinical history, such as treatments, cultures and stays. We extend the Electronic Health Record (EHR) visualization of WASPSS, integrating events of the patient's clinical history (antibiotic administration, blood tests, etc.). Moreover, this view enriches the representation of the temporal perspective related to process and decision diagrams obtained from the guideline. Figure 1b (top) shows the implementation of the iteractive timeline: basic information about the patient is displayed at the top of the picture, while the timeline view below shows all the stays, laboratory tests, treatments and cultures performed, including a view of the guideline tasks at the end.

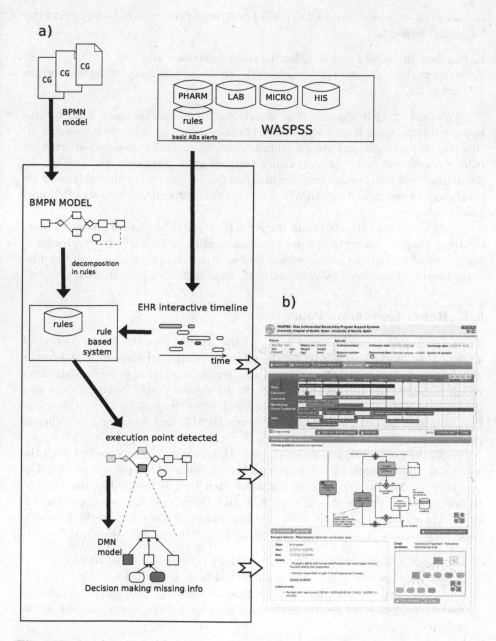

Fig. 1. Tool architecture (a) and snapshot of current implemented version (b). (Color figure online)

3.3   Guideline and BPMN Model

In this work we shall focus on the CPG knowledge components that support the following decisions:

1. the recommended steps to follow to treat infections and
2. decision rules regarding the antibiotic to be applied according on certain symptoms.

We consider that the use of generally accepted standards in industry for process design, since it provides solid technology for long-term maintenance. To this end, key knowledge from guidelines is obtained, under medical supervision, using a semi-automatic process using technology available in the market. In particular, this tool version implements the standard notation currently used for business process modelling (BPMN 2.0) to model procedural aspects of clinical guidelines.

The knowledge extracted from the guidelines refers to clinical processes coordinating people, resources and information dealing with patients. A process is composed of activities (tasks), events and splitting/merging points, and can be considered and managed by using suitable approaches such as BPMN.

3.4   Rules: Excecution Point

The second goal of our proposal is to put the patient record into the context of a CPG that might be followed by the clinician. Our tool aims to visualize the all steps (using the BPMN graph) of the recommendation process, indicating which might be the current step, called the execution point. However, detecting the current execution point of a CPG for a given patient is a complex issue. Our approach consists in checking for every BPMN task whether it is either in progress, completed or omitted.

From the computational point of view, this problem means to deal with the automatic map of each BPMN task with the elements of the patient record. The key issue is the way the current status of each task is inferred in the BPMN. In our proposal, we decompose the whole BPMN process in a set of production rules. Therefore, a rule-based system is implemented according to the following aspects:

1. the input is the current state of the patient (visualised in the timeline),
2. the knowledge base has the rules extracted from the BPMN,
3. and a forward-chaining reasoning engine is used. Its outcome is an inferred fact for each task (or several, if the task is inside a loop) containing the status inferred.

The implementation has been carried out by using Drools [19] as a rules engine, a consolidated solution in industry that is easy to integrate with Java code. Figure 1b (middle) shows the BPMN process and the execution point.

3.5   DMN: Decision Support

The last goal of this tool is to support a specific set of decisions of antibiotic therapy. Unlike indicating the execution point of the CPG, a general set of recommendations, the tool aims to visualize the elements required to deal with some clinical actions. We propose the use of a new standard, the Decision Model and Notation (DMN 1.1) [15], to represent process-related decision making. This notation makes it possible to model complex decisions by depicting the data requirements and the previous decisions that must be considered to obtain the final recommendation.

Similarly to the execution point, we use production rules to make knowledge represented in DMN executable. Detailed explanations about any decision status are possible using rule-based inference. All the rules include metadata regarding their origin (guideline, task, etc.) and all the facts generated include, in a human-readable way, the complete history of rules launched to generate them. Clinicians may therefore check each suggestion made by the system and validate its foundation. DMN visualization and suggestions are shown in Fig. 1b (bottom). If the box representing the decision is green, this means that all the required input data are available, and the user can then request a suggestion about the decision based on available knowledge. These rules will subsequently be fired to generate the suggested decision.

4   Case of Use: Vancomycin

The survey of Vancomycin administration is essential due to its resistance to many health-care associated strains. In this case of study, we propose BPMN and DMN models of the public guidelines for the Vancomycin treatment proposed by the Johns Hopkins Hospital [9].

– Firstly, we face the modelling of CPG using BPMN. Usually, two main objectives can be pursued when creating a computer-interpretable model from a CPG. On the one hand, the model should be as detailed as possible, in order to cover as many aspects from the CPG as possible. On the other hand, the model should be as simple as possible for fostering interpretation by domain experts. Unlike current computerized CPG methodologies, which are based on a comprehensive description, we present the modelling of those parts that are critical for decision-making and for.which we have sufficient data to provide proper decision support.

  We propose a BPMN diagram (Fig. 2) representing the main steps to be performed during the treatment. Only the main tasks are modelled, and we focus on the need to carry out periodic controls so as to ensure the appropriate dosage of antibiotics. Activities are represented by means of rounded-corners rectangles. Gateways are used to define splitting/merging points, and are represented as diamonds with a "+" for parallel branching points, and an "×" for that data-based branching points where it is needed to choose an exclusive path. The decision activities are represented using activity rectangles but

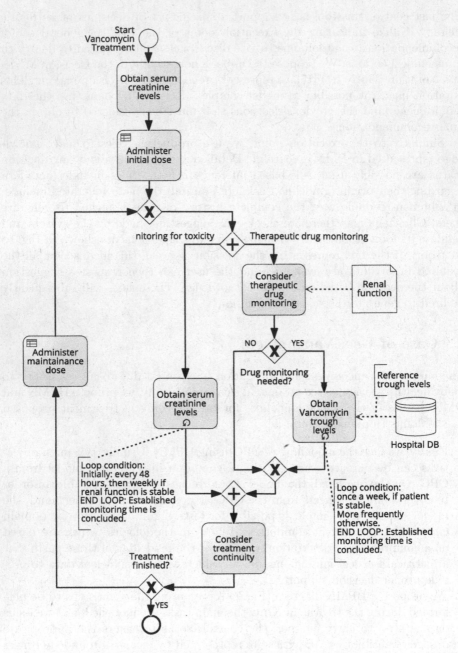

Fig. 2. Example of Vancomycin treatment: BPMN

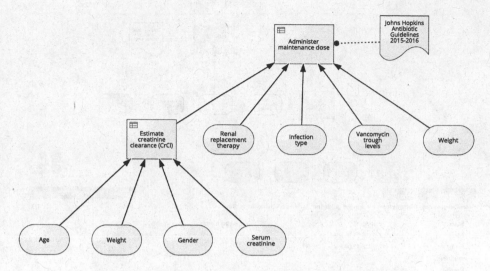

Fig. 3. Example of Vancomycin treatment: DMN model.

including an specific mark (a small table) located at the up-left. As shown in Fig. 2 the represented part of the CPG is a simple BPMN diagram composed of 5 activities and 2 decision activities.

– Secondly, we model the decision of *administer maintenance dose* using DMN. This decision depends on available information (e.g. renal replacement therapy or patient weight) and *estimation creatinine clearance*, a second decision to me made. Figure 3 shows a DMN decision requirements diagram for the main decision *administer maintenance dose*. As shown, decision activities are represented as rectangles and are related to the needed information, that are depicted as rounded rectangles. Other knowledge sources, such as authority and related published documents, are shaped as wavy-sided rectangles.

– Figure 4 shows how the tool supports a decision for *Administer maintenance dose* using DMN visualization. The first component visualizes the DMN model. In green the available components are highlighted. For example, the *Age, Weight, Gender* and *Serum creatinine* components are available and, therefore, *Estimate creatinine clearance (CrCl)* is possible. The second component of the tool shows the DMN selected element, in this case *Administer maintenance dose*, and the information available in the health record (e.g. timestamped 12/18/2016 12 pm). The third module helps the physician by providing a suggestion. In this example, the tool, according to the guideline, suggest an initial Vancomycin dose of 1000 mg.

– Finally, Fig. 1b depicts a real example of a ICU patient for the Vancomycin problem and how the visualization tool aims to support decisions. The interactive timeline shows the current state of the patient, indicating the Vancomycin details (750 mg every 12 h, intravenous). The BPMN panel depicts the current guideline execution modelled in Fig. 2. The *Administer maintenance dose* task has been selected, and the interface therefore shows a detailed

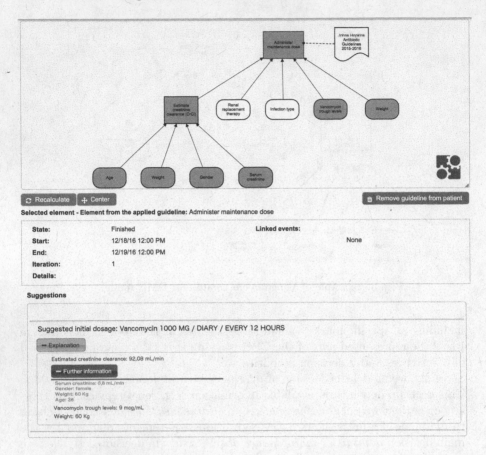

Fig. 4. Visualization tool snapshot: decision supported using DMN. (Color figure online)

description (including the linked DMN model), showing the missing information to make a decision.

The supervision of Vancomycin using our visualization tool is currently under evaluation by the ASP team of the University Hospital of Getafe.

5   Conclusions

In this work we propose a tool to support decisions for infection management considering the visualization of: the current state of the patient, the context of a potential CPG in use and specific medical actions.

There is a myriad of models to approach this problem. However, part of the originality of this work relies on the assumption of using solid technologies tested in the industry, avoiding unstandardized models, in order ease its integration in hospital systems and to assure its maintenance in the long term.

The presented tool is integrated the WASPSS platform [16] and patient information is visualized using an interactive timeline, a simple and widely extended model.

We use the BPMN to model processes contained in the CPGs and the novel DMN model to represent decision tasks. We also use BPMN/DMN for visualisation when a CPG is applied to a specific patient, colouring the elements of the model in different ways depending on its adherence. We use production rules to: (1) provide the user the context of a adherence of a CPG by inferring the state of each task of the CPG (in progress, completed or omitted) and (2) support decision based on the tasks modelled by DMNs. On the one hand, the BPMN and DMN provide a standard formalism to express and share different types of task process and rationale. On the other hand, production rules are widely used antibiotic recommender systems in the industry. Its use also allows us to infer helpful information for the physician to make a decision.

The tool is currently under evaluation in a hospital to assess on the management of Vancomycin therapy, and we plan to incorporate mechanisms with which to facilitate the linking of tasks and data.

Acknowledgments. This work was partially funded by the Spanish Ministry of Economy and Competitiveness under the WASPSS project (Ref: TIN2013-45491-R), PhD grant (Ref: BES-2014-070682) and grant for short stays (Ref: EEBB-I-16-10856); and by the European Fund for Regional Development (EFRD, FEDER).

References

1. Beilken, C., Spenke, M.: Visual, interactive data mining with InfoZoom – the medical data set. In: Workshop Notes on Discovery Challenge. Proceedings of the 3rd European Conference on Principles and Practice of Knowledge Discovery in Databases, Prague, pp. 49–54, 15–18 September 1999
2. Cánovas-Segura, B., Campos, M., Morales, A., Juarez, J.M., Palacios, F.: Development of a clinical decision support system for antibiotic management in a hospital environment. Prog. Artif. Intell. **5**(3), 181–197 (2016)
3. Carling, P., Fung, T., Killion, A., Terrin, N., Barza, M.: Favorable impact of a multidisciplinary antibiotic management program conducted during 7 years. Infect. Control Hosp. Epidemiol. **24**(9), 699–706 (2003)
4. Chittaro, L., Combi, C., Trapasso, G.: Data mining on temporal data: a visual approach and its clinical application to hemodialysis. J. Vis. Lang. Comput. **14**(6), 591–620 (2003)
5. Combi, C., Keravnou-Papailiou, E., Shahar, Y.: Temporal Information Systems in Medicine. Springer, Boston (2010)
6. Garcia-caballero, H., Campos, M., Juarez, J.M., Palacios, F.: Visualization in clinical decision support system for antibiotic treatment. In: Actas de la XVI Conferencia de la Asociación Española para la Inteligencia Artificial, CAEPIA 2015, Albacete, 9–12 Noviembre 2015, pp. 71–80 (2015)
7. Gustafson, T.L.: Practical risk-adjusted quality control charts for infection control. Am. J. Infect. Control **28**(6), 406–414 (2000)
8. Institute of Medicine: Health IT and Patient Safety: Building Safer Systems for Better Care. National Academies Press, Washington, D.C., March 2012

9. Johns Hopkins Medicine: Antibiotic Guidelines 2015-2016 (2015). http://www. hopkinsmedicine.org/amp

10. Klimov, D., Shahar, Y., Taieb-Maimon, M.: Intelligent interactive visual exploration of temporal associations among multiple time-oriented patient records. Methods Inf. Med. **48**(3), 254–262 (2009)

11. Lins, L., Heilbrun, M., Freire, J., Silva, C.: Viscaretrails: visualizing trails in the electronic health record with timed word trees, a pancreas cancer use case. In: AMIA Workshop on Visual Analytics in HealthCare (2013)

12. Magill, S.S., Edwards, J.R., Bamberg, W., Beldavs, Z.G., Dumyati, G., Kainer, M.A., Lynfield, R., Maloney, M., McAllister-Hollod, L., Nadle, J., Ray, S.M., Thompson, D.L., Wilson, L.E., Fridkin, S.K.: Multistate point-prevalence survey of health care-associated infections. N. Engl. J. Med. **370**(13), 1198–1208 (2014)

13. Nathan, C., Cars, O.: Antibiotic resistance — problems, progress, and prospects. N. Engl. J. Med. **371**(19), 1761–1763 (2014)

14. National Research Council: Computational Technology for Effective Health Care: Immediate Steps and Strategic Directions. National Academies Press, Washington, D.C., February 2009

15. Object Management Group: Decision Model and Notation, Version 1.1 (2016). http://www.omg.org/spec/DMN/1.1/

16. Palacios, F., Campos, M., Juarez, J.M., Cosgrove, S.E., Avdic, E., Cánovas-Segura, B., Morales, A., Martínez-Nuñez, M.E., Molina-García, T., García-Hierro, P., Cacho-Calvo, J.: A clinical decision support system for an antimicrobial stewardship program. In: HEALTHINF 2016, pp. 496–501. SciTePress, Rome (2016)

17. Peleg, M.: Computer-interpretable clinical guidelines: a methodological review. J. Biomed. Inf. **46**(4), 744–763 (2013)

18. Pinciroli, F., Portoni, L., Combi, C., Violante, F.F.: WWW-based access to object-oriented clinical databases: the KHOSPAD project. Comput. Biol. Med. **28**(5), 531–552 (1998)

19. Proctor, M., Neale, M., Lin, P., Frandsen, M.: Drools Documentation, pp. 1–297. JBoss (2008)

20. Rind, A.: Interactive information visualization to explore and query electronic health records. Found. Trends® Hum. Comput. Interact. **5**(3), 207–298 (2013)

21. Schentag, J.J., Ballow, C.H., Fritz, A.L., Paladino, J.A., Williams, J.D., Cumbo, T.J., Ali, R.V., Galletta, V.A., Gutfeld, M.B., Adelman, M.H.: Changes in antimicrobial agent usage resulting from interactions among clinical pharmacy, the infectious disease division, and the microbiology laboratory. Diagn. Microbiol. Infect. Dis. **16**(3), 255–264 (1993)

22. Shabo (Shvo), A., Peleg, M., Parimbelli, E., Quaglini, S., Napolitano, C.: Interplay between clinical guidelines and organizational workflow systems experience from the mobiguide project. Methods Inf. Med. **55**(6), 488–494 (2016)

23. Shahar, Y., Goren-Bar, D., Boaz, D., Tahan, G.: Distributed, intelligent, interactive visualization and exploration of time-oriented clinical data and their abstractions. Artif. Intell. Med. **38**(2), 115–135 (2006)

24. Wang, T.: Interactive visualization techniques for searching temporal categorical data. Ph.D. thesis, University of Maryland (2010)

Automatic Recording and Analysis of Somniloquy Through the Use of Mobile Devices to Support the Diagnosis of Psychological Pathologies

Virginia Aparicio-Paniagua[1], Jorge Pérez-Muñoz[1],
Alejandro Rodríguez-González[2,3(✉)] (iD), Ángel García-Pedrero[2],
Juan Miguel Gomez-Berbis[1], Consuelo Gonzalo-Martin[2,3],
Ernestina Menasalvas-Ruiz[2,3], and Giner Alor-Hernández[4]

[1] Computer Science Department, Universidad Carlos III de Madrid,
Leganes, Madrid, Spain
[2] Escuela Técnica Superior de Ingenieros Informáticos,
Campus de Montegancedo Boadilla del Monte,
Universidad Politécnica de Madrid, 28660 Madrid, Spain
alejandro.rg@upm.es
[3] Centro de Tecnología Biomédica, Campus de Montegancedo,
Universidad Politécnica de Madrid, Pozuelo de Alarcón, 28223 Madrid, Spain
[4] Division of Research and Postgraduate Studies,
Instituto Tecnológico de Orizaba, Orizaba, Mexico

Abstract. Somniloquy is a parasomnia that refers to talking aloud while sleep. This parasomnia usually happens during transitory arousals from NREM sleep. The recording of these parasomnias could be useful to help in the diagnosis of certain psychological pathologies given that they can reflect a state of anxiety or some behaviors which could be identified as psychological diagnosis criteria. In this work-in-progress paper, a mobile platform which only records sleep-talking (excluding other noises or sounds) and analyze them to identify the main emotion in the voice, allowing making a transcription of the conversation, is presented.

Keywords: Somniloquy · Mobile devices · Diagnosis · Psychology

1 Introduction

Somniloquy consists in the pronouncing of words during sleep, without any subjective and simultaneous notion by the subject. Usually, it is an infrequent short-term process, which is most commonly experienced by males. It can switch between unintelligible and incoherent sounds and long speeches, and it can happen several times during sleep.

According to the American Sleep Disorders Association [1], it belongs to the group of parasomnias. This group is composed by episodic disorders that burst

R. Valencia-García et al. (Eds.): CITI 2017, CCIS 749, pp. 169–180, 2017.
DOI: 10.1007/978-3-319-67283-0_13

in the process of sleep and are characterized by vegetative and motor phenomena as a manifestation of the central nervous system activation. It is common among children, particularly between 3 and 10 years of age and it becomes less frequent during adolescence [2]. Most adults with this disorder have done so since childhood, however if the age of onset is over around 25 years it could be related to factors as stress and sleep deprivation [2] or to underlying pathologies [3]. In this regard, somniloquy may represent part of a prodrome in REM sleep behavior disorder or coincide with obstructive sleep apnea [4]. Therefore it requires a detailed analysis to have a better understanding of what happens when we sleep.

Speaking in dreams can take place in REM and NREM phases. There are several studies such as those performed by Arkin [5] and Rechlschaffen [6] which show that there is a relationship between the somniloquy produced in REM phase with an emotional time.

This paper presents an intelligent recording platform which also allows to analyzing the recorded audio with the aim of isolating the main emotions of the recording. The recording process was optimized, avoiding file generation with long silences and therefore be very heavy. The recording process allows detecting the voice, discarding snoring noises, cries, etc. The emotions studies from the audio files are performed through acoustic analysis of voice signal. Also, transcription of the audio files will be provided.

The remainder of the paper is organized as follows. In Sect. 2 the related works is presented. In Sect. 3 the main parameters of sound analysis are shown. Section 4 presents the System overview of the system, including architecture and internal behavior. Finally, in Sect. 5 main conclusions and future work are summarized.

2   Related Works

There are many studies about the relationship between somniloquy and emotional lived occurrences. One of the oldest and most important is presented in Andriani's work in 1892 [7], in which the author declared that "the content speech during sleep is emotional usually, and it reveals a desire, an unsatisfied desire, an expected pleasure, a lament, or a fear state, anxiety or terror". The book [8] contains a classification of sleep-talking types available, depending on the relationship with other psychological or organic:

A. Primary idiopathic sleep-talking: sleep-talking unaccompanied by other sleep disorder, significant psychopathology, or an organic disease.
B. Sleep-talking accompanying and/or reflecting serious psychic conflict, environmental stress, and/or classical psychiatric conditions but occurring in the absence of other sleep-disorder syndromes.
C. Sleep-talking accompanying other sleep-disorder syndromes.
D. Sleep-talking occurring with post-traumatic states.
E. Sleep-talking with headache syndromes.
F. Sleep-talking related to seizure phenomena.
G. Sleep-talking with organic disease or abnormality.

Speech not only allows communicating. It is also a biological signal that contains extra-linguistic information about physical, physiological and emotional states. According to Darwin [9], emotions and its expression are innate or instinctive. He also pointed out that non-verbal voice can be a means of expressing emotions.

From this research, several other studies emerge in this field. Nowadays there are two big groups focused on the study of voice expressions. The first one has the basic goal of determine how an emotion is expressed or exteriorized through the voice of a person. In this field we have several remarkable studies.

Fairbanks and Pronovost [10] analyzed voice to detect five emotional expressions (i.e., contempt, anger, fear, grief, and indifference). The study concluded that emotions expressed by the voice can be easily identifiable by means of the pitch characteristics. In [11], four different works for analyzing pitch features were presented, main conclusions established emotions are identifiable from pitch patterns (e.g. pitch level, rate of pitch change). Fairbanks and Hoaglin [12] analyzed the durational characteristics of the voice during the expression of emotions. They found that anger, fear and indifference can be distinguished from contempt and grief due to the slow rate of latter ones, being the slowest the pattern of contempt.

Skinner [13] analyzed the pitch, force and quality of vocal tones expressing two emotions: happiness and sadness. He found that the tone of the voice is generally significantly higher than the ordinary tone or representative tone of sad states. Williams et al. [14, 15] examined the correlation between the speech signal and the emotions. Their study concluded that anger, fear, and sorrow situations tend to produce characteristic differences in the speech signal, particularly, in the contour of fundamental frequency, average voice spectrum, temporal characteristics, articulation accuracy and regularity of the successive glottal pulse waveform. In [16], Levin and Lord developed a computer-aided instruction system based on pitch analysis for analyzing emotions. Their results showed the effectiveness for detecting emotional stress by using an octave range detection method. France et al. [17] studied the emotional contents of a patient's speech as a diagnosing tool for various disorders, in particular, as an indicator of depression and suicidal risk.

On the other hand, the studies focused on how voice recognition deal with the aim of knowing to which extent the receiver is able to identify, from non-verbal aspects of the speaker voice, its emotional status. The main problem of these methods stems from separating the verbal channel from the vocal channel, to avoid being conditioned by linguistic content. Several techniques have been developed, but the method which has provided better results consists in keeping constant a sentence with neutral content when the process tries to identify the emotions as were demonstrated by several works [10, 18, 19].

Inside of the world of systems related with the content of this paper we can provide some examples about mobile applications to record a somniloquy. In Android, we have the application called DreamCatcher [20] which uses an advanced system for the recording, allowing controlling the level of noise during sleeping. Similar to this application, we found Dream Talk Recorder [21] which records only when a person is talking or snoring, filtering automatically silence. In Windows Mobile platform, it is possible to use the Sleep Recorder [22] system, which works in an efficient way detecting when noise is produced, allowing recording only these parts. Also, it allows adjusting some configuration parameters, such as the microphone sensitivity, among others. In iOS-based systems we can observe the application called Sleep Talk Recorder [23], which allows to monitoring the sounds while we are sleeping, and it is waiting to some talking to start the recording process. Dream Talk Recorder is also available on iOS platform offering the same functionalities as its Android version.

As we can see from the state of the art, the recording of a somniloquy could be used in several psychological processes to diagnose certain pathologies or help in the diagnosis process. The systems which have been developed on this topic are interesting, but they have several drawbacks. The main drawback is that they are not capable to analyze the captured audio in order to provide some insights about data that could be relevant for understanding what is happening while a person is sleeping such as the emotions that are experimented.

In this paper, a new system composed of mobile software and a web platform is presented. The mobile platform provides several other functionalities that other system does not address in the past such as:

- Automatic detection of speech
- Text transcription
- Emotion recognition

Apart from these features, a web platform will be provided to allow users to manage and download the speeches recorded by the mobile platform facilitating its analysis.

3   Physical Sound Magnitudes

Sound [24] is a vibrating phenomenon which is transmitted in wave form. As every wave movement, the sound could be represented as a sum of sinusoid curves, which can be characterized with the same magnitudes that each frequency wave: wave length (λ), frequency (f) or period inverse (T) and amplitude. In the following sections a brief description of each of these parameters will be done with the aim of helping in the understanding of the paper.

3.1   Amplitude, Frequency, Intensity and Sound Pressure

The amplitude defines the wave intensity. It should not be confused with acoustic volume or power, which is the amount of energy radiated in wave form for each unit of time.

The frequency gives us a measurement of the number of waves that we can find in a certain time. A sound with a higher frequency implies that more waves has been produced in a unit of time, and for hence, this will represent a more high-pitched sound. Lower tones correspond to lower frequencies.

The intensity is the amount of acoustic energy that contains a sound. For the development of this system it is necessary to focus in auditory intensity, which is supported by the psychophysics law of Weber-Fechner [25]. This law establishes a logarithmic relation between the physical intensity of the sound which is captured and the minimal physical intensity audible by the human ear.

The acoustic pressure comes from the sound propagation. The Sound Pressure Level (SPL) [26] is measured in decibels (dB). In mathematical terms, the SPL is the logarithmic measurement of the sound pressure mean with respect a reference level. It is calculated as follows:

$$SPL = 20 \times Log\left(\frac{P}{P_o}\right) \tag{1}$$

where P_o is the reference sound pressure. This value is fixed to 2×10^{-5} N/m^2. P represents the sound pressure being measured, which is calculated as follows:

$$P = \sqrt{2 \times Z \times I} \tag{2}$$
$$I = 2 \times Z \times \pi^2 \times F^2 \times A^2 \tag{3}$$

where Z is the acoustic impedance, equivalent to 406.2 for air at 30 °C, and F and A represent the frequency and amplitude, respectively.

3.2 Digital Sound Audio

In digital audio, the amplitude and frequency changes are stored in form of numbers, taking values to register the height of the wave in each moment. To do that, the scale is divided in a set of parts which correspond to a numerical value between 0 and the maximum number of parts considered.

This maximum number of parts is defined by the number of sound bites which we are working. Hence, with 8 bits, we can handle up to 256 possible values whereas with a sound of 16 bits we have 65536 values. This means that when we are working with 16 bits, the precision obtained when we play the sound is much higher. Apart from having different altitude scales, when a sound is digitalized, we can also take samples of this altitude with higher or lower frequency. This is called sampling rate, and indicates how many measurements of the sound which is being digitalized have in a second. For example, if we have a frequency of 44.1 KHz, we are taking 44.100 measurements per second.

4 System Overview

To define the system functionality we should consider two different parts: the mobile platform and the web platform. Through the mobile platform users can record their somniloquy audios and play them. During recording time the application will detect the existing voice patterns during sleep, removing uninteresting fragments such as silences, snoring or crying, among others.

The audio files generated are sent to the web platform through web services in order to be stored. Also, the web platform is in charge of generating the text transcriptions and to perform the emotion analysis, sending back the results to the mobile device.

The aim of this section is to present the design of the system, focusing on the architecture design, the technologies used, and finally, the application programming interfaces (APIs) which were used for implementation.

4.1   Architecture

The system is mainly divided into two parts, following client-server architecture. In this model, the tasks are distributed between the resource providers or services (servers) and service requesters (clients). In this case, the client is the mobile device, which makes requests to another process, where the server responds.

The structure of the mobile application is based on three-tier architecture [27]. This architecture consists in a hierarchical organization where each tier provides services to the upper tier, working with the tier which is immediately below.

The presentation tier shows the system to the user, communication the information and capturing the inputs. The logic tier provides the functionality, and data tier provides the data access. With this, we allow the communication between the three tiers, except the presentation and data tier.

The component "Web Platform" is structured following to Model-View-Controller pattern (MVC) [27], which clearly separates the domain modeling, presentation and actions based on data entered by the user. The Model layer manages the behavior and data of the application domain, responds to requests for information about its state, and responds to instructions of state change. The view layer renders the model into a user interface element and Controller layer interprets user actions. This separation allows building and testing the model independently of visual representation, but adds system complexity. Figure 1 shows the architecture diagram.

4.2   Mobile Platform

The development of the mobile platform was based on Android operating system. The reason of choosing this platform was based on technological perspective, given that most of the APIs which allows us to recording and processing audio, have been developed for Android devices. Furthermore, Android is becoming one of the most popular and used smartphone operating systems.

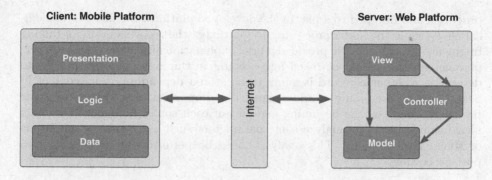

Fig. 1. Client-Server architecture design.

Android. As it was described before, Android is an operating system for mobile devices that consists of a core based on the Linux kernel. Android is an open-source platform that allows controlling the device via Google-developed Java libraries.

The internal architecture in Android platform is basically composed of five components: Applications, Applications Framework, Libraries, Android Runtime and Linux Kernel. Android applications run in its own process, with its own instance of the Dalvik virtual machine.

The most interesting features of Android for our project are listed in Table 1. For the development of the main application Eclipse IDE as well as the Android SDK and the plugin for the development of Android applications for Eclipse (ADT) will be used.

Table 1. Main Android features.

Storing	SQLite as relational database
Connectivity	It supports the following technologies: GSM/EDGE, IDEN, CDMA, EV-DO, UMTS, Bluetooth, WIFi, LTE and WiMAX
Java Support	Java bytecode is executed on Dalvik Virtual Machine
Virtual Machine	Dalvik is a specialized virtual machine designed for Android and optimized for mobile devices
DevelopmentEnvironment	It includes a device emulator, debugging tools and software development analysis

AudioRecord. The AudioRecord [28] class is in charge of managing the audio resources in Java applications which needs to be recorded from the input audio hardware of a device. An AudioRecord object initiates its audio buffer associated with the aim of being filled with the data audio recorded. Once these data have been recorded using the audio data device, this information should be read, processed and dumped to a file. In the developed platform the main technological challenge is the audio processing to guarantee the recording only of talking fragments. Hence, we have provided a brief explanation about the different audio parameters that should be taken into account in the audio analysis process to determine whether a record is going to be stored depending on its content in Sect. 2. In the processing of audio signal it is important also to measure some parameters such as the beginning and end of each sound fragment. The main idea behind this is to analyze some parameters such as frequency, amplitude or sound level pressure. This analysis could be performed in real time or as post-processing.

4.3 Web Platform

The web platform developed allows the users to manage the different recordings performed through the mobile application, allowing interacting with them. However, the main aim of this platform is to provide the capabilities of analyze and process the audio files to provide emotion analysis and text transcription. The following sections will show how these goals were fulfilled from a technological point of view.

Emotion Analysis. The emotion analysis was focused mainly on analyzing primary emotions such as anger, joy, sadness and fear. We used as base for the development of this module some studies performed in the past [29,30], which will help us understanding what the main features of the primary frame alterations are. Physical measures of human speech and vocal sound are based on three perceptual dimensions: time, pitch and loudness [13]. Based on these factors, we present what are the fundamental features of each sound-emotional model.

Anger: Anger is characterized by a half-high tone (around 229 Hz), a wide range of tone and a quick speech (190 words per minute), with 32% of pauses.

Happiness: Happiness is manifested as an increase in mid tone that varies between 10% and 50% also in its range, as well as an increase in speech rate and intensity.

Sadness: Sadness lows the average intensity between 10 and 25%, it has a narrow range and a slow speech rate.

Fear: Fear has a half tone higher (around 254 Hz), the range is greater, there are a several changes in the tone curve and it has a fast speech rate.

The analysis of the audio files which contain the talks performed during the somniloquy is analyzed using the parameters mentioned as a reference to identify the emotions during the talk. If some of the emotions are identified during the talk, the audio file is categorized, performing searches in the web platform from several parameters, including the emotion of the talk.

Speech to Text. Speech to Text (STT) technology is integrated in computers and mobile devices [31] to enable the user the actual control of the applications without the need of interacting directly with the device, such as in dictation systems.

As it could be seen in Fig. 2, the STT mechanism consists in processing the audio input through spectral analysis and acoustic models with the aim of obtaining a phonetic representation of the signal. The application of statistical models and phonetic dictionaries in the obtained phonemes, such as Speech Assessment Methods Phonetic Alphabet (SAMPA) [32], allows converting these phonemes in words with high similitude accuracy. SAMPA is a legible phonetic alphabet which is represented using 7 bits ASCII characters. SAMPA is one of the most used alphabets in STT environments.

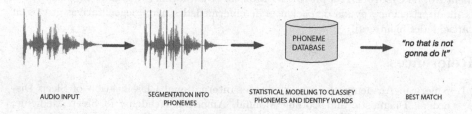

AUDIO INPUT   SEGMENTATION INTO   STATISTICAL MODELING TO CLASSIFY   BEST MATCH
                 PHONEMES   PHONEMES AND IDENTIFY WORDS

Fig. 2. Basic scheme of a Speech to Text mechanism.

The lack of punctuation in speech makes necessary to perform a syntactic analysis to make a separation between sentences. Finally, STT usually performs an orthographic analysis in order to increase the process accuracy.

The design of the proposed system includes the aforementioned mechanisms. The STT platform was integrated in the system by means of using the following open-source modules: CMUSphinx library [33], HTK toolkit [34], and Java Speech API [35].

5 Conclusions

This paper describes the development of a platform for the recording and analysis of somniloquys. The system is able to record somniloquys while a patient is sleeping, being able to isolate the fragments where the patient is talking, allowing to discard these fragments which contains noises or silences. This capability is quite important in order to select the fragments interesting to the user.

Other of the important features of the proposed system is the ability of automatically classify the emotion which is behind the recorded talk. This is quite important to allow finding previous recordings using as search parameter a concrete emotion. For psychological purposes this is very interesting given that the psychologist will be able to play only the fragments with a concrete emotion.

Another important feature of this system is the ability of automatically convert the talk recorded into text. This is again very important to allow better searches, using keywords as search parameter, or to be able to read the content of a somniloquy instead of listening to it.

As future work, a study will be performed in order to validate the proposed system in terms of precision. Speech databases will be used to evaluate voice analysis and emotion recognition as well as the implemented STT which will be compared with APIs such as Google Cloud Speech [36] and Watson Speech to Text [37].

Acknowledgements. This paper is supported by European Union's Horizon 2020 research and innovation programme under grant agreement No. 727658, project IASIS (Integration and analysis of heterogeneous big data for precision medicine and suggested treatments for different types of patients). The paper is also supported by the Spanish Ministry of Economy, Industry and Competitiveness under the grant agreement No, RTC-2016-4922-1 project NDMonitor (Plataforma Integral de bajo coste para la monitorización y ayuda de pacientes de enfermedades neurodegenerativas graves en capacidades mentales).

References

1. American Academy of Sleep Medicine: International Classification of Sleep Disorders: Diagnostic and Coding Manual. American Academy of Sleep Medicine, Westchester, Illinois, 2nd edn. (ICSD-2) (2015)
2. Chokroverty, S., Allen, R.P., Walters, A.S., Montagna, P.: Sleep and Movement Disorders. Oxford University Press, New York (2012)
3. Shneerson, J.M.: Sleep Medicine: A Guide to Sleep and Its Disorders. Wiley, New York (2009)
4. Thorpy, M.J., Plazzi, G.: The Parasomnias and Other Sleep-Related Movement Disorders. Cambridge University Press, New York (2010)
5. Arkin, A.M., Toth, M.F., Baker, J., Hastey, J.M.: The frequency of sleep talking in the laboratory among chronic sleep talkers and good dream recallers. J. Nerv. Mental Dis. **151**(6), 369–374 (1970)
6. Rechtschaffen, A., Goodenough, D.R., Shapiro, A.: Patterns of sleep talking. Arch. Gen. Psychiatry **7**(6), 418–426 (1962)
7. Andriani, G.: Fisiología psicológica del sonniloquio. Ann. Neurol. **10**, 299–308 (1892)
8. Arkin, A.M.: Sleep-Talking: Psychology and Psychophysiology. Lawrence Erlbaum Associates, Hillsdale (1981)
9. Darwin, C.: The Expression of the Emotions in Man and Animals. Oxford University Press, Oxford (1998)
10. Fairbanks, G., Pronovost, W.: An experimental study of the pitch characteristics of the voice during the expression of emotion. Commun. Monogr. **6**(1), 87–104 (1939)
11. Fairbanks, G.: Recent experimental investigations of vocal pitch in speech. J. Acoust. Soc. Am. **11**(4), 457–466 (1940)
12. Fairbanks, G., Hoaglin, L.W.: An experimental study of the durational characteristics of the voice during the expression of emotion. Commun. Monogr. **8**(1), 85–90 (1941)
13. Skinner, E.R.: A calibrated recording and analysis of the pitch, force and quality of vocal tones expressing happiness and sadness; and a determination of the pitch and force of the subjective concepts of ordinary, soft, and loud tones. Commun. Monogr. **2**(1), 81–137 (1935)

14. Williams, C.E., Stevens, K.N.: Emotions and speech: some acoustical correlates. J. Acoust. Soc. Am. **52**(4B), 1238–1250 (1972)
15. Williams, C.E., Stevens, K.N.: Vocal correlates of emotional states. In: Speech Evaluation in Psychiatry, pp. 221–240 (1981)
16. Levin, H., Lord, W.: Speech pitch frequency as an emotional state indicator. IEEE Trans. Syst. Man Cybern. **2**, 259–273 (1975)
17. France, D.J., Shiavi, R.G., Silverman, S., Silverman, M., Wilkes, M.: Acoustical properties of speech as indicators of depression and suicidal risk. IEEE Trans. Biomed. Eng. **47**(7), 829–837 (2000)
18. Zuckerman, M., Lipets, M.S., Koivumaki, J.H., Rosenthal, R.: Encoding and decoding nonverbal cues of emotion. J. Pers. Soc. Psychol. **32**(6), 1068 (1975)
19. van Bezooijen, R.: The characteristics and recognizability of vocal expression of emotions (1984)
20. Buckley, C.: Dreamcatcher. Version 1.2 (2011). https://market.android.com/details?id=com.buck.SleepTalker&hl=es
21. MobiUtil: Dream talk recorder. Android version (2016). https://play.google.com/store/apps/developer?id=MobiUtil&hl=en, Version 3.6. iOS version. https://itunes.apple.com/us/app/dream-talk-recorder/id445472628?mt%3D8, Version 7.0
22. Asleroid: Sleep recorder (2017). https://www.microsoft.com/en-us/store/p/sleep-recorder/9wzdncrfhmw3
23. MadinSweden: Dreamcatcher (2011). http://www.sleeptalkrecorder.com. https://itunes.apple.com/WebObjects/MZStore.woa/wa/viewSoftware?id=391767653, Version 2.1.2
24. Corominas, R.: Audio digital: amplitud, frecuencia, ruido y normalización (2005)
25. Fontes, S., Fontes, A.: Consideraciones teóricas sobre las leyes psicofísicas. Revista de psicología general y aplicada: Revista de la Federación Española de Asociaciones de Psicología (Internet) **47**(4), 391–395 (1994)
26. Instituto de Salud Pública. Gobierno de Chile: Instructivo para la aplicación del d. s n° 594/99 del minsal, título iv, parrafo 3° agentes fisicos - ruido (1999)
27. Reynoso, C., Kicillof, N.: Estilos y patrones en la estrategia de arquitectura de microsoft. Universidad de Buenos Aires, Buenos Aires (2004)
28. Android Developers: android.media.audiorecord (2009). http://developer.android.com/reference/android/media/AudioRecord.html
29. Rodríguez Bravo, Á., Lázaro Pernias, P., Montoya Vilar, N., Blanco Pont, J.M., Bernadas Suñé, D., Oliver, J.M., Longhi, L.: Modelización acústica de la expresión emocional en el español. Procesamiento del lenguaje natural, no. 25 (Septiembre 1999), pp. 159–166 (1999)
30. GilMartín, V.F., Gómez-Navarro, P.G., Ballesteros, R.H.: Análisis y síntesis de expresión emocional en cuentos leídos en voz alta. Procesamiento del lenguaje natural **35**, 293–300 (2005)
31. Zaykovskiy, D., Minker, W.: Speech recognition for mobile phones. Int. J. Speech Technol. **11**(2), 63–72 (2012). Springer
32. Wells, J., Barry, W., Grice, M., Fourcin, A., Gibbon, D.: Standard computer-compatible transcription. Esprit project 2589 (SAM), Doc. no. SAM-UCL 37 (1992)
33. Project by Carnegie Mellon University: Cmusphinx - open source toolkit for speech recognition (2017). https://cmusphinx.github.io
34. Speech Vision, Robotics Group of the Cambridge University Engineering Department: The hidden Markov model toolkit (htk) (2017). http://htk.eng.cam.ac.uk
35. Sun Microsystems: Java speech API (2017). http://www.oracle.com/technetwork/java/speech-138007.html

36. Google: Cloud speech API (2017). https://cloud.google.com/speech
37. IBM: Watson developer cloud (2017). https://www.ibm.com/watson/developercloud/speech-to-text.html

Clinical Assessment Using an Algorithm Based on Fuzzy C-Means Clustering

Alfonso A. Guijarro-Rodríguez[1](✉), Lorenzo J. Cevallos-Torres[1],
Miguel Botto-Tobar[1,2], Maikel Leyva-Vazquez[1], and Jessica Yepez Holguin[1]

[1] Universidad de Guayaquil, Guayaquil, Ecuador
{alfonso.guijarror,lorenzo.cevallost,miguel.bottot,
maikel.leyvav,jessica.yepezh}@ug.edu.ec
[2] Eindhoven University of Technology, Eindhoven, The Netherlands
m.a.botto.tobar@tue.nl

Abstract. The Fuzzy c-means (FCM) algorithms define a grouping criterion from a function, which seeks to minimize iteratively the function up to until an optimal fuzzy partition is obtained. In the execution of this algorithm each element to the clusters is related to others that belong in the same n-dimensional space, which means that an element can belong to more than one clusters. This proposal aims to define a fuzzy clustering algorithm which allows the patient classifications based on the clinical assessment of the medical staff. In this work 30 cases were studied using the Glasgow Coma Scale to measure the level of awareness for each one which were prioritized by triage Manchester method. After applying the FCM algorithm the data is separated data into two clusters, thus, verified the fuzzy grouping in patients with a degree of membership that specifies the level of prioritization.

Keywords: Fuzzy logic · Clinical assessment · Fuzzy grouping · Triage · Glasgow

1 Introduction

Fuzzy c-means (FCM), are algorithms that operate with a non-supervised grouping criteria, their aim is to find out hidden patterns from a given set [1]. This algorithm for its processing defines an objective function which seeks to minimize the function in an iterative way in order to obtain an optimal fuzzy partition, therefore, the elements of the same class could be similar to others.

In the medical field fuzzy logic has being handled for many years ago, where enough evidence has been found in experimental programs aiming to improve the accuracy degree among them for decision-making, staff selection, and the clinical assessment process, where ambiguity and uncertainty are mostly handled [1].

This article presents a fuzzy grouping method for patient classification at the moment of coming to the doctor medical appointment [2]. GCS is a method to assesses the level of consciousness through nomenclatures, assessing the state of

© Springer International Publishing AG 2017
R. Valencia-García et al. (Eds.): CITI 2017, CCIS 749, pp. 181–193, 2017.
DOI: 10.1007/978-3-319-67283-0_14

alertness and the cognitive status of a person [2]. The Manchester Triage System model determines the level of urgency based on the information obtained from a patient, allowing its prioritization and classification according to the severity of his/her case [3].

From the sample considered in this research, an evaluation with the GCS method on each of one of 30 patients was performed in order to prioritize them and group them according to their level of severity, and regarding to the fuzzy grouping, the FCM algorithm was applied.

The paper is organized as follows: Sect. 2 discusses the fuzzy logic. Section 3 presents the research method. Section 4 describes the results obtained, and finally, Sect. 5 presents our conclusions and suggest areas for further investigation.

2   Fuzzy Logic

Fuzzy logic is considered as a technique to developing decision-making process using ambiguous variables [2], representing uncertainty mathematically, is worth to note that the ambiguous terms are not the logic, rather the objective to be analyzed [4]. Other definitions consider the fuzzy logic as a form of multi-valued logic that deals with approximate and non-precise reasoning [2].

This concept was proposed by Lofti Zadeh, who posed the fuzzy sets theory, and afterwards, he published the fuzzy logic theory and approximate reasoning in 1974. However, the diffuse logic unlike traditional logic has an unconcrete limit, it proposes a range of possibilities of veracity between (0-1), it may exist that an assertion is partially true or partially false. As a multivalued logic uses continuous values between zero (pretends completely facts) and one (totally certain) [3]. One example of information that uses the fuzzy logic is as follow: slightly low temperature, half-wet clothes, low speed, etc. making use of fuzzy terms for representing ambiguous data.

In classical sets elements belong or not to an established set, whereas in fuzzy sets the elements are related to a linguistic value, which is a word or phrase written in an artificial language. For instance, a linguistic variable could be the position of a balloon and its linguistic values could be: almost nothing, little, balanced, large, huge. The sentences can be formed between linguistic variables and linguistic terms. In this way the traditional logic can be observed as a particular event of the fuzzy logic (see Fig. 1).

2.1   Fuzzy Sets

Fuzzy sets are those elements that have a certain belonging degree, where an element can have a value of one or zero of the total elements. In [5] they define that a fuzzy set is a mathematical tool to address uncertainties that are free of difficulties. Unlike classical sets, where an element can just belong to a single class or group, whereas the elements of a fuzzy set, an individual may belong to more than one group in certain way. For the manipulation of fuzzy sets, two fundamental elements are applied.

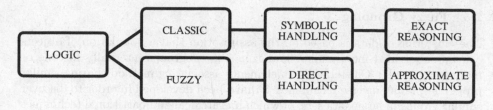

Fig. 1. Differences between classical and fuzzy logic.

2.2 Universe of Discourse

It is defined as all possible values that a variable can take, indicating all the elements that are classified by a belonging degree, it is represented by X. A clear example would be the classification of a group of people according to their height. In this case, the totality would be all the people that make up the group.

2.3 Membership Function

Also called belonging function $\mu(x)$, it is a curve that determines the membership degree of the set components, the graphs of the function are values $\mu(x) \in [0,1]$.

In medical environments, many people handle fuzzy terms that include some imprecision, those terms, are not handled by doctors and information systems directly. When a patient is interviewed, the obtained information is classical logic, these data are subtly fitted into two sets: "with pain", "without pain". Applying the theory of diffuse sets the degrees of pain belonging are determined, such as for example: "strong pain", "moderate pain", "half pain", "low pain".

2.4 Fuzzy Driver

It is a complete and diffuse decision-making system that uses fuzzy sets theory [4]. It includes three important steps: fuzzification, the inference, and defuzzification. The [6] fuzzification aims to transform the input data into output linguistic variables. The rule or inference engine is carried out in the grouping of input data according to output data. The final step is the deffuzzification, its procedure is to transform the diffuse data into an arithmetical value (See Fig. 2).

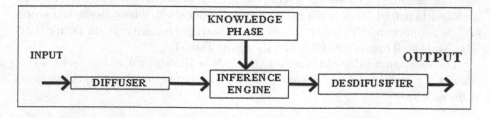

Fig. 2. Fuzzification and Defuzzification.

2.5   Fuzzy Grouping

The clustering of data is based on the assumption that a population of objects can be subdivided into smaller, homogeneous subgroups internally for one or more functions [7]. Clustering is an elements associating method sharing similar properties. Many diverse techniques [8] have been developed in order to discover similar groups in large data sets, of which hierarchical and partitional techniques are being widely practiced. The group is much more natural than conventional set theory, since the objects that are at the borders of these groups, may not necessarily be forced to belong to one of them [9].

3   Research Method

In order to carry out the clinical assessment process to diffuse grouping, we used the FCM algorithm formulated by Dunn and Bezdek. The case study data were assessed, applying three aspects of level of SGA awareness to the 30 patients with brain injury traumatism. According to obtained results from the assessment scale, we identified patients with a high degree of consciousness and patients who are completely unconscious, which ones were classified using the Manchester triage system method. For the data processing, Orange Canvas tool [10] was used to apply the clustering algorithms and to observe the separated results in two clusters

3.1   Glasgow Coma Scale (GCS)

GCS [11] is considered as an instrument with high sensitivity for the assessment of patients with brain damage, the level of consciousness of a person is measured through three parameters: the ocular, verbal and motor response. The ocular response has a maximum value of 4 and a minimum score of 1, the maximum score is obtained when the patient responds by spontaneously opening the eyes. To assess the motor response, it gives the following scores: 6 if the patient captures the orders, 5 if the patient locates the pain, 4 if the patient responds in a retreat to the response to the pain, 3 if he/she makes an abnormal flexion, 2 if he/she makes an abnormal extension and 1 if there are responses absences. Regarding to verbal assessment the values are as follow: 5 if the answer is oriented, 4 if the patient responds confused, 3 if responds inconsistently, 2 if speech incomprehensible, if no answer a score of 1. In the out-of-hospital setting, GCS is an important tool for decision-making and classification, where the initial score acts as an important prognostic indicator following traumatic brain injury [12]. The Nomenclatures of the GCS are shown in Table 1.

The maximum value obtained on the scale is 15, which it indicates that the patient is conscious, and on the other hand, the minimum value is 3, the patient is unconscious.

Table 1. Parameters of GCS with their nomenclatures.

LEVEL	ANSWER	VALUE
Opening Eyes	Spontaneous, flashing	4
	For verbal stimulation, speech	3
	For pain only	2
	No response	1
Verbal	Oriented	5
	Answer to confuse questions	4
	Inappropriate words	3
	Incomprehensible speech	2
	No response	1
Motor response	Obey orders for movement	6
	Pain stimulus movement	5
	Pain response is withdrawn	4
	Bending in response to pain	3
	Extension in response to pain	2
	No response	1

3.2 Process of the Manchester Triage System (MTS)

Triage has emerged as a method to optimize care and minimize damage caused by overcrowding by identifying patients who need immediate care [13]. The MTS is a method of prioritization and classification that was raised in the English city Manchester by professionals in emergency services. Nowadays, this method of prioritizing patients in the emergency room is applied in public hospitals, which is implemented at the IESS: Teodoro Maldonado Carbo hospital and at the University Hospital of the Guayaquil city. In [14], the classification levels of the MTS are presented. The highest level means that a patient is probably suffering from a life-threatening illness, so immediate attention is provided. Such patients are assigned the red color category. Urgent conditions are assigned the orange color category, they are able to wait a time limit of 10 min. Less urgent patients are assigned a yellow color category. Non-urgent patients, green category with time limit of 2 hours. Other patients are given a blue triage level, which means they can wait for 4 hours. The MTS process will then be displayed in Table 2.

In general terms, this method attempts to provide diagnosis, elimination or clinical priority.

3.3 FCM Clustering Method

It is one of the most used algorithms in diffuse grouping. It assigns to each data a membership value within each cluster and therefore, specific data may belong to more than one cluster [15]. A fuzzy partition determines the intervention of each

Table 2. Classification of the Manchester Triage System.

Priority	Attention	Time	Color
1	Immediate	0 min	Red
2	Very urgent	10 min	Orange
3	Urgent	60 min	Yellow
4	Standard	120 min	Green
5	Non-urgent	240 min	Blue

sample in the clusters using membership functions that take values of [0,1]. FCM performs a soft distribution known as soft partition, such partition elements are hierarchically integrated to all clusters. A mathematically smooth partition is defined:

$$X = \text{data set}$$

$$xi = \text{element corresponding to } X$$

$P = \{C_1, C_2, ..., C_c\}$ soft partition X, whether only if the following is true:

$$\forall xi \in X \quad \forall C_j \in P \qquad 0 \leq \cup_{cj}(xi) \leq 1 \tag{1}$$

For all Xi which belongs to X, for all cluster C_j which belongs to P, the belonging coefficient $\cup_{cj}(xi)$ must be between [0-1].

$$\forall xi \in X \quad \exists C_j \in P \qquad \text{such that} \qquad \cup_{cj}(Xi) > 0 \tag{2}$$

For all xi which belongs to X, there is a cluster which belongs to P, such that the belonging coefficient $\cup_{cj}(xi)$ is greater than zero. FCM minimizes function:

$$J_m = \Sigma_{i=1}^{N} \Sigma_{j=1}^{C} \cup_{ij}^{m} ||x_i - c_j||, 1 \leq m \leq \infty \tag{3}$$

known as the objective function where:
$m =$ is some arithmetic value greater than 1.
$\cup_{ij} =$ is the belonging degree x_i in the group j.
$x_i = i$ of the measured data.
$c_j =$ cluster dimension center.
$|| * || =$ similarity between measured data and center.

The calculation is done updating the belonging coefficients $\cup_{ij}$, and the centroids C_j. A diffuse partition $\{C_1, C_2, ..., C_k\}$ can be a local minimum of the objective function J^m only if the following conditions are fulfilled [15].

3.4 FCM Grouping Algorithm

Step 1.

- Initialize the centroids.
- Choose the number of cluster C.
- Choose the exponent m.
- Initialize the array of partition $\cup$ randomly.

Step 2. Calculate the belonging functions of n clusters, through the use of:

$$\cup_{cj}(x) = \frac{1}{\Sigma_{k=1}^{C}(\frac{||x_i - v_i||^2}{||x_i - v_j||^2})^{\frac{1}{m-1}}} \tag{4}$$

Step 3. Sum each of belongings in both clusters which complies with:

$$\Sigma_j \cup_{ci}(x_i) = 1 \quad \forall x_i \in X \tag{5}$$

In case of error, the belonging grade should be calculated once more.

Step 4. Update the n centroids $C = C_j$.

$$v_i = \frac{\Sigma_{k=1}^{N} \cup_{ci}(x)^m . x}{\Sigma_{k=1}^{N} \cup_{ci}(x)^m} \tag{6}$$

Note: Once the number of clusters and the value of m have been defined, the centroids and the core initialized the then FCM algorithm performs 2 steps: first, the belonging functions are calculated using the equation in step 2, and second, the prototypes are updated by means the equation in step 4.

3.5   Case Study

There is a table evaluating the Glasgow valuation process and triage prioritization of 30 patients with head trauma. These data were stored in an Excel table, then it was taken to the orange application [10], where the evaluation was performed (see Table 4).

Once the results were obtained, a close value to 1 indicated that the patient is consent and did not need immediate attention, and on the other hand, a close value to 0 showed that the patient is unconscious and needed immediate attention. Depending on the case we should expect a time limit according to the Manchester Triage system. It is desired to separate the data set into two groups (clusters) to visualize those patients with different characteristics. For this case, centroids or prototypes are initially defined.

Data: The cluster quantity is 2, the parameter m is 2, centroids: $v1 = (0.3, 0.6)$ and $v2 = (0.9, 0.6)$.

Note: We designed and worked with a table according to the Manchester triage system in fuzzy level (Table 3) in order to classify the patients according to the result obtained in the Glasgow scale assessment.

As indicated above we grouped those patients who have a belonging degree close to 1 in a cluster which meant that they did not need immediate attention, and on the other hand, the patients with a lower degree of belonging in another cluster, needed immediate attention.

Table 3. Manchester Triage System with fuzzy levels.

Fuzzy prioritation	Color	
[0–0.20]	Red	Immediate attention
[0.21–0.47]	Orange	Immediate attention
[0.48–0.65]	Yellow	Non-immediate attention
[0.66–0.80]	Green	Non-immediate attention
[0.81–100]	Blue	Non-immediate attention

4   Results

Table 4 shows the results of the Glasgow evaluation of 30 patients with craniofemoral trauma, we applied 3 parameters in order to measure the level of consciousness, identifying those who need immediate attention or not, resulting in random values between [0-1].

Table 5 shows the final results of the evaluation process, the sum is the result of the clinical assessment for each one of the 30 patients, for that reason was generated an approximation value, indicating the priority of the Clinical assessment by means of an algorithm based on clustering Fuzzy c-means.

For this case study, the first iteration of the algorithm, the belonging coefficient in the first element is calculated. An important elements to consider in the fuzzy clustering algorithm are the centroids. This value allows to represent all the possible characteristics belonging to a diffuse set. It is worth noting that the value to be considered as centroid oscillates between 0 and 1. Therefore, for this research we considered referential values $v1 = (0.3, 0.6)$ and $v2 = (0.9, 0.6)$, and the following formula was applied:

$$\cup_{c1}(X1) = \frac{1}{\Sigma_{j=1}^{2}(\frac{||x_i-v_i||^2}{||x_i-v_j||^2})^2} \tag{7}$$

The sum of the centroids $v1 = (0.3, 0.6)$ is calculated. The first point is subtracted with centroid $v1$. $0.67 - 0.3 = 0.37$, and $0.53 - 0.6 = 0.07$. With that same point we subtracted the second centroid $v2 = (0.9, 0.6)$ to obtain the values of 0.2 and 0.07.

$$||x1 - v1||.^2 = 0.37^2 + 0.07^2 = 0.1369 + 0.0049 = 0.1418 \tag{8}$$

$$||x1 - v2||.^2 = 0.23^2 + 0.07^2 = 0.0529 + 0.0049 = 0.0578 \tag{9}$$

$$\cup_{c1}(x1) = \frac{1}{\frac{0.1418}{0.1418} + \frac{0.1418}{0.0578}} \tag{10}$$

$$\cup_{c1}(x1) = \frac{1}{1 + 2.4533} \tag{11}$$

$$\cup_{c1}(x1) = 0.2896 \tag{12}$$

Table 4. Glasgow valuation.

Patient	Eye response	Verbal response	Motor response
1	0,27	0,07	0,33
2	0,07	0,33	0,13
3	0,07	0,13	0,13
4	0,13	0,33	0,07
5	0,20	0,20	0,33
6	0,07	0,20	0,07
7	0,07	0,20	0,20
8	0,07	0,13	0,33
9	0,20	0,13	0,07
10	0,13	0,20	0,27
11	0,27	0,07	0,13
12	0,07	0,07	0,13
13	0,07	0,20	0,13
14	0,20	0,13	0,07
15	0,20	0,13	0,40
16	0,07	0,20	0,27
17	0,20	0,27	0,20
18	0,27	0,13	0,40
19	0,27	0,20	0,27
20	0,27	0,13	0,40
21	0,07	0,33	0,40
22	0,13	0,33	0,40
23	0,07	0,33	0,07
24	0,07	0,13	0,33
25	0,27	0,27	0,33
26	0,27	0,07	0,07
27	0,27	0,27	0,40
28	0,20	0,33	0,40
29	0,27	0,07	0,07
30	0,13	0,07	0,27

Similarly, the values of the other membership functions are calculated, beside the complete results are shown in Table 6. For the calculation of the belonging values of both clusters, we used a source code of the FCM algorithm implemented in C# [16].

Table 5. Final results.

Patient	Health status	Priority
	Glasgow	Medical attention
1	0,67	0,53
2	0,53	0,60
3	0,33	0,53
4	0,53	0,53
5	0,73	0,33
6	0,33	0,67
7	0,47	0,33
8	0,53	0,47
9	0,40	0,67
10	0,60	0,19
11	0,47	0,47
12	0,27	0,80
13	0,40	0,67
14	0,40	0,87
15	0,73	0,53
16	0,53	0,40
17	0,67	0,93
18	0,80	0,60
19	0,73	0,53
20	0,53	0,67
21	0,80	0,28
22	0,87	0,12
23	0,47	0,12
24	0,53	0,87
25	0,87	0,52
26	0,40	0,98
27	0,93	0,05
28	0,93	0,43
29	0,40	0,09
30	0,47	0,25

Table 6 shows the belonging values obtained in 2 cluster by compiling the program, and it provided as a result the approximation values of the clinical assessment in 30 patients.

The grade of belonging 1 indicates the maximum of belonging, whereas 0 indicates that the data does not belong to the cluster, thus, the data with greater

Table 6. Values of belonging for each data/cluster.

Priority - Medical attention	Cluster 1	Cluster 2
0,53	0,2896	0,7104
0,60	0,7213	0,2787
0,53	0,9827	0,0173
0,53	0,7104	0,2896
0,33	0,2831	0,7169
0,67	0,9827	0,0173
0,33	0,8488	0,1512
0,47	0,6878	0,3122
0,67	0,9448	0,0552
0,19	0,5000	0,5000
0,47	0,8150	0,1850
0,80	0,9144	0,0856
0,67	0,9448	0,0552
0,87	0,7957	0,2043
0,53	0,1512	0,8488
0,40	0,6557	0,3443
0,93	0,3970	0,6030
0,60	0,0385	0,9615
0,53	0,1512	0,8488
0,67	0,7104	0,2896
0,28	0,2418	0,7582
0,12	0,2941	0,7059
0,12	0,3844	0,6156
0,87	0,6251	0,3749
0,52	0,0216	0,9784
0,98	0,7187	0,2813
0,05	0,3026	0,6974
0,43	0,0654	0,9346
0,09	0,6538	0,3402
0,25	0,6700	0,3300

belonging in cluster 1 are 2, 3, 4, 6, 7, 8, 9, 11, 12, 13, 14, 16, 20, 23, 26, 29, 30 while the remaining data has a greater belonging in cluster 2. These values were represented using Open Source Orange Canvas tool [10]. In Fig. 3, the data were loaded into the program by means of the widget field. Widget Data Table allowed to visualize the simulated data, and the widget Scatter Plot showed the results of the dispersion of the data. The first cluster brings together patients who are aware and do not need medical attention thus they would wait for a time limit, while the second cluster brings together all patients who need immediate care.

Based on the sample applied with the Manchester triage system, 17 patients obtained non-immediate priority, which had to wait the time limit according to

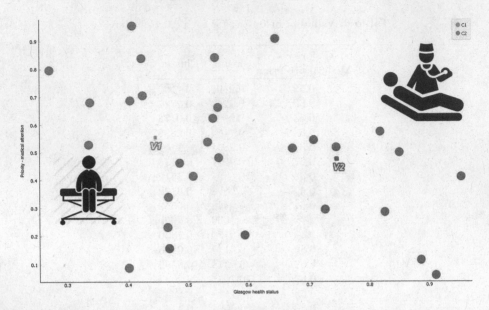

Fig. 3. Dispersion of data and in Orange Canvas [10] separated in 2 cluster.

their level of urgency, meanwhile the remaining patients were considered as cases of immediate attention.

According to the experts, the case study allowed us to glimpse the fuzzy grouping, as well as a proposed classification of the patients in the emergency room of the University Hospital, which indicates that the prioritization and the classification of the patient has improved significantly through the use of Fuzzy c-means algorithm.

5   Conclusions

The clinical assessment work was performed with five groups of 30 patients in approximately 30 days in the emergency room of the University Hospital. Afterwards, a case study was generated with 30 patients from a total of 150, with the intention of generalizing the method and making the respective suggestions of the use Fuzzy c-means algorithm, the results obtained allows to segment patients groups form high to low priority.

After the application of the Fuzzy c-means algorithm to the clinical evaluation process, an effective contribution was obtained by allowing the medical staff and their work team to obtain a better data visualization, therefore, they can make better decisions regarding prioritization of the patient.

References

1. Gudino-Penaloza, F., González-Mendoza, M., Mora-Vargas, J.: Uso de técnicas de agrupamiento en la clasificación de estilos de aprendizaje. Res. Comput. Sci. **95**, 135–146 (2015)
2. Hazelzet, J.A.: Can fuzzy logic make things more clear? Crit. Care **13**(1), 116 (2009)
3. Horgby, P.J.: Risk classification by fuzzy inference. GENEVA Pap. Risk Insur. Theory **23**(1), 63–82 (1998)
4. Lim, C.H., Vats, E., Chan, C.S.: Fuzzy human motion analysis: a review. Pattern Recogn. **48**(5), 1773–1796 (2015)
5. Çelik, Y., Yamak, S.: Fuzzy soft set theory applied to medical diagnosis using fuzzy arithmetic operations. J. Inequalities Appl. **2013**(1), 82 (2013)
6. Velarde, E.S.S., Sotelo-deÁvila, A.A., Rico-Asención, I.O., Alemán, N.R., González, R.S., Ramírez-Sotelo, M.G., Cabrera-Llanos, A.I.: Fuzzy-state machine for triage priority classifier in emergency room. In: Jaffray, D. (ed.) World Congress on Medical Physics and Biomedical Engineering, June 7–12, 2015, Toronto, Canada, pp. 1488–1491. Springer, Cham (2015)
7. Fu, L., Medico, E.: Flame, a novel fuzzy clustering method for the analysis of dna microarray data. BMC Bioinf. **8**(1), 3 (2007)
8. Sandra, A.K., Sarkar, A.K.: Application of fuzzy logic and clustering techniques for pavement maintenance. Transp. Infrastruct. Geotechnol. **2**(3), 103–119 (2015)
9. Plata, E.C., Plata, C.C.: Análisis de los algoritmos de agrupamiento borroso para detectar asimetría de información. Economía y Administración **45**(70), 7–22 (2008)
10. Demšar, J., Curk, T., Erjavec, A., Gorup, Č., Hočevar, T., Milutinovič, M., Možina, M., Polajnar, M., Toplak, M., Starič, A., et al.: Orange: data mining toolbox in python. J. Mach. Learn. Res. **14**(1), 2349–2353 (2013)
11. Muñana-Rodríguez, J.E., Ramírez-Elías, A.: Escala de coma de glasgow: origen, análisis y uso apropiado. Enfermería universitaria **11**(1), 24–35 (2014)
12. Heim, C., Schoettker, P., Gilliard, N., Spahn, D.R.: Knowledge of glasgow coma scale by air-rescue physicians. Scand. J. Trauma Resuscitation Emerg. Med. **17**(1), 39 (2009)
13. Azeredo, T.R.M., Guedes, H.M., de Almeida, R.A.R., Chianca, T.C.M., Martins, J.C.A.: Efficacy of the manchester triage system: a systematic review. Int. Emerg. Nurs. **23**(2), 47–52 (2015)
14. Forsgren, S., Forsman, B., Carlström, E.D.: Working with manchester triage-job satisfaction in nursing. Int. Emerg. Nurs. **17**(4), 226–232 (2009)
15. Porras, J.C.C., Laverde, R.M., Diaz, J.R.: Tecnicas de logica difusa aplicadas a la mineria de datos. Sci. Tech. **3**(40), 1–6 (2008)
16. Jurado, J., Penagos, D.: Fuzzy C Means Presentation (2013)

Kushkalla: A Web-Based Platform to Improve Functional Movement Rehabilitation

Fabián Narváez[1]([✉]), Fernando Arbito[1], Carlos Luna[2], Christian Merchán[3], María C. Cuenca[1], and Gloria M. Díaz[4]

[1] Biomedical Engineering Research Group, School of Electronic Engineering, Universidad del Azuay, Cuenca, Ecuador
frnarvaeze@uazuay.edu.ec
[2] Faculty of Health Sciences, Universidad Técnica de Ambato, Ambato, Ecuador
[3] School of Physical Therapy, Universidad Católica de Santiago de Guayaquil, Guayaquil, Ecuador
[4] Faculty of Engineering, Instituto Tecnológico Metropolitano, Medellín, Colombia

Abstract. Telerehabilitation is a growing alternative to traditional face-to-face therapy, which uses technological solutions to cover rehabilitation care in both clinical centers and in-home programs. However, the current telerehabilitation systems are limited to deliver a set of exercise programs for some specific locomotor disability, without including tools that allow a quantitative analysis of the rehabilitation progress, in real-time, as well as the medical condition of patients. This paper presents the design and development of a novel web-based platform, named "Kushkalla", that allows to perform movement assessment for creating personalized home-based therapy routines, integrating hardware and software tools for a quantitative analysis of locomotor movements based on motion capture, preprocessing, monitoring, visualization, storage and analysis, in real-time. The platform combines two motion capture strategies, the Kinect-based and IMU-based motion capture. In addition, a set of 2D and 3D graphical models, virtual environments, based on WebGL technology, and videoconference module are included to allow the interaction between user and clinician for enhancing the capability of the clinician to direct rehabilitation therapies.

Keywords: Telerehabilitation · Motion capture analysis · Depth sensor · Inertial sensors · WebGL

1 Introduction

According to the World Health Organization, at least 15% of world people could present musculoskeletal disabilities, which present difficulties to access appropriate management even in diagnosis, treatment or follow-up stages. Particularly, it is estimated that between 76% and 85% of disabled people have not accessed to treatment programs in developing countries [17]. Conventionally, when a musculoskeletal disability is diagnosed, a clinical specialist designs a specific functional

© Springer International Publishing AG 2017
R. Valencia-García et al. (Eds.): CITI 2017, CCIS 749, pp. 194–208, 2017.
DOI: 10.1007/978-3-319-67283-0_15

rehabilitation program, according to the analysis of the strength, flexibility and other biomechanical aspects of the patient; then, a team of therapists is responsible for its execution and follow-up. Both diagnosis and follow-up require quantifying those biomechanical aspects in order to guarantee that the designed program is suitable for the patient. This workflow demands an important number of therapists and technologies, such as strength platforms, to ensure the quality of the rehabilitation program. Additionally, the patient location could be a major obstacle for this purpose. This is the case of some rehabilitation programs to restore functional movements of elderly people, which are constantly suffering locomotor impairment caused by aging. Thus, functional movement rehabilitation programs evaluate the movement patterns from each patient to establish what parts of the human body may be treated. An improper movement pattern or imbalances throughout the human body allow determining postural and motor issues, which are used to develop different rehabilitation programs by the therapist. Therefore, functional movement rehabilitation programs are able to rehabilitate the human body that is weak, tight or unbalance by using a combination of functional movement correction and classic rehabilitation exercises.

Recently, telerehabilitation has emerged as an alternative that allows to perform functional movement rehabilitation activities from the comfort of the patient location, which are monitored by the physician from the specialized medical center [14]. This is possible by the use of the Internet and emerging technologies such as inertial sensors, optical motion capture devices, robots, virtual reality environments, among others [4]. In general, telerehabilitation strategies can be classified as: telepresence-based rehabilitation, which are supported by videoconference tools that allow a continuous communication between patient and physician [3]; robotic-based rehabilitation, which uses autonomous robots or exoskeletons for guiding patient movements [7]; interactive-based rehabilitation, which uses interactive environments for motivating patient to perform exercises while playing [12,15,21] and; rehabilitation based on a precision analysis, which provides movement analysis tools for supporting the physician decisions [11].

This paper describes the design and development of a novel web-based platform that integrates telepresence, interactive environments, and movement analysis tools, for providing the technology to carry out functional movement assessment and to create personalized home-based therapy routines. The proposed Web-based platform was developed on a service-oriented architecture (SOA), a client/server software design approach in which an application consists of software services and software service consumers that are provided between software components through several network communication protocols [16]. It is composed of two main software parts: a client and a cloud server components. Additionally, two applications conform the client component: the patient application, and the physician application. The patient application includes a bimodal human motion capture module that allows to integrate both a wearable inertial sensor system and a depth camera sensor (Kinect); a visualization module provided with a virtual environment with an interactive interface in which patient can see in two 3D avatars how an exercise must be executed and how they execute it; and an assistance module provided with a videoconference tool and videotutorials about the platform. The Physician application includes an exercise visualization module, synchronized with the patient interface, in which real-time patient movements are displayed, and a motion analysis module, which displays graphically the movement measurements generated by the analysis of captured data. Finally, the server component, implemented as a software as a service cloud component that it includes a web-server, a websocket server, a webRTC (web with Real-Time Communications) server, and relational and non-relational databases.

This paper is organized as follows. The next section presents a brief summary of related works. In the Sect. 3 the main hardware/software components of the proposed platform are described. Section 4 presents a preliminary evaluation that shows the reliability of the proposed architecture and finally, Sect. 5 presents the conclusions and discuss the future work.

2   Related Works

In the last 15 years, telerehabilitation systems have been developed as an alternative for individuals with limited access to comprehensive medical and rehabilitation outpatient services. Originally, these kind of systems have been implemented by using basic videoconference strategies for establishing a communication between patients and specialist [3,5]. However, the need of know some relevant measurements performed in clinical practice for monitoring the rehabilitation progress, it has motivated the development of technologies that allow to capture the patient movement and transfer it to the physician. Robot based technologies have shown a very good performance; however, its high costs doing it unimplementable for real in-home rehabilitation programs. Therefore, low-cost technologies such as those based on Kinect and inertial movement unities (IMUs) have shown to be more feasibility and cost-effective option [21].

Telerehabilitation platforms using the Microsoft Kinect sensor are the most common in the state-of-the-art, due to its low price and easy integration with programming technologies [6]. One of the most recognized platforms using it is VirtualRehab[1], a web-based platform that provides a set of games designed for Kinect, which can be used by therapists to prepare a personalized plan of exercises for each patient and the to monitor and assess the progress from a control center. Nevertheless, Kinect-based platforms have some limitations, the first one is that the Kinect sensor must be fixed to a specific location and has a limited range of capture; so, data could be lost if patient move out of this range. Moreover, performance of movement measurements may be low because they depend on the angle of vision of the camera. IMU's based telerehabilitation had shown to be more precise in the estimation of these measurements. However, mapping movements on virtual characters requires extra processing in comparison with those using Kinect. Additional, due that it is required to localize the IMU on any body part, this technology could be unsuitable for using with disabled or specific people [2].

---

[1] http://www.virtualrehab.info.

In the last years, the fusion of information provided for Kinect and IMUs sensors has been proposed [1,20,22]. However, integrating it into end user platforms is still a challenging problem.

3   Overview of Kushkalla Platform

The proposed telerehabilitation platform, named "Kushkalla" (means "together" in Quechua), is devised as a model of high interaction between patient-physician for real-time functional movement rehabilitation. The platform is provided with several clinical tests (e.g. Tinetti and Mini-mental tests) that allow to establish an initial medical condition of patients in a remote way. In order to offer a quantitative analysis of the movement disorders, a scheme of multi-modal motion analysis is introduced by combining a set of wearable inertial sensors and a depth video sensor (Kinect camera). Thus, this information is used to animate two 3D graphical models (avatars) under a virtual environment on a Web browser, providing visual information to support and monitoring therapy sessions by the physicians. In addition, this movement information is stored and used to prepare clinical records, which should be analyzed for constructing personalized therapy sessions, for which a set of graphical tools is also developed on the Web. The emerging technologies introduced in our platform are integrated into a service-oriented architecture (SOA), where each component of the proposed system (hardware/software components) provides services to the other component through several communication protocols over a network. Therefore, the proposed platform is composed of two main components: (a) client applications and (b) cloud component, as is illustrated in Fig. 1.

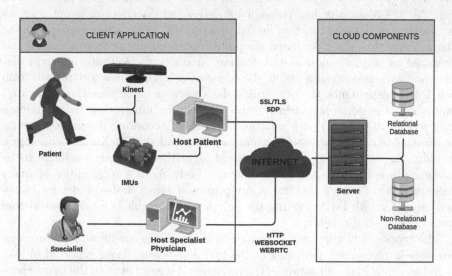

Fig. 1. General framework of Kushkalla: Telerehabilitation platform

3.1   Client Applications

This component was developed to establish the remote interaction between the patient and the physicians. This is divided into two applications, the patient and physician application, respectively. In the patient application, three modules have been integrated: *(1) Motion capture module, (2) Visualization module and (3) Video-assistance module.* While, in the physician application, two additional modules have been developed: *(4) Graphical tools module and (5) Human motion analysis module.*

Motion Capture Module: This module is composed of a set of hardware and software tools, and it was implemented for capturing the patient movements based on both *orientation and position* of the body joints, for which a biomechanical human model is proposed as an articulated rigid-body model. In order to obtain the oriented information of body joints, a set of seven wearable inertial sensors (from XSens technology[2]) was integrated. Each IMU-Xsens sensor (Inertial Measurement Unit) is a combination of 3-axis magnetometer, gyroscope and accelerometer sensors, which are combined and fused to track rapidly orientations changes in 3D. It measures the directions of gravity and magnetic north to provide a stable reference. The fused information of each IMU is carried out by using the Extended Kalman Filter [18]. These sensors were chosen due to reliable performance in medical applications and their highly accurate reported in state-of-art [10,13,18]. On the other hand, this set of inertial sensors is configured as the MTW-awinda Development Kit from Xsens technology, which allows users to take full advantage of the possibilities and the integration of the IMUs-Xsens with your own system. In our case, a software, implemented in C++, was developed to capture body segment orientation in real-time. These data are captured from the MTW-awinda kit, through its driver, which offers different formats for orientation data as rotation angles, quaternion, orientation matrix, among others. From this, the data based on quaternion representation was chosen and organized as a quaternion matrix format, in order to facilitate later calculations and avoids confusion about the order of arbitrary quaternion data from each IMU-sensor. Once the quaternion data were available, another software's component was developed, which is responsible for integrating it into human body model (3D avatar) on a web browser, scaled according to anthropometric measurements of the patient (which are recommended from Xsens technology). In addition, this software contains several algorithms that are available to be configured according to the pre-set human body models (e.g. upper or lower limbs models). Figure 2 illustrates our proposed lower limbs model for movement analysis with IMUs (a) and the animated 3D graphics model over virtual environments on the web (b).

The proposed biomechanical human model and its coordinate reference system were implemented according to the ISB recommendations reported in [25]. Therefore, an initial calibration of the reference systems between the biomechanical and 3D graphic models was also implemented to accurately move the virtual

---

[2] https://www.xsens.com/products/mtw-awinda/.

Fig. 2. Panel (a) illustrates motion capture process based on Xsens technology for extracting the body joints orientation. Panel (b) shows the joints position extracted by kinect sensor.

body models. This algorithm is based on the quaternion algebra [23], allowing the avatar's movement as well as the computing of relevant clinical information extracted from the proposed biomechanical model. This relevant clinical information includes flexion-extension, abduction-adduction and rotation angles of each body segment, their maximums and minimums values, their velocities, among others. Thus, our proposed algorithm also convert from quaternion information of joints of the body model to clinical angle information of each body segment under measurement. Finally, the implemented software is capable of inserting the avatar's movement into the virtual reality scenario and reporting relevant clinical information to the physician application through the web service interface. The information is structured and sent as a JSON (JavaScript Object Notation) format through Websockets technology. All package of our software was written in C++, JavaScript and HTML5.

On the other hand, as it is illustrated in Fig. 2(b), the positions of 3D joints of the patient are obtained by using a Kinect sensor. This device is a low-cost RGB-Depth sensor introduced by Microsoft for human-computer interface applications, which provide images with a resolution of 320×240 pixels and a maximum frequency of 30 Hz, approximately. In our platform, a software package publically available was integrated (OpenNi/NITE[3]) for driving this device. Specifically, the Kinect V1 was used to capture videos based on depth imaging information. For this, the human skeleton is extracted from the displayed silhouette based on a distance map approach [19]. Then, an image preprocessing stage was development to extract fifteen coordinate points, corresponding to the joint position of the body. Likewise, the position of each joint is used to insert the avatar's movements into the virtual reality scenario. This information allows to compute rotation of each body segment as well as to establish their clinical information. For computing quantitative measurements from the captured human movements based on image processing techniques, the well-known OpenFrameworks was included. In the same way, the captured information is structured and sent as a JSON format through Websockets technology to the cloud components.

---

[3] http://openni.ru/files/nite/index.html.

Unlike conventional telerehabilitation systems that are implemented with any of these two motion capture technologies, the motion capture module herein developed is available to fuse the movement information extracted from both modalities, the orientation (from Kinect sensor) and the position of joints (from Inertial sensors), allowing more accurate of the clinic measurements. This fused information is archived by implementing a quaternion-based Kalman Filter algorithm as described in [24]. This algorithm was implemented in OpenCV package and introduced in our software package. Finally, each motion capture strategy can also be used in an independent way according to some functional rehabilitation program.

Visualization System: This module aims to provide several graphical user interfaces such as Web interface, avatar animation, virtual environment and video-assistance elements, as it is shown in Fig. 3. All of them allow a real-time interaction between the patient and the physician during the functional rehabilitation process. This module is responsible for establishing a bidirectional communication of both client applications and cloud components, which were defined in the general platform framework. Once the patient movements are captured and processed, this information is visualized on a Web browser as graphical information in 2-D or 3-D. Thus, this information is available for display on the Web and it can be acceded in a remote way, for which two profiles were developed, the patient and physician. For the patient profile, a Web interface is provided with two avatars under a virtual environment as a therapy scenario. The two avatars represent the patient and the therapy instructor, respectively. The avatar instructor is included to produce different sequences of movement according to personalized rehabilitation program, for instance, physical exercises previously designed by the physician. Basically, the patient and physician profiles allow to control the movements for each avatar. However, unlike the user profile, the physician Web interface includes a monitoring system based on clinical information computed from the aforementioned biomechanical human model.

Computer graphic models, avatar animation, and 3D visualization were developed on a WebGL technology, for which, several software frameworks under open-source philosophy were implemented. The animation and visualization of 3D computer graphics were performed using JavaScript 3D Libraries. Particularly, the ThreeJS framework was implemented, which allows the creation of GPU-accelerated 3D animations using the JavaScript language as part of a website, without relying on proprietary browser plugins. Avatars were designed and constructed in the well-known graphical Motor Blender and exported to WebGL technology. In the case of tempo-spatial signals (2D signals for clinical measurements), these were displayed using an additional javascript package, the canvas.JS. All these graphical components were interconnected through JSON formats and were communicated mean of structured WebSockets.

Video-Assistance Module: In order to establish a real patient-physician interaction, the developed platform is provided with a multimedia resource (audio-video), which allows a direct interaction during the whole rehabilitation plan. In addition, this resource stimulates to patients and their caregiver to perform

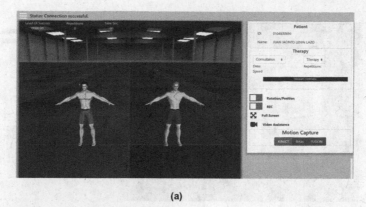

(a)

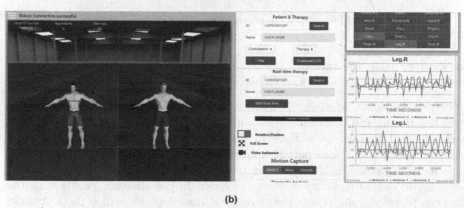

(b)

Fig. 3. Panel (a) illustrates the web interface for patient profile. Panel (b) depicts a screenshot of web interface for Physician Profile.

rehabilitation sessions as a traditional face-to-face therapy. Besides, this resource may be used for caregiver training purposes. For doing that, a videoconference system was implemented, which is based on WebRTC open-source (JavaScript) and it allows to transmit audio/video streams in many-to-many style, allowing setups multiple peer connections to support multi-user connectivity feature. The videoconference system may be activated in anytime between the User and Clinician profiles, as is shown in Fig. 4.

Graphical Tools Module: This module provides a control panel with several graphics resources to manipulate the 3D graphic model (Instructor Avatar) at the (x, y, z) coordinate system. Each body segment from avatar was assigned to a drop-down bar, allowing to manipulate some of its spatial parameters such as rotation angles and x, y, z positions for each joint into the avatar. In general terms, this tool was implemented to construct and storage different personalized rehabilitation programs by the specialist. The software package was written in

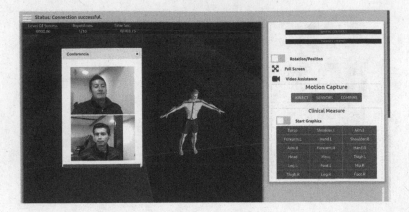

Fig. 4. Figure illustrates a connection through videoconference module

JavaScript, using the three.JS library for WebGL. Therefore, these graphical resources are only available into physician Profile.

Motion Analysis Module: A quantitative analysis of patient movements is essential during the functional rehabilitation. This reveals the performance of each physical therapy as well as it allows to support the diagnosis process. Clinical information from patient movements, which was extracted with capture motion module, is visualized as temporal-spatial signals, in other words, an array of canvas environments was included in the clinician profile with the purpose to graphically report the movement disorders, for which the CanvasJS package was also included in our system. Moreover, the clinician graphically may support his diagnosis reporting. This module allows printing the whole reporting of each exercise session in a .pdf file. Figure 3(b) shows an example of the canvas environment into the physician profile.

3.2 Cloud Components

This component is composed of the servers (each provides a service) to stay heterogeneous information, which was implemented as a service-oriented architecture (SOA). Basically, the cloud contains a web-server, a websocket server, a webRTC (web with Real-Time Communications) server, and relational and non-relational databases. In order to maintain an asynchronous communication among events providing for each server and to unify a single programming language (JavaScript code), our main server is based on NODEJS with an infrastructure of web applications based on Express.JS, Three.JS for WebGL applications, WebSockets and WebRTC. All of them were implemented in JavaScript and used on HTML5 for controlling some graphical interfaces. Each event was packaged as JSON format by channels WebSockets among client/servers. On the other hand, a relational database was created to collect and save the personal information of each patient, which is based on MySql [8]. However, to avoid some delays during the access to information, a non-relational database was used to collect and store the clinical information related to motion analysis, also each patient, which are based on a MongoDB architecture [9], this due to the huge amount of data obtained from each patient and the therapy sessions. All these aforementioned components were integrated into a single web-based platform, called Kushkalla, which can be acceded by the link: https://kushkalla.cedia.org.ec

4 Experimental Evaluation

The performance of the proposed web-based platform depends directly on data acquired by the motion capture system. Thus, clinic information is essential for a reliable estimation of 3D motion at each joint. To evaluate the accuracy in the definition of the clinic measurements (e.g. flexion-extension angles), a comparative analysis was performed using the joint angles data captured from the lower-limb of the same patient by our motion capture module respect to data captured by a camera-based motion system, a well-known gold standard widely used for human motion capture. In this work, the camera-based motion system provides information of the joint angles, which is computed and extracted from a sequence of video by the open-source software "KINOVEA", a semi-automated tracking tool to follow points or trajectories from optical tracking systems[4]. The experiment consists of a sequence of movements defined as follows: the patient starts moving from a stationary position (seating-down), then he takes a step and the leg climbs a stool, as is shown in Fig. 5. In order to measure the flexion-extension angle in the sagittal plane at the knee joint with both capture systems, a set of optical markers are placed on the patient to define some anatomical landmarks according to ISB recommendations [25], in the same way, wearable inertial sensors are placed in the same patient. Therefore, both inertial and video information are recorded together for comparative purpose. The inertial motion capture was configured to capture joint angle data to a rate of 60 Hz. Unlike, KINOVEA captures sequences of videos to a rate of 30 Hz (30 fps). In order to compare the joint angle information a metric was calculated to define curves similarity, based on, the well-known, coefficient of multiple correlation (CMC), which takes values between 0 and 1; with a value of 1 indicating that exact similarity was found. In this case, CMC was computed as presented in [26], and defined as follows:

$$CMC = \sqrt{1 - \frac{\sum_{g=1}^{G}[\sum_{p=1}^{P}\sum_{f=1}^{F}(\theta_{gp}(f) - \bar{\theta}_{gf})^2/GF_g(P-1)]}{\sum_{g=1}^{G}[\sum_{p=1}^{P}\sum_{f=1}^{F}(\theta_{gp}(f) - \bar{\theta}_{g})^2/G(PF_g-1)]}} \tag{1}$$

where θ_{gpf}, is the joint angle at frame f that is measured by method p (our method or Kinovea) at sequence cycle g; $\bar{\theta}_{gf}$ is the mean angle at frame f between angles measured by the two systems for the sequence cycle g:

$$\bar{\theta}_{gf} = \frac{1}{p}\sum_{p=1}^{2}\theta_{gpf} \tag{2}$$

---

[4] https://www.kinovea.org.

$\bar{\theta}_g$ is the grand mean for the sequence cycle g among these two methods:

$$\bar{\theta}_g = \frac{1}{2F} \sum_{p=1}^{2} \sum_{f=1}^{F} Y_{gpf} \tag{3}$$

where $P = 2$ is the number of evaluated methods. $F = 103$ is the total number of frames. G is the number of cycles corresponding to a procedure (trial), which is one cycle for all trials in this evaluation.

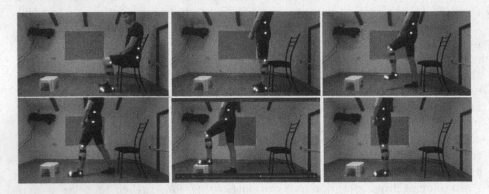

Fig. 5. Sequence of movements (trial) defined to compute the joint angle in sagittal plane using Optical and our fused motion capture. Figure illustrates sequence of movements, which can be viewed from top-left to right frames

In the experiment, a group of 10 normal healthy subjects (age range of 22–27 years, 5 males and 5 females) with no previous history of musculoskeletal problems were evaluated. In order to assess the repeatability of motion data, the subjects were evaluated three times with both the proposed system and optical system using kinovea. The results of this preliminary evaluation report an average of $CMC = 0.98$, approximately.

Figure 6 shows the average of Flexion-Extension vs. (%) Percentage of movements curves obtained for the complete designed circuit evaluated on the group of subjects. Both curves show how our fused motion capture (blue line) approach coincide when the knee-angles are estimated by the optical tracking system (red line) during the different stage of the sequence of movements, receptively.

On the other hand, for the case of ankle and hip Flexion-Extension angles, an average of $CMC = 0.87$ and $CMC = 0.97$ was obtained, respectively. These results reveal that ankle angles measures are more variable when they are captured with our proposed platform. Figure 7(a) shows the average of hip Flexion-Extension angle obtained from the group of subjects used for evaluation. In the same way, Fig. 7(b) reports the average of Ankle Flexion-Extension angles obtained in the experiment.

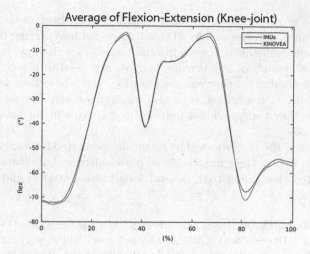

Fig. 6. Average of Knee flexion-extension during the complete sequence of movements (Color figure online)

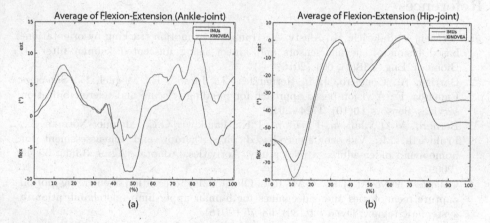

Fig. 7. Panel (a) shows the Average of Ankle flexion-extension during the complete sequence of movements. Panel (b) depicts the average of hip flexion-extension during the same complete sequence of movements

5   Conclusions and Future Works

As seen above in the experimental evaluation section, the use of combined motion capture modalities allows to obtain accurate clinical measures that can be implemented into any telerehabilitation system and used to restore different types of functional disability. This type of technologies are feasible and are acceptable to physicians. The emerging technologies, such as wearable inertial sensor, Kinect sensor, virtual environments, are getting more and more common in our daily routine, and this opens up new possibilities for systems such as the one proposed.

The ease of use is one of the advantages of this system. Besides the integration of computer graphics on the web by 3D avatars model for carrying out the rehabilitation at home, simulating the traditional face-to-face therapy, is a great step forward in users' quality of life, because they do not need to travel, they do not need to wait for treatment, they can decide when and where they want to carry out their rehabilitation sessions. It is also an improvement for medical professionals because they can provide a personalized treatment for several patients at the same time.

As future work, the platform will be integrally evaluated for a specific locomotor disability as well as the effectiveness of personalized rehabilitation programs will be evaluated. For doing that, several longitudinal studies and clinic trials will be performed.

Acknowledgment. This work was partially funded by the Ecuadorian Consortium for Advanced Internet Development (CEDIA) through the CEPRA projects. Specifically, under grants CEPRA-X-2016 project; "Tele-rehabilitation platform for elderly with dementia disorders, based on emerging technologies". [Grant number: X-2016-02].

References

1. Atrsaei, A., Salarieh, H., Alasty, A.: Human arm motion tracking by orientation-based fusion of inertial sensors and kinect using unscented kalman filter. J. Biomech. Eng. **138**(9), 091 (2016)
2. Barriga, A., Conejero, J.M., Hernández, J., Jurado, E., Moguel, E., Sánchez-Figueroa, F.: A vision-based approach for building telecare and telerehabilitation services. Sensors **16**(10), 1724 (2016)
3. Bernard, M.M., Janson, F., Flora, P.K., Faulkner, G.E., Meunier-Norman, L., Fruhwirth, M.: Videoconference-based physiotherapy and tele-assessment for homebound older adults: a pilot study. Activities, Adaptat. Aging **33**(1), 39–48 (2009)
4. Callejas-Cuervo, M., Díaz, G.M., Ruíz-Olaya, A.F.: Integration of emerging motion capture technologies and videogames for human upper-limb telerehabilitation: a systematic review. Dyna **82**(189), 68–75 (2015)
5. Clark, P.G., Dawson, S.J., Scheideman-Miller, C., Post, M.L.: Telerehab: stroke teletherapy and management using two-way interactive video. J. Neurol. Phys. Ther. **26**(2), 87–93 (2002)
6. Da Gama, A., Fallavollita, P., Teichrieb, V., Navab, N.: Motor rehabilitation using kinect: a systematic review. Games Health J. **4**(2), 123–135 (2015)
7. Díaz, I., Gil, J.J., Sánchez, E.: Lower-limb robotic rehabilitation: literature review and challenges. J. Robot. **2011**(i), 1–11 (2011). doi:10.1155/2011/759764
8. DuBois, P.: MySQL Cookbook: Solutions for Database Developers and Administrators. O'Reilly Media Inc., Sebastopol (2014)
9. Edward, S.G., Sabharwal, N.: MongoDB architecture. Practical MongoDB, pp. 95–157. Apress, Berkeley, CA (2015). doi:10.1007/978-1-4842-0647-8_7

10. Helten, T., Muller, M., Seidel, H.P., Theobalt, C.: Real-time body tracking with one depth camera and inertial sensors. In: Proceedings of the IEEE International Conference on Computer Vision, pp. 1105–1112 (2013). doi:10.1109/ICCV.2013. 141

11. Joukov, V., Karg, M., Kulic, D.: Online tracking of the lower body joint angles using IMUs for gait rehabilitation. In: Conference Proceedings of Annual International Conference on the IEEE Engineering in Medicine and Biology Society. IEEE Engineering in Medicine and Biology Society. Annual Conference 2014, pp. 2310–2313 (2014). doi:10.1109/EMBC.2014.6944082

12. Kurillo, G., Koritnik, T., Bajd, T., Bajcsy, R.: Real-time 3D avatars for telerehabilitation in virtual reality. Stud. Health Technol. Inf. **163**, 290–296 (2011). doi:10.3233/978-1-60750-706-2-290

13. Laudanski, A., Brouwer, B., Li, Q.: Measurement of lower limb joint kinematics using inertial sensors during stair ascent and descent in healthy older adults and stroke survivors. J. Healthc. Eng. **4**(4), 555–576 (2013). doi:10.1260/2040-2295.4. 4.555

14. Moffet, H., Tousignant, M., Nadeau, S., Merette, C., Boissy, P., Corriveau, H., Marquis, F., Cabana, F., Ranger, P., Belzile, E.L., Dimentberg, R.: In-home telerehabilitation compared with face-to-face rehabilitation after total knee arthroplasty: a noninferiority randomized controlled trial. J. Bone Joint Surg. **97**(14), 1129–1141 (2015). doi:10.2106/JBJS.N.01066

15. Muñoz-Cardona, J.E., Henao-Gallo, O.A., López-Herrera, J.F.: Sistema de rehabilitación basado en el uso de análisis biomecánico y videojuegos mediante el sensor kinect. Tecno Lógicas (2013)

16. Natis, Y., Schulte, R.: Introduction to service-oriented architecture. Gartner Group, 14 April 2003

17. World Health Organization, et al.: World report on disability. World Health Organization (2011)

18. Roetenberg, D., Luinge, H., Slycke, P.: Xsens MVN: full 6DOF human motion tracking using miniature inertial sensors. Xsens Technologies White Paper, 1–7, January 2009. (2013)

19. Sosa, G.D., Sanchez, J., Francoy, H.: Improved front-view tracking of human skeleton from Kinect data for rehabilitation support in multiple sclerosis. In: Conference Proceedings of the 2015 20th Symposium on Signal Processing, Images and Computer Vision, STSIVA 2015 (2015). doi:10.1109/STSIVA.2015.7330422

20. Spasojević, S., Ilić, T., Milanović, S., Potkonjak, V., Rodić, A., Santos-Victor, J., et al.: Combined vision and wearable sensors-based system for movement analysis in rehabilitation. Methods Inf. Med. **56**(2), 95–111 (2017)

21. Tanaka, K., Parker, J., Baradoy, G., Sheehan, D., Holash, J.R., Katz, L.: A comparison of exergaming interfaces for use in rehabilitation programs and research. Loading **6**(9), 69–81 (2012)

22. Tian, Y., Meng, X., Tao, D., Liu, D., Feng, C.: Upper limb motion tracking with the integration of imu and kinect. Neurocomputing **159**, 207–218 (2015)

23. Vargas-Valencia, L., Elias, A., Rocon, E., Bastos-Filho, T., Frizera, A.: An IMU-to-body alignment method applied to human gait analysis. Sensors **16**(12), 2090 (2016). doi:10.3390/s16122090

24. Wang, L., Zhang, Z., Sun, P.: Quaternion-based Kalman Filter for AHRS using an adaptive-step gradient descent algorithm. Int. J. Adv. Rob. Syst. **12**(9), 1–12 (2015). doi:10.5772/61313

25. Wu, G., Van Der Helm, F.C.T., Veeger, H.E.J., Makhsous, M., Van Roy, P., Anglin, C., Nagels, J., Karduna, A.R., McQuade, K., Wang, X., Werner, F.W., Buchholz, B.: ISB recommendation on definitions of joint coordinate systems of various joints for the reporting of human joint motion - Part II: shoulder, elbow, wrist and hand. J. Biomech. **38**(5), 981–992 (2005). doi:10.1016/j.jbiomech.2004.05.042

26. Zhang, J., Novak, A.C., Brouwer, B., Li, Q.: Concurrent validation of Xsens MVN measurement of lower limb joint angular kinematics. Physiol. Meas. **34**(8), N63–N69 (2013). doi:10.1088/0967-3334/34/8/N63

E-learning

Competences as Services in the Autonomic Cycles of Learning Analytic Tasks for a Smart Classroom

Alexandra González-Eras[1], Omar Buendia[2], Jose Aguilar[1,2(✉)],
Jorge Cordero[1], and Taniana Rodriguez[2]

[1] DCCE, Universidad Técnica Particular de Loja, Loja, Ecuador
{acgonzalez, jmcordero}@utpl.edu.ec
[2] CEMISID, Universidad de Los Andes, Mérida, Venezuela
{omarbuendia, aguilar, taniana}@ula.ve

Abstract. Learning Analytic is a useful tool in the context of the learning process, in order to improve the educational environment. In previous works, we have proposed autonomic cycles of learning Analytic tasks, in order to improve the learning process in smart classrooms. One aspect to be considered by the autonomic cycles is their adaptability to the formation of competences, assuming that a student has competences that must be strengthened during the learning process. In this paper, we propose the utilization of competences to guide the adaptation process of a learning environment. Particularly, we propose the extensions of the autonomic cycles for smart classrooms, using the idea of competences. In this case, we define the competences as a service, to help the autonomic cycles in their processes of adaptation.

Keywords: Learning analytics · Smart classroom · Educational competences · Autonomic cycles

1 Introduction

The dynamism of the competences in the work environment, which establishes the capabilities of a professional in the work, brings complications with the planning of the educational institutions that must handle the appearance of new positions and the growing need for experts in certain areas [1]. As a result, the content of curriculum courses should be reviewed in order to keep up-to-date with skills and knowledge required by the labor market [2, 3].

On the other hand, the Ambient Intelligence (AmI) is based on the new advances in ubiquitous, autonomic and pervasive computing, to allow the interaction of the different components of software and hardware in the environment, to reach global goals. In [4] defines an Ambient Intelligence for education as any space where ubiquitous technology helps the learning process in an unobtrusive manner. Smart Classroom (called SaCI, Salón de Clase Inteligente, for its acronym in Spanish) is the challenge of Ambient Intelligence in this area. Smart Classroom redefines a classroom with the integration of sensor technology, communication technology, artificial intelligence, etc., into classrooms. The idea

© Springer International Publishing AG 2017
R. Valencia-García et al. (Eds.): CITI 2017, CCIS 749, pp. 211–226, 2017.
DOI: 10.1007/978-3-319-67283-0_16

is to exploit the Ambient Intelligence to improve the learning process, considering aspects of the educational domain (e.g., learning styles) and the advances in the information technologies (e.g., augmented reality, ubiquitous computing).

Moreover, the Learning Analytic (LA) is a very important discipline of the artificial intelligence, due to their ability to mine learning data, in order to generate information and knowledge to improve the learning process. LA has emerged fundamental for the optimization of learning environments; for the adaptation of the strategies, resources and tools for teaching to the learning styles and abilities of the students [5]. There are several studies on LA [6, 17], but in general, the utilization of LA has been understood as a process of isolated designing (a task for a specific problem), and the current works do not consider the integration of a set of LA, to solve complex learning problems. Recently, we have integrated LA tasks in the context of smart classrooms, in order to integrate the large quantity of information about the learning processes generated in it [7, 37]. For that, we have proposed the concept of "Autonomic Cycle Of Learning Analysis Tasks" (ACOLAT) in [37], to organize the different types of tasks of Learning Analysis to be applied to this environment. An autonomous cycle is a closed loop of tasks of LA, which supervises constantly the learning process under study, where the multiple LA tasks have different roles: observes the learning process, analyses it, makes decisions.

One main aspect to improve the adaptability of the autonomic cycles is to consider the concept of competences, assuming that a student has competences that must be strengthened during the learning process. In this sense, the autonomic cycles can be guided by learning trajectories that establish states of skills and knowledge to be reached. In this way, the set of LA tasks of the autonomic cycles must use the competences like sources of knowledge (knowledge and skills) and goals (acquisition of these competences), to improve the learning process [18]. In this paper, we propose the extension of the autonomic cycles in order to include the competences as a service to guide the process of adaptation of the smart classrooms.

Thus, the purpose of this research is the definition of services for the management of competences in Autonomic Cycle of LA Tasks, applied to smart classrooms, so that autonomous cycles exploit the information of the competences to improve the learning process. The present work is made up as follows. First, the theoretical aspects of the proposal are presented, then the approach to include the competences in the context of Smart Classrooms is presented, then a case study is presented, from which preliminary results are obtained that validate our approach of Competences as a Services.

2   Related Works

Some studies reveal the importance of the LA techniques to support learning process in ubiquitous environments [10, 12, 13, 16]. In [19] is proposed a framework, which allows capturing and visualizing traces of learning activities, in order to analyze them, enabling learners to define goals and track progress towards these goals. In [20] proposes a dashboard that predicts and visualizes learning outcomes based on grades in the course, time on task and past performance. The environment's feedback is given by the combination of these variables with thresholds to predict the student performance. In contrast, in [21], the authors develop an environment that presents indicators calculated based on self-assessments activities that are part of the online course. In [22] introduces SAM (Student Activity Meter) that provides statistics about student's activity.

There are works about competency management systems for learning environments [8, 9, 11, 14, 15]. In [23] presents a framework for personalizing and adapting MOOCs designed in a collaborative-networked pedagogical approach by identifying participant's competence profile, previous knowledge, and mobile communication preference, to generate matching personalized learning. In [24] introduces CUSP (Course and Unit of Study Portal), a system that uses a set of frameworks for the mapping of learning objectives through ontologies, where the knowledge gaps of the student are identified at a specific time in the Curriculum. In [25] proposes a conceptual approach that aims at supporting a learner-centered learning process in virtual environments, through a self-regulated learning model, a model of competence-based personalization and a LA approach for capturing relevant learner information required by the competence evaluation. There are not previous works about the utilization of the competences in smart classroom, neither to guide autonomic cycles of LA, nor to propose the determination of the competences as a service. In this paper, we propose an approach that considers these aspects.

3 SaCI and LA

In previous works, we have defined a SaCI based on the paradigm of Multi-agent Systems (MAS), called SaCI [4]. SaCI is a smart student-centered classroom, which supports the learning process through collaborative devices and applications, working together to form an intelligent environment in the context of educational learning. SaCI proposes two types of separate agent's frameworks, one to represent the software components of SaCI and other to represent its hardware components. For example, among the main hardware devices are: smart boards, cameras, sensors, etc., among the main software components are: Virtual Learning Environment (VLE), academic system, recommender system of Educational Resources, etc. In [26–28] were developed the middleware based on a MAS, to allow the management of SaCI. This middleware proposes three levels, one for the management of the multi-agents community, another to manage the access to services, applications, etc., and the last one to characterize the different components (software and hardware) of SaCI.

Particularly, in SaCI is generated many data about the learning processes, which can be exploited by its agents to improve the learning process. Thus, SaCI must use LA tasks to extract the knowledge hidden in the data, in order to produce useful information about the students, the learning resources, among other things, which can be used by the agents of SaCI. The components of SaCI provide the data about the learning process. The VLE and the academic system are the main data sources of an educational institution, but SaCI stores a lot of academic information, interaction data, and personal data, among others, which must be used to extract knowledge about the teaching-learning process.

In previous works, we have proposed the utilization of the LA paradigm in SaCI, to integrate artificial intelligence technology in the educational process [6, 7, 29]. For example, in [30] we have proposed to use the business intelligence paradigm to analyze the online tutoring process, based on the data collected on the interactions of students and teachers in a VLE. On the other hand, in [6, 26–28] is presented an extension of the middleware for SaCI, based on the paradigm of cloud computing, which provides services of LA in the cloud. In [31] is presented a paper to identify factors that influence the decision of a student to abandon their studies. Finally, a general framework about how the LA paradigm can be used in SaCI was introduced in [7, 37]. In [37], we have proposed the concept of ACOLAT, to organize the different types of tasks of LAs to be applied to SaCI. An autonomous cycle defines a closed loop of tasks of LA, which constantly supervises the learning process under study. With our concept of ACOLAT, we aspire to solve the complex problems present in a SaCI that require the integration of multiple LA tasks, with different roles.

The use of autonomic cycles to handle the large volume of tasks in SaCI is an efficient methodology, which is executed with a minimum of human intervention and that is capable of handling large amounts of data from SaCI, automatically. It is a supervision cycle of processes based on LA tasks, to permanently improve them. Specifically, the roles of each LA analysis task in the autonomous cycle are: observe the system, analyze the system, and make decisions to improve the learning process. In [37] has been defined the next set of ACOLAT for SaCI:

- ACOLAT 1: it defines the current learning paradigm. In this case, the goal is to define a suitable learning paradigm for a class in a given course based on the data of the students.
- ACOLAT 2: it determines the educational resources for a given student. The goal, in this case, is to identify the ideal educational resources that can be provided to a student in a determinate time.
- ACOLAT 3: it identifies of students with special needs. The goal is to determine students who need more attention and needs.
- ACOLAT 4: it avoids the student desertion. In this case, the goal is to provide a learning process that motives the students, in order to increase their interest to continue their studies.

In this paper, we extend the autonomic cycles, enriched with competences that will be available as a service. These competences will provide knowledge.

4 Competences in SaCI

4.1 Specification of Autonomic Cycle with Competences

The concept of competence is a learning outcomes defined as the knowledge and skills that the students must demonstrate at the end of the educational process [32]. Thus, the main elements of the competences are the skills and knowledge. The knowledge comprises the set of topics and themes that are part of a profession and that the students need to develop, while the skill represents the abilities to use the knowledge in the development of activities [25].

In the learning contexts, we need to define objective competences [3]. Depending on the current objective competence, can be set the knowledge and skill levels required, and with the learner's current knowledge and skill state, ACOLAT can determine the learning trajectory to follow in SaCI (see Fig. 1). Based on this learning trajectory, personalized learning paths and adequate learning resources can be defined by the ACOLAT. In this way, the ACOLAT can be enriched using the learning trajectory defined by the competences. The learning trajectory is used like a source of knowledge for the Autonomic Cycles. Specifically, the knowledge and skills required to fulfill the objective competence is the goal to reach, taking as a starting point the previous competences and skills that the student possesses. The tasks of the Autonomic Cycles must define the strategies, activities, etc. in the learning process to reach the objective competence, and must monitor the evolution of the student in its learning trajectory to modify the learning process, if it is required, to reach the objective competence. In the next section, we are going to extend one of the Autonomic Cycles defined in [37] with the incorporation of competences like sources of knowledge.

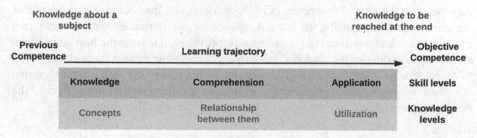

Fig. 1. Learning trajectory to reach an objective competence.

4.2 Autonomic Cycle with Competences

According to [37], an ACOLAT is composed of the next set of tasks:

- Observe the system: This set of tasks must monitor the learning process. Specifically, in our case, some of the information to monitor are the knowledge and skill levels of the students. That means, ACOLAT must define specific LA tasks to determine the current knowledge and skill levels of the students.
- Analyze the system: This set of tasks interprets, understands, diagnoses, among other things, the current situation in the learning process. Specifically, it must determine the evolution of the learning trajectories of the students, to determine the difference between the current competences of the students and the objective competence. Additionally, based on this difference, it is necessary to define the set of strategies and activities to be included in the learning process. All this is carried out by the different LA tasks of the ACOLAT.
- Make decisions to improve the learning process: These tasks impact the dynamic of the learning process because they introduce the strategies and activities in order to reach the objective competence.

Additionally, it includes a general service about the competences, called competences as a service, to support the ACOLAT anytime with information of the competences (required and objective). For testing this extension in the ACOLAT, we are going to consider the ACOLAT defined in [37] "to determine the educational resource for a given student". This ACOLAT is defined by the next set of LA tasks:

1. Classify the students by their scores, participations, etc.
2. Determine the relationship between the classification of the students and the educational resources used.
3. Determine the best educational resource for a given student, according to the previous results and its learning style.
   The ACOLAT extended includes the next task, which describes the competences as a service for the rest of LA tasks of this ACOLAT (see Fig. 2):
4. Competence as a Service: this task gives support to any LA task on the cycle, in order to generate all the knowledge necessary about the competences.

Now, the first task of observation must monitor the students' knowledge and skill levels of the students. The next task analyzes the learning trajectories to determine the gaps between the current competences of the students and the objective competence of the learning process. Finally, the last task defines the appropriate educational resources for a given student, considering the previous information. It defines the best educational resources according to the students' performance, and their current competences. The "Competence as a Service" task gives support to the rest of the tasks, to analyze the information around the competences. It determines the current competences, the objective competence, and the learning trajectories, among other things.

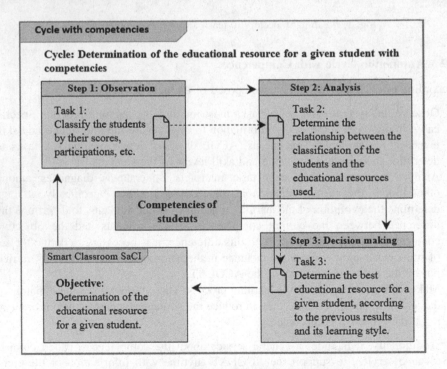

Fig. 2. Autonomic Cycle with Competences task.

4.3   Tasks Description of This Cycle

Step 1: Observation

Task 1: it classifies the students by their scores, participations, etc. In this task, the goal is to establish a ranking of the students according to their performance. For that, it is necessary to observe and monitor the behavior of the students in SaCI. Another aspect that is monitored in this task are the competences of the students, and particularly, the evolution of their knowledge and skills. Now, the task groups the students by their participation using different aspects, such as their scores, participation, but additionally, their current competences. Table 1 shows the description of the task.

Table 1. Description of the task "Classify the students by their scores, participations."

Task name	Classify the students by their scores, participations, competences
Data source	VLE, academic system, etc.
Data analytic techniques	Data mining
Role	Observation

Step 2: Analysis

Task 2: it determines the relationship between the classification of the students and the educational resources used. It is a task for analyzing the matching between the educational resources with the performance of the students, in order to determine the education resource used by the best students (see Table 2). The performance of the students includes the current profile of competences of the student (see the previous task). Additionally, this task analyzes the learning trajectories, in order to determine the gap between the objective competence and the competences of the students. With this information are determined the ideal educational resources.

Table 2. Description of the task "Determine the relationship between the classification of the students and the educational resources used."

Task name	Determine the relationship between the classification of the students and the educational resources used
Data source	Previous results, VLE, repositories of education resources, etc.
Data analytic techniques	Data mining
Role	Analysis

Step 3: Decision making

Task 3: it determines the best educational resources for a given student, according to the previous results and its learning style. The educational resources are selected by evaluating different aspects: the student characteristics (their current profile of competences), the educational resources used by the students with the best scores, the gap between the objective competence and the current competences of the students, among other things. Table 3 shows the general description of the task.

Table 3. Description of the task "Determine the best educational resource for a given student, according to the previous results and its learning style."

Task name	Determine the best educational resource
Data source	Previous results, academic systems, repositories of educational resources, etc.
Data analytic techniques	Data Mining
Role	Decision

Task 4: Competences as a service: This task works as a service for any task in the cycle. Its goal is to generate information and knowledge about the current competences of the students, and particularly, about their evolution on their learning trajectories (see Table 4). It determines the objective competence to be reached.

Table 4. Description of the task "Competences as a service for obtaining knowledge".

Task name	Competences as a service
Data source	Previous results, academic systems, repositories of educational resources, current profile of competences, etc.
Data analytic techniques	Data Mining
Role	Analysis

The Data Model of this autonomic cycle is defined in Fig. 3. We can see the fact table and the dimensions, in order to support the LA tasks of the cycle. The data model considers the variables about the students, the web page, among others, and the results of the LA tasks, such as the preferences of the students on the web, the web browsers actions, etc. Additionally, it includes the information about the competences of the students, and especially, their knowledge and skills (it is included in the "users" dimension).

4.4   Competences as a Service (CaaS)

In this work, we propose to include the management of competences within the autonomic processes, like a task that gives this service for the rest of LA tasks of ACOLAT. This task creates the competences profile of a student, and determine the evolution of the learning trajectory of the students. For that, it uses different sources of information, based on the monitoring and analysis of the learning context, such as the current skills and knowledge of the students, the professional career, among others. Specifically, for the ACOLAT under study, this task provides the next set of services to the "classification of the students" and "determination of the relationship between students and educational resources" LA tasks (see Fig. 4):

- *Create a profile of competences*: this service builds the current competences of a student using two aspects: its skills and knowledge (see Table 5). This task search different sources of information about the student in order to determine his/her its

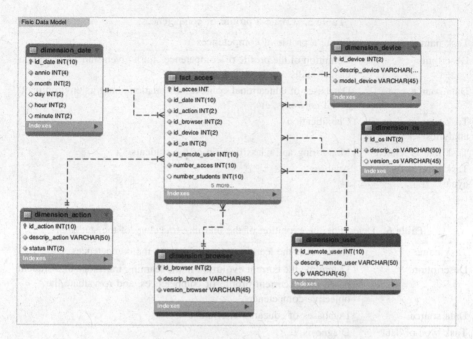

Fig. 3. Data model of the autonomic cycle.

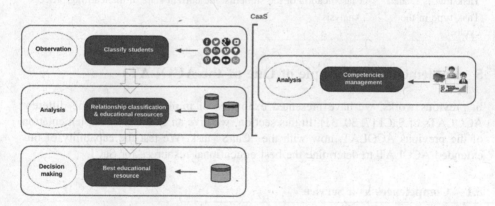

Fig. 4. Autonomic Cycle with Competences as a Service (CaaS)

skills and knowledge. For that, it can use academic sources (where there are information about his/her academic path), but also, it can use information from other sources outside of the educational context (it is important to determine the skills).

- *Determine the evolution of the learning trajectory of the students*: this service determines the current state in the trajectory of formation of the student, considering two aspects: its current competences and the objective competence (see Table 6). Also, this service can determine the objective competence, based on the skills and knowledge that must be reached in a given domain. This service uses different sources, especially from the educational context and professional profiles.

Table 5. Create a profile of competences.

Task name	Create a profile of competences
Description	Definition of the profile of competences for a given student, based on his/her skills and knowledge
Data source	Databases of educational context, information about its environment, social networks, etc.
Task type of data analytics	Classification
Task that is related	Monitoring and Classification of the students
Task type in the cycle	Analysis

Table 6. Determine the evolution of the learning trajectory of the students.

Task name	Analysis of the learning trajectory using the competences
Description	Determine the current evolution in the learning trajectory of a student based on its current profile of competences, and reevaluate the objective competence
Data source	Databases of educational context
Task type of data analytics	Diagnosis
Task that is related	Classification of the students and current state of the learning process
Task type in the cycle	Analysis

5   Implementation Sample of One of the ACOLATs

In previous works, we have presented examples of implementation of the different ACOLATs of SaCI [7, 30, 31]. In this section, we give an example of implementation of the previous ACOLAT, now with the "CaaS" task. We test the capability of this extended ACOLAT to determine the best educational resources for SaCI.

5.1   Competences as a Service

The first task is to determine the learning trajectory to follow. For that, it is required to determine the current profile of competences of the student, and the objective competences. The objective competences is based on the goal of the course. For that, we suppose a vegetarian cooking course, which is described in Table 7.

Now, we need to specify the competences of the students, in order to determine the learning trajectory of each one. Table 8 gives an example of a profile of competences of a student. We see that the student has basic competences.

With this information can be established the learning trajectory, using the profile of competences of a student like the initial state, and the objective competence of the vegetarian cooking course like the state to be reached (see Fig. 5). We can see the skills

Table 7. Vegetarian Cooking course.

Course activities	- Select vegetables and other ingredients (input)
	- Prepare mixture (process)
	- Cooking vegetables according to their characteristics
Content of the virtual course	*Ingredients:* the mechanism to select the vegetables and other required ingredients
	Preparation: the procedure, step by step, to prepare a dish
Objective competences (knowledge)	- Extensive knowledge of vegetables
	- The dishes that can be generated from vegetables
Objective competences (Skill)	- Handling of cooking utensils, so as not to mistreat vegetables
	- Establish the difference between vegetarian dish and any other

Table 8. Example of profile of competences of a student.

Current knowledge	- Basic knowledge of vegetables
Current Skills	- Basic Handling of cooking utensils

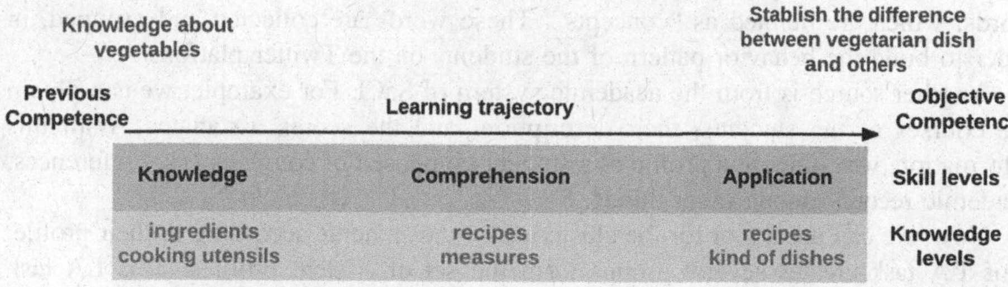

Fig. 5. Learning Trajectory for the case study (source [36]).

and knowledge that must be acquired during the learning process. This acquisition of competences must be carried out evolutionary.

5.2 Classify the Students by their Scores, Participations, etc.

The general procedure of this LA task is:

- To determine the profile of the students.
- To cluster according to their similarities.

In this case, we use different sources of knowledge to determine the profile of each student. One of them are the results of the previous task (it gives the profiles of competences of each student). Other sources are from social LA tasks to discover the profile of the students [33–35]. These tasks analyze the texts left by the students on the Internet, how on the social networks (Twitter, Facebook, etc.), emails, blogs, websites, among others, to determine how they think, act and feel. These tasks apply linguistic analysis, among other things, to infer certain attributes from the unstructured texts written by students on the Internet, about their experiences, thoughts, and answers. The general procedure of these LA tasks is:

- To determine the sources of texts from the Internet to be analyzed.
- To execute the text analysis.

One example of these LA tasks is: suppose that Twitter is the source of information (but it is similar for other sources: Facebook, etc.). The Macro-algorithm is:

1. Capture tweets
2. Filter the captured tweets
3. Generate patterns based on the captured data

The first step captures the tweets. This step requires a program that invokes the API Tweepy API. The second step reduces the number of tweets by filtering them by keywords that allow us to describe student behavior, such as '<student name>', 'preferences', '<course name>'. This allows to get information about what students are doing on social networks, but also things like their interests, etc. Finally, patterns are generated based on the captured data, using the IBM SPSS Text Analytics tool for text mining, which can extract key concepts from unstructured data and group into categories. This tool analyzes all data from the tweets and finds the frequently appeared words, which are defined as "concepts". These words are collected and grouped, in order to build the behavior pattern of the students on the Twitter platform.

Another source is from the academic system of SaCl. For example, we can obtain the courses of the students, their description, and the scores associated. With this information, we compose a profile of a student composed of competences, preferences, academic record, among other things.

Now, we can use a tool for the clustering of the students according to their profile. This LA task creates several groups from the set of student profiles. This LA task provides the source of information for the next LA tasks of our autonomic cycle, which is the centroid of each group that will be analyzed for the next tasks. This centroid describes the main learning characteristics of the students that belong to it. This algorithm must be executed each time an educational period has finished, to update the groups. In this way, the knowledge model is always updated.

5.3 Determine the Relationship Between the Classification of the Students and the Educational Resources

With the centroid of the previous groups, we can use the model of Learning Styles of Felder-Silverman to determine the characteristics of the learning resources required for each one. Specifically, with the information contained in the centroids of the groups (the pattern of preferences, competences, etc.), we determined the Learning Styles of each group; and with this information, we can determine the activities, tools, among other things, that must contain the learning resources to be selected for each group. Figure 6 represents an example of the determination of the learning style for the groups of students, where it is observed that there is a group with 41% of the students with a Sensitive Learning Style, another group of 36% of students with a Reflexive Learning Style, and a group of 23% of students with a Global Learning Style.

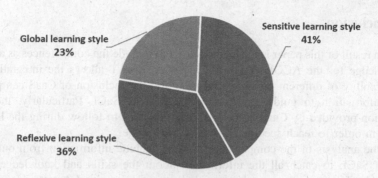

Fig. 6. Learning styles.

With the information of the models of Learning Styles of the students, we define the Educational Resources to be used by SaCI. Specifically, we use the standard LOM (https://standards.ieee.org/develop/wg/LOMWG12.html) to describe the Educational Resources, which defines their interactivity characteristics (exercise, simulation, questionnaire, etc.), among other things. This information is used to match it with the information from the style of learning of each group (centroid). Table 9 shows an example of the Educational Resources recovered by this task. The general procedure of this LA task is:

- To obtain the Learning Styles of the groups of students.
- To match each Learning Style of each group with a set of learning resources.

Table 9. Example of educational resources matched.

Educational resources	Attributes
LO1: Interactive virtual course, where the apprentice must follow the instructions and prepare the requested plate	book, exercises, syllabus, didactical guide
LO2: Digital multimedia content with a catalog of vegetables, classified by edible and non-edible vegetables	video, exercises, evaluations, simulation software

5.4   Determine the Best Educational Resource for a Given Student

This task provides high-quality recommendations of educational resources to students in SaCI, to assist the learning process. This task uses the information extracted in the previous task (the educational resources) and ranks them using knowledge about how the item features meet user needs and preferences, the rating of the items by their classmates, the score obtained in this course by previous similar students, among other things. This last task closes the loop with the agents of SaCI. Specifically, the VLE agent uses these recommendations of learning resources to organize the learning process. The VLE is the main agent that consumes the knowledge generated by the closed loop, but eventually, the recommender system (RS) agents can use this information to improve their searches, or the Student Profile (SP) to update its information, among other agents.

6 Conclusion

The main result of this paper is the methodology to include the competences as a source of knowledge for the ACOLATs of SaCI. An ACOLAT allows the integration and interoperability of different possible LA tasks, and the inclusion of CaaS can provide useful information to guide the learning process of SaCI. Particularly, the main information provided by CaaS is the learning trajectory to follow during the learning process, in order to reach specific skills and knowledge.

For the analysis of the competences, we can include information from outside or inside of SaCI, to catch all the information about the skills and knowledge of the students. In this way, we can mix social data analysis with LA tasks, in order to discover this information.

The results of the extension of one of the ACOLAT indicate that CaaS generates useful knowledge for the SaCI agents. For example, the determination of the appropriate learning resources for the students, to be used by the VLE agent, which defines the appropriate activities to introduce in the learning process of SaCI according to the objective competence to be reached. In previous works, this aspect has not been considered. Future work must extend the rest of ACOLATs because the competences are an important source of knowledge. Other future work must define a generic platform with the techniques and tools required by the CaaS in its tasks.

Acknowledgment. Dr. Aguilar has been partially supported by the Prometeo Project of the Ministry of Higher Education, Science, Technology and Innovation (SENESCYT) of the Republic of Ecuador.

References

1. De Leenheer, P., Christiaens, S., Meersman, R.: Business semantics management: a case study for competency-centric HRM. Comput. Ind. **61**(8), 760–775 (2010)
2. Dorn, J., Pichlmair, M.: A competence management system for universities. In: Proceedings of the European Conference on Information Systems (2009)
3. Malzahn, N., Ziebarth, S., Hoppe, H.: Semi-automatic creation and exploitation of competence ontologies for trend aware profiling, matching and planning. Knowl. Manage. E-Learn. **5**(1), 84–103 (2013)
4. Valdiviezo-Díaz, P., Aguilar, J., Cordero, J., Sánchez, M.: Conceptual design of a smart classroom based on multiagent systems. In: ICAI 2015 International Conference on Artificial Intelligence, pp. 471–477 (2015b)
5. Siemens, G.: Learning analytics: envisioning a research discipline and a domain of practice. In: Proceedings of the 2nd International Conference on Learning Analytics and Knowledge, pp. 4–8 (2012)
6. Aguilar, J., Valdiviezo-Díaz, P.: Learning analytic in a smart classroom to improve the eEducation. In: Proceedings of Fourth International Conference on eDemocracy and eGovernment, pp. 43–50 (2017)

7. Aguilar, J., Valdiviezo, P., Cordero, J., Riofrio, G., Encalada, E.: A general framework for learning analytic in a smart classroom. In: Valencia-García, R., et al. (eds.) Technologies and innovation. Communications Computer and Information Science Series, vol. 658, pp. 214–225. Springer, Cham (2016)

8. Brooks, C., Greer, J., Gutwin, C.: The data-assisted approach to building intelligent technology-enhanced learning environments. In: Larusson, J., White, B. (eds.) Learning Analytics, pp. 123–156. Springer, New York (2014)

9. Cruz-Benito, J., Therón, R., García-Peñalvo, F.J., Lucas, E.P.: Discovering usage behaviors and engagement in an Educational Virtual World. Comput. Hum. Behav. **47**, 18–25 (2015)

10. García-Saiz, D., Zorrilla, M.: E-learning web miner: a data mining application to help instructors involved in virtual courses. In: Educational Data Mining 2011 (2010)

11. Gómez-Aguilar, D.A., Hernández-García, Á., García-Peñalvo, F.J., Therón, R.: Tap into visual analysis of customization of grouping of activities in eLearning. Comput. Hum. Behav. **47**, 60–67 (2015)

12. Hershkovitz, A., Nachmias, R.: Learning about online learning processes and students' motivation through web usage mining. Interdisc. J. E-Learn. Learn. Objects **5**(1), 197–214 (2009)

13. Kalles, D., Pierrakeas, C.: Analyzing student performance in distance learning with genetic algorithms and decision trees. Appl. Artif. Intell. **20**(8), 655–674 (2006)

14. Krumm, A.E., Waddington, R.J., Teasley, S.D., Lonn, S.: A learning management system-based early warning system for academic advising in undergraduate engineering. In: Larusson, J., White, B. (eds.) Learning Analytics, pp. 103–119. Springer, New York (2014)

15. Muñoz-Merino, P.J., Ruipérez-Valiente, J.A., Alario-Hoyos, C., Pérez-Sanagustín, M., Kloos, C.D.: Precise effectiveness strategy for analyzing the effectiveness of students with educational resources and activities in MOOCs. Comput. Hum. Behav. **47**, 108–118 (2015)

16. Papamitsiou, Z.K., Economides, A.A.: Learning analytics and educational data mining in practice: a systematic literature review of empirical evidence. Educ. Technol. Soc. **17**(4), 49–64 (2014)

17. Pardo, A.: Designing learning analytics experiences. In: Larusson, J., White, B. (eds.) Learning analytics, pp. 15–38. Springer, New York (2014)

18. Gonzalez, A., Aguilar, J.: Semantic architecture for the analysis of the academic and occupational profiles based on competences. Contemp. Eng. Sci. **8**(33), 1551–1563 (2015)

19. Verbert, K., Govaerts, S., Duval, E., Santos, J.L., Van Assche, F., Parra, G., Klerkx, J.: Learning dashboards: an overview and future research opportunities. Pers. Ubiquitous Comput. **18**(6), 1499–1514 (2014)

20. Arnold, K.E., Pistilli, M.D.: Course signals at Purdue: Using learning analytics to increase student success. In: Proceedings of the 2nd International Conference on Learning Analytics and Knowledge, pp. 267–270. ACM (2012)

21. Dollár, A., Steif, P.S.: Web-based statics course with learning dashboard for instructors. In: Proceedings of Computers and Advanced Technology in Education (CATE) (2012)

22. Govaerts, S., Verbert, K., Duval, E., Pardo, A.: The student activity meter for awareness and self-reflection. In: CHI 2012 Extended Abstracts on Human Factors in Computing Systems, pp. 869–884. ACM (2012)

23. Teixeira, A., Mota, J., García-Cabot, A., García-Lopéz, E., de-Marcos, L.: A new competence-based approach for personalizing MOOCs in a mobile collaborative and networked environment. RIED Revista Iberoamericana de Educación a Distancia, **19**(1), 143–160 (2016)

24. Gluga, R., Kay, J., Lever, T.: Foundations for modeling university curricula in terms of multiple learning goal sets. IEEE Trans. Learn. Technol. **6**(1), 25–37 (2013)

25. Nussbaumer, A., Hillemann, E.C., Gütl, C., Albert, D.: A competence-based service for supporting self-regulated learning in virtual environments. J. Learn. Anal. **2**(1), 101–133 (2015)
26. Sánchez, M., Aguilar, J., Cordero, J., Valdiviezo-Díaz, P., Barba-Guamán, L., Chamba-Eras, L.: Cloud computing in smart educational environments: application in learning analytics as service. In: Rocha, Á., Correia, A., Adeli, H., Reis, L., Teixeira, M.M. (eds.) New Advances in Information Systems and Technologies. Advances in Intelligent Systems and Computing, vol. 444. Springer, Cham (2016). doi:10.1007/978-3-319-31232-3_94
27. Sánchez, M., Aguilar, J., Cordero, J., Valdiviezo, P.: A smart learning environment based on cloud learning. Int. J. Adv. Inf. Sci. Technol. 39(39), 39–52 (2015a)
28. Sánchez, M., Aguilar, J., Cordero, J., Valdiviezo, P.: Basic features of a reflective middleware for intelligent learning environment in the cloud (IECL). In: 2015 Asia-Pacific Conference on Computer Aided System Engineering, pp. 1–6 (2015b)
29. Aguilar, J., Sánchez, M., Cordero, J., Valdiviezo-Díaz, P., Barba-Guamán, L., Chamba-Eras, L.: Learning analytics tasks as services in smart classrooms. Universal Access in the Information Society (2017)
30. Valdiviezo-Díaz, P., Cordero, J., Reátegui, R., Aguilar, J.: A business intelligence model for online tutoring process. In: Proceedings - Frontiers in Education Conference, FIE, vol. 2015 (2015a). http://doi.org/10.1109/FIE.2015.7344385
31. Riofrío, G., Encalada, E., Aguilar, J.: Learning analytics focused on student behavior. case study: dropout in distance learning institutions. CLEI Electron. J. **20**(1) (2017)
32. Paquette, G.: A competency-based ontology for learning design repositories. Int. J. Adv. Comput. Sci. Appl. **5**(1), 55–62 (2014)
33. De Laat, M., Prinsen, F.R.: Social learning analytics: navigating the changing settings of higher education. Res. Pract. Assess. **9**, 51–60 (2014)
34. Ferguson, R., Shum, S.B.: Social learning analytics: five approaches. In: Proceedings of the 2nd International Conference on Learning Analytics and Knowledge, pp. 23–33 (2012)
35. Shum, S.B., Ferguson, R.: Social learning analytics. Educ. Technol. Soc. **15**(3), 3–26 (2012)
36. Guevara, C., Aguilar, J., González-Eras, A.: The model of adaptive learning objects for virtual environments instanced by the competences. Adv. Sci. Technol. Eng. Syst. J. **2**(3), 345–355 (2017)
37. Aguilar, J., Cordero, J., Buendía, O.: Specification of the autonomic cycles of learning analytic tasks for a smart classroom. J. Educ. Comput. Res. (2017). Accepted for publication

A Cloud-Based Architecture for Robotics Virtual Laboratories

Raquel Gómez-Chabla[1]([⊠]) [iD], Karina Real-Avilés[1,2] [iD],
and Jorge Hidalgo[1] [iD]

[1] Escuela de Ingeniería en Computación e Informática,
Facultad de Ciencias Agrarias, Universidad Agraria del Ecuador,
Av. 25 de Julio y Pio Jaramillo, P.O. Box 09-04-100, Guayaquil, Ecuador
{rgomez,kreal,jhidalgo}@uagraria.edu.ec
[2] Carrera de Ingeniería en Networking y Telecomunicaciones,
Facultad de Ciencias Matemáticas y Físicas, Universidad de Guayaquil,
Salvador Allende entre, 1er Callejón 5 NO,
P.O. Box 09-06-13, Guayaquil, Ecuador
karina.reala@ug.edu.ec

Abstract. Nowadays, robotics plays a very important role in the improvement of the quality of life, because it helps to automate tasks from several fields such as services, production, housing, and education. However, robotics projects in Higher Education require a big investment. To save resources, a big group of students must work on the same project. This fact does not allow students to develop their abilities because they are not involved in all the stages of the project. Thanks to the advance of technology, learning trends such as virtual laboratories have arisen. These laboratories bring advantages such as flexibility, scalability, collaborative tools, and better communication among students. In this work, we propose a three-layer architecture for virtual laboratories which uses basic principles of Cloud computing and virtualization. This platform was used for the development of robotics projects within the Agrarian University of Ecuador. The platform has proven to be creative, modern, and accessible for universities.

Keywords: Robotics · Virtual laboratories · Architecture · Simulators

1 Introduction

Higher education institutions have been contributing to the meaningful learning approach. In this approach, teachers must connect previous knowledge with new knowledge, thus achieving significant learning where all knowledge is connected. It is important to emphasize that this kind of learning allows students to increase their self-esteem and motivation to learn more. To achieve this goal, materials and resources contribute greatly to produce this type of learning [1].

Nowadays, robotics plays a very important role in the improvement of the quality of life, because it helps to automate tasks from several fields such as services, production, housing, and education. Robotics projects in Higher Education require a big investment. To save resources, a big group of students must work on the same project. This fact does not allow students to develop their abilities because they are not

© Springer International Publishing AG 2017
R. Valencia-García et al. (Eds.): CITI 2017, CCIS 749, pp. 227–238, 2017.
DOI: 10.1007/978-3-319-67283-0_17

involved in all the stages of the project. Thanks to the advance of technology, learning trends such as virtual laboratories [2] have arisen. This kind of laboratories has been used for years in countries like Spain. Hence, this country can contribute to the creation of virtual and remote laboratories for science and engineering education [3]. In these laboratories, a computer simulation can be carried out through an Internet communi- cation infrastructure. This software and hardware infrastructure allows users to remotely control real or simulated devices, thus allowing students to perform their practices without being physically present in the laboratory. At the same time, these laboratories bring advantages such as flexibility, scalability, collaborative tools, and better communication among students. Finally, it should be mentioned that these laboratories foster the development of multidisciplinary research groups.

Although virtual laboratories have been widely used in other countries [4], in Ecuador these laboratories are used in disciplines [5, 6] other than robotics. In this sense, the Agrarian University of Ecuador as an Institution of Higher Education seeks to contribute to the scientific and professional community. Therefore, it implemented a virtual laboratory [7] for designing robotic prototypes that satisfy a specific need considering the parameters proposed in class. Thanks to these practices, students obtain valuable tools that will allow them to integrate current knowledge with previous knowledge, thus achieving pedagogical effectiveness, which enables students to develop practical and multidisciplinary skills.

2 Related Works

ICT (Information and Communication Technology) provides education with a tool that enables teachers and students to work collaboratively. The use of software for virtual simulations encourages students to interact with new technologies by improving the teaching-learning process in different fields such as robotics [8]. Furthermore, this software allows students to develop critical thinking to take advantage of current technologies including distributed systems in areas such as chemistry, physics and robotics. At the UNED (University of Distance Education) in Spain, the use of practical laboratories is a key factor in engineering education. Considering the approach followed by this university, i.e. the lack of physical interactions among teachers and students, this university implemented a system for managing remote virtual laboratories [9] to improve the way in which practical tasks are performed. This system provides each student a virtualization-based virtual laboratory that can be accessed through the Internet.

Lab4CE [10] is a remote virtual laboratory that adopts a modular, flexible and distributed architecture that integrates a set of tools and services focused on teachers and students. On the other hand, NetLab [11] is a remote laboratory developed at the University of South Australia that improves the flexibility of access to students and increases their learning experience. The UOC (Open University of Catalonia) implemented a structure of virtual laboratories [12] that integrates technological, strategic and academic resources in a virtual learning environment considering the features that are important for the development of practical activities.

In Ecuador, there are industrial, chemical and physical remote laboratories that are using a methodology [6] based on working with virtual laboratories. This methodology arose to improve the sharing of research results with potential users. On the other hand, there are some initiatives in schools and colleges for the creation of virtual laboratories. For instance, the Educational Unit Lady of the Swan has a physic virtual laboratory [13] where children can perform different academic activities.

There are local and remote virtual laboratories. On the one hand, in local virtual laboratories, resources are executed in a server from which academic resources are downloaded to a personal computer. In this scenario, the virtual laboratory can be only one computer in which there is no communication with the teacher. Even, in this kind of laboratories, students can perform their tasks without Internet access. The main advantage of local virtual laboratories is that students can directly interact with all resources. However, its main disadvantage is that it requires many resources, a physical space, maintenance, and the physical presence of students and teachers. On the other hand, in remote virtual laboratories [9], a remote server executes all different processes. In this scenario, students carry out their practices in a collaborative way, where teachers and other students are involved. Furthermore, although these laboratories do not require a great investment, students cannot interact with real equipment [14]. These laboratories cannot be applied to certain experiments that require specific resources and organization. Furthermore, sometimes the presence of the teacher is required. Another disadvantage is that students do not manipulate real equipment. However, some advantages of remote laboratories are [15] the possibility of performing practices from remote places, the access to different equipment without time restrictions, observation of sessions by many users, reduction of the costs associated with real practical laboratories, simulated processes by means of Software, as well as the possibility of acquiring a better understanding of the hardware. Furthermore, remote laboratories allow disable people to have access to these resources.

Table 1 summarizes the classification of local experimental environments. Real laboratories have physical systems with which people have interaction. These systems allow obtaining real data, however, they require space and maintenance. Regarding local virtual laboratories, these ones have simulated systems. The main advantage of virtual laboratories is that the investment costs are lower than real experimental environments.

Table 1. Classification of local experimental environments.

Type	Description
Real	Laboratories with real physical systems
Virtual	Laboratories with simulated systems

Table 2 summarizes the classification of remote experimental environments. Thanks to remote laboratories, students can perform experiments at the most convenient time for them, thus allowing them to make an efficient use of their time. Furthermore, this kind of systems allows students to perform a wide variety of practices. In remote environments, students can work on software-simulated systems, which make them an ideal tool for experimentation.

Table 2. Classification of remote experimental environments.

Type	Description
Real	Teleoperation of a real systems
Virtual	Remote laboratories with simulated systems

3 Open-Source Tools

3.1 Open-Source Cloud-Based Platforms

There are cloud-based remote laboratories for mechatronics [16] that facilitate the access to a large amount of computing and storage resources. These platforms transform an informatic infrastructure into a private or hybrid cloud [17]. In this work, two open-source platforms were analyzed namely, OpenNebula [18] and Yellow Circle. The first platform allows managing heterogeneous infrastructures of distributed data sources which are integrated at different functionality levels through KVM and VMware [19]. Figure 1 presents the general architecture of these platforms. Such architecture is composed of several interfaces that enable the interaction and management of physical and virtual resources.

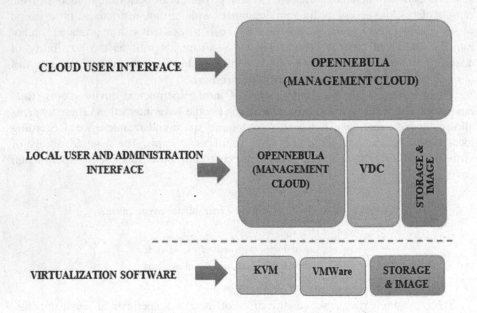

Fig. 1. OpenNebula architecture.

The user interface allows the management of virtual machines (VM), networks and virtual images. There are two kinds of interfaces: end-user interfaces and expert users' management interface. The system interface provides a general perspective of all functionalities given by OpenNebula. Some of these functionalities are: infrastructure customization, and the management of resources such as virtual machines, networks, virtual images, users, nodes and clusters [18].

On the other hand, Yellow Circle is an IT-based platform that provides Cloud computing features for creating learning environments for students and for implementing real-world TI-based infrastructures without having to worry about the associated costs. With this platform, students can create, manage and customize their own virtual datacenter. The number of network jumps between the end user and the Cloud is a key element to evaluate the Cloud performance [20]. Yellow circle generates 19 jumps between the Cloud and the end user, which indicates that this platform has a good performance.

3.2 Free Software Tools for Robotics

Software and hardware play an important role for constructing robots. Hence, it is important to address different requirements of the application which depend on several limitations such as performance and soundness [21]. Generally, the software system of the robot is concurrent, distributed, embedded, real-time and data-intensive. However, due to the increasing complexity of robotics applications, the modularity, reusing, and compatibility are also considered important factors at the moment of selecting the software [22]. In this work, the open-source software for robotics V-REP [22], ROBOTICS-STUDIO [23, 24] and GAZEBO [25] were analyzed. Table 3 presents a general description of the features provided by software above mentioned.

Table 3. Features of open-source software for robotics.

Software	Operating system	License	Programming language	Calculation modules
V-REP	Windows, Linux, MacOS	Commercial license, GNU GPL	C/C++, Python, Java, MATLAB, Octave, Urbi	Kinematics module, dynamics module, collision detection module, mesh-mesh distance calculation module, path/motion planning module
ROBOTICS STUDIO	Windows	CTP	.NET platform, VBasic, C/C++	Visual Programming Language, RDS 3D simulation environment, the Kinect sensor
GAZEBO	Linux	Apache 2.0	Python	ROS Integration, world Modelling, Robot Model Modifications, Programmatic Control

4 Case Study

This section describes a case study that was developed at the Agrarian University of Ecuador, more specifically, in the Computer Science degree. This process involved 50 students from the course Introduction to the Robotics.

Nowadays, there is no a robotics laboratory in this university. This fact makes it difficult the teaching-learning process as students do not have the correct tools to perform the corresponding robotics practices, which demands a great investment for acquiring the required resources. Based on these facts, in this work, we propose a free architecture for implementing robotics virtual laboratories that help students create and test their own robotics design in a cheap and simple way.

From the open-source software for robotics analyzed in the previous section, the Yellow circle platform was selected for implementing the virtual laboratory proposed in this work. The main reason why Yellow circle was selected is that it generates a smaller number of network jumps than OpenNebula, which generates around 30 network jumps. Therefore, a private environment was created to have physical nodes [26] with a wide set of infrastructure services, storage options, 25 operating systems and networks. Among the operating systems and software supported by Yellow Circle are Windows Server, Microsoft SQL Server, Red Hat Enterprise, Linux, Oracle Enterprise, Java Application Server, to mention but a few.

The virtual laboratory implementation was performed in public Cloud environment by Yellow circle. This environment consists of 50 virtual machines with Windows 7. The hardware specification of all virtual machines is a VCPU-4, 8 Gb RAM, 35 Gb storage, and the necessary software for carrying out the robotics practices was based on V-REP [27].

Students can access to the Cloud-based robotics simulator from anywhere with the corresponding user and password for authentication. Once students have logged into the system, they can perform configured practices or create new practices to work in collaboration with other students. Figure 2 shows the Cloud-based architecture for robotics virtual laboratories proposed in this work. This architecture is composed of three layers namely virtual classroom (Web application), Virtual laboratory and the Yellowcress-based technology infrastructure.

The virtual classroom promotes the e-learning process as well as the teacher-student interactions. In this layer, tasks, practice guidelines, and partial and final evaluations are created. Furthermore, it is possible to register all students' activities. Students can access the system from anywhere by using their corresponding username and password. The virtual classroom is related to the virtual laboratory, which represents the students' working area. The virtual laboratory is composed of virtual machines with the software for robotics V-REP. The technological infrastructure of Yellow circle learning platform provides resources such as router, networks, servers, firewalls and load balancers to design virtual laboratories. This environment contributes to the development of students' skills. Figure 3 presents the virtual laboratory with a network where students perform their robotics practices.

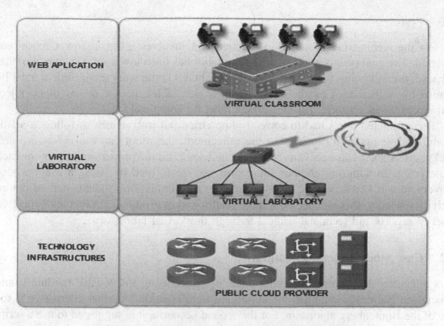

Fig. 2. Technological architecture proposed.

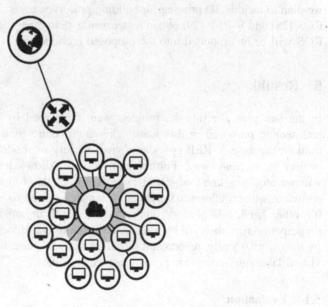

Fig. 3. Virtual laboratory.

4.1   Tests

To test the architecture proposed, a practice that involves a line follower robot was selected. The goal of this practice is that the robot has to follow a set of points. For this purpose, the following parameters were established: (1) the work environment must be limited by walls, i.e., it can be a room with chairs, tables, people or any other object that represent an obstacle; (2) the surface must be completely flat.

The simulated robot had to correctly implement all instructions to follow a set of established points. With regards to the movement, the robot can move forward and backward. Also, it was necessary to define the speed and the proper orientation for each route point. In addition, another simulation was performed by using a robot whose movement was like a person. After completing the simulation, students carried out an activity related to this practice both individually and in groups. Finally, they generated a set of reports and technical manual through the virtual laboratory.

4.2   Case Study Recommendations

It is suggested to perform the route planning tasks using the V-REP module (route generation engine) to establish the initial and final position. Another alternative is the use of the Braitenberg algorithm. For the second scenario, it is suggested to use a script to establish the movements of legs and arms along the route. In future works, more complex robotic designs that include more sensors will be implemented. Furthermore, we plan to include 3D printing for building prototype parts. According to this research, ROS [28] and V-REP [29] obtain better results than other robotics software. Therefore, ROS will be incorporated into the proposed architecture.

5   Results

In the last year, the robotics projects were developed by the students by using the architecture proposed in this work. This architecture motivates critical and creative thinking because V-REP provides a great variety of models that can be used in the project in an easy way. Furthermore, V-REP allows importing XML-based files without requiring knowledge and expertise about this format. Another feature of this software is that it allows using different sensors as well as a graphic visualization. On the other hand, this platform improves the group organization due to the students' participation was observed by teachers concluding that students learn to solve problems by teamwork. Finally, reports and technical manuals generated by students through the virtual laboratory complement the practical activities.

5.1   Evaluation

To evaluate the architecture here proposed, we carry out a survey by using the EVA criteria, in which students evaluated the practical experience and functionalities of V-REP, the virtual laboratory, and the virtual classroom. Table 4 shows all survey questions that were asked to the students that were involved in the case study.

Questions 2, 9, 10 and 11 are focused on measuring usability, question 12 measures interaction, and the rest measure the utility of the architecture. Students rated each question from 1 to 5, where 1 means strongly disagree, 2 disagree, 3 neutral, 4 agree and 5 strongly agree.

The results of the survey (questions 1 to 10) are shown in Fig. 4. Regarding usability, more than 50% of the students think that both the platform and the software V-REP are friendly and easy to use. According to the results obtained from question 12, 76% of the students think that the virtual laboratory makes it easy the interaction, design and programming of the robots. Regarding the availability provided by the virtual laboratory, 82% of the students think that this feature contributes to their academic training. This fact is confirmed by question 5, whose results indicate that the virtual laboratory is very useful. Finally, the time students spent on performing the robotics practice proposed was around 30 min, which is the average time for this kind of practices.

Table 4. Survey questions.

No.	Question
Q1	The environment and tools provided by the virtual laboratory facilitate the design and implementation of robots
Q2	The working platform provided by the virtual laboratory is friendly
Q3	The use of the virtual laboratory improves the learning process during the course Introduction to robotics
Q4	The 24/7 availability of the virtual laboratory helps the academic training
Q5	Indicate the utility of the virtual laboratory
Q6	Indicate the access frequency to the virtual laboratory from the physical laboratory
Q7	Indicate the access frequency to the virtual laboratory from the University
Q8	Indicate the access frequency to the virtual laboratory from home
Q9	The complexity degree of the virtual laboratory is low
Q10	Do you think that the V-REP software is easy to use?
Q11	The time you spent performing the practice was around 30 min
Q12	The virtual laboratory provides features to interact with other students
Q13	Which kind of Internet access do you have to perform the practices?
Q14	Which kind of problems did you find performing the practices?

Figure 5a shows that most students (80%) access to the platform using WIFI, whether from the university or from home (questions 6 and 7). This fact, in conjunction with the shown in Fig. 5b, denotes a decrease in speed access. However, when fiber optics is used, this problem is solved.

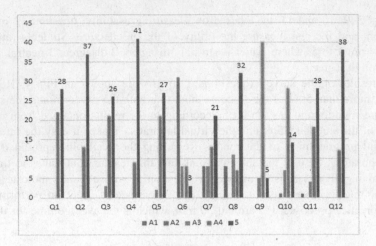

Fig. 4. Survey results.

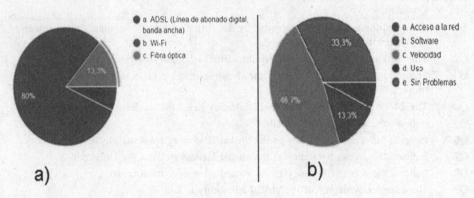

Fig. 5. A graphical representation of (a) types of access and (b) types of problems.

6 Conclusions

The three-layer architecture for virtual laboratories proposed in this work uses basic principles of Cloud computing and virtualization. Thanks to these technologies, the architecture provides features such as fault tolerance, scalability, among others. Therefore, we can conclude that this platform represents a creative, modern, and accessible option for universities, both distance and face-to-face. Using the teaching tools provided by the virtual classroom, the teacher can customize the robotics practices to be developed by the students, thus increasing the students' critical thinking as well as improving teamwork among students. One of the main advantages of this platform is the fact that virtual laboratories are always available. What is more, it has been proven to be easier to use than Gazebo [30].

Current robotics designs used by the students are not so complex. Therefore, as future work, we plan to add to the platform the robotics operating system ROS, which will allow developing better movement simulations thanks to the nodes, tools, libraries, messages definition, services definition, and configurations provided by this software. The implementation of such functionality will allow obtaining a better teleoperation when the simulated model is implemented in real-world scenarios. Finally, we plan to integrate to the platform 3D design functionalities, by means of which students can design and print components of the robotic prototypes.

References

1. Gadzhanov, S., Nafalski, A.: Pedagogical effectiveness of remote laboratories for measurement and control. World Trans. Eng. Technol. Educ. **8**, 162–167 (2010)
2. Tawfik, M., Salzmann, C., Gillet, D., Lowe, D., Saliah-Hassane, H., Sancristobal, E., Castro, M.: Laboratory as a service (LaaS): a model for developing and implementing remote laboratories as modular components. In: 2014 11th International Conference on Remote Engineering and Virtual Instrumentation (REV), pp. 11–20. IEEE (2014)
3. Esquembre, F.: Facilitating the creation of virtual and remote laboratories for science and engineering education. IFAC-PapersOnLine **48**, 49–58 (2015)
4. Gomes, L., Bogosyan, S.: Current trends in remote laboratories. IEEE Trans. Ind. Electron. **56**, 4744–4756 (2009)
5. Stefanovic, M.: The objectives, architectures and effects of distance learning laboratories for industrial engineering education. Comput. Educ. **69**, 250–262 (2013)
6. Vivanco Cruz, L., Salazar, X., Cordero, M.F.: Laboratorio virtual de ciudad y territorio (2014)
7. Kotzer, S., Elran, Y.: Learning and teaching with Moodle-based E-learning environments, combining learning skills and content in the fields of Math and Science & Technology (2012)
8. Stefanovic, M., Tadic, D., Nestic, S., Djordjevic, A.: An assessment of distance learning laboratory objectives for control engineering education. Comput. Appl. Eng. Educ. **23**, 191–202 (2015)
9. Caldas Pinto, J.R., Sä da Costa, J.M.G.: Virtual and remote laboratories for industrial automation e-learning. IFAC Proc. **46**, 286–290 (2013)
10. Broisin, J., Venant, R., Vidal, P.: Lab4CE: a remote laboratory for computer education. Int. J. Artif. Intell. Educ. **27**, 154–180 (2017)
11. Nafalski, A. (1948-): Remote laboratories: developments in electrical engineering: guide through his research outcomes (2012)
12. Prieto-Blazquez, J., Herrera-Joancomarti, J., Guerrero-Roldán, A.-E.: A Virtual Laboratory Structure for Developing Programming Labs. Kassel Univ. Press, Kassel (2009)
13. Liu, D., Valdiviezo-Díaz, P., Riofrio, G., Sun, Y.-M., Barba, R.: Integration of virtual labs into science e-learning. Procedia Comput. Sci. **75**, 95–102 (2015)
14. Coito, F., Palma, L.B.: A remote laboratory environment for blended learning. In: Proceedings of the 1st ACM International Conference on PErvasive Technologies Related to Assistive Environments – PETRA 2008, p. 1. ACM Press, New York (2008)
15. Pitzer, B., Osentoski, S., Jay, G., Crick, C., Jenkins, O.C.: PR2 remote lab: an environment for remote development and experimentation. In: 2012 IEEE International Conference on Robotics and Automation, pp. 3200–3205. IEEE (2012)
16. Han, T., Sim, K.: An ontology-enhanced cloud service discovery system. In: Proceedings of International MultiConference, vol. 1, pp. 17–19 (2010)

17. Rodriguez-Gil, L., Orduna, P., Garcia-Zubia, J., Angulo, I., Lopez-de-Ipina, D.: Graphic technologies for virtual, remote and hybrid laboratories: WebLab-FPGA hybrid lab. In: 2014 11th International Conference on Remote Engineering and Virtual Instrumentation (REV), pp. 163–166. IEEE (2014)
18. Gutiérrez, S., de la Fé Herrero, J., de Armas, Y.: Desarrollo de un driver LXC para opennebula. informaticahabana.cu
19. Varrette, S., Guzek, M., Plugaru, V., Besseron, X., Bouvry, P.: HPC performance and energy-efficiency of Xen, KVM and VMware hypervisors. In: 2013 25th International Symposium on Computer Architecture and High Performance Computing, pp. 89–96. IEEE (2013)
20. Khalid, A., Shahbaz, M., Khan, I.A.: Intelligent decision making for Packet-Processing-Location selection between Cloud and Fog Devices
21. Vahrenkamp, N., Kröhnert, M., Ulbrich, S., Asfour, T., Metta, G., Dillmann, R., Sandini, G.: Simox: a robotics toolbox for simulation, motion and grasp planning. In: Lee, S., Cho, H., Yoon, K.J., Lee, J. (eds.) Intelligent Autonomous Systems 12. Advances in Intelligent Systems and Computing, vol 193, pp. 585–594. Springer, Heidelberg (2013). doi:10.1007/978-3-642-33926-4_55
22. Gherardi, L., Brugali, D.: Modeling and reusing robotic software architectures: the HyperFlex toolchain. In: 2014 IEEE International Conference on Robotics and Automation (ICRA), pp. 6414–6420. IEEE (2014)
23. Tacué, J.J., Tacué, G.: Simulación del Ciclo de Marcha del Robot Bipedo Bioloid en el Entorno Virtual V-REP. In: XVII Congreso Mexicano de Robótica (2015)
24. Rosa, S., Russo, L.O., Bona, B.: Towards a ROS-based autonomous cloud robotics platform for data center monitoring. In: Proceedings of the 2014 IEEE Emerging Technology and Factory Automation (ETFA), pp. 1–8. IEEE (2014)
25. Nogueira, L.: Comparative Analysis Between Gazebo and V-REP Robotic Simulators. dca.fee.unicamp.br
26. Kaur, K., Raj, G.: Comparative analysis of Black Hole attack over Cloud Network using AODV and DSDV. In: Proceedings of the Second International Conference on Computational Science, Engineering and Information Technology, CCSEIT 2012, pp. 706–710. ACM Press, New York (2012)
27. Rohmer, E., Singh, S.P.N., Freese, M.: V-REP: A versatile and scalable robot simulation framework. In: 2013 IEEE/RSJ International Conference on Intelligent Robots and Systems, pp. 1321–1326. IEEE (2013)
28. Barros, J.J.O., dos Santos, V.M.F., da Silva, F.M.T.P.: Bimanual Haptics for humanoid robot teleoperation Using ROS and V-REP. In: 2015 IEEE International Conference on Autonomous Robot Systems and Competitions, pp. 174–179. IEEE (2015)
29. Olivares-Mendez, M.A., Kannan, S., Voos, H.: V-REP and ROS Testbed for Design, Test, and Tuning of a Quadrotor Vision Based Fuzzy Control System for Autonomous Landing (2014)
30. Meyer, J., Sendobry, A., Kohlbrecher, S., Klingauf, U., von Stryk, O.: Comprehensive simulation of quadrotor UAVs using ROS and Gazebo. In: Noda, I., Ando, N., Brugali, D., Kuffner, James J. (eds.) SIMPAR 2012. LNCS, vol. 7628, pp. 400–411. Springer, Heidelberg (2012). doi:10.1007/978-3-642-34327-8_36

A Reference Framework for Empowering the Creation of Projects with Arduino in the Ecuadorian Universities

Raquel Gómez-Chabla(✉) , Maritza Aguirre-Munizaga ,
Teresa Samaniego-Cobo , Jhonny Choez ,
and Néstor Vera-Lucio

Escuela de Ingeniería en Computación e Informática,
Facultad de Ciencias Agrarias, Universidad Agraria del Ecuador,
Av. 25 de Julio y Pio Jaramillo, P.O. BOX 09-04-100, Guayaquil, Ecuador
{rgomez,maguirre,tsamaniego,nvera}@uagraria.edu.ec,
jhonnyjcb@gmail.com

Abstract. There has been a shift in the Higher Education model, especially at the university level, where distance education and remote laboratories for teaching and training have been incorporated. On the other hand, popular interest in robotics, as well as research around this technology, have increased in the last years. In this sense, Arduino is a platform that helps teachers and students to develop robotics-based solutions without a great investment, since its use does not require special robotics labs. Considering these facts, in this work, we present a reference framework that allows the fast development of robotic projects based on Arduino. This framework was used for developing several projects that solve multidisciplinary and real-life problems. Furthermore, this framework was used regardless the students' expertise level in robotics. Considering the students' opinions about the use of the framework, we noted that it helped students to provide solutions for a wide range of problems based on a critical thinking approach.

Keywords: Arduino · Embedded systems · Educational projects · Robotics

1 Introduction

In last years, there has been a shift in the Higher Education model, especially at the university level, where distance education and remote laboratories for teaching and training have been incorporated [1]. The research presented in this work goes from a teaching-centered model to a learning-centered model as it is described in some active methodologies for the formation of competences [2]. Within the framework of university reform, technological innovation cannot be ignored because it represents an outstanding tool for building knowledge and perform distance and flexible learning.

Popular interest in robotics, as well as research on this technology, have increased astonishingly in the last years [3]. In this context, free hardware and software for robot designing are used to provide solutions in domains such as medicine [4], industry [5],

© Springer International Publishing AG 2017
R. Valencia-García et al. (Eds.): CITI 2017, CCIS 749, pp. 239–251, 2017.
DOI: 10.1007/978-3-319-67283-0_18

space exploration [6], and education [7]. Some of the functionalities that these robots can perform are to obtain environmental information and to make tasks based on this data through embedded systems [8].

An embedded system is a general-purpose system that combines hardware and software to perform predefined functions based on specific requirements. Furthermore, this kind of systems is integrated within a larger system. Embedded systems have been applied in contexts such as communication, transport, medicine, home automation, and robotics. Examples of embedded systems are the temperature sensors [9], the Sony Ericsson T68, and the NIOS II processor [10], among others.

The Agricultural University of Ecuador, as an Institution of higher education, has as its main mission the formation of high qualified professionals able to identify current problems from social and industrial contexts. Furthermore, it is important to encourage students to research and apply their knowledge in the development of robotics-based projects that provide solutions for the problems identified, thus promoting their entrepreneurial capacity. Considering the above-discussed facts, we propose a reference framework that promotes the development of educational robotics prototypes focused on solving a specific need or problem. This framework takes as reference the research work presented in [11], where a low-cost educational mobile robot based on Android and Arduino is described. The reference framework was implemented at the Computer Engineering career at the Agricultural University of Ecuador.

There are research works such as the presented in [12], that encourage students to create robotics projects by means of open hardware and software. Furthermore, this type of work helps students to develop competences which will be reflected in their educational level and their future working world. Hence, the framework proposed in this work allows students to design and implement robots. These processes start with the draft of the project as a case study based on free software and hardware, technologies that are being promoted worldwide [13].

To sum up, this work aims to provide students with a framework that allows the fast development of robotic projects based on embedded systems, Arduino [14] and sensors, as well as the low-level hardware management and software accessibility. With regard to teachers, this framework provides them with a useful tool to get the student to develop skills and competences, thus encouraging entrepreneurship, teamwork, leadership and learning.

2 Related Works

In the robotics field, it is interesting to study control algorithms and process automation, which are widely used in teaching tasks. A clear example of robotics technologies that support this task is Arduino, an open-source platform which provides an environment for controlling, simulating and monitoring communication interfaces between a robot and a computer. In this sense, there have been several studies that address the integration of robotics to solve society problems. Some of these works are focused on improving the education. For instance, in [15], authors identify the challenges and analyze several case studies focused on improving the capacities and skills of children with autism using robots. This work emphasizes the importance of integrating robotics into education.

Regarding the integration of robotics into education, the free software plays a very important role since it encourages students to share knowledge that can be improved by other people. This fact is remarked in [16], where authors conclude that open source appropriate technology has marked a milestone in the software society because it allows students to work by using standards that promote open knowledge.

Free software, together with free hardware, allow the development of a wide range of projects. Therefore, it is important to use both technologies in education. For example, the project presented in [17] proposes a distributed laboratory with remote access for the teaching of robotics. This project represents a learning tool for robotics that contributes to the reconstruction of cognitive schemes, while it improves the way in which students acquire knowledge. It is worth noting that free hardware-based modules generated in this project -namely, its specifications and diagrams- are publicly accessible. This research encourages the use of free software and hardware.

On the other hand, in [18], authors evaluate the use of remote laboratories for secondary school science education. This evaluation comprises the conduction of trials addressing the use of remote laboratories that enable students to experience science through carefully designed practices, which includes performing procedures under controlled conditions.

The goal of competence-based education is to guide students to be entrepreneurs and to generate technological solutions, thus establishing a knowledge base for future works. Regarding this fact, in [19], a knowledge-based model for curricular design in Ecuadorian universities is presented. This model, which is based on competences, not only focuses on the concept of learning but also it emphasizes the importance of this kind of projects for supporting learning while specific curricular requirements are fulfilled [20].

There has been proven, that open source platforms and robotics platforms help students to develop their skills and attitudes to solve a real-world problem. For instance, in [21], low-cost printable robots for Education are presented. According to the authors, this project can be easily adapted to other university contexts.

Barcia-Quimí et al. [5] present an Arduino-based project for the automation of a distillation column of packed bed for an ethanol solution. This practical application was developed at the Polytechnic School of the Coast, Ecuador, more specifically, at the chemistry laboratory of the Campus Prosperina. It is worth mentioning that this project uses free hardware and software, and it involves other disciplinary areas. Also, the work presented in [22] proposes the use of an Arduino microcontroller in fields such as physics.

In this section, we carried out a brief review of the related works considering the application of Arduino in several areas and levels. The works mainly emphasize how Arduino is used in education applied to other multidisciplinary areas. This information will allow students who have worked with these hardware and software tools to expand their professional possibilities.

3   Free Hardware and Software

Arduino is an open-source hardware and software platform that is being used in many countries all around the world, including Ecuador. This technology is very useful for both teachers and students who start in the electronics and robotics. Thanks to Arduino, students can develop interactive prototypes whose microcontroller performs different tasks by running a program stored in its memory. This program processes data and interacts with the environment in real time through input and output interfaces. These interfaces allow collecting data, environmental monitoring, sending alarms and controlling the motor, among other activities.

The architecture of Arduino UNO is composed of an ATMEGA controller that is recorded in firmware. This controller is designed to control devices such as servos, sensors, as well as to read their position and execute instructions from the computer. Regarding the Arduino firmware, it can run programs stored in the EEPROM (Electrically Erasable Programmable Read-Only Memory) memory.

4   Case Study

4.1   Design and Implementation of a Robot Architecture

This section describes the design and implementation of the reference framework for developing Arduino-based projects that is proposed in this work. Firstly, we performed an analysis of the components to be used in the prototype. Next, the logic architecture of the robot circuits was designed by using the software Proteus [23]. This software allows simulating the performance of the mechanism in real time. The last task consisted in assembling all components to the Arduino UNO board [24] following the design generated. Regarding the use of the Arduino-based robot, it is controlled by means of a PlayStation 2 videogame controller.

4.2   Robot Morphology

In this work, we present the project Carrobots, which is composed of two cars that interact between them simulating a soccer game. Figure 1 depicts the components of the robotics system. The robots are composed of a microcontroller ATM328 [25], an H-bridge (L293D), motors, LEDs, servomotors, and ultrasonic sensors.

Fig. 1. Morphology of the project Carrobots.

The simulation of each actuator that compose the project was simulated by means of the Proteus Software. This simulation specifies the connection among them, how Arduino UNO pins and actuators are connected, and how the robot circuit was implemented. Some of the circuits that are part of Carrobots are: ATM328 connections, voltage divider and control, H-bridge, as well as the connections of motors, servo-motors, LEDs, and ultrasonic sensors. The architecture of the Carrobots project is presented in Fig. 2. The Arduino UNO board is composed of five main components namely: (1) an ATmega328 microcontroller, which in turn, has 14 digital input/output pins (of which 6 can be used as PWM outputs); (2) a 16 MHz quartz crystal; (3) a power jack; (4) a USB port for data communication; and (5) a reset button. The design of the pins that compose the robot was carried out with Proteus, specifically, by using Arduino libraries.

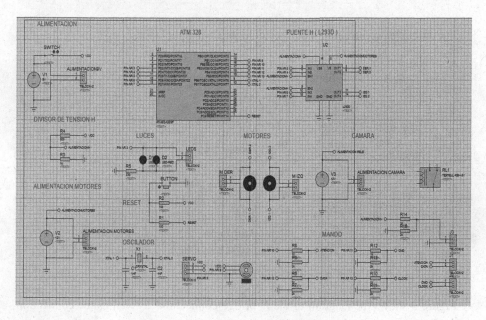

Fig. 2. Architecture of the project Carrobots.

Table 1 describes the connections of the pins used for sending signals and data to the different elements that are part of the robot. The robot has 3.3 and 5 volts ground pins that are used to ensure the correct performance of the actuators and to avoid discharges of energy. Furthermore, a PlayStation 2 wireless lever was used for con-trolling the movement of the robot. This lever uses a voltage divider circuit to avoid that Arduino UNO board burns the receiver. The voltage divider is an electrical circuits configuration that distributes electrical voltages throughout the circuit. This voltage divider is necessary because sometimes it is necessary to obtain higher or lower tension levels. Finally, an H-bridge was used to allow DC motors to run forward or backward.

Table 1. Arduino pins connections.

Arduino pin	Element	Action
3	LEDs	
4	H-Bridge pin 7	Forward
5	H-Bridge pin 2	Backward
6	H-Bridge pin 10	Forward
7	H-Bridge pin 15	Backward
9	Servomotor	
10	Lever handle: attention command	
11	Lever handle: CMD command	
12	Lever handle: Data command	
13	Lever handle: Clock command	

The H-bridge connections are structured as shown in Table 2.

Table 2. H-bridge (L293D) connections.

H-bridge pin	Element
1	H-bridge pin 9
1	H-bridge pin 16
4	Ground pin
4	H-bridge pin 5
4	H-bridge pin 12
4	H-bridge pin 13
11	Left motor
14	Left motor
3	Right motor
6	Right motor

Figure 3 shows the diagram of the H-bridge connections as well as the connection of the motors.

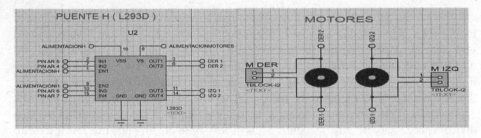

Fig. 3. H-bridge and motors connections.

The project presented in this work also integrates a servomotor, which is a DC motor that helps to determine the position of the robot and it works within predetermined time intervals. The servomotor is composed of an amplifier, a motor, a reduction system, sprockets and a feedback circuit. The operating angle of the servomotor is of 180%. The brown ground wire is connected to the ground pin of Arduino and to the batteries, the 5 v red cable is connected to the pin 1 of the Arduino UNO, and the orange wire is connected to the pin 9 of the Arduino UNO. The LEDs simulates left and right lights of a car. The signal is emitted by pin 3 of the Arduino UNO, the LEDs are connected in series and each of them has two connectors, the longest one is connected to positive and the smaller one to a 330 Ω resistor.

To identify the proximity of an object with respect to the car, an ultrasonic sensor is used. This sensor measures the distance by means of ultrasonic waves. For this purpose, the PIN 9 (TRIG), PIN 8 (ECHO) and the PIN (2) of the Arduino UNO are used. Once the schema of the robot was designed in Proteus, internal connections were made for the operation of the robot.

Test Cases. Once the framework has been implemented, a set of test cases were performed. These test cases included smooth and irregular surfaces, as well as the forward, backward, right, left, and stop commands. Furthermore, the test cases were done with the serial monitor that is included in Arduino. Some test cases were focused on verifying the emission of signals to the Arduino board. When the actions programmed were successfully executed, it was considered that the robot has a good communication. The distance at which the robot could be controlled was up to 15 meters. Regarding the batteries, they had an average duration of one hour. The result was a robot capable of monitoring areas through RF communication and simulating a soccer game.

Considering the above scheme, two robots were implemented as development and learning prototypes in robot technology. The communication speed was acceptable since there were no visible delays by part of the robot in the execution of the instructions.

Recommendations. This project can be improved in several aspects: (1) replacing the use of batteries by a solar panel and a current converter in order to cooperate with environmental protection, (2) increasing the distance range using radiofrequency repeaters, and (3) designing a new architecture that includes robotic applications with Android and Cloud Computing referring to new trends such as the internet of things (IoT) [26]. IoT technology allows internet-connected objects to collect, utilize and share data. The smart home is a popular IoT application where domotic and security concepts are involved, which can be perfectly achieved with Arduino and Android [27].

5 Results

In the last two years, several robotics projects were developed following the framework proposed in this work. It is worth mentioning that some of these projects were adapted to the application domain, the complexity of the project, the sensors to be used, and the expertise level of the student. Furthermore, some projects cover the development of a

Table 3. Projects developed by using our framework.

Expertise level	Project	Sensors	Programming language
Basic	Robotic arm	No	Arduino C/C++
Basic	Traffic light	No	Arduino C/C++
Medium	Smart cars	HC-SR04 Ultrasonic sensors, HC-06 Bluetooth	Arduino C/C++, AppInventor2
Medium	Home automation	HC-05 Bluetooth	Arduino C/C++, AppInventor2
Advanced	Agricultural vehicle	HC-SR04 sensor, temperature sensor, gas sensor, HC-06 Bluetooth	Arduino C/C++, AppInventor2
Advanced	Eco-boat	HC-SR04 ultrasonic sensor, DHT11 temperature and humidity sensor, DS18B20 Water temperature sensor, MQ4 gas sensor, HC-06 Bluetooth	Arduino C/C++, AppInventor2

mobile application to interact with Arduino. Table 3 shows the projects developed at different education levels.

Students with a basic level of expertise in robotics developed a robotic arm and a traffic light by using Arduino C/C++ [28]. These projects allowed them to understand the operation of a microcontroller and to verify the signal sending for specific elements. Students with a medium level of expertise could incorporate the use of sensors and mobile applications through the free tool AppInventor2 [29]. The proposed solutions at this level were more complex. For instance, the smart cars included ultrasonic distance sensors and a mobile application which allowed users to interact with Arduino from their smartphone through Bluetooth. In the other hand, the home automation project included sensors for lighting control, control security alarm in doors and windows, thus contributing to improving the feeling of security and comfort of the user.

Students with an advanced level of expertise developed 2 prototypes that integrated mobile applications. First project consisted in an agricultural vehicle with the ability to identify soil type and plant pepper seeds. These features allow automating daily activities, reducing time and effort, saving resources, and obtaining relevant data about crops. The agricultural vehicle integrates sensors for analyzing the soil type, an HC-SR04 sensor, which incorporates a pair of ultrasound transducers, which in turn were used to measure the distance between the vehicle and other objects. The second project was an Eco-boat that integrates sensors for monitoring the temperature of water and air, and for measuring the pollution level. The sensors used by this project are presented in Fig. 4. Specifically, these sensors are: (a) HC-SR04(a) ultrasonic sensor, (b) DHT11 temperature and humidity sensor, which incorporates an NTC thermistor to obtain temperature metrics, (c) DS18B20 temperature and water sensor, and (d) MQ4 gas sensor, which collects information about the environment. Furthermore, this project integrates a mobile application for controlling the vehicle by means of a Bluetooth HC-06 based module.

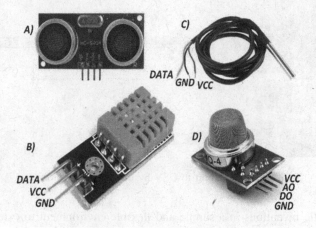

Fig. 4. Eco-boat sensors.

The Eco-boat project required a greater level of expertise on robotics because it integrated the following components: (1) a photocell for the capture of photons in the area, and (2) a servomotor (also known as servo), which is like a DC motor, and which can determine its position within its operating range. Furthermore, this project took advantage of the Android operating system to drive the vehicle, i.e., the smartphone contains a motion sensor that enables executing actions by rotating the mobile device.

Based on the above discussion, AppInventor2 is an easy to learn multiplatform language that allows incorporating several functionalities without requiring a great expertise. For instance, Fig. 5 shows the connection of the application to the Bluetooth module through the address "98:D3:36:00:97:D1". If the connection is successful, the robot can be operated from the mobile device.

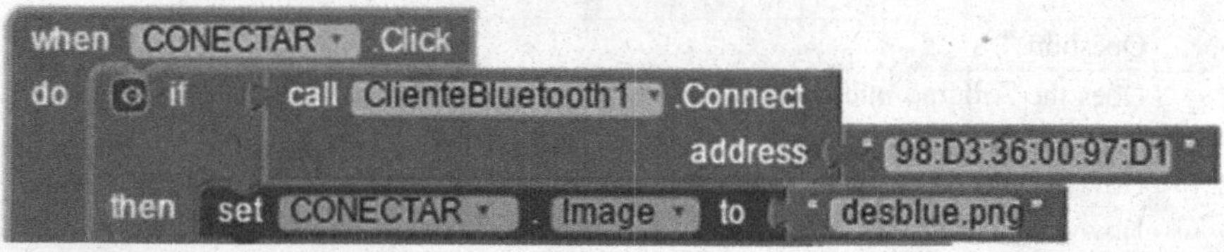

```
when  CONECTAR ▾ .Click
do    ⊙ if      call  ClienteBluetooth1 ▾ .Connect
                            address ( " 98:D3:36:00:97:D1 "
      then   set  CONECTAR ▾ . Image ▾ to (  " desblue.png"
```

Fig. 5. Bluetooth connections from AppInventor2.

Meanwhile, Fig. 6 shows the way to export the data collected into a CSV file, the same one that is generated from the data stored in TinyDB [30], a database system of spatial sensors.

The projects developed by using our framework run on Windows and Android since Arduino and AppInventor2 are cross-platform. This advantage allows educators

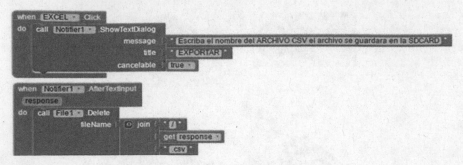

Fig. 6. Data export to CSV by using AppInventor2.

to share didactic inventions in a simple and flexible environment to extend the basic capabilities of the microcontroller, thus achieving projects with useful applications in an educational environment in which there is short time and low economic budget.

5.1 Students Evaluation

A survey was performed to analyze the students experience regarding the development of the Arduino-based projects. Survey questions are presented in Table 4. Each student answered all questions based on a scale running from 1 to 5, being 1 strongly disagree, 2 disagree, 3 neutral, 4 agree, and 5 strongly agree. The objective of this survey is to evaluate the Arduino platform around the compatibility and interaction, reuse of the code, and its application in different areas to automate a specific task.

Figure 7 shows the survey results. As we can see, 72% of the population agree with the assertion that Arduino allows to productively use the time allotted to a project.

Table 4. Survey questions.

No.	Question
Q1	Does the Arduino microcontroller help to productively use the time allotted to the project?
Q2	How do you rate Arduino compatibility with other devices and programs?
Q3	How do you rate the integration of the Arduino board with other market available boards?
Q4	How do you rate the interaction level with Arduino C/C++?
Q5	How do you rate use of open-source in Arduino?
Q6	Do you think Arduino platform is better than closed hardware regarding educational purposes?
Q7	Does Arduino improve the understanding of connections between I/O devices and controllers?
Q8	Could the knowledge acquired by using Arduino be used in future projects?
Q9	Do you recommend the use of Arduino for developing robotics projects?
Q10	How easy do you think Arduino would be integrated in other careers?

Regarding the use of microcontrollers, students mentioned that its use was relatively easy. This fact was due to their previous experience with the C/C++ programming languages. With regards to the interaction level (Q4), most students think the use of Arduino is not complicated. In fact, the available documentation about Arduino helped to understand in an easy way the use of the platform. Finally, it must be noted that most students provided values over 4 regarding all questions. This fact indicates that most students think that Arduino makes it easier the development of robotics projects, while it contributes to the improvement of skills and competences of students.

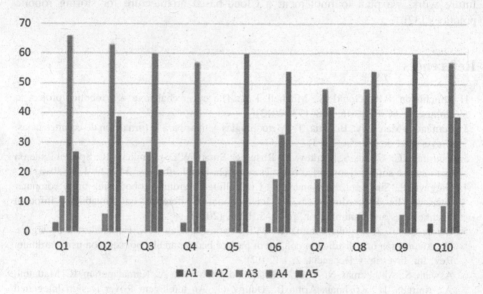

Fig. 7. Survey results.

6 Conclusions

The learning approach based on the development of robotics projects by means of Arduino was adopted to improve the skills and competences of students. Arduino platform is a technology that helps teachers and students to develop robotics project without a great investment since its use does not require robotics labs or special physical spaces. Based on these observations, we agree with other authors [31] that this technology is easy-to-use and provides great benefits such as the ones discussed in [16] [22]. Arduino allows people to use its source code and improve it, as well as to provide new ideas. This advantage allows students to work optimally and understand easily the interaction with the outside world using sensors and actuators.

Along the development of the projects, roles were assigned to each member of the groups. This approach allowed teachers to help students, to detect common problems and to provide timely solutions. The projects were focused on solving real-life problems from different areas, thus providing them a multidisciplinary approach.

The framework here proposed was used in all projects regardless of the expertise level of the students. This framework allowed students to solve multidisciplinary and real-life problems, take decisions, work in group, as well as to acquire the skills and knowledge that will allow them to face future job challenges.

The projects presented in this work involves an autonomous and face-to-face learning. This feature allowed students to develop a critical thinking framework to perform analysis and synthesis tasks, as well as to solve different kinds of problems. Other abilities that students developed are the organization and planning when working in a team, where communication is a critical factor for the success of the project. As future work, we plan to implement a Cloud-based architecture for storing robotic practices [32].

References

1. Minchinton, P.R., Gould, S., Mitchell, R.J.: The cyber challenge – a robotics project to enthuse. IFAC Proc. **46**, 168–173 (2013)
2. Fernández-March, A., Bolonia, T.: Metodologías activas para la formación de competencias. Universidad de Murcia (2005)
3. Pantofaru, C., Chitta, S., Gerkey, B., Rusu, R., Smart, W.D., Vaughan, R.: Special issue on open source software-supported robotics research. Auton. Robots. **34**, 129–131 (2013)
4. Gargava, P., Sindwani, K., Soman, S.: Controlling an arduino robot using brain computer interface. In: Proceedings of 3rd International Conference on Reliability, Infocom Technologies and Optimization, pp. 1–5. IEEE (2014)
5. Barcia-Quimi, A., Aguirre-Munizaga, M.E., León-Munizaga, N., Hernández, L., Vergara, V.: Automation of a distillation column of packed bed for an alcohol solution using arduino. Rev. Int. Investig. y Docencia. **2**, 1 (2017)
6. Aswath, S., Ajithkumar, N., Tilak, C.K., Saboo, N., Suresh, A., Kamalapuram, R., Mattathil, A., Anirudh, H., Krishnan, Arjun B., Udupa, G.: An Intelligent Rover Design Integrated with Humanoid Robot for Alien Planet Exploration. In: Kim, J.-H., Yang, W., Jo, J., Sincak, P., Myung, H. (eds.) Robot Intelligence Technology and Applications 3. AISC, vol. 345, pp. 441–457. Springer, Cham (2015). doi:10.1007/978-3-319-16841-8_41
7. Ishikawa, M., Maruta, I.: Rapid prototyping for control education using arduino and open-source technologies. IFAC Proc. **42**, 317–321 (2010)
8. Palacio, L.G.: Modelo de requisitos para sistemas embebidos (2008)
9. McRoberts, M.: Temperature sensors. In: Beginning Arduino, pp. 279–291. Apress, Berkeley (2010)
10. Tutorial IV: Nios II processor hardware design. In: Rapid Prototyping of Digital Systems, pp. 323–343. Springer, New York (2006)
11. López-Rodríguez, F.M., Cuesta, F.: Andruino-A1: low-cost educational mobile robot based on android and arduino. J. Intell. Robot. Syst. **81**, 63–76 (2016)
12. Díaz Sánchez, J.: Open Hardware y Software, Herramientas para el desarrollo de competencias educativas (2015). http://www.pag.org.mx/index.php/PAG/article/view/504
13. Viseur, R.: From Open Source Software to Open Source Hardware. In: Hammouda, I., Lundell, B., Mikkonen, T., Scacchi, W. (eds.) OSS 2012. IAICT, vol. 378, pp. 286–291. Springer, Heidelberg (2012). doi:10.1007/978-3-642-33442-9_23
14. Drymonitis, A.: Introduction to arduino. In: Digital Electronics for Musicians, pp. 51–96. Apress, Berkeley (2015)

15. Dautenhahn, K.: Roles of Robots in Human Society: Challenges and Case Studies. In: Jacquart, R. (ed.) Building the Information Society. IIFIP, vol. 156, p. 745. Springer, Boston, MA (2004). doi:10.1007/978-1-4020-8157-6_78
16. Pearce, J.M.: The case for open source appropriate technology. Environ. Dev. Sustain. **14**, 425–431 (2012)
17. Caicedo Bravo, E., Bacca Cortés, E.B., Andrés Calvache, B., Evelio Cardona, J., Buitrago, J. A.: Laboratorio distribuido con acceso remoto para la enseñanza de la robótica. Rev. Educ. en Ing. **4**, 51–61 (2009)
18. Lowe, D., Newcombe, P., Stumpers, B.: Evaluation of the use of remote laboratories for secondary school science education. Res. Sci. Educ. **43**, 1197–1219 (2013)
19. Vergara, V., Lagos-Ortiz, K., Aguirre-Munizaga, M., Aviles, M., Medina-Moreira, J., Hidalgo, J., Muñoz-García, A.: Knowledge-Based Model for Curricular Design in Ecuadorian Universities. In: Valencia-García, R., Lagos-Ortiz, K., Alcaraz-Mármol, G., del Cioppo, J., Vera-Lucio, N. (eds.) CITI 2016. CCIS, vol. 658, pp. 14–25. Springer, Cham (2016). doi:10.1007/978-3-319-48024-4_2
20. Rubio, M.Á., Mañoso, C., Romero Zaliz, R., Ángel, P. de M.: Uso de las plataformas LEGO y Arduino en la enseñanza de la programación (2014)
21. Armesto, L., Fuentes-Durá, P., Perry, D.: Low-cost printable robots in education. J. Intell. Robot. Syst. **81**, 5–24 (2016)
22. Galeriu, C.: An Arduino-Controlled Photogate. Phys. Teach. **51**, 156–158 (2013)
23. Wu, F., He, T.: Application of Proteus in Microcontroller Comprehensive Design Projects. In: Zhang T. (eds.) Instrumentation, Measurement, Circuits and Systems. Advances in Intelligent and Soft Computing, vol 127. Springer, Heidelberg (2012)
24. Ramos, E.: Arduino basics. In: Arduino and Kinect Projects, pp. 1–22. Apress, Berkeley (2012)
25. Badamasi, Y.A.: The working principle of an arduino. In: 2014 11th International Conference on Electronics, Computer and Computation (ICECCO), pp. 1–4. IEEE (2014)
26. Skiba, D.J.: The Internet of Things (IoT). Nurs. Educ. Perspect. **34**, 63–64 (2013)
27. Barbon, G., Margolis, M., Palumbo, F., Raimondi, F., Weldin, N.: Taking Arduino to the Internet of Things: The ASIP programming model. Comput. Commun. **89–90**, 128–140 (2016)
28. Warren, J.-D., Adams, J., Molle, H.: Arduino for robotics. In: Arduino Robotics, pp. 51–82. Apress, Berkeley (2011)
29. Tutorials for App Inventor: Anyone Can Build Apps That Impact the World. http://appinventor.mit.edu/explore/ai2/tutorials.html
30. Kim, D.-O., Liu, L., Shin, I.-S., Kim, J.-J., Han, K.-J.: Spatial TinyDB: a spatial sensor database system for the USN environment. Int. J. Distrib. Sens. Netw. **9** (2013). 10.1155/2013/512368
31. Jamieson, P.: Arduino for teaching embedded systems. are computer scientists and engineering educators missing the boat? In: Proceedings FECS, pp. 289–294 (2010)
32. Chao, K.-M., James, A.E., Nanos, A.G., Chen, J.-H., Stan, S.-D., Muntean, I., Figliolini, G., Rea, P., Bouzgarrou, C.B., Vitliemov, P., Cooper, J., van Capelle, J.: Cloud E-learning for mechatronics: CLEM. Futur. Gener. Comput. Syst. **48**, 46–59 (2015)

Ontology Model for the Knowledge Management in the Agricultural Teaching at the UAE

Ana Muñoz-García[1]([✉]) ⓘ, Javier Del Cioppo[2] ⓘ,
and Martha Bucaram-Leverone[2] ⓘ

[1] Los Andes University, Mérida 5101, Venezuela
anamunoz@ula.ve
[2] Agrarian University of Ecuador, Guayaquil 090112, Ecuador
{jdelcioppo,mbucaram}@uagraria.edu.ec

Abstract. This work aims to propose a model for the design and construction of a knowledge management model for agricultural education based on ontologies. It proposes, through the business model identification, the business processes, the intellectual capital and the ontologies, to develop a model which can identify intelligent technological tools based on ontologies. The relationship between each part of the model is shown and explained, and the technological elements that support it arise. From the combination of elements such as: knowledge management, the university as capitalizer of knowledge, the ontology as elements to represent the knowledge and the intelligent technologies as support to all the above, develops the ontological model that leads to the innovative university, where the Milagro campus of the Agrarian University of Ecuador (UAE) is the case of study. This model incorporates the "know-how" of knowledge management, agriculture production and collaborative learning articulated with Information Communication and Technology (ICT) applied to educational management in the agricultural sector. The ontology is developed as the main mechanism to represent knowledge, which defines the meaning of the terms and the language used as well as the relationship between them. The application of this model is expected to structure the technological and knowledge bases required for agriculture teaching.

Keywords: Ontology · Agriculture · Teaching · Business process · Knowledge management

1 Introduction

The history of agricultural systems modeling shows that major contributions have been made by different disciplines, addressing different production systems from field to farms, landscapes, and beyond. In addition, there are excellent examples in which component models from different disciplines have been combined in different ways to produce more comprehensive system models that consider biophysical, socioeconomic, and environmental responses. For example, there are examples where crop, livestock, and economic models have been combined to study farming systems as well as to

© Springer International Publishing AG 2017
R. Valencia-García et al. (Eds.): CITI 2017, CCIS 749, pp. 252–266, 2017.
DOI: 10.1007/978-3-319-67283-0_19

analyze national and global impacts of climate change, policies, or alternative technologies for different purposes. History shows that the development of agricultural system models is still evolving through efforts of an increasing number of research organizations worldwide and through various global efforts demonstrating that researchers in these groups are increasingly interested in contributing to communities of science. However, it is clear that there is a need for a more focused effort to connect these various agricultural systems modeling, database, harmonization and open-access data, and DSS efforts together, so that the scientific resources being invested in these different initiatives will contribute to compatible set of models, data, and platforms to ensure global public goods [24].

The knowledge society has given birth to a new economy based on "know and know-how to do with knowledge" of people and organizations that in the growing challenges of current market behavior require strengthening the construction of that knowledge to be competitive in today's changing world [2]. The knowledge society is considered a new era, leading to changes mainly in educational institutions that must find ways to incorporate technologies into learning processes, to achieve new knowledge [3].

From the combination of elements such as: knowledge management, the university as a capitalizer of knowledge [7], the ontologies as elements to represent the knowledge [5] and the intelligent technologies as support to all the above, the agricultural knowledge model that guides towards the innovative university it developed, where the Milagro campus of the Agrarian University of Ecuador (UAE) is the case of study. This model describes the elements that define the knowledge of an agricultural production unit from the university. The idea of this model is to allow it to incorporate the "know-how" of agricultural knowledge management [14] and collaborative learning [10] articulated with intelligent technology.

An ontology is a formal and explicit specification of a shared conceptualization [6]. It provides a formal representation of structure knowledge in a reusable and sharable way. Ontologies offer common vocabulary with different levels of formality for a domain. Also, they define the semantics of the terms and the relationships between them. The knowledge management process requires determining the structure of the knowledge in order to facilitate the problems solution. The ontology is used as the main mechanism to represent knowledge, to define the meaning of the terms and language used as well as the relationships in the knowledge system of the UAE Milagro campus. The ontology is developed under the methodology Methontology [8].

This research presents a description of the agricultural knowledge management model, then discusses the most relevant investigations of the topic addressed. The following section describes the methodology used for model development and concludes with the ontology model obtained, the conclusions and future research work to be carried out.

2 State of the Art

In [10] summarize the background and current state of agricultural models, methods and data that are used for a range of purposes. It summarizes a history of events that contributed to the evolution of agricultural system modeling. It includes process-based bio-physical models of crops and livestock, statistical models based on historical observations, as well as economic optimization and simulation models at household and regional to global scales. This history is followed by an overview of the characteristics of agricultural systems models and the wide range of purposes that various researchers in different disciplines had when developing and using them. These purposes have led to systems being defined, modeled and studied at a wide range of space and time scales. They also summarize the capabilities and limitations associated with these models, data, and approaches relative to what may be needed for future generation models.

In [9] presents ideas for a new generation of agricultural models and data that could meet the needs of a growing community of end-users exemplified by a set of use cases. They envision new models and knowledge products that could accelerate the innovation process that is needed to achieve the goal of achieving sustainable local, regional and global food security. They identify desirable features for models, and describe some of the potential advances that they envisage for model components and their integration. They also discuss possible advances in model evaluation and strategies for model improvement. They conclude with a multi-pronged implementation strategy that includes more through testing and evaluation of existing models, the development and testing of modular model components and integration, improvements in data management and visualization tools, and development of knowledge-products for end users.

In [16] identify the possible areas of knowledge management intervention in agricultural projects and how they can contribute to the achievement of their impacts. The areas of intervention of the knowledge management that they identified are: research planning, use of knowledge management tools, management of the information generated in the research processes, sharing of research processes, use of information technologies and communication, co-creation of information and knowledge products, and communication for development. At the beginning of each project the implementers carry out a planning involving the immediate partners, with the first results and in a collaborative way with the partners, they develop tools and methodologies that adapt to multiple audiences. Through strategic networks, these products are shared and their use is generated at scale, and the social media are used to make visible the solutions developed.

Based on the needs identified in [10] and [9] and the [16] vision of knowledge management for agricultural projects, this paper develops the knowledge management model for agricultural education using ontologies as a means of representing knowledge.

3   Ontology Model for the Knowledge Management in the Agricultural Teaching at the UAE

The Milagro campus is an academic-research campus with an approximate area of 90 hectares belonging to the Agrarian University of Ecuador in which the degrees of the third level of agronomic engineering, agricultural engineering mention agro-industrial, agricultural economy and the engineering in computation and informatics are imparted. The learning-teaching system is carried out by applying the learning-by-doing methodology as well as project-based learning. This is done through the management of agricultural production in their facilities and the development of projects with the communities.

The Milagro Campus manages three major areas: academic, administrative and production area. In the academic area, they define projects for the learning in the agricultural area and have carried out projects of: horticulture, fruit-growing and irrigation systems, as well as crops of tomato, cucumber, watermelon and melon. In the productive area, projects are developed on productive land of short-cycle crops: rice, soy, beans cotton and maize; and perennial and semi-permanent crops are developed such as cocoa, African palm and sugarcane. The administrative area supports production activities such as the administration and sale of processed foods from the cultivation projects. The learning process is carried out according to the production process and then the teaching is replicated by students in their practices with the community.

The methodology used to develop the model proposed in this work was adapted from the presented in [11] and [12]. The structure of this model is composed of three layers: business model and processes, knowledge management, and knowledge management technologies. These layers are represented by means of ontological models. The business model describes how the organization creates, delivers, and captures value [14]. This concept of business model is used to describe the business model ontology of Milagro campus, as shown below.

It is important to note that the Ontology for Knowledge Management of the Milagro campus was developed with the methodology Methontology [7] and its implementation was carried out with the Protégé-OWL ontology editor.

3.1 Business Model Ontology of Milagro Campus

Osterwalder [15] defines the business model as an abstract representation of the business logic of an organization through an ontology for the business model, consisting of three large blocks, a block representing the resources, activities and third parties that act as allies, necessary to produce and maintain the value offered. A second group of blocks represent the revenue and cost reflection of the previous set, and a third block of customer-related activities.

This model is aimed at students, professors, researchers and workers of the Milagro campus, as well as surrounding communities. The value proposition is the creation of an agricultural knowledge management model that guides innovation in the Milagro campus. This model will indicate know-how through the processes of knowledge management, and support the generation of new learning and innovation. Key activities are defined in the following areas:

- **Academic.** The activities of teaching learning, and research and innovation.
  - *Teaching learning* is formed by activities such as academic planning, planning and project management, creation of learning objects (supports to the theoretical and practical classes) and evaluation.
  - *Research and innovation* are all activities required before starting the production project of learning activities.

- **Agriculture**, the different components of the agricultural value chain [10] are:
  - *Technology Inputs*. This process describes the technological solutions or applications that support agriculture process. Physical: Seeds, fertilizer, water, fuel, weed, insect and disease control. Information: Precision farming (Yield mapping, UAVs, on-the-go sensors, diagnostics and analytic packages).
  - *Crop Production*: Equipment (Tillage, irrigation, harvesting, storage, etc.). Management Strategies (conservation tillage, crop rotation, integrated pest management). Marketing of production.
  - *Animal Production*: Livestock and aquaculture: genetics, precision feedings, nutrition, healthcare, animal wellness, diagnostics, drug delivery.
  - *Transformation*: Processing: carbohydrate, protein, fiber, meat-milk-eggs, food and feeds safety, logistics, bioenergy, biomaterials.
  - *Distribution*: Production, packaging, transportation, distribution, product development, supply chain management, traceability, retail.
  - *Consumption*: Food, Feed, Fiber, Fuel.

The business model ontology is show in the Fig. 1.

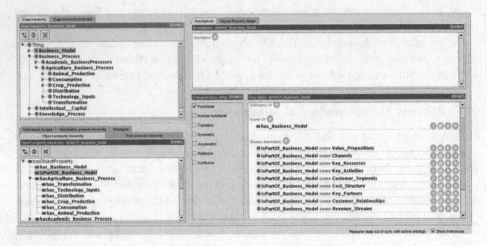

Fig. 1. Business model ontology of milagro campus.

3.2 Business Process of Milagro Campus

This section describes each of the business processes of the Milagro campus, obtained from the key activities of the business model. These business processes are modeled from the ontologies as shown below.

- **Academic Process.** In this process, as shown in Fig. 2, the activities of teaching learning, and research and innovation are described, which support the projects that develop in each lapse that make up the careers. This process is supported by project-based learning methodologies and learning by doing. It is divided into two major threads: teaching learning, and research and innovation. The learning sub-process is formed by the activities of academic planning, project planning, creation of learning objects (supports to the theoretical and practical classes) and evaluation. The research, development and innovation sub-process is formed by the activities such as promotion work, creation of new products and services, publications, management of research lines, thesis of degree.

- **Agriculture Production Processes.** The different components of the agricultural value chain [10], is shown in the Fig. 2.

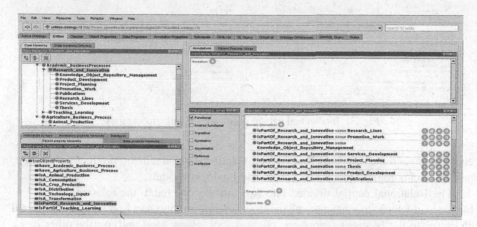

Fig. 2. Ontology of academic and agriculture process at the milagros campus

3.3 Knowledge Management Model

Davenport and Prusac [2] consider knowledge as a fundamental asset for higher education, and they say that knowledge management is a business model that uses knowledge as the organization's asset to achieve competitive advantage, as well as the tools of knowledge management support and promote evaluation, utilization, creation, expansion, protection, Division and application of the intellectual capital of the organization. From this vision and using the Model Euroforum [1] to represent the intellectual capital of an organization, the Fig. 3 shows the model of intellectual capital and its structure for the Milagro campus.

This model defines the elements of knowledge that create value and describe how the organization behaves.

Human capital is formed by professors, students and researchers from an academic perspective. Within the productive frame there are roles such as: Experts in food, veterinarians, livestock experts and experts in agricultural and livestock management. These roles are to be complemented by the sense of belonging and learning to do collaborative work within the organization.

The Structural capital is formed by the organizational capital, associated with the structural scope of the designs, processes and culture of the Organization; such as the business model, organizational memory and systems that support the organization. And the technological capital linked with the effort in R&D, the use of technological

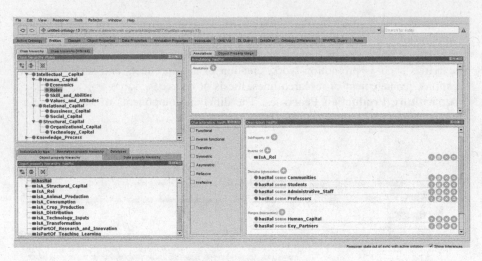

Fig. 3. Intellectual capital ontology for milagro campus

endowment and the results of R&D in organizational management, product technology, process technologies, social innovation and business models.

The Relational capital divided into two, on the one hand, the relational capital of business in which they have to see the flows of information and knowledge of external character to the business (suppliers, clients-users, allies, etc.) and, on the other hand, social relational capital, which has to do with relationships outside the business sphere (social commitment, public image, reputation, prestige, social action, etc.). All of them allow us to obtain a panoramic view of the intangible assets that the miracle extension possesses, thus generating the information necessary for the decision-making.

The knowledge processes are composed of a group of strategic processes that occur cyclically [13]. The knowledge creation cycle, covers all phases where it can intervene knowledge management tools, allowing a total link between them. Designed knowledge creation cycle is based on the following phases.

- *Knowledge Identification*. Determine the knowledge necessary for the operation of the knowledge processes and ensure the conformity of products or services. The knowledge audit should be at this stage. Knowledge management has various tools to identify knowledge: directories and yellow pages experts, knowledge maps, topographies of knowledge, assets of knowledge maps, maps of sources of knowledge, which are used interchangeably depending on the objectives, but all with results proven in different contexts.
- *Knowledge Acquisition*. It is performed through the fault log and successes, capturing undocumented experiences, improvement in processes, products and services. As well as the acquisition of external knowledge that should be sought through existing elements as external sources: standards, academic institutions, conferences, knowledge compiled with customers or suppliers. Information and document management systems are used for this purpose.

- *Knowledge Maintenance.* This lesson-learned system can be used for example. Threads are inside this process:
- *Knowledge Use.* Through creation of knowledge platforms, intranets, portal, scenarios, among other tools.
- *Knowledge Retention.* This can be done through a document management system to support the work of the organization and facilitate an inquiry at the necessary time.
- *Knowledge Measurement.* The process of evaluation and measurement of knowledge can be determined through various parameters established by the organization.
- *Knowledge Distribution (Share).* Produce measures to make available the knowledge to those who need it at the right time (for example, with communities of practice).

3.4 Technology Architecture for Knowledge Management Model of Milagro Campus

From the definition of the business model, business processes, the model of intellectual capital and knowledge management processes the technological architecture that supports it is defined. Figure 4 shows the architecture and its components.

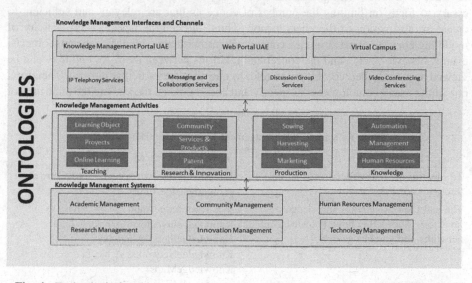

Fig. 4. Technological architecture to management knowledge model for milagro campus.

Interfaces and channels are the elements that provide the input interface to the knowledge management of the Milagro campus and are the Web and Knowledge Portals and Virtual Campus. Business processes are those that represent key activities for knowledge management. And the knowledge management layer in which academic management, communities, human resources, research and innovation and technology management are carried out, which in turn are supported by elements such as:

- Content management systems to manage the content and Knowledge Portal, as well as wiki, blogs and manage users (yellow pages and white pages to find out who knows what and for collaborative work).
- Learning Management Systems (LMS) that will support the management of watercourses. The management systems of learning contents (LCMS) for the creation, reusability, location, development and management of learning content.
- Systems of document management will enable to carry out the registration and tracking of documents generated during the academic activities and production of Milagro Campus. System of registration activities indicating what makes who, how and with what tools to record experiences.
- Organizational memory that holds elements that make up the organization, workflow, and projects that are being carried out. A first version of this report for projects is shown below, developed through a database.

All these elements are linked and target by the ontologies represented as shown below.

3.5 Ontology of Knowledge Management of Milagro Campus, UAE

In order to produce some phenomenon or part of the world, called domain, it is necessary to focus on limiting the number of concepts that are relevant and sufficient to create an abstraction of the phenomenon. Thus, the central aspect of any activity of modeling consists of performing a conceptualization; that is, identify concepts (objects, events, behaviors, etc.) and the conceptual relations between them An ontology can be viewed as a controlled vocabulary to refer to entities of a particular domain. Therefore, one of the uses of ontologies is to specify and communicate the knowledge of an area of

Table 1. Knowledge management process of milagro campus

Natural language	First-order predicate logic (FOPL)
To identify the knowledge is carried out through knowledge audit	$\forall$ x IdentifyKnowledge(x) = > isCarriedOut (x, KnowledgeAudit)
The audit knowledge has knowledge inventory, knowledge flow, knowledge networks and knowledge map	$\forall$ x KnowledgeAudit (x) = > has (x, KnowledgeInventory) $\wedge$ has (x, KnowledgeFlow) $\wedge$ has (x, KnowledgeNetworks) $\wedge$ has (x, KnowledgeMaps)
The knowledge inventory has role and has business process	$\forall$ x KnowedgeInventory (x) => has (x, BusinessProcess) $\wedge$ has (x, Rol)
The knowledge flow has a knowledge transfer that is shared between knowledge networks	$\forall$ x KnowledgeFlow(x) => has (x, KnowledgeTransfer) $\wedge$ has (x, Rol) $\wedge$ has (x, KnowledgeNetworks)
A knowledge network is defining who does what within the Organization, and who knows what each process	$\forall$ x ReddeConocimiento (x) => isDefined (x, BusinessProcess) $\wedge$ isIntegrated (x, Rol) $\wedge$ isRegistered (x, YellowPagesRepository)

(continued)

Table 1. (*continued*)

Natural language	First-order predicate logic (FOPL)
The knowledge acquisition is to record by not documented experiences in the practice log repository	∀ x KnowledgeAdquisition (x) => isA (x, NoDocumentedExperience) ∧ isRegistered (x, PracticeLogRepository)
Not documented experiences are videos and results of meetings, and learning	∀ x NoDocumentedExperience (x) => isA (x, Video) V isA (x, ResultofMeeting) V isA (x, ResultofLearning)
Knowledge Maintenance is the knowledge use, is a knowledge retention, or is a knowledge measurement	∀ x KnowledgeMaintenance (x) => isA (x, KnowledgeUse) V isA (x, KnowledgeRetention) V isA (x, KnowledgeMeasurement)
The knowledge retention has learned lessons and this are registered in knowledge repository	∀ x KnowledgeRetention (x) => have (x, LearnedLesson) V registeredIn (x, KnowledgeRepository)
The knowledge use is an application platform or is a storage repository or is an artificial intelligence technologies or is a network technologies	∀ x KnowledgeUse (x) => isA (x, ApplicationPlatform) V isA (x, StorageRepository) V isA (x, ArtificialIntelligenceTechnology) V isA (x, NetworkTecnologies)
Application platform is a content learning management platform or user management platform or content management platform or knowledge management platform or online learning platform	∀ x ApplicationPlatform (x) => isA (x, ContentManagementLearningPlatform) V isA (x, UserManagementPlatform) V isA (x, KnowledgeManagementPlaform) V isA (x, OnlineLearningPlatform)
Storage Repository is a knowledge repository or an organizational memory repository or a practice log repository or a yellow pages repository	∀ x StorageRepository (x) => isA (x, KnowledgeRepository) V isA (x, OrganizationalMemoryRepository) V isA (x, PracticeLogRepository) V isA (x, YellowPagesRepository)
Network Technologies is an extranet or a Portal or an Intranet or an Internet	∀ x NetworkTecnologies (x) => isA (x, Extranet) V isA (x, Portal) V isA (x, Intranet) V isA (x, Internet)
Artificial Intelligence Technologies is an expert system or a semantic web or a machine learning or an ontology or a multiagent systems or a knowledge based systems	∀ x ArtificialIntelligencetechnologies (x) => isA (x, ExpertSystem) V isA (x, SemanticWeb) V isA (x, MachineLearning) V isA (x, Ontology) V isA (x, MultiAgentSystem) V isA (x, KnowledgeBasedSystem)
Knowledge retention is an organizational memory	∀ x KnowledgeRetention (x) => isA (x, OrganizationalMemory)
Knowledge measurement has measurement parameters	∀ x KnowledgeMeasurement (x) => have (x, MeasurementParameters)
The knowledge distribution is a community of practice, or a forum or a training or an event	∀ x KnowledgeDistribution (x) => isA (x, CommunityofPractice) V isA (x, Forum) V isA (x, Training) V isA (x, Event)

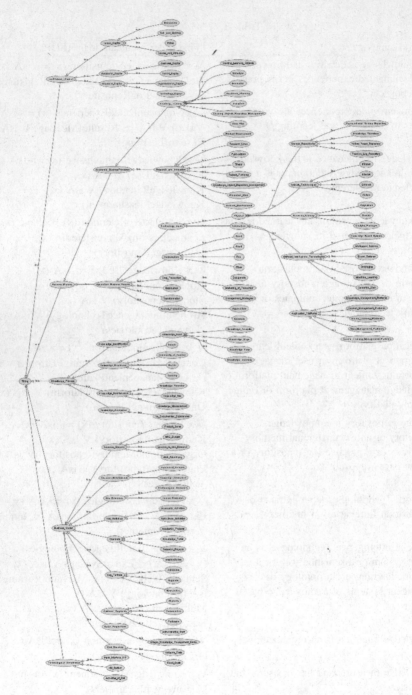

Fig. 5. Ontology for the knowledge management in the teaching of agricultural sciences of milagro campus

knowledge, generically, that are very useful to structure and define the meaning of the terms. The ontologies to represent knowledge, require the following components [6]: concepts, relations, functions, instances and axioms. If you specify the components and their relationships of a field of knowledge following a strict formalism encoded in a computer language (no programming, but description), then it is an ontology.

The following Table 1 describes formally the knowledge management processes at Milagro Campus. These processes are shown in the form of sentences in natural language and first-order predicate logic, which allows the formalization of the axioms that will give support to the reasoning to find new knowledge.

Using the concepts, properties, relations and axioms defined above we find below the ontological model for the knowledge management of Milagro Campus UAE, using Protégé OWL extension, which allows its representation and validation. Figure 5 shows the Ontology for the Knowledge Management in the Teaching of Agricultural Sciences of Milagro Campus and Fig. 6 shows the class hierarchy and object property of Ontology.

The ontology is classified using the Fact++ reasoner, which is executed as part of the Protege OWL. The classification of the ontology in OWL 2 is supported by the Manchester Syntax (Fig. 7)[1].

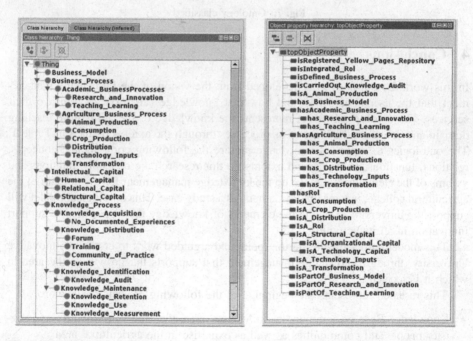

Fig. 6. Class hierarchy and object property of ontology for the knowledge management in the teaching of agricultural sciences of milagro campus

---

[1] https://www.w3.org/TR/owl2-manchester-syntax/.

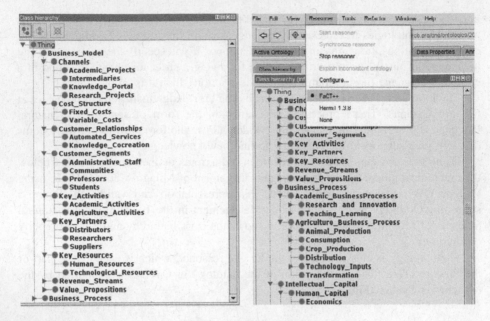

Fig. 7. Ontology classified

4   Conclusions

In this work the ontology was developed from the vision of the knowledge management that the user should use, and how that knowledge can serve to improve their services. The ontological model represents the knowledge of the agriculture teaching domain and describes the logic of its processes through the axioms defined in Table 1. The ontologies to represent knowledge require the following components: concepts, relations, functions, instances and axioms. In this research are concepts, relations and axioms of the elements that make up the knowledge management for the domain of the agricultural college, using Milagro Campus as a study case. This ontological model will support the university to define the elements of knowledge that it requires to support innovation in all its activities.

This model represents the starting point and a guided work to create an innovative University, through knowledge management that supports the growth of the area in which it is located.

This research represents the beginning of the following projects to develop:

- Knowledge Base of communities in Milagro area, that allows to identify and register people and communities as well as expertise in the agricultural area.
- Organizational Projects Memory that are carried out between the communities and the University to perform logging practices and measure the quality of them. This project is starting.

- Portal of knowledge for agricultural production in Milagro area, this portal manages the repositories of knowledge, ontologies and practices between the University and the community.
- Integration ontologies for the Knowledge Management Model.

Ontologies are used in bio-health, e-science, and Semantic Web applications to capture the meaning of terms. Designing ontologies is a non-trivial task that requires sophisticated tool and service support. One of the most important services for logic based ontologies. In this work, through the axioms proposed in Table 1, the formal logic of the Milagro Campus knowledge model is represented.

The growing presence of ICTs in agriculture chains tends to generate automation and efficiency, either through the use of machinery and equipment, or in the knowledge fields, to facilitate the productivity of crops. Its main objective in agriculture is to support the improvement of processes and products, together with the intermediation of the people who develop and operate. Technology may be within the reach of everyone, but it is necessary to have the adequate training to use it, without forgetting the capabilities of people. That is why this ontological model of knowledge management describes the processes and intelligent technologies that support teaching in the agricultural area from vision learn making and collaborative work in conjunction with the communities.

Acknowledgment. The authors wish to express our deepest gratitude to Dr. Jacobo Bucaram Ortíz, founding rector of the Agrarian University of Ecuador for his experience and knowledge.

References

1. Campo, E.B. (ed.): Gestión del Conocimiento en Universidades y Organismos públicos de Investigación. Dirección General de Investigación, Consejería de Educación (2003)
2. Davenport, T., Prusak, I.: Working Knowledge How Organizations Manage What they Know. Harvard Business School Press, Boston (1999)
3. Fainholc, B., Rasgos con los que la Gestión del Conocimiento debería caracterizar a Universidades y Organizaciones de Educación Superior para una Sociedad del Conocimiento. Signos Universitarios, 25(2) 2014
4. Gómez, A., Fernández-López, M., Corcho, M.: Ontological Engineering. Springer, London (2004)
5. Gruber, T.R.: The role of common ontology in achieving sharable, reusable knowledge bases. In: Allen, J.A., Fikes, R., Sandewall, E. (eds.) Principles of Knowledge Representation and Reasoning: Proceedings of the Second International Conference, Cambridge, pp. 601–602 (1991)
6. Gruber, T.: A translation approach to portable ontology specifications. Knowl. Acquisition 5(2), 199–220 (1993)
7. Kende, G., Noszkay, E.: Role of the knowledge management in modern higher education – the e-learning (2011)
8. Fernandez, L., Gomez-Perez, A., Jurista, N.: METHONTOLOGY: from ontological arts towards ontological engineering. In: Symposium on Ontological Engineering of AAAI Stanford University, pp. 33–40 (1997)

9. Janssen, S., Porter, C.H., Moore, A.D., Athanasiadis, I.N., Foster, I., Jones, J.W., Antle, J.M.: Building an open web-based approach to agricultural data, system modeling and decision support. AgMIP. Towards a New Generation of Agricultural System Models, Data, and Knowledge Products, 91 (2015)

10. Jones, J.W., Antle, J.M., Basso, B.O., Boote, K.J., Conant, R.T., Foster, I., Godfray, H.C.J., Herrero, M., Howitt, R.E., Janssen, S., Keating, B.A., Munoz-Carpena, R., Porter, C.H., Rosenzweig, C., Wheeler, T.R.: State of Agricultural Systems Science. Towards a New Generation of Agricultural System Models, Data, and Knowledge Products, p. 91 (2015)

11. Muñoz-García, A., Lagos-Ortiz, K., Vergara-Lozano, V., Salavarria-Melo, J., Real-Aviles, K., Vera-Lucio, N.: Ontological model of knowledge management for research and innovation. In: Valencia-García, R., Lagos-Ortiz, K., Alcaraz-Mármol, G., del Cioppo, J., Vera-Lucio, N. (eds.) CITI 2016. CCIS, vol. 658, pp. 51–62. Springer, Cham (2016). doi:10.1007/978-3-319-48024-4_5. http://www.springer.com/series/7899

12. Muñoz, A., Lopez, V., Lagos, K., Vásquez, M., Hidalgo, J., Vera, N.: Knowledge management for virtual education through ontologies. In: Ciuciu, I., Panetto, H., Debruyne, C., Aubry, A., Bollen, P., Valencia-García, R., Mishra, A., Fensel, A., Ferri, F. (eds.) OTM 2015. LNCS, vol. 9416, pp. 339–348. Springer, Cham (2015). doi:10.1007/978-3-319-26138-6_37

13. Nonaka, I., Takeuchi, H.: The Knowledge-Creating company. The Oxford University Press, New York (1995)

14. Osterwalder, A., Pigneur, Y.: Business Model Generation: A Handbook for Visionaries, Game Changers, and Challengers. Wiley (2010)

15. Osterwalder, A.: The business model ontology: A proposition in a design science approach (2004)

16. Staiger-Rivas, S., Alvarez, S., Arana, J.A., Howland, F., Cunha, F., Valencia, B., Muñoz, L.A., Feijóo, K.: Diseño de intervenciones de gestión de conocimiento en la investigación agrícola para el desarrollo: Metodología, experiencias y lecciones aprendidas. Knowl. Manag. Dev. J. **10**(1), 36–51 (2014). http://journal.km4dev.org/journal/index.php/km4dj/article/viewFile/180/273

ICT in Agronomy

The Current State and Effects of Agromatic: A Systematic Literature Review

William Bazán-Vera[✉] [iD], Oscar Bermeo-Almeida [iD],
Teresa Samaniego-Cobo [iD], Abel Alarcon-Salvatierra [iD],
Ana Rodríguez-Méndez [iD], and Valeria Bazán-Vera [iD]

Computer Science Department, Faculty of Agricultural Sciences,
Agrarian University of Ecuador, Av. 25 de Julio y Pio Jaramillo,
P.O. BOX 09-04-100, Guayaquil, Ecuador
{wbazan, obermeo, tsamaniego, jalarcon,
arodriguez}@uagraria.edu.ec, v-bazan90@hotmail.com

Abstract. IT (Information Technology) has been used to solve problems from different domains. In the context of agriculture, IT is being applied for increasing the productivity as well as for empowering farmers to make decisions. Some of the technologies used in agriculture are the Decision Support Systems, Semantic Web, Cloud computing, Internet of Things and Big data. There are a lot of agriculture processes where IT solutions can be implemented. In this sense, it is important to provide a general perspective on the role of IT in agriculture, emphasizing its effects on agriculture. This work presents a systematic literature review that aims to obtain a solid background in the use of IT in agriculture. The results obtained depicts the need of integrating IT solutions to agriculture as well as the need for allowing farmers and experts work in cooperation to generate systems that combine different technologies for providing low-cost solutions.

Keywords: Systematic literature review · Agriculture · Information system · Decision Support System

1 Background

IT (Information Technology) has been used for responding to a wide range of problems from different domains such as communication, transportation, and health, to mention but a few. In the context of agriculture, IT is being applied as a tool for increasing the productivity as well as a tool for empowering farmers to make decisions based on quality information.

Taking decisions involves farmers and experts who can diagnose the real state of the agricultural system, estimate possible scenarios, evaluate the impact of crop rotation, as well as to predict crop yield, among other tasks. Each process involves obtaining, processing and sharing information from several and heterogeneous agriculture data sources. Therefore, the methodology necessary to perform these activities must consider this important feature. In this sense, the agromatics arise as a new field that consists in applying the informatics applications and computational principles and techniques to the theories and management of agricultural systems [1].

Some of the technologies used in agriculture are the DSS (Decision Support Systems), Semantic Web, Cloud computing, IoT (Internet of Things) and Big data, among others. With regards to DSS, these are focused on tasks such as irrigation management and water conservations. The Semantic Web is used to facilitate the knowledge sharing, as well as to provide a shared lexicon that improves the communication among farmers and experts. Regarding Cloud Computing and IoT, these ones are used to implement crop monitoring systems and precision agriculture. Finally, Big data helps precision agriculture and weather forecasting, among other tasks.

As can be seen, there are a lot of agriculture processes where IT solutions can be implemented. In this sense, it is important to provide a general perspective on the role of IT in agriculture, emphasizing its effects. This information could help farmers to know technologies and approaches that are being used for optimizing farming operations and for getting a better management of resources such as water, which in turn reduces costs.

Considering the facts discussed above, we have carried out a literature review considering the systematic review approach proposed by Kitchenham [2]. This review aims to obtain a solid background in the use of IT in different agriculture processes such as crop rotation process, precision agriculture, irrigation management, agricultural productivity and disease recognition.

The rest of this work is structured as follows. Section 2 presents the execution of the systematic review, from planning to result analysis. Section 3 provides a discussion about the use of IT to agriculture. Finally, Sect. 4 sets out the conclusions obtained.

2 Systematic Review

The execution of a systematic review allows identifying, evaluating and analyzing all the significant studies concerning a given research question, topic area, or phenomenon of interest. Some of the advantages provided by a systematic review are: the summarization of evidence about a specific technology, and the identification of any existing gap in current research, which in turn, allows establishing future research directions.

A systematic review follows a defined research strategy whose main goal is to detect all relevant literature in the subject area. The systematic review presented in this work was carried out by following the guidelines proposed by Kitchenham [2], which are appropriate for software engineering community. Furthermore, this review was performed based on the review protocol template suggested by Biolchini et al. [3], which aims to facilitate the planning and execution of this kind of research.

The systematic review presented in this work consisted of three stages, namely planning, execution and result analysis. The first stage consists in planning the review, identifying its needs and defining its protocol. The second stage refers to the execution of the established plan i.e., the corresponding search in the defined sources are performed according to specific criteria, and the main studies are compared by using a formal framework. In the final stage, we provide our conclusions and identify the need for additional research efforts. Next sections provide a description in detail of the above-mentioned phases.

2.1 Systematic Review Planning

In this phase, we define the research objectives as well as the way the systematic review will be performed. For this purpose, we formulated research questions to be addressed, and planned how the information sources and studies will be selected. In summary, this phase is composed of three tasks, namely question formulation, sources selection, and studies selection.

Question Formulation

This task refers to the clear definition of the research objectives, which are composed of two items: question focus and question quality and amplitude. Regarding question focus, it must be defined what we expect to be answered by executing the systematic review. Therefore, the research questions that were addressed by our work are:

- Which agriculture activities have been typically supported by IT solutions?
- Which IT technologies have been used to support the activities identified?

With respect to the question quality and amplitude, we define the syntax of the research questions above as well as its semantics specificity. The research works to be analyzed in this work are those ones proposing IT solutions that support agriculture. Hence, we define a set of keywords and related concepts to be used during the review execution. These terms, which are presented in Table 1, were considered to be the most representative for discovering the research works that help us to answer the research questions.

Table 1. Keywords and related concepts used during the systematic review.

Area	Keywords	Related concepts
Agriculture	Agriculture, Agricultural	Agricultural
		Climate
Information technology		Decision support system
		Big Data
		Information system

Sources Selection

The objective of this phase was to identify the sources where searches for primary studies were performed. To achieve this goal, we defined the selection criteria as follows: (1) the possibility of searching for digital version of journals and conference papers on agriculture and IT topics by using the established keywords; (2) the sources had to count with a search engine that allows executing advanced search queries; and (3) the studies had to be written in English.

Considering the selection criteria above, we performed the search for primary studies on the digital research libraries: SpringerLink, ScienceDirect and IEEE Xplore Digital Library. Although these digital sources index the most relevant research, we include other information sources such as web pages of communities and research groups related to IT applied on the agricultural domain.

Studies selection

Once information sources were defined, the process and criteria for studies selection and evaluation must be described. Firstly, the search for primary studies was performed by combining the keywords presented in Table 1 with AND and OR connectors. Thus, the resulting search chain that we use is the following:

```
(Agriculture OR Agricultural AND ((Information systems) OR
(Decision support system) OR (Big data) OR (Climate)))
```

According to Biolchini [3], before executing the systematic review, it is necessary to evaluate the planned review. In this sense, the validity of our plan was assessed by a group of experts on Computer Science and Agriculture domains (full-time professors from the Agrarian University of Ecuador). This group concluded that the list of information sources as well as the search chain defined were sufficient and complete to achieve the expected results.

Regarding the strategy of studies selection, it began with the execution of the search chain in the search engine of each digital library. Then, we obtained a set of results to which was applied studies inclusion criteria to select potential candidates for primary studies. The criteria by which studies were evaluated are: (1) only the studies published in the last five years; (2) the studies must clearly depict the integration of IT solutions to agriculture systems.

Once the search chain was executed against each digital library, the set of results obtained was reduced by applying the inclusion criteria described above. Then, we applied exclusion criteria focused on analyzing titles, keywords and abstract of the works obtained. The goal of this task was to ensure the study was related to the topic of the publication. When there was no certainty about this relation, the full-paper was accessed and sections such as introduction and conclusion were read to detect which studies provide important contributions to the field of agriculture.

2.2 Systematic Review Execution

This phase consisted in executing the search in the information sources selected to evaluate the retrieved studies considering the criteria above mentioned. The result of this process was a set of about 550 studies which were filtered by using the inclusion criteria established to give a set of about 120 relevant studies. This set of works was again filtered according to the exclusion criteria.

As a result of evaluating each one of the primary studies, a set of 30 studies was finally obtained. The inclusion and exclusion criteria help us to ensure that the studies were relevant for the research questions established at the planning stage.

2.3 Information Extraction

This phase aims to extract relevant information from the primary studies that were selected. To standardize the way in which this information will be presented, the definition of the kind of information that must be obtained from selected primary studies was performed. Therefore, following objective information we extracted from studies (1) basic information (publication title and authors), (2) information related to the study (main purpose, information technologies used), and (3) results (agricultural processes to which they are focused, and their effect on agricultural processes support).

Table 2 provides a general perspective of all studies selected. It aims to summarize and contrast these studies in an integrated way.

Table 2. Primary studies classified by area

Work	Data source	Objective
Brandt et al. [4]	ScienceDirect	Aid the targeting of climate-smart agriculture (CSA)
Giusti and Libelli [5]		Improve the irrigation based on information related to the crop and site characteristics
Navarro et al. [6]		Manage irrigation in agriculture based on soil measurements and climatic variables
Tan [7]		Increasing agricultural productivity while preserving natural resources
Senthilvadivu et al. [8]		Give better yields considering associations and patterns under climatic influence for geographical segmentation
Longo et al. [9]		Provide software to transform and scale up the applications using Grid infrastructures
Zhang et al. [10]		Develop a cucumber disease recognition approach able to recognize a greater number of diseases
Pérez-Gutiérrez et al. [11]		Validate the hypothesis that on-farm water storage (OFWS) could mitigate downstream nutrient-enrichment pollution
Aiello et al. [12]		Help managers taking more effective decisions thus increasing the efficiency of farming operations
Bernardi [13]	SpringerLink	Improve the communication between public and private agricultural partners
Lan [14]		Design a precision agricultural system based on GIS and GPS technologies
Liu et al. [15]		Establish an accurate tobacco agricultural precision positioning application
Lindblom et al. [16]		Increase sustainability and facilitate innovation by means of experts' knowledge
Wang and Gao [17]		Realize the agricultural production automation and precision agriculture
Yuan et al. [18]		Implement Semantic Web technologies to precision agriculture (citrus crops)
Hu et al. [19]		Describe and extract semantics of agriculture devices and reuse that knowledge to solve semantic interoperation problem
Malche and Maheshwary [20]		Monitor water level and control the water pump accordingly in agricultural and farm production

(*continued*)

Table 2. (*continued*)

Work	Data source	Objective
Lokers et al. [21]		Allow efficient discovery and unified querying of agricultural and forestry resources
Bendre et al. [22]		Implement a model for the use of ICT services in agricultural environment for collecting Big data
Zhang [23]		Provide an agricultural supply chain optimization approach based on IoT
Bansal and Malik [24]	IEEE Xplore Digital Library	Define a framework to provide contextual and scientifically information about crop production lifecycle
Bendre et al. [25]		Discover additional insights from precision agriculture data through Big Data approach
Salleh [26]		Overcome the uncertainty during the development of agriculture DSS
Shah et al. [27]		Reduce the technological gap between rural communities and agriculture information through DSS
Shikalgar et al. [28]		Help farmers to stay on track, avoid troubles, and receive information related to the agriculture
Shyamaladevi et al. [29]		Help agricultural development planning and formulating agricultural policies
Suakanto et al. [30]		Define a model and a DSS of smart farming with network sensors applications
Tan and Zhang [31]		Improve the scalability and reliability of agricultural DSS
Trogo et al. [32]		Help farmers to identify the best day to start planting, harvest, and the predicted yield of the crop
Viani et al. [33]		Reduce the waste of water and to maximize the crop yield according to weather conditions

2.4 Result Analysis

Table 3 shows the studies selected in this work, as well as a comparison of them regarding the relevant information established in the previous section. The way in which they are listed is random, i.e., its order doesn't determine its importance regarding the goals of this work.

It is important to highlight that most of these works propose the use of DSS for support agriculture tasks such as climate-smart agriculture, irrigation and water conservation. Another technology they employ is the Big Data, which is mainly used for crop rotation process, precision agriculture, as well as weather forecasting, where a lot of information is necessary to obtain accurate results. A third type of technology from which these types of approach take advantage is the IoT, which helps monitoring crops as well as supporting precision agriculture. Finally, an outstanding technology that is

Table 3. Summary of contributions

Work	IT's used	Agricultural process	Main contribution	Effect in agriculture processes
Brandt [4]	Multicriteria DSS	Climate-smart agriculture	A framework for obtain value insights to the development of policy and planning tool to consensually target and implement CSA	Better practices for improving fertility and soil management
Giusti [5]	Fuzzy-based DSS, Web services	Irrigation and water conservation	A fuzzy soil moisture model, and an Irrigation Web service	Water saving was confirmed
Navarro [6]	DSS, Machine learning	Irrigation management	A DSS to manage irrigation agriculture based on continuous soil measurements	Improve the performance of using only weather information
Tan [7]	DSS, Cloud computing, Web services, IoT	Agricultural productivity and natural resources preserving	An extensible software architecture for precision agriculture	Versatile and safe control of field devices from a Cloud platform
Senthilvadivu et al. [8]	Big Data Analytics	Crop rotation process	A crop rotation methodology	No validation method is provided
Longo et al. [9]	Simulation software	Resource agricultural simulation	A software for resource-intensive agricultural simulation	A faster software for agricultural simulation
Zhang et al. [10]	Image processing, Data mining	Disease recognition	A cucumber disease recognition algorithm	A greater number of cucumber diseases can be automatically recognized
Pérez-Gutiérrez et al. [11]	Data mining	Seasonal water quality	A study about the behavior of OFWS that helps enhance the management of agroecosystems	A better insight into the behavior of OFWS systems
Aiello et al. [12]	Rule-based DSS, IoT	Pest management	An easy-to-use and low cost to reduce the use of pesticides and fertilizers in protected crops	Better management of pesticides and fertilizers in small scale production systems
Bernardi [13]	Semantic Web,	Knowledge sharing and exchange	A specification of suitable ontologies for agriculture	Improvement of the communication between

(continued)

Table 3. (*continued*)

Work	IT's used	Agricultural process	Main contribution	Effect in agriculture processes
				agricultural partners
Lan [14]	GIS, GPS, Databases	Precision agriculture	A precision agriculture information system based on GIS and GPS	No validation method is provided
Liu [15]	GPS, Databases	Precision agriculture	A tobacco agricultural precision positioning application	Accurate system for the measurements of tobacco production
Lindblom [16]	DSS, Human Computer Interaction	Precision agriculture	A review of decision support systems for precision agriculture	Contribute to long-term sustainable development
Wang [17]	IoT. Wireless Network	Precision agriculture	A wireless temperature and humidity network system	No validation method is provided
Yuan [18]	Semantic Web, DSS, IoT	Precision agriculture	Ontologies for citrus fertilizing and citrus diseases	Increase yield of citrus and avoid plant disease
Hu et al. [19]	IoT, Semantic Web, Cloud computing	Record of grain lifecycles	Ontology for the agriculture based on IoT	Integration of heterogeneous data sources
Malche and Maheshwary [20]	IoT, Cloud computing	Water level monitoring	A prototype of a IoT-based water level monitoring system	Better management of water source
Lokers et al. [21]	Big Data, Linked Data, Semantic Web	Discovery and querying of agricultural resources	A semantic-based platform to access to agro-forestry data for research	A research infrastructure for agriculture
Bendre et al. [22]	Big Data analytics, Neural networks	Precision agriculture (weather forecasting)	A model for the use of ICT services in agriculture environments	Possibility of improving productivity and reduce investment costs
Zhang [23]	IoT	Agricultural supply chain	An IoT-based approach for optimizing supply chain costs	Reduce supply chain costs
Bansal and Malik [24]	Semantic Web	Crop production lifecycle	An ontology for agricultural information systems	Integration of heterogeneous agricultural data sources

(*continued*)

Table 3. (*continued*)

Work	IT's used	Agricultural process	Main contribution	Effect in agriculture processes
Bendre et al. [25]	Big Data	Weather forecasting	A distributed algorithm for data processing and weather forecasting	Reduce agricultural investments costs
Salleh [26]	Fuzzy modelling, DSS	Crop selection	Algorithms and analysis for planting material classification	High return in planting material breeders
Shah et al. [27]	Big data, DSS	Crop yield prediction	A big data analytics architecture for an agro-advisory system	Possibility of alternative crops
Shikalgar et al. [28]	Cloud computing	Agriculture task scheduling	A mobile expert system for agriculture task scheduling	Better control of financial income and expenses
Shyamaladevi et al. [29]	HCI, Web services, Semantic Web	Formulating agricultural policies	A Semantic web based farmer helper system	Improve the share and reuse of data across applications
Suakanto et al. [30]	IoT	Smart farming (Task management)	An IoT-based model for smart farming	No validation method is provided
Tan and Zhang [31]	DSS, Cloud computing	Precision agriculture	A meta-model-based data acquisition and integration module	Optimization of farming operations
Trogo et al. [32]	SMS, DSS	Precision agriculture	An SMS-based solution for precision agriculture	Help farmers with limited Internet connection
Viani et al. [33]	DSS, IoT, Fuzzy Logic	Irrigation management	A wireless monitoring and SS for water saving	Reduce the waste of water

used by some of these approaches is the Semantic Web. This technology has been successfully applied in domains such as natural language processing [34], finances [35], and Cloud computing [36]. Furthermore, Semantic Web has proven to be effective for integrating and reusing high-quality information from distributed and heterogeneous agricultural data sources.

Regarding how these works have contributed to the agriculture domain, it is important to remark that most of the works analyzed have improved several agriculture tasks such as irrigation systems, crop rotation process, disease diagnosis, precision agriculture and pest management, among others.

3 Result Analysis: Discussion

Taking into account the results obtained from the systematic literature review presented in this work, nowadays, there are several IT solutions for improving agriculture processes which go from crop selection to climate-smart agriculture. DSS represent the technologies that have been widely used to address problems such as irrigation management, natural resources preserving, and pest management. As can be noted, this technology is used to deal with problems that requires expertise that helps farmers to make correct decisions, thus avoiding a waste of time and resources. Furthermore, DSS has allowed improving fertility and soil management as well as getting a better management of resources such as pesticides, fertilizers and water.

Also, as it can be observed from Table 2, Big data has arisen as a new technology that allows dealing with tasks that requires a lot of data such as weather forecasting and precision agriculture. Big data is expected to have a large impact on smart farming [37]. Furthermore, it involves the whole supply chain, and it can be combined with technologies such as Cloud computing and IoT to collect information from smart sensors and devices to support agriculture tasks such as crops monitoring, agricultural supply chain, irrigation management, among others.

Precision agriculture is an agricultural process on which several researchers are focusing their efforts. This process is very popular in developed countries, and some of the technologies used in this process are IoT, geographical information systems, Big data and Cloud computing. The combination of these technologies contributes to agricultural productivity. For example, it is possible to alternate crops based on a lot of weather forecasting data, improving productivity and reducing investment costs, as well as establishing a research infrastructure for agriculture.

With regards to the effect of IT on agriculture, IT solution has been applied with positive results. To name a few, some of its effects are: improved fertility and soil management, improved decision making, resources saving (including water, pesticides, fertilizers, etc.), community involvement, better management of plant diseases, and the integration of heterogeneous data sources, and finally, agriculture for everyone (farmers and experts) thanks to the use of Semantic Web technologies.

Regarding Semantic Web technologies, they have been used to formally represent the domain knowledge in such a way that this information can be automatically processed by machines and these ones can infer new knowledge. Some of the specific domains where ontologies have been implemented are geo data, fertilizing, diseases treatment and agriculture based on IoT. Finally, it should be remarked that ontologies have been used as an important part of DSS.

To sum up, farmers need to consider the endless possibilities that IT solutions can bring to agriculture, i.e., they need to be involved in a new method for agriculture. It is well known that farmers can benefit from some of the agricultural advancements analyzed in this work. Furthermore, it is important to encourage farmers to take part in the positive change that IT solutions promote for agriculture.

4 Conclusions and Future Work

This work describes the planning, execution and evaluation of several studies that aim to improve agriculture processes. Considering the results obtained, we conclude that the research questions established at the beginning of this systematic literature review (planning stage) were successfully answered.

The results obtained depicts the necessity of integrating IT solutions to all agriculture processes to optimize them and reduce investment costs. Also, it is necessary for farmers and experts to work in cooperation in order to generate systems that combine different technologies for providing low-cost and accessible solutions to farmers independently of the economic resources they have. A kind of technology that can help people to work in cooperation are ontologies, which can be used to ensure broad understanding of the agriculture domain. This understanding will allow farmers and agriculture organizations to develop IT solutions focused on the agriculture application, service and consulting.

We expect this work could contribute to reduce the gap existing between farmers and current technological solutions for agriculture, and could represent a complementary guideline for farmers and experts about which technologies they can implement in their farms.

As future work, we plan to extend this work by including a wider set of digital libraries such as the ACM Digital Library. Furthermore, we expect this systematic literature review to include more innovative technologies. In this sense, we expect this future work results in more findings on the implementation of IT solutions in real-world scenarios. Finally, we plan to investigate the use of techniques that help us to contrast the results obtained from the systematic literature.

References

1. D'Angelo, C.: Notas sobre la Ordenación del Territorio. Rev. Perspect. **4**, 14–18 (2006)
2. Kitchenham, B., Charters, S.: Guidelines for performing systematic literature reviews in software engineering, version 2.3. Keele University. 45, 1051 (2007)
3. Biolchini, J., Mian, P.G., Natali, A.C.C., Travassos, G.H.: Systematic review in software engineering. Systems Engineering and Computer Science Department COPPE/UFRJ (2005)
4. Brandt, P., Kvakić, M., Butterbach-Bahl, K., Rufino, M.C.: How to target climate-smart agriculture? Concept and application of the consensus-driven decision support framework "targetCSA". Agric. Syst. **151**, 234–245 (2017)
5. Giusti, E., Marsili-Libelli, S.: A fuzzy decision support system for irrigation and water conservation in agriculture. Environ. Model. Softw. **63**, 73–86 (2015)
6. Navarro-Hellín, H., Martínez-del-Rincon, J., Domingo-Miguel, R., Soto-Valles, F., Torres-Sánchez, R.: A decision support system for managing irrigation in agriculture. Comput. Electron. Agric. **124**, 121–131 (2016)
7. Tan, L.: Cloud-based decision support and automation for precision agriculture in orchards. IFAC-PapersOnLine **49**, 330–335 (2016)
8. Senthilvadivu, S., Kiran, S.V., Devi, S.P., Manivannan, S.: Big data analysis on geographical segmentations and resource constrained scheduling of production of agricultural commodities for better yield. Procedia Comput. Sci. **87**, 80–85 (2016)

9. Longo, M., Arroqui, M., Rodriguez, J., Machado, C., Mateos, C., Zunino, A.: Extending JASAG with data processing techniques for speeding up agricultural simulation applications: a case study with Simugan (2016)

10. Zhang, S., Wu, X., You, Z., Zhang, L.: Leaf image based cucumber disease recognition using sparse representation classification. Comput. Electron. Agric. **134**, 135–141 (2017)

11. Pérez-Gutiérrez, J.D., Paz, J.O., Tagert, M.L.M.: Seasonal water quality changes in on-farm water storage systems in a south-central U.S. agricultural watershed. Agric. Water Manag. **187**, 131–139 (2017)

12. Aiello, G., Giovino, I., Vallone, M., Catania, P., Argento, A.: A decision support system based on multisensor data fusion for sustainable greenhouse management. J. Clean. Prod. (2017)

13. Bernardi, A.: iGreen—intelligent technologies for public-private knowledge management in agriculture. KI - Künstliche Intelligenz. **27**, 347–350 (2013)

14. Lan, B.: The establishment of agriculture information system based on GIS and GPS. In: Qu, X., Yang, Y. (eds.) IBI 2011, Part II. CCIS, vol. 268, pp. 506–511. Springer, Heidelberg (2012). doi:10.1007/978-3-642-29087-9_78

15. Liu, T., Bi, L., Chen, H., Qian, C., Li, L.: Study on precision positioning technology in digital tobacco agriculture. In: Du, W. (ed.) Informatics and Management Science II. LNEE, vol. 205, pp. 167–174. Springer, London (2013). doi:10.1007/978-1-4471-4811-1_23

16. Lindblom, J., Lundström, C., Ljung, M., Jonsson, A.: Promoting sustainable intensification in precision agriculture: review of decision support systems development and strategies. Precis. Agric. **18**, 309–331 (2017)

17. Wang, X., Gao, H.: Agriculture wireless temperature and humidity sensor network based on ZigBee technology. In: Li, D., Chen, Y. (eds.) CCTA 2011, Part I. IFIP AICT, vol. 368, pp. 155–160. Springer, Heidelberg (2012). doi:10.1007/978-3-642-27281-3_20

18. Yuan, Y., Zeng, W., Zhang, Z.: A semantic technology supported precision agriculture system: a case study for citrus fertilizing. In: Wang, M. (ed.) KSEM 2013. LNCS, vol. 8041, pp. 104–111. Springer, Heidelberg (2013). doi:10.1007/978-3-642-39787-5_9

19. Hu, S., Wang, H., She, C., Wang, J.: AgOnt: ontology for agriculture Internet of Things. In: Li, D., Liu, Y., Chen, Y. (eds.) CCTA 2010, Part I. IFIP AICT, vol. 344, pp. 131–137. Springer, Heidelberg (2011). doi:10.1007/978-3-642-18333-1_18

20. Malche, T., Maheshwary, P.: Internet of Things (IoT) based water level monitoring system for smart village. In: Modi, N., Verma, P., Trivedi, B. (eds.) Proceedings of International Conference on Communication and Networks. AISC, vol. 508, pp. 305–312. Springer, Singapore (2017). doi:10.1007/978-981-10-2750-5_32

21. Lokers, R., van Randen, Y., Knapen, R., Gaubitzer, S., Zudin, S., Janssen, S.: Improving access to big data in agriculture and forestry using semantic technologies. In: Garoufallou, E., Hartley, R.J., Gaitanou, P. (eds.) MTSR 2015. CCIS, vol. 544, pp. 369–380. Springer, Cham (2015). doi:10.1007/978-3-319-24129-6_32

22. Bendre, M.R., Thool, R.C., Thool, V.R.: Big data in precision agriculture through ICT: rainfall prediction using neural network approach. In: Satapathy, S.C., Bhatt, Y.C., Joshi, A., Mishra, D.K. (eds.) Proceedings of the International Congress on Information and Communication Technology. AISC, vol. 438, pp. 165–175. Springer, Singapore (2016). doi:10.1007/978-981-10-0767-5_19

23. Zhang, G.: Research on the optimization of agricultural supply chain based on Internet of Things. In: Li, D., Chen, Y. (eds.) CCTA 2013, Part I. IFIP AICT, vol. 419, pp. 300–305. Springer, Heidelberg (2014). doi:10.1007/978-3-642-54344-9_36

24. Bansal, N., Malik, S.K.: A framework for agriculture ontology development in semantic web. In: 2011 International Conference on Communication Systems and Network Technologies, pp. 283–286. IEEE (2011)

25. Bendre, M.R., Thool, R.C., Thool, V.R.: Big data in precision agriculture: weather forecasting for future farming. In: 2015 1st International Conference on Next Generation Computing Technologies (NGCT), pp. 744–750. IEEE (2015)
26. Salleh, M.N.M.: A fuzzy modelling of decision support system for crop selection. In: 2012 IEEE Symposium on Industrial Electronics and Applications, pp. 17–22. IEEE (2012)
27. Shah, P., Hiremath, D., Chaudhary, S.: Big data analytics architecture for agro advisory system. In: 2016 IEEE 23rd International Conference on High Performance Computing Workshops (HiPCW), pp. 43–49. IEEE (2016)
28. Shikalgar, S., Kolhe, M., Bhalerao, N., Pansare, S., Laddha, S.: A cross platform mobile expert system for agriculture task scheduling. In: 2016 International Conference on Computing, Communication and Automation (ICCCA), pp. 835–840. IEEE (2016)
29. Shyamaladevi, K., Mirnalinee, T.T., Trueman, T.E., Kaladevi, R.: Design of ontology based ubiquitous web for agriculture — a farmer helping system. In: 2012 International Conference on Computing, Communication and Applications, pp. 1–6. IEEE (2012)
30. Suakanto, S., Engel, V.J.L., Hutagalung, M., Angela, D.: Sensor networks data acquisition and task management for decision support of smart farming. In: 2016 International Conference on Information Technology Systems and Innovation (ICITSI), pp. 1–5. IEEE (2016)
31. Tan, L., Hou, H., Zhang, Q.: An extensible software platform for cloud-based decision support and automation in precision agriculture. In: 2016 IEEE 17th International Conference on Information Reuse and Integration (IRI), pp. 218–225. IEEE (2016)
32. Trogo, R., Ebardaloza, J.B., Sabido, D.J., Bagtasa, G., Tongson, E., Balderama, O.: SMS-based smarter agriculture decision support system for yellow corn farmers in Isabela. In: 2015 IEEE Canada International Humanitarian Technology Conference (IHTC 2015), pp. 1–4. IEEE (2015)
33. Viani, F., Bertolli, M., Salucci, M., Polo, A.: Low-cost wireless monitoring and decision support for water saving in agriculture. IEEE Sens. J., 1 (2017)
34. Paredes-Valverde, M.A., Rodríguez-García, M.Á., Ruiz-Martínez, A., Valencia-García, R., Alor-Hernández, G.: ONLI: an ontology-based system for querying DBpedia using natural language paradigm. Expert Syst. Appl. **42**, 5163–5176 (2015)
35. del Pilar Salas-Zárate, M., Valencia-García, R., Ruiz-Martínez, A., Colomo-Palacios, R.: Feature-based opinion mining in financial news: an ontology-driven approach. J. Inf. Sci. **43**, 458–479 (2016). doi:10.1177/0165551516645528
36. Rodríguez-García, M.Á., Valencia-García, R., García-Sánchez, F., Samper-Zapater, J.J.: Ontology-based annotation and retrieval of services in the cloud. Knowl. Based Syst. **56**, 15–25 (2014)
37. Wolfert, S., Ge, L., Verdouw, C., Bogaardt, M.-J.: Big data in smart farming – a review. Agric. Syst. **153**, 69–80 (2017)

A Photogrammetry Software as a Tool for Precision Agriculture: A Case Study

Carlota Delgado-Vera[1](✉) ⒾⒹ, Maritza Aguirre-Munizaga[1] ⒾⒹ,
Manuel Jiménez-Icaza[2] ⒾⒹ, Nadia Manobanda-Herrera[3] ⒾⒹ,
and Ana Rodríguez-Méndez[1]

[1] Facultad de Ciencias Agrarias, Escuela de Ingeniería
en Computación e Informática, Universidad Agraria del Ecuador,
Avenue 25 de Julio y Pio Jaramillo, P.O. BOX 09-04-100, Guayaquil, Ecuador
{cdelgado,maguirre,arodriguez}@uagraria.edu.ec
[2] Facultad de Ciencias Agrarias, Escuela de Ingeniería en Agronómica,
Universidad Agraria del Ecuador, Avenue 25 de Julio y Pio Jaramillo,
P.O. BOX 09-04-100, Guayaquil, Ecuador
mjimenez@uagraria.edu.ec
[3] Facultad de Ciencias, Campus Universitario de Rabanales,
Universidad de Córdoba, Ctra. Madrid-Cádiz Km. 396, 14071 Córdoba, Spain
z62mahen@uco.es

Abstract. Traditionally, agriculture is practiced by performing tasks such as planting or harvesting against a predetermined schedule. However, collecting real-time data can help farmers to make the best decisions about planting, fertilizing and harvesting crops. This approach is known as precision agriculture. In this context, interest in technological tools to adapt crop management strategies is growing. Hence, this research aims to analyze and compare the photogrammetry-based tools for the treatment of images in the agricultural domain. Furthermore, a case study of the land of the Agrarian University of Ecuador Experimental Research Center based in Mariscal Sucre, located in Milagro is presented. This study involves taking several photos by means of a drone and analyzing them with a photogrammetric software to obtain an orthophoto. This product can help to perform relative biomass analysis, drought stress, irrigation scheduling, predicting agricultural production, monitoring nutrition, pests and diseases that are affecting the photographed crop.

Keywords: Agriculture · Photogrammetry · Software

1 Introduction

Since several years ago, several researchers have analyzed the potential capacities of knowledge engineering and the use of technological systems for solving poorly structured agricultural problems [1].

Photogrammetry [2] has become an indispensable tool in the production of the cartographic base of all countries of the world. It allows delimiting and describing the crops, and make the best use of the soil of a territory. In fact, most of the topographic

© Springer International Publishing AG 2017
R. Valencia-García et al. (Eds.): CITI 2017, CCIS 749, pp. 282–295, 2017.
DOI: 10.1007/978-3-319-67283-0_21

mapping of the planet has been carried out by means of this type of technique, which allows obtaining innovative results in the agricultural sector using information and communication technologies.

A photogrammetric station is an instrument defined by a set of hardware and software that applies several techniques for the treatment of digital images. These methods use a mathematical model which is based on analytical photogrammetry calculations in a systematic way.

Photogrammetry techniques have been implemented in areas such as archeology, architecture, hydrogeology, land management, geology, environmental, forestry, and agriculture. The most used licensed software applications are Agisoft-PhotoScan, Pix4d, and Ensomosaic, as well as, free software OpenDroneMap, Insight3d, Mic Mac, VisualSFM, and Qgis.

In recent years, the use of photogrammetry in several areas has increased. In addition, current computers with processors of high-performance have contributed to the improvement and execution of the components used in the image processing of the photogrammetry stations.

In this paper, we carried out an analysis and comparison of most used applications in the agriculture area. This analysis aims to characterize the most used photogrammetry tools as a technological alternative to coupled photographs taken from a dron or images taken from satellites. First, the functionalities, limitations, and scope of both free and licensed software for photogrammetry are defined. Second, this paper describes the ways in which precision agriculture is impacting on agriculture with the use of airborne vehicles as drones for image capture, processing, and analysis [3].

The application of technological tools to adapt crop management strategies is defined as precision agriculture [4, 5].

The remainder of this paper is organized as follows. Section 2 presents a review of the literature concerning agriculture and photogrammetry. Section 3 presents an analysis and comparison of the most used applications in agriculture. A case study is described in Sect. 4. Finally, our conclusions and future work are presented in Sect. 5.

2 Related Works

In this work, a review of works concerning to research of agriculture and photogrammetry is presented. Specifically, techniques that incorporate the use of the technologies towards precision agriculture. These research works affirm that remote sensing technology is playing a key role in the precision agriculture [3].

For instance, Gillan et al. [6] mentioned that traditional methods for monitoring erosion (sediment traps, erosion pins, and bridges) require a lot of labor and they are generally limited to the intensity of parameters and/or spatial extent. The authors demonstrated through photogrammetric differentiation technique of DEM (digital elevation model) that this technique can provide information and a complete assessment of soil loss and movement than any single technique alone.

Some works are based on techniques that evaluate the topography of the terrain using orthophotos. For example, Rokhmana [7] presented some practical experiences of the use of the platform based on unmanned aerial vehicles (UAV) for supporting remote sensing in precision agriculture cartography.

Precision agriculture can be used for analysis of fields infested by weeds [8, 9]. These works have achieved to map small weeds in wheat at a very early phenological stage. Also, this technique has been used to analyze agricultural river basins [10].

The knowledge of the advantages and disadvantages of existing technologies may be useful information for selecting the appropriate technology.

In addition to the analysis of the state of the art presented above, in this paper, an analysis and comparison of the tools for the treatment of images using the photogrammetry technique is performed. The photogrammetry technique acts as a support tool for precision agriculture.

Precision agriculture is used by farmers to map their lots and improve whole-farm management. For example, citrus fruit is an important agricultural product for farmers in Florida USA [11]. Therefore, several authors have used these fruits to perform photogrammetry study to predict the production of citrus fruit. The authors developed a camera system, which registers thermal images with normal visible images. The fusion of these images helps to obtain information to detect immature fruits and locate the places of the land that these fruits need more attention.

In [12], the authors show that hyperspectral data provide information about following: (1) the biophysical and biochemical properties of vegetation and agricultural crops; (2) the detection of biotic and abiotic stress, and (3) the estimation of biomass and yield. In this work, the authors introduced cameras of light hyperspectral snapshots, which register the spectral information as a two-dimensional image with each exposure. Specialized workflows based on photogrammetric algorithms allow the reconstruction of the 3D topography of a surface and thus recover structural and spectral information at the same time.

Icaros-Demeter company [13] developed a lightweight and compact remote sensing system with the potential to produce thematic maps of 100,000 acres (400 km^2) for a day with high-resolution RGB/CIR CMOS digital sensors using photogrammetry. The Icaros-Demeter system allows a quick and accurate location of multiple areas and types of points. The system's ability to produce high-precision digital surface models (DSM) over large areas provides a direct method for calculating agricultural biomass through volume calculations rather than common indirect methods.

This work presents a comparison of the tools for image treatment using the photogrammetry technique. These tools are used as a support tool for precision agriculture.

3   Analysis and Comparison of the Most Used Applications in Agriculture

Nowadays, there is software for the processing of images for agriculture of high precision which can be classified into two main types:

- Payment software: They are provided as software packages with a license of a certain price according to the operations to be performed, for example, generation of ortho-mosaics, processing, and interpretation of images or calculation of vegetative indexes, among others.

• Free software: They are free software packages. However, they use Cloud-based processing platforms which have an established price according to the amount of information to be processed.

To obtain the photos, it is necessary the small unmanned aerial systems (UVA). For instance, Duncan and Murphy [14] use fixed-wing dron for the acquisition of images.

Both licensing software and free software have advantages and disadvantages. License software requires high-performance computers which imply a high economic cost, although this provides the possibility of independent studies at any moment. Free software requires payments for each task to be carried out, however, if the task is of low complexity and not performed frequently, it can be a better option than the previous one [15].

Agisoft PhotoScan was developed by Agisoft LLC from St. Petersburg, Russia (http://www.agisoft.com). It is used for the processing of aerial images, which allows performing high-resolution digital image processing [16] as well as the generation of 3D information. Furthermore, these functionalities can be performed in multiple GIS applications. Agisoft PhotoScan is suitable for the photogrammetric documentation of buildings, archaeological sites, deposits, and agriculture. In the context of agriculture, Agisoft PhotoScan has obtained excellent results. There are two versions of Agisoft PhotoScan, the professional and standard edition. The professional version includes improved features of the standard edition [17].

Pix4d is a software to produce cartography. It is based on images taken with low weight cameras, transported by UAV [18]. This software supports input image resolutions from 1 to 200 megapixels and it processes up to 10,000 RGB, infrared or thermal images at the same time. A requirement for using this software is an accurate GPS location of the images. The developers of this software teamed up with the company Parrot to create Pix4Dmapper Ag, an exclusive software for the application of precision agriculture [19]. It converts multispectral images into maps of specific uses in the agriculture for better analysis and crop management. Among its main features are a calculator of vegetative indexes such as SAVI and some other less common ones, formulae edition, editor of maps of reflectance, automatic generation of NDVI, automatic segmentation of the indices and creation of maps of application for the Agricultural machinery. A good example of the use of this software is the work presented in [20], where this software was used for the analysis of photos taken from a dron.

Insight3d is a free software, which allows creating orthophotos in 3d by means the coincidence of the common points of several photos taken from several angles. The application calculates the position in the space obtained from the optical parameters of the camera. However, a limitation of the application is that it does not support a large volume of images because storing all characteristics of the images at the same time for the calibration of the same ones in high resolution requires enough memory resource. Furthermore, it does not perform the transformation of the point clouds to the real coordinate system. Therefore, it is necessary to rely on free software for coordinate transformation.

Ensomosaic was developed by MosaicMill. It is a photogrammetry software which can create distortion-free ortho mosaics in areas with marked terrain undulations. The software requires as input three main elements: (1) images in any common format (jpg, png, among others), (2) GPS coordinates (Global Positioning Systems) and (3) the parameters of the camera used. In addition, there is a specialized version of this software for the agriculture, the Ensomosaic Agri, which provides, among other functionalities, the calculation of vegetative indexes, with a high effectiveness in the NDVI. This software has UAV (Unmanned Aerial System) licenses which capture unlimited photos.

OpenDroneMap is an open source toolkit that provides a full photogrammetric solution for small Unmanned Aircraft (Drones), balloons, and kites [21]. This software acts as a tool to process highly overlapping unreferenced imagery, including colorized point clouds, digital surface models, textured digital surface models and orthophotography [22]. It is important to mention that once OpenDroneMap performs the images union, the presentation of the orthophoto can be visualized through Meshlab, Phyton, and on the Web with WebOdm which adds more functions such as user authentication, map visualizations, 3D screens, an API, and the ability to organize multiple processing nodes (run parallel jobs). Processing nodes are servers running node-OpenDroneMap.

VisualSFM is a GUI (graphical user interface) application that allows creating a 3D point cloud using SFM (Motion Structure) [23]. They are formed by simple points described by a space coordinates XYZ and RGB values that will be responsible for restoring the original texture through dense point cloud [24]. The SfM production of VisualSFM incorporates tools such as Yasutaka Furukawa's PMVS (Patch-based Multiview Stereo)/ CMVS (Clustering Views for Multi-View Stereo), Michal Jancosek's CMP-MVS, MVE by Michael Goesele's research group, which are algorithms to handle the cluster for manipulating the entire image in 2D or 3D.

Micmac is a collection of open-source tools, developed by Marc Pierrot-Desseilligny who has designed "depth maps" from a set of images and about a master image [25]. A "depth map" is an image where each pixel represents the corresponding depth with a point of view, relative to an image or master scene. Micmac, as well as others photogrammetry field tools, is based on the epipolar geometry (stereoscopic vision geometry) but does not support multi-stereoscopy. This fact implies a certain specialization in quasi-planar scenarios, such as land images, facades, facings, reliefs, etc., excluding objects or artifacts of the round bundle type.

QGIS is a distributed system for crop monitoring developed in Ukraine [26]. QGIS was implemented to work with the SQLite databases and the creation of vectorized maps of the fields. This software is specific to the management of geospatial data with support for most data formats and vendors. Also, it has an open source software interface for the programming languages C++ and Python to implement additional components and extend its functionality as the case of orthophoto. Furthermore, it provides two ways to calculate indices: (1) the Raster Calculator that allows the introduction of the specific formula, and (2) the radiometric indices that contain the most used vegetation indices in agriculture today.

Figure 1 shows the criteria used in photogrammetry software such as ease of use, processing time, image quality, and cost. With respect to the free software before mentioned, it is necessary internet connection since the program works by obtaining data from the web to apply the photogrammetry procedure. Regarding the ease of use, it has a graphical user interface that allows obtaining the ortho-photo. However, it is necessary to have some skills on Linux commands for the installation. The visual quality of the resulting orthophoto does not show distortions or voids, thus obtaining an image of excellent quality.

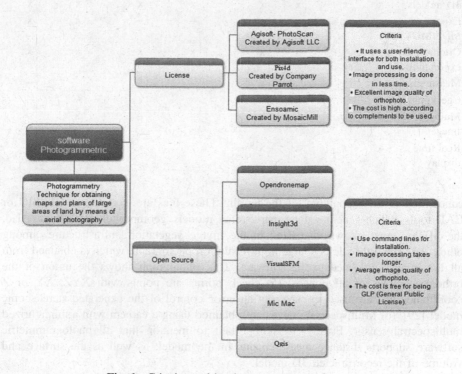

Fig. 1. Criteria used in photogrammetry software.

Table 1 shows the main functionalities of the photogrammetric software. In this table, several functional criteria of license and free software are presented. As can be observed, most open source programs do not provide the relevant functions for the application of the photogrammetric technique. However, Open-DroneMap is a free software that provides 90% of the functions of a licensed software. Therefore, this software is the most suitable to process images applying the technique of this study.

Next, the main features of the photogrammetric software are presented: (1) the triangulation process involves the automatic measurement of the union points and the interactive measurement of the control points to obtain a better adjustment of the image [27]. (2) cloud is an automatic process where the homologous points between the images are joined through correlation algorithms [28], which allows obtaining three-dimensional images, i.e. images more real. (3) Export to MDT format means to generate a file type "Raster", where each pixel has values of XYZ coordinates

Table 1. Comparison of photogrammetry software.

Feature	Pix4d	Agisoft Photos Can Pro	Enso amic	OpenDrone Map	Insight3d	VisualSFM	MicMac	Qgis
Triangulation	x	x	x	x	x	–	x	x
Point cloud	x	x	x	x	x	x	x	x
3D models	x	x	x	x	x	x	x	x
Export MDS/MDT	x	x	x	x	–	–	x	x
Ortomosaico exportation	x	x	x	x	x	x	x	x
Measurements	x	x	x	x	–	–	–	–
Checkpoints	x	x	x	x	x	–	–	–
Multispectral Images	x	x	x	x	–	–	x	–
Real-time display	x	x	x	x	x	x	x	–

concerning to the topography of the terrain. These files are exported to GIS/SIG or CAD tools, which generate slope maps, relief models, geomorphological maps. Also, the MDS format allows visualized in the image vegetation, infrastructure, among others. (4) The orthosaic is a large high-resolution photograph, which is obtained from all the images uploaded to the software. This photograph shows the union of the orthogonal areas of all images. (5) check points are points with XYZ, XY or Z coordinates that are used to carry out an error control of the generated stereoscopic model [29]. (6) Multispectral images are obtained using a camera with a miniaturized multispectral sensor. Finally, it is important to mention that all photogrammetric software supports distance measurements in the model, as well as the surface and volume of the reconstructed 3D model.

4   Case Study

The Agrarian University of Ecuador has agricultural fields for the training of agricultural engineers, one of them is the Experimental Center of Investigations with headquarters in Mariscal Sucre, Milagro. It is an estate, with an extension of 5 hectares, in which field practices are carried out with several crops of the region. Some of these crops are plots of horticultural crops, fruit trees, bananas, and pastures.

4.1   Collection of Images

Two flights with different sensors were carried out with the collaboration of the company Sensefly [23], who facilitated a UAV model Ebee Ag to obtain the images in the Experimental Mariscal Sucre field of the Agrarian University of Ecuador ($-79.5019°$, $-2.1144°$). The first sensor used was with an NIR camera and the second one with a Multispectral camera. A total of 51 NIR and 49 multispectral images were obtained. Figure 2 shows a collage of photos obtained in one of the overflights of the crops, which were in the stage of filling the grain. An ortho-photo was created by using software that uses photogrammetry techniques namely Opendronemap. This software was used to carry out through an image a topographical survey, and consecutively a more advanced analysis of the images.

Fig. 2. Images of the Mariscal Sucre farm for further processing. These images were collected by the UAV.

4.2   Software Installation

An experimental research was carried out with the Open-dronemap image processing software. OpenDroneMap is an open source software that works on operating systems with Linux kernel. The installation of the software was done through the virtualization of Ubuntu Server 14.0 using Oracle Virtualbox. The specifications of the computer used are a 4th Generation Intel® Core ™ i7 processor of 3.40 GHz and 4 cores with an 8 GB Ram memory. The first steps were performed through the lines of code that allow access to Opendronemap repositories. Once the software was installed, some Phyton libraries were used to correctly execute the projects created. There are some environmental variables that need to be established in relation to the project that must be performed.

4.3   Images Processing

Aiming to process the images with Opendronemap, the graphical interface WebODM was installed. Then, the orthophoto was created. The result obtained was a quality product, where the field can be clearly seen, as shown in Fig. 3. This image allowed obtained some primordial data to make the determination of the total area of the land of existing crops. With the aim to establish a real comparison of the image processing, a trial license of the Agisoft-Photoscan software was obtained. The photos used in OpenDrome-Map were imported as an input obtaining an orthophoto of similar characteristics to the free software analyzed in this case of study.

Fig. 3. Images obtained with Opendronemap.

Figure 4 shows the union of the images. The time spent in this process was 5 h 30 min, which represents an acceptable time compared to the commercial Photoscan software whose time was of 2 h 20 min.

Agisoft PhotoScan allows creating professional-quality 3D content using fixed images. This software incorporates latest multi-view 3D reconstruction technologies. It works with arbitrary images and it is optimal under controlled and uncontrolled

Fig. 4. Images obtained with Agisoft-Photoscan.

conditions. The photos can be taken from any angle in order to create the orthophoto. However, the object to be reconstructed must be visible in at least two photos. Both image alignment and 3D model reconstruction are fully automated. Unlike the afore-mentioned software, OpenDroneMap is a set of open source tools for processing aerial drones images. Typical drones use simple cameras, i.e. non-metric images. Open-DroneMap converts these simple images into three-dimensional geographic data that can be used in combination with other geographic data sets [30].

4.4 Validation and Results

With the resulting image, several processes can be performed between different bands such as the differential vegetation index (NDVI), which can determine the nutritional status of the crops. Through these procedures, it was possible to obtain practical data to 4 main objectives: (1) combat the weeds, (2) determine the presence of pests,

(3) visualize the deficiency of nutrients, and (4) monitor in a reliable way the necessary times and thus to take control of the crops.

Maize and pineapple are cultivated in the land used for the experiment. Figure 5 shows a series of tracings made on the orthophoto, obtaining the perimeter of the land with a surface of 4.95 ha, where it is visualized lots of crops with 1 ha and buildings with 0.48 ha. The topographic survey has been carried out in an agile way, saving personnel resources, time and money, in the same way, that the conventional methods with topographic instruments.

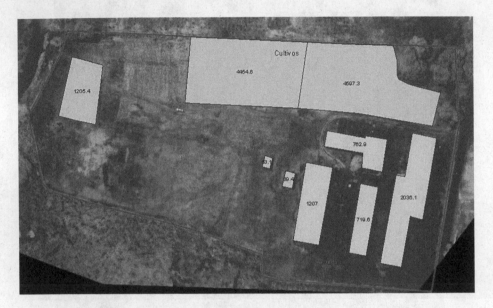

Fig. 5. Topographic survey based on the multispectral image.

To validate the results of the case study, field measurements were made with high precision topographic survey equipment by using the South 362N Total Station. Subsequently, the data were processed in AutoCAD. Table 2 shows the results obtained and the margin of error. These data show a difference of 19 m^2 in the perimeter of the land, which indicates a margin of error less than 1%. With respect to the measurement values of buildings, there is a margin of error of 1.71%. Finally, considering the crop lots an error of 0.59% is estimated. Regarding the data mentioned above, it can be stated that the software generates an estimated error of less than 2%.

Table 2. Comparison among real data and data obtained by the software.

Parameter	Open-DroneMap	Real	Error rate
Perimeter of the property	49539 m^2	49520 m^2	0.038%
Lots of crops	10257 m^2	10196 m^2	0.59%
Buildings	4868 m^2	4786 m^2	1.71%

5 Conclusions and Future Work

Photogrammetry is a technique that is being applied in precision agriculture since it allows obtaining information of the land in three dimensions. This feature has allowed implementing applications for the monitoring and analysis of the agricultural parcels.

Furthermore, a comparison of the different photogrammetry software applied to agriculture has been performed. OpenDroneMap software was the most suitable to be applied in the processing of NIR and RGB images based on criteria such as time, ease of use, visual quality and cost.

The application of this software in the case study presented in this work allowed to obtain a high-quality image, through which it was possible to perform a planimetric survey of the land in a suitable way.

The image obtained through the software analyzed in this work provides a mean for the analysis of the techniques obtained. For example, the techniques for efficient water management, which helps to improve the localization of agricultural inputs and practices, and the quality detection and crop production that helps to improve the productivity in a sustainable way.

As future work, we plan to perform an in-depth analysis of software for photogrammetry focused on increase the efficiency of agricultural production [31]. This process will require the performance of practices that allow students to use OpendroneMap as a tool in the different experimental centers of the University. Among the main tasks that we are considering are: irrigation programming, predict the agricultural production, monitor nutrition, and detect pests and diseases that are affecting the crop, among other practices.

Also, we plan to use the photogrammetry technique in the following: (1) quantification of the number of cultivated plants [32], (2) detection of the crowns of plants in 3D, and (3) phenotypic identification [33]. Furthermore, we are interested in the implementation of short-range photogrammetry and computer vision in order to determine the productivity, through the measurement of the volume, mass, and number of crops of the plants [34].

References

1. Barrett, J.R., Jones, D.D., Thompson, T.L.: Knowledge systems development in U.S. agriculture. Expert Syst. Appl. **4**, 45–51 (1992)
2. Shekhar, S., Xiong, H.: Encyclopedia of GIS. Springer, New York (2008)
3. Abdullahi, H.S., Mahieddine, F., Sheriff, R.E.: Technology impact on agricultural productivity: a review of precision agriculture using unmanned aerial vehicles (2015)
4. Thorp, K.: Precision Agriculture (2014)
5. Chang, Y.K., Zaman, Q.U., Farooque, A., Chattha, H., Read, S., Schumann, A.: Sensing and control system for spot-application of granular fertilizer in wild blueberry field. Precis. Agric. **18**, 210–223 (2017)
6. Gillan, J.K., Karl, J.W., Barger, N.N., Elaksher, A., Duniway, M.C.: Spatially explicit rangeland erosion monitoring using high-resolution digital aerial imagery. Rangel. Ecol. Manag. **69**, 95–107 (2016)

7. Rokhmana, C.A.: The potential of UAV-based remote sensing for supporting precision agriculture in Indonesia. Procedia Environ. Sci. **24**, 245–253 (2015)

8. Lamb, D.W., Brown, R.B.: PA—Precision Agriculture. J. Agric. Eng. Res. **78**, 117–125 (2001)

9. Gómez-Candón, D., De Castro, A.I., López-Granados, F.: Assessing the accuracy of mosaics from unmanned aerial vehicle (UAV) imagery for precision agriculture purposes in wheat. Precis. Agric. **15**, 44–56 (2014)

10. Ouédraogo, M.M., Degré, A., Debouche, C., Lisein, J.: The evaluation of unmanned aerial system-based photogrammetry and terrestrial laser scanning to generate DEMs of agricultural watersheds. Geomorphology **214**, 339–355 (2014)

11. Gan, H., Lee, W., Alchanatis, V.: A photogrammetry-based image registration method for multi-camera systems. In: Proceedings of 14th International Conference on Precision Agriculture

12. Aasen, H.: The acquisition of Hyperspectral Digital Surface Models of crops from UAV snapshot cameras (2016)

13. Ram, E., Shechter, M., Sela, E.: High capacity system for precision agriculture reconnaissance and intelligence. In: 13th International Conference on Precision Agriculture, St. Louis, MO, USA (2016)

14. Duncan, B.A., Murphy, R.R.: Comparison of flight paths from fixed-wing and rotorcraft small unmanned aerial systems at SR530 mudslide Washington state. In: 2015 IEEE International Conference on Robotics and Automation (ICRA), pp. 3416–3421. IEEE (2015)

15. Schwind, M.: Comparing and characterizing three-dimensional point clouds derived by structure from motion photogrammetry (2016). http://gradworks.umi.com/10/24/10247379.html

16. Staller, J.E., Thompson, R.G.: A multidisciplinary approach to understanding the initial introduction of maize into Coastal Ecuador. J. Archaeol. Sci. **29**, 33–50 (2002)

17. Agisoft - User Manuals. http://www.agisoft.com/downloads/user-manuals/

18. Visockiene, J.S., Brucas, D., Ragauskas, U.: Comparison of UAV images processing softwares. J. Meas. Eng. **2**, 111–121 (2014)

19. Pix4D - Offline Getting Started and Manual. https://support.pix4d.com/hc/en-us/articles/204272989-Offline-Getting-Started-and-Manual-pdf-#gsc.tab=0

20. Govorcin, M., Pribicevic, B., Dapo, A.: Comparison and analysis of software solutions for creation of a digital terrain model using unmanned aerial vehicles. In: 14th International Multidisciplinary Scientific GeoConference SGEM 2014 - Geoconference on Informatics (2014)

21. Psirofonia, P., Samaritakis, V., Eliopoulos, P., Potamitis, I.: Use of unmanned aerial vehicles for agricultural applications with emphasis on crop protection: three novel case-studies. Int. J. Agric. Sci. Technol. **5**, 30–39 (2017)

22. Park, J.W., Jeong, H.H., Kim, J.S., Choi, C.U.: Development of open source-based automatic shooting and processing UAV imagery for Orthoimage Using Smart Camera UAV. ISPRS Int. Arch. Photogramm. Remote Sens. Spat. Inf. Sci. **XLI-B7**, 941–944 (2016)

23. Micheletti, N., Chandler, J.H., Lane, S.N.: Structure from motion (SFM) photogrammetry. In: Book Chapters (Civil and Building Engineering). Zenrin (1995)

24. Morgan, J.A., Brogan, D.J., Nelson, P.A.: Application of Structure-from-Motion photogrammetry in laboratory flumes. Geomorphology **276**, 125–143 (2017)

25. Brocks, S., Bareth, G.: Evaluating dense 3D reconstruction software packages for oblique monitoring of crop canopy surface. ISPRS Int. Arch. Photogramm. Remote Sens. Spat. Inf. Sci. **XLI-B5**, 785–789 (2016)

26. Shelestov, A.Y., Kravchenko, A.N., Skakun, S.V., Voloshin, S.V., Kussul, N.N.: Geospatial information system for agricultural monitoring. Cybern. Syst. Anal. **49**, 124–132 (2013)
27. Tempelmann, U., Borner, A., Chaplin, B., Uebbing, R.: Photogrammetric software for the LH Systems ADS40 Airborne Digital Sensor. ISPRS (2000)
28. James, D., Eckermann, J., Belblidia, F., Sienz, J.: Point cloud data from Photogrammetry techniques to generate 3D Geometry (PDF Download Available). In: ACME 2015 (2015)
29. Şanlıoğlu, İ., Zeybek, M., Karauğuz, G.: Photogrammetric survey and 3D modeling of Ivriz rock relief in late Hittite Era. Mediterr. Archaeol. Archaeom. **13**, 147–157 (2013)
30. Pokrovenszki, K., Vágvölgyi, B., Tóth, Z.: Practical experience with the 3D photogrammetric methods used at the excavation of Csókakő castle. J. F. Archaeol. **40**, 325–346 (2015)
31. Machovina, B.L., Feeley, K.J., Machovina, B.J.: UAV remote sensing of spatial variation in banana production. Crop Pasture Sci. **67**, 1281 (2016)
32. Miserque Castillo, J.Z., Laverde Diaz, R., Rueda Guzmán, C.L.: Development of an aerial counting system in oil palm plantations. IOP Conf. Ser. Mater. Sci. Eng. **138**, 12007 (2016)
33. An, N., Welch, S.M., Markelz, R.J.C., Baker, R.L., Palmer, C.M., Ta, J., Maloof, J.N., Weinig, C.: Quantifying time-series of leaf morphology using 2D and 3D photogrammetry methods for high-throughput plant phenotyping. Comput. Electron. Agric. **135**, 222–232 (2017)
34. Herrero-Huerta, M., González-Aguilera, D., Rodriguez-Gonzalvez, P., Hernández-López, D.: Vineyard yield estimation by automatic 3D bunch modelling in field conditions. Comput. Electron. Agric. **110**, 17–26 (2015)

Search for Optimum Color Space
for the Recognition of Oranges
in Agricultural Fields

José Luis Hernández-Hernández[1]([⊠]) [iD],
Mario Hernández-Hernández[1] [iD], Severino Feliciano-Morales[1] [iD],
Valentín Álvarez-Hilario[1] [iD], and Israel Herrera-Miranda[2] [iD]

[1] Academic Unit of Engineering,
Autonomous University of Guerrero, Guerrero, Mexico
Joseluis.hernandez4@um.es, mhernandezh@uagro.mx,
sevefelici72@gmail.com, valentin_ah@yahoo.com
[2] Center for Research and Postgraduate in Socio-Territorial Studies,
Autonomous University of Guerrero, Guerrero, Mexico
israel_hm@hotmail.com

Abstract. Artificial vision systems are powerful tools for automatic recognition of fruits and vegetables in Mexican agricultural fields. This research presents the image capture, cropping and process for the recognition of fruits found in trees. The design and implementation of a recognition system based on color is proposed. For this research, experiments were carried out with the following color spaces: Hue Lightnes Saturation (HLS), Hue Saturation Value (HSV), Luma Chrominance-red Chrominance-blue (YCrCb), Luminance Chrominance-U Chrominance-V (YUV), Luminance red/green yellow/blue (L * a * b *), Luminance Chromaticity-u Chromaticity-v (L * u * v *), Tonality Saturation Lightness (TSL), Intensity-red Intensity-green Intensity-blue (I1I2I3) and XYZ. In each color space, different alternatives emerge, for example: what channels to use, reduction of the image, size of the histograms, etc. A varied set of images were selected to test these techniques for the color recognition of orange fruit. The results showed that some color spaces are the most appropriate for the recognition of oranges.

Keywords: Artificial vision · Orange segmentation · Orange recognition and color spaces

1 Introduction

One of the most important senses of human beings is the vision which is used to obtain visual information from the physical environment. According to Aristotle, "vision is to know what objects exist and where they are by sight." Vision is the most important sense that the human being has. The eye is responsible for capturing the images and sending them to the brain to be processed and interpreted appropriately [9].

The color is a property of the objects that depends on the wavelengths that the objects are able to absorb or to reflect in the visible spectrum in such a way that, in a

© Springer International Publishing AG 2017
R. Valencia-García et al. (Eds.): CITI 2017, CCIS 749, pp. 296–307, 2017.
DOI: 10.1007/978-3-319-67283-0_22

white object no frequency component is absorbed and in a black object none is reflected. Color is a very important attribute for the recognition of objects in images. Figure 1.a shows an image of an orange tree and Fig. 1.b the same image is shown but in greyscale. In the second image it is more difficult to identify the oranges; hence the importance of using the color attribute for the recognition of oranges [11].

Fig. 1. Oranges images in the tree (a. Color image and b. Grayscale image).

Artificial vision is a field of artificial intelligence that, through the use of appropriate techniques, allows the gathering, processing and analysis of different type of information obtained from digital images. The artificial vision is composed of a set of processes used to carry out the analysis of images. These processes are: gathering data from images, memorization of data, processing and interpretation of results.

Companies require applications that enhance their productivity and optimize the way employees collaborate and interact, whether from the organization's internal network or from a remote point through a mobile device and from the cloud infrastructure. The purpose of such applications is to guarantee the delivery of data and information in a simple and synchronous manner.

In fruit growing many applications have been developed using artificial vision. Computer vision systems not only recognize the size, shape, color and texture of objects, but also provide numerical attributes of the objects or scenarios that are examined [1].

There are many processes in the fruit growing processes where decisions are made depending on the appearance of the product. The applications to classify the fruit by its quality, size or maturity stage are based on its appearance, helping to asses if the fruit is not ripe, mature or rotten. Humans are able to perform tasks such as planting, pruning and harvesting using basically the visual sensory mechanism. This suggests that a system based on a visual sensor should be able to emulate the process of the human visual recognition system [6].

One of the fundamental problems that can be solved by digital image analysis is the segmentation of fruits, that is, the detection of pixels belonging to fruits or to the ground - leaves, stems or other objects [10]. The technique is always related to image analysis and processing which is largely dependent on the segmentation procedure [17].

The problem of fruit segmentation has been extensively studied in a previous research [7]. This technique must be able to solve non-trivial sensing conditions such as the appearance of shadows, image noise, pixel saturation (very light or very dark values), light shortage, differences between fruit varieties and intrinsic camera parameters such as white balance.

Quality assessment of fruits and vegetables is done based on the analysis of external features like color, size, shape, texture and presence of damage. As consumers are mostly influenced to choose or reject a particular fruit by its color, it is the most important attribute for assessing the quality of fruit. The traditional labor intensive manual inspection process which is subjective in nature is gradually being replaced by computer vision techniques [14].

Some studies have shown the importance of selecting an optimum color space for each application domain [8]. A comparative study of several color models applied to a problem of plant and soil classification in lettuce crops is described [5]. Therefore, automation and use of image processing methods in agriculture have become a major issue in recent years [15].

The increase in computer power at affordable prices and the introduction of multiple core processors allow to process complex images in a short time and to use more complex algorithm [17].

2   Materials and Methods

This section describes the suggested method to find the most optimum color space for the fruit image recognition and specifically, images of oranges. First, we identify the color spaces that have been considered for this study, the algorithm of color classification, image acquisition, and the creation of the orange-background image model and the recognition of oranges in the images.

2.1   Color Spaces Analyzed

Color is a subjective sensation of the human being, derived from the ability of our eyes - in particular, the photoreceptors - known as cones - for capture light in different spectral ranges [8]. The different color models are mathematical models for these subjective perceptions, which describe how to represent perceptible colors with a tuple of values. It is called a color space to the set of values that are generated with all possible tuples of each model. Since the spaces are mostly nonlinear transformations of the RGB space, the way in which the colors are distributed is different in each color space.

A color space is a model that attempts to describe human perception, that is, a specific organization of colors in a photo or video. Depending on the color model in combination with the physical devices that allow the color representations in the images, as well as those used as analogue signals (color television) or digital representations. A color space can be arbitrary, with particular colors assigned according to the system, in addition to being mathematically structured.

A color space is an abstract mathematical model that describes how colors can be represented as tuples of numbers, usually as three or four values as color components.

However, a color model that does not have a mapping function associated with an absolute color space is more or less an arbitrary color system without connection to a color interpretation system.

In the present work the following color spaces were analyzed: HLS, HSV, YCrCb, YUV, L * a * b *, L * u * v *, TSL, I1I2I3 and XYZ [4] [8]. The following paragraphs detail each of these spaces:

- Color space HSL (Hue, Lightness, Saturation) defines a color model in terms of its constituent components. The HLS color space is represented graphically as a double cone or a double hexagon. The two vertices in the HSL model correspond to white and black, the angle corresponds to the hue, the distance to the axis with saturation and the distance to the white-black axis corresponds to the luminance.
- Color space HSV follows a representation more similar to the cylindrical coordinates. It is also a representation closer to the way humans perceive the colors and their properties, because the color tones are grouped, which is different from the RGB case where the colors are not necessarily so grouped.
- Color space YCrCb it is a model oriented to compression and transmission of images. It is based on the separation of one Y-channel of luminance (or light intensity), and two chrominance channels (or color tone, independent of its luminosity). The channels Cr and Cb correspond, to the channels R and B normalized in intensity, respectively [3].
- Color space YUV is a model which defines a color space in terms of a luminance component and two chrominance components. The YUV model is used in PAL and NTSC television broadcast systems, which is the standard in most of the countries. The YUV model is closer to the human perception model than the RGB standard used in computer graphics hardware.
- Color space L*a*b* also referred to as CIELAB, is currently one of the most popular and uniform color spaces used to evaluate the color and object. This color space is widely used because it correlates numerical color values consistently with human visual perception. Researchers and manufacturers use it to evaluate color attributes, identify inconsistencies, and accurately express their results to others in numerical terms.
- Color space L*u*v* (also called the CIELUV space) is one of the uniform color spaces defined by the CIE in 1976.
- Color space TSL. This model was created to address human skin detection problems [12].
- Color space I1I2I3. This color space was proposed by Ohta for color segmentation, as a correlation of RGB components using the Karhunen-Loeve transform.
- Color space XYZ. This color space, also defined by the CIE, is essentially based in a trichromatic model of the human retina. Although in the individual channels of XYZ very low classification results are achieved by themselves, the combinations of two channels have been found to be very accurate [5].

The representation of the nine color spaces described above can be seen in Fig. 2.

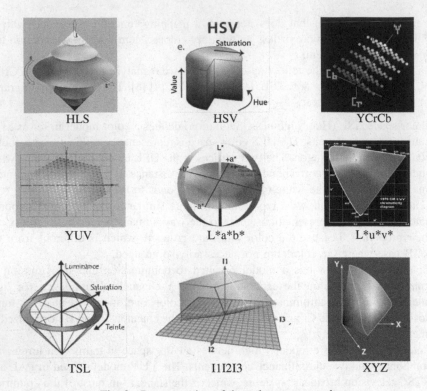

Fig. 2. Representation of the color spaces used.

2.2   Color Classification Algorithm

The individual pixel on orange process segmentation is based on the pixel classification, which is repeated in images of interest.

The classification or segmentation is based on a probabilistic method, in which it is estimated the probability of a particular color is orange color or background color (elements other than orange). The probability density functions are approximated by histograms in the color model and with the chosen channels. This technique has several advantages: it can be adapted to complex distributions, it can be trained with a small number of examples, and it is computationally very efficient.

From each of the pixels, we can define the conditional probabilities based on whether a pixel is orange, **P**(orange | color), or background **P**(background | color). Using the Bayes rule, these probabilities can be computed through the probability density functions, **P**(orange | color) and **P**(background | color), which indicate the distribution, with the formulas (1) and (2):

$$P(orange|color) = \frac{p_{orange}(color)}{p_{orange}(color) + p_{background}(color)} \tag{1}$$

$$P(background|color) = \frac{p_{background}(color)}{p_{orange}(color) + p_{background}(color)} \tag{2}$$

With the equations of García-Mateos, we obtain the pixels that correspond to plant and soil respectively. This is a process of mathematical morphology, consisting of moving all pixels of the image from left to right and from top to bottom to find isolated pixels, which are considered noise [5]. This noise is eliminated by applying the erosion and dilation with the following equations:

$$Open = (B \otimes E) \oplus E \tag{3}$$

$$Close = (B \oplus E) \otimes E \tag{4}$$

The open operation eliminates the fine points or fine structures and the close operation fills the black holes of a certain size.

Subsequently various arithmetic calculations are performed to obtain the percentages of orange and background of processed image. (Fig. 3)

INPUT: **I**: set of n training images and orange/background masks
   M : set of color spaces
   C : set of channels selections
   T : set of histogram sizes
OUTPUT: m^*, c^*, t^* : optimal color space, channels and size
   $p_{orange}, p_{background}$: trained models for orange and background

1. Let **A**= $\{i_1, i_3...\}$ and **B**= $\{i_2, i_4...\}$.
2. For each color space m in **M** do:
3.   Convert **A** and **B** images from RGB to space m.
4.   For each channels selection c in **C** do:
5.   For each size t in **T** do:
6.   Compute p_{orange} and $p_{background}$ from **A**, with size t, channels c.
7.   Classify **B** with p_{orange} and $p_{background}$, computing $error_1$.
8.   Compute p_{orange} and $p_{background}$ from **B**, with size t, channels c.
9.   Classify **A** with p_{orange} and $p_{background}$, computing $error_2$.
10.   Calculate mean error: $error(m,c,t) = (error_1 + error_2)/2$.
11. Select (m^*, c^*, t^*) with: $\text{argmin}_{m,c,t} \, error(m,c,t)$.
12. Obtain p_{orange} and $p_{background}$ from **I**, with size t^*, channels c^*, space m^*.

Fig. 3. Algorithm for optimum selection of color space.

2.3   Image Acquisition

The previous images were used to check the efficiency of the color spaces and were taken from the web network. These orange images are in a mean resolution level, and different focus variations, light, shadow and brightness were considered in order to have a wide range of orange pixel colors. The images were stored in png image format. To do the recognition, the probability of the maximum value between P(orange | color) and P(background | color) was searching for each pixel in order to identify if it was orange, background or they were not undefined for recognition. This probability is a function of the Bayes' theorem which is shown in Fig. 4.

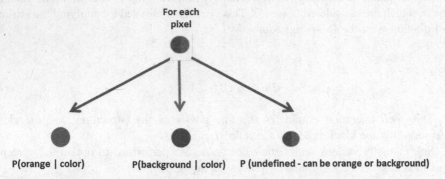

Fig. 4. Probability of being orange or background according to Bayes' theorem.

2.4   Creating the Model Orange-Background

For the orange-background model creation, 10 images were taken and some places were marked in rough orange light where there was orange and green and where there is not orange to generate the orange class and the background class. The 2 classes remain in a single file where the model is generated. This process can be seen in Fig. 5.

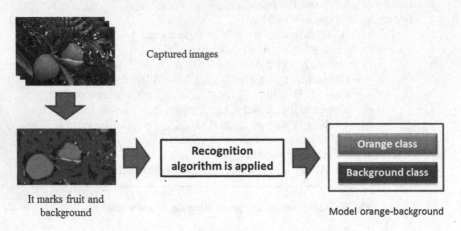

Fig. 5. The orange-background model Creation.

In the process model creation, histograms were generated by each of the following color spaces and each color space were also made from the combinations of its 3 channels (channel 1, channel 2, channel 3, channels 1-2, Channels 2-3, channels 3-1 and channels 1-2-3). During the process of creating the model, several recognition errors were found, which are shown in Fig. 6. In this figure it can be seen that the color space that has the smallest error is the YCrCb in its Cr channel.

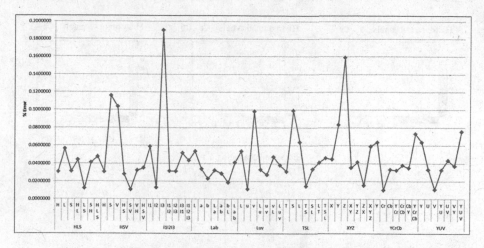

Fig. 6. Recognition errors when creating the orange-background model.

63 histograms (9 color spaces per 7 channel combinations) were generated. When creating the histograms, the images and the errors recognition were piled up. The histograms were normalized so that the major and minor peaks were shown in aesthetic form but showing the literal results.

For each histogram, we generated: the orange class, the background class and a recognition error statistics (where it was not possible to specify if it was orange or background).

In the program runs that were carried out to show the recognition operation, it was obtained that the color space that best does the recognition of oranges and background was the YCrCb color space with the combination of Cr channels. The other three color spaces which have a smaller recognition error are: (i) HSV with the combination of S-V channels, (ii) YUV on channel V and (iii) Luv on channel u.

The generated histograms of the YCrCb color space are shown in Fig. 7.

The orange and background recognition errors of the 7 combinations of the YCrCb color space obtained from the histograms of Fig. 7 are shown in Table 1.

In Table 1, three columns are shown; the first column, shows the optimal color space that shows less error in the recognition; the second column shows all possible combinations of channels and the third column shows the recognition error when creating the orange-background model. The lowest recognition error is the Cr channel, which is shown in Yellow background in Table 1.

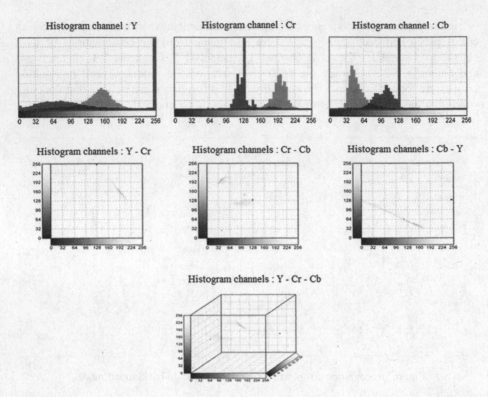

Fig. 7. Histograms of the 3 individual channels of the YCrCb color space of and their combinations.

Table 1. Errors of the 7 combinations of the YCrCb color space.

Color space	Channels	Error
YCrCb	Y	0.0637151
	Cr	0.0101590
	Cb	0.0331156
	Y Cr	0.0322010
	Cr Cb	0.0379072
	Cb Y	0.0348894
	Y Cr Cb	0.0730170

2.5   Recognition of Oranges in Images

Based on several program runs that were carried out, it was observed that the Cr channel gave good results for the segmentation of the regions where there were oranges. The Cr plane is not affected by variations in light. Therefore it has been concluded that using only the Cr channel of the YCrCb color space gives a very robust algorithm regardless the illumination variation.

To perform the recognition of oranges, various photos were taken. With the model referred above, we calculated the orange coverage that exists in each image. In Fig. 8, three orange recognition examples are shown.

Original Images   **Recognition of oranges**

Fig. 8. Recognition of orange in images using the orange-background model.

3 Conclusions

Image processing has been proved to be an effective tool for analysis in various fields and applications [18].

Artificial vision systems are powerful tools for the automatic pattern recognition of fruits and vegetables, including classification by internal and external parameters that determine the quality of the product. In addition, these systems favor adequate automatic supervision strategies to sense the processes of post-harvest, until the fruits reach the final consumer. Artificial systems not only replace human recognition, but also improve accurate an in-time fruit and vegetable classification [2].

In the last years automatic horticulture has been one of the most important research objects in many universities in the world. We have found that the main research projects are committed to the recognition of fruits, counting, detection of plants, monitoring of irrigation needs, etc.

In this research, the OpenCV (Open Source of Computer Vision) libraries were used. These libraries provide a set of image processing functions as well as pattern and image analysis functions.

The processing was implemented in a desktop application using the Windows 8 operating system. In the experiments carried out, the feasibility and efficiency of the method have been verified. The segmentation method based on color segmentation accurately detects the fruits regions in the processed images.

It was verified that there are 4 color spaces in which the recognition of fruits was successfull:

- The YCrCb color space in the Cr channel.
- The HSV color space, with the combination of S-V channels.
- The YUV color space in the V channel.
- The Luv color space in channel u.

Other applications for mobile devices and compact controllers using these models are currently being developed.

Future research lines include the application of dimensionality reduction techniques, as well as the Linear Dimensionality Analysis (LDA). This could improve the quality of classification tasks and avoid the subordination in the color space used. On the other hand, although this paper focuses mainly on color analysis, more advanced techniques could be used for normalizing the obtained binary images instead of using a mathematical morphology, like graph-cuts-based techniques. This could override many errors in situations when color is not detected sufficiently in order to discriminate the actual classes.

Acknowledgments. Authors are grateful to Academic Unit of Engineering of Autonomous University of Guerrero for supporting this work.

References

1. Chen, Y.R., Chao, K., Kim, M.S.: Machine vision technology for agricultural applications. Comput. Electron. Agric. **36**(2), 173–191 (2002)
2. Cubero, S., Aleixos, N., Moltó, E., Gómez-Sanchis, J., Blasco, J.: Advances in machine vision applications for automatic inspection and quality evaluation of fruits and vegetables. Food Bioprocess Technol. **4**(4), 487–504 (2011)
3. Farhad, D., Abdolhossein, S.: An adaptive real-time skin detector based on Hue thresholding: a comparison on two motion tracking methods. Pattern Recogn. Lett. **27**(2), 1342–1352 (2006)
4. Enriquez, I.J.G., Bonilla, M.N.I., Cortes, J.M.R.: Segmentación de rostro por color de la piel aplicado a detección de somnolencia en el conductor. Congreso Nacional de Ingeniería Electrónica del Golfo CONAGOLFO, pp. 67–72 (2009)
5. García-Mateos, G., Hernández-Hernández, J.L., Escarabajal-Henarejos, D., Jaen-Terrones, S., Molina-Martínez, J.M.: Study and comparison of color models for automatic image analysis in irrigation management applications. Agric. Water Manage. **151**, 158–166 (2015)

6. Jiménez, A.R., Jain, A.K., Ceres, R., Pons, J.L.: Automatic fruit recognition: a survey and new results using range/attenuation images. Pattern Recogn. **32**(10), 1719–1736 (1999)
7. Lin, K., Chen, J., Si, H., Junhui, W.: A review on computer vision technologies applied in greenhouse plant stress detection. Adv. Image Graph. Technol. **363**, 192–200 (2013)
8. Luszczkiewicz-Piatek, M.: Which color space should be chosen for robust color image retrieval based on mixture modeling. Adv. Intell. Syst. Comput. **233**, 55–64 (2014)
9. Machuca Arias, S.: Uso de Técnicas Avanzadas de Visión Artificial aplicado a la Industria Frutícola. Universidad Tecnológica Metropolitana, Chile (2009)
10. McCarthy, C.L., Cheryl, N.H., Hancock, S.R.: Applied machine vision of plants - a review with implications for field deployment in automated farming operations. Intell. Serv. Robot. **3**(4), 209–217 (2010)
11. Pajares, G., De la Cruz, J.: Visión por computador. Imágenes digitales y aplicaciones. Alfaomega Grupo Editor (2003)
12. Terrillon, J.C., Akamatsu, S.: Comparative performance of different chrominance spaces for color segmentation and detection of human faces in complex scene images. In: International Conference on Face and Gesture Recognition, pp. 54 − 61 (2000)
13. Lu, J., Sang, N.: Detecting citrus fruits and occlusion recovery under natural illumination conditions. Comput. Electron. Agric. **110**, 121–130 (2015)
14. Ashok, V., Vinod, D.S.: Automatic quality evaluation of fruits using Probabilistic Neural Network approach. In: 2014 International Conference on Contemporary Computing and Informatics (IC3I). IEEE (2014)
15. Thendral, R., Suhasini, A., Senthil, N.: A comparative analysis of edge and color based segmentation for orange fruit recognition. In: 2014 International Conference on Communications and Signal Processing (ICCSP). IEEE (2014)
16. Yamamoto, K., et al.: On plant detection of intact tomato fruits using image analysis and machine learning methods. Sensors **14**(7), 12191–12206 (2014)
17. Pham, V.H., Lee, B.R.: An image segmentation approach for fruit defect detection using k-means clustering and graph-based algorithm. Vietnam J. Comput. Sci. **2**(1), 25–33 (2015)
18. Syal, A., Garg, D., Sharma, S.: A survey of computer vision methods for counting fruits and yield prediction. Int. J. Comput. Sci. Eng. **2**(6), 346–350 (2013)

Predictive Models for the Detection of Diseases in Crops Through Supervised Learning

Cristina Páez Quinde[1]([⊠]), Margarita Narváez Ríos[1], Segundo Curay Quispe[2],
Marco Pérez Salinas[2], Francisco Torres Oñate[1], Daniel Sánchez Guerrero[3],
Javier Sánchez Guerrero[1], and Carlos A. Morales F.[1]

[1] Facultad de Ciencias Humanas y de la Educación,
Universidad Técnica de Ambato, Ambato, Ecuador
{mc.paez,mm.narvaez,cf.torres,jsanchez,carlosamoralesf}@uta.edu.ec
[2] Facultad de Ciencias Agropecuarias,
Universidad Técnica de Ambato, Ambato, Ecuador
{se.curay,mo.perez}@uta.edu.ec
[3] Departamento de Ciencias de la Vida,
Universidad Estatal Amazónica, Puyo, Ecuador
dsanchez@uea.edu.ec

Abstract. This paper proposes a methodology for the application of
prediction algorithms for the development of diseases in crops using data
mining techniques, which incorporate validation mechanisms based on
data analysis requirements including verification of the method of selection and presentation of the results, as well as mechanisms of validation
of the results based on metrics of quality of the information, which guarantee the effectiveness in the construction of the knowledge. The conditions for the establishment and proliferation of diseases are used as a case
study in the analysis and contrasted with the favorable meteorological
conditions for the different diseases, using methods that allow the collection of data for the prognosis of the disease. The models relate indicators
of occurrence with meteorological data collected from the National Institute of Meteorology and Hydrology located in Querochaca Experimental
Farm of the Technical University of Ambato whose geographical coordinates are: Latitude: -1.353543; Longitude: -78.617175. The data analysis techniques used were able to predict crop diseases in 78.80% with the
J48 algorithm and 79.18% with the Logistic Regression algorithm based
on data collected and analyzed from the meteorological station of the
year 2015–2016, allowing the iterative search of correlations of consec-
utive day records, agro-climatic variables and biological variables. Our
study is an initial proposal taking as parameters the temperature and
humidity from previous works that qualify this line of research.

Keywords: Supervised learning · Agroclimatic variables · Disease ·
Cultivation · Agriculture

© Springer International Publishing AG 2017
R. Valencia-García et al. (Eds.): CITI 2017, CCIS 749, pp. 308–318, 2017.
DOI: 10.1007/978-3-319-67283-0_23

1 Introduction

Agriculture is one of the productive activities of the human being that depends heavily on the behavior of the climate, associated with it, are the presence of pests and diseases, nutritional efficiency and water demand [24]. The world population growth with the consequent increase in the demand of food has exerted on the agriculture world-wide, a pressure in the sense of maximize the production. One of the well-known effects is the huge increase in the use of chemical synthesis fertilizers.

Solanaceae represent an important economic resource for several countries in the region, especially for the cultivation of the main species of food, such as tomato, pepper, eggplant and especially potatoes [6,9]. Globally potatoes, together with rice, maize and wheat, are the four most important crops for human consumption. In 2013, more than 10 million hectares of potatoes were planted in the world with a production of 300 million tons. The main potato producing countries are Russia, China, India, Poland and the United States [23].

Due to the importance of complementary cultures for human food, studies are necessary with new products that favor the growth and induction of resistance mechanisms, which can confer protection against the presence of pathogens. Tomato (Solanum lycopersicum L.) is a crop of national preference and in great demand worldwide due to its high content of vitamins C and E, potassium and its antioxidant properties [19].

Environmental conditions are a determining factor in the appearance of phytopathogenic diseases affecting susceptible plants, leading to the appearance of several types of symptoms that alter the normal physio-metabolism of plants. This causes tissue necrosis and finally death of the host, as manifested by [13], indicating that the environmental conditions favor disease development. The objective of this research is to apply supervised algorithms to predict cultivar diseases based on data collected and analyzed from the meteorological station of the year 2016 and its relationship with agriculture. Research on this problem shows that data mining has the potential to be a great resource in obtaining knowledge and generate patterns and originate models that allow predicting results. These techniques organize behavior in trends, and this allows data mining to give effect to information of great interest that other media cannot detect. [21]. On the other hand, there are learning algorithms that build regression and classification models with supervised learning. These algorithms allow, through a set of training data, to predict or detect a new input data; several are the alternatives to generate models of prediction of diseases in plants that are subject to algorithms or mechanisms of Artificial Intelligence [18], either Automatic Learning, Knowledge Engineering, Fuzzy Logic, Artificial Neural Networks, Expert Systems, Bayesian Networks, which are the ones that are most attached to the management of Big Data related to the conditions or factors of the crops [4].

The present research presents a brief description of the algorithms used in the experimentation, presents a discussion on more relevant researches of the topic addressed, and describes the methodology used for the prediction of diseases and will conclude with the results obtained, conclusions and some recommendations on future research work.

2   State of the Art

Diseases affecting horticultural crops have a high environmental and economic impact due to the losses they cause in crop yield and quality [10,12]; among these we have Phytophthora, Phytium, Peronospora, Oidium, Botrytis and others that directly affect the Solanaceae because this pathogens develop under favorable meteorological conditions [22]. For the control of these phytopathogens a great amount of fungicides are being used that generate resistance to the molecules and pollute the environment [7,8].

Diseases cause the greatest losses and increase of costs due to the need for greater care; the disease management strategy includes a series of measures including chemical control, being an alternative that brings biological problems in the organisms involved and a high-risk factor in human health [3]. Knowledge of meteorological conditions and their relationship to disease development are key factors in reducing impacts. The new production systems must be designed with environmental changes in mind, seeking to reduce the excessive use of agrochemicals [11].

[15] aim to generate models for use in sustainable agriculture, in order to efficiently control diseases and thus preserve the ecosystem and human health. The losses caused by pests and diseases to the production of all the crops in the world are estimated at 35%; insect pests cause 13% of losses, diseases 12% and weeds 10%. Annually, an estimated 2.5 million tonnes of pesticides are used worldwide. Of the total pesticides applied, 59–60% are herbicides, 20–30% insecticides and 10–20% fungicides [12].

The area of study of the epidemic triangle is the conceptual basis of epidemiology research, being one of the greatest research potential in Phytopathology, regarding the construction of predictive models in crops [1,2].

The processing of data obtained from temperatures, humidity, precipitation and dew point is done by means of techniques such as J48, KDD and Tree distribution, which are handled by the software tool WEKA. This is supported by the technique of selection of attributes, which results in a classification scheme of decision trees with the mining algorithms J48, Logistic Regression, Multilayer Perceptron and RBF [20].

Losses in production that affect Solanaceae, especially potato, tomato and tamarillo crops, are caused by the different diseases that occur due to changes in environmental conditions. Likewise, the incidence and severity of these diseases depends on the organism that causes them, the susceptibility of the plant and the environment. The application of Artificial Intelligence in the commercialization of agricultural products is an alternative not widely used in food distribution, it recognizes only a prototype expert system, directed to the marketing of agricultural products, where [4] uses a system that forecasts the sales time for perishable products using neural networks and evolutionary computing where it is a very useful system to avoid the loss in the commercialization of grains.

The agricultural case study for the learning of Bayesian networks (BNs) in the prediction of coffee rust [14], which causes premature defoliation that weakens the plant and reduces its subsequent yield, is commonly controlled by chemical fungicides that must be applied before the symptoms of infection, but with prediction system the use of fungicides would be reduced, obtaining a quality product, healthy and with lower costs [16].

[14] indicate that the use of neural and multiple regression networks predict diseases in various plant populations; their limited use by the user means that there is no online tool available to assist researchers or farmers in planting with adequate control measures. In the work cited the researcher presents a method based on vector machines, which is a support for the development of predictive models based on the climate to avoid the development of plant diseases [17].

[8] propose the use of sensor networks to analyze organic compounds and to know if tomato crops are healthy or infected. For this purpose, the inclusion of predicted meteorological data for the evaluation of the different crop management techniques is very important. Their work is intended to predict time using a modified k-nearest neighbor approach and then use parameters such as humidity and temperature to predict disease outbreaks in grapes. Such predictions could warn growers of significant developments expected in grape disease through e-mail or text messages.

The diseases that affect Solanaceae, especially potato, tomato and tamarillo crops, are caused by the environmental conditions that reduce their production. The incidence and severity of these diseases depends on the organism that causes them, the susceptibility of the plant and the environment [5]. In each disease, a description of symptoms and integrated management of the disease will be given. Integrated disease management includes: proper identification of the organism causing the disease, use of resistant cultivars, crop rotation, sanitation measures, avoidance of plantings at times favorable to disease development, and inappropriate use of pesticides; it is desired to know the diseases and pests that occur in the cultivation of Solanaceae.

3   Methodology

For this research, a case-control study was developed with data obtained by INAMHI (National Institute of Meteorology in Hydrology) in the periods 2015–2016 that determine the factors to be considered primordial for the procedure to which they were subjected. The aim was to correct them before being processed by the computer tool WEKA to allow the prediction of diseases in the cultivation of Solanaceae.

The selection of the factors is of vital importance for the development of the predictive model in the crop, therefore the most important variables taken into consideration are: humidity, maximum and minimum temperature, the parts of the plant to which the disease affects (Stem, leaves, flowers, root), diseases (Phytophthora, Phytium, Peronospora, Botitrys, Oidio, Roya, Alternaria, Septoria, Colletotrichum, Bacteriosis) and estimated times in which diseases are generated that particularly better predict the class (disease).

3.1   Method

The initial sample is a total of 2930 data, using as main variables humidity and temperature.

The algorithms used for the prediction of these diseases were: Neural Network, RBF, MLP, Logistic Regression and J48 (Fig. 1).

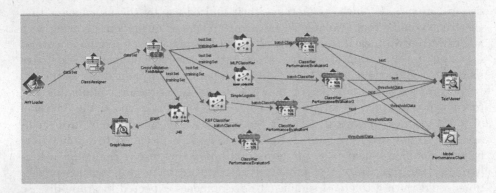

Fig. 1. Structure of models with the algorithms analyzed

Using the Weka tool and its Knowledge Flow functionality, the model was constructed with the algorithms to be analyzed. This tool allows graphical visualization of the scheme, connecting the dataset between each of the elements, adding diverse types of classifiers, whether supervised or not supervised. In this case, algorithms like Neural Network, RBF, MLP, Logistic Regression and J48 were used, creating training and evaluation connections to be visualized through links and the creation of a tree with all the data.

Table 1 shows the performance of each algorithm selected for the tests, in addition to providing sensitivity and specificity, considering that the sensitivity is the percentage of the data correctly classified and the specificity shows the percentage of data not classified correctly; of the algorithms analyzed, the ones with the highest prescience and recall were Logistic Regression and J48 in a range of 79.18% and 78.80%, respectively.

Table 1. Results of the Analyzed Models in the test set.

Model	Sensitivity	Specificity	%Correct
RBF	0.77	0.66	77.03%
MLP	0.78	0.67	77.88%
Logistic regression	0.79	0.74	79.18%
J48	0.79	0.77	78.80%

Of all the algorithms analyzed the algorithm J48 was selected by the favorable results obtained from a series of tests in the evaluation; the sensitivity and specificity to this study depends on the data that are being analyzed as: temperature, humidity, precipitation, dewpoint.

Figure 2 shows the relationship between temperature and humidity since these two factors are directly linked in the cultivation of Solanaceae, stressing that at higher temperature and humidity the crops are affected by dry and moist diseases, the colors are represented according to the diseases mentioned above, Alternaria-blue; Bacteriosis-red; Botrytis-Green; Colletotrichum-cyan; Oidium-pink; Peronospora-magenta; Phytium-yellow; Phytophthora-red; Rust-green; Septoria-gray. The values to be considered in the graph are determined by minimum and maximum, in the axis of the x temperature is located, and humidity in the axis of the y.

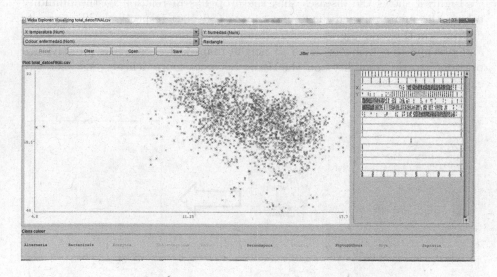

Fig. 2. Temperature-humidity ratio (Color figure online)

Figure 3 shows a relationship between diseases and temperature, taking as an example the month of March where it has a maximum temperature of 15.2 and a humidity of 73.0, precipitation of 6.8, heliophania (light) of 7.3 and a dewpoint of 9.9; as there is no light, the environmental humidity is increased, the tissue of the crop becomes more delicate and therefore exposed to more diseases, as shown in the example where the crop is affected by Botrytis.

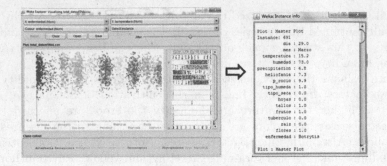

Fig. 3. Disease-Temperature Ratio

Figure 4 shows the diseases that the crop has in relation to the humidity taking the minimum and maximum ranges (80–100) respectively; The results obtained in this example were with a temperature of 12.7 and humidity of 66.0, and precipitation was considered to be the main factor, which is directly proportional to the humidity and the tissue becomes more delicate and therefore exposed to diseases.

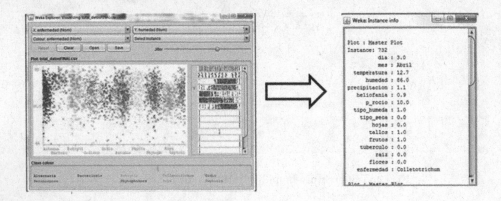

Fig. 4. Disease-moisture ratio

Figure 5 shows a direct relationship between crop diseases and precipitation (rainfall). It should be remembered that at lower rainfall the pests and diseases are more propitious to sprout in the plant.

As the example shows a precipitation of 0 to 20.3, the rains affect the yield of the crops in cold seasons, generally the crops with excess of water are not very productive since the humid conditions and the lack of sun affect the yield of the crops.

Figure 6 determines the dew point which indicates the temperature at which the air with a relative humidity percentage can no longer hold the water, thereby

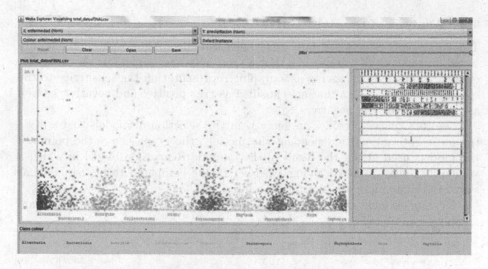

Fig. 5. Disease-precipitation ratio

producing condensation, i.e., at the lowest dewpoint in this case between 0–6 would rule out diseases in crops. Both the dew point and the absolute humidity are interrelated.

When the air is at dew point it is said that the relative humidity is 100%, the dew point varies and occurs at different times, as is the case of dry seasons in which dew point is shown by the nights and in which diseases such as Phythoph-thora develop in the leaves of the plant despite no rain or precipitation.

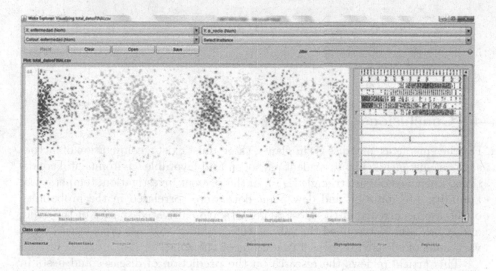

Fig. 6. Disease - dew point

3.2   Analysis of the ROC Curve

This analysis is done for a data comprehension effect, the results obtained are based on the case of the diseases that a crop acquires, depending on the result of the diagnostic tests, giving as a graphic representation the sensitivity to the specificity with the data that are classified as true positive and negative, as well as false positives and negatives.

The ROC curve provides an analysis in the selection of models that will be the most optimal and independent sub models, the graph shows the points of the models used giving the result of the Logistic Regression model in which a value of 1.0 was obtained giving a perfect rating compared to model J48 that shows optimal values and greater than 0.5.

The models located above the main diagonal represent good results to obtain a good prediction (Fig. 7).

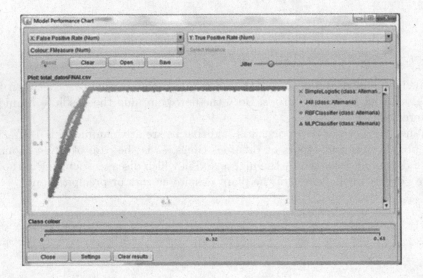

Fig. 7. ROC Curve

4   Conclusions

For the emergence of a disease in plants, there must exist a conjugation of factors such as: susceptible plant, virulent pathogen and favorable environmental conditions, known as disease triangle (DT); in the present investigation, temperature, humidity, precipitation and dew point data were correlated in the probability of disease occurrence in the most representative cultivated species of the zone, and it has been determined that about 80% of biotic diseases are caused by the variations of the environmental conditions of the zone.

This article reviews the research on the prediction of diseases and pests in Solanaceae crops using supervised learning algorithms; the algorithms were compared in order to observe the performance, considering that temperature and humidity are the variables most used to generate the probabilities correctly and interpretably.

Algorithms J48 and Logistic Regression are the most accurate algorithms when predicting or classifying diseases and pests in Solanaceae crops. On the other hand, RBF and MLP are rarely used in an agricultural context. However Multilayer Perceptron is an algorithm that stands out for its training learning speed. Regarding the future work, it is recommended to combine a set of classifiers for the measurement of water according to crop yield, as well as to obtain parameters of height, altitude and soil characteristics that are other factors that influence the appearance of pests and diseases in cultivars. This would increase the accuracy of prediction results by using techniques commonly referred to as set methods.

References

1. Bombelli, E.: Modelado para la predicción de enfermedades en los cultivos de alto valor comercial. Universidad Tecnologica Nacional, Buenos Aires (2011)
2. Bombelli, E., Moschini, R., Wright, E., López, M.V., Fabrizio, M.: Modelado para la predicción de enfermedades en cultivos de alto valor comercial. In: Proyecciones, pp. 47–59 (2013)
3. Borrás, O., Hernández, I., Portieles, R., Silva, Y., Pujol, M., Oliva, O.: Desarrollo de una alta protección frente a hongos y oomycetes en plantas mediante genes involucrados en la inhibición de patrones moleculares asociados a patógenos. In: Revista Anuales de la Academia de Ciencias de Cuba, pp. 1–14 (2014)
4. Bustos, J.: Inteligencia Artificial en el Sector Agropecuario. In: Seminario de Investigación, pp. 1–8 (2005)
5. Recuperado el 12 de Septiembre de 2016 (2016). de Infopankki.fi, http://www.infopankki.fi/es/informacion-sobre-finlandia/informacion-basica-sobre-finlandia/historia-de-finlandia
6. Corrales, D.C., Corrales, J.C., Figueroa Casas, A.: Hacia la detección de plagas y enfermedades en cultivos a través de aprendizaje supervisado, pp. 207–228 (2015)
7. Egea, J.M., Catalá, M., Egea, M.: Nuevos datos sobre variedades locales de solanáceas de la región de Murcia como base para la producción ecología, VIII Congreso SEAE Bullas (Murcia) (2008)
8. Ghaffari, R., Zhang, F.: Early detection of diseases in tomato crops: an electronic nose and intelligent systems approach. In: Control Decision and Information Technologies, pp. 753–757 (2010)
9. Gil, J., Cotes, J., Marín, M.: Incidencia visual de síntomas asociados a enfermedades virales en cultivos de papa de Colombia. In: Biotecnología en el Sector Agropecuario y Agroindustrial, pp. 101–110 (2013)
10. González, D., Costales, D., Falcón, A.: Influencia de un polímero de quitosana en el crecimiento y la actividad de enzimas defensivas en tomate (Solanum lycopersicum L.). In: Cultivos Tropicales, pp. 35–42 (2014)
11. Guerra, G., De Rossi, R., Plazas, M., Marquez, N., Ducasse, D.,& Brucher, E.: La protección vegetal en los cultivos. Aportes desde la fitopatología para el manejo de las enfermedades. In: Biología, epidemiología, manejo y control de hongos y bacterias fitopatógenas asociados a cultivos (2014)

12. Hernández, L., Montezuma, H., Vidal, N., Ruíz, R., Castillo, D., Chiquito, R.: La situación de las annonaceae en México: principales plagas, enfermedades y su control. In: V Congresso Internacional & Encontro Brasileiro sobre Annonaceae: do gene á exportao, pp. 044–054 (2014)

13. Jimenez, H.: Identificación de fitopatógenos asociados a las principales enfermedades del cultivo de sábila en los municipios de Agua de Dios y Ricaurte (Cundinamarca). In: Revista Tecnología y Productividad. Girardot, Regional Cundinamarca, pp. 35–50 (2015)

14. Kaundal, R., Kapoor, A., Raghava, G.: Machine learning techniques in disease forecasting: a case study on rice blast prediction. BMC Bioinf. (2016)

15. Morales, E., Gutierrez, J., Cerna, W., Chavez, L.: Muestreo secuencial de spodoptera frugiperda cogollero en el cultivo de zea mays para determinar límites de confianza. In: Repositorio Digital Universidad José Faustino Sánchez, pp. 1–6 (2013)

16. Pérez, C., Nicholson, A., Flores, J.: Prediction of coffee rust disease using Bayesian networks. In: Sixth European Workshop on Probabilistic Graphical Models, pp. 259–266 (2012)

17. Kaundal, R., Kapoor, A.S.: Machine learning techniques in disease forecasting: a case study on rice blast prediction. BMC Bioinf. (2007)

18. Tendencias, R., Comercio, E.: Big Data, El Futuro Agrícola? Obtenido de El Comercio (30 de Mayo de 2015). http://especiales.elcomercio.com/planeta-ideas/planeta/mayo-31-del-2015/big-data-el-futuro-agricola

19. Robles, Á., Salinas, D., Armijos, W., Sánchez, A., Torres, R.: Estudio de la variabilidad morfológica de aislados fúngicos asociados con la enfermedad de la marchitez vascular del babaco (Vasconcellea heilbornii var. pentagona) Loja - Ecuador. In: Centro de Biotecnología, pp. 34–44 (2013)

20. Tello, M., Eslava, H., Tobías, L.: Análisis y evaluación del nivel de riesgo en el otorgamiento de créditos financieros utilizando técnicas de minería de datos. In: Vision Investigadora, pp. 13–26 (2012)

21. Rosado, A., Verjel, A.: Minería de datos aplicada a la demanda del transporte aéreo en Ocaña, Norte de Santander. In: Tecnura, pp. 101–113 (2015)

22. Rueda, E., Hernández, L., Peña, J., Ruiz, F., López, J., Huez, M., Jiménez, J., Borboa, J., Ortega, J.: Ralstonia solanacearum: Una enfermedad bacteriana de importancia cuarentenaria en el cultivo de Solanum tuberosum L., pp. 24–36 (2014)

23. Sannakki, S., Rajpurohit, V.: A neural network approach for disease forecasting in grapes using weather parameters. IEEE (2014)

24. Sifuentes, E., Ruelas, J., Macías, J., Talamantes, I., Palacios, C., Valenzuela, B.: Fenología y tiempo en el manejo del riego y fertilización del cultivo de papa. In: Revista de Ciencias Biológicas y de la Salud, pp. 42–48 (2015)

Selection of Agricultural Technology:
A Multi-attribute Approach

Jorge L. García-Alcaraz[(✉)] [iD], Valeria Martínez-Loya [iD],
Aide Maldonado-Macias [iD], and Liliana Avelar-Sosa [iD]

Universidad Autónoma de Ciudad Juárez,
32310 Ciudad Juárez, Chihuahua, Mexico
{jorge.garcia,amaldona,liliana.avelar}@uacj.mx,
al160648@alumnos.uacj.mx

Abstract. The evaluation and selection process of agricultural technology traditionally is focused on economic aspects, delegating to third parties and ignoring several attributes in the analysis. This article presents a multicriteria model that integrates the TOPSIS technique, based on a similarity index to an ideal alternative performed by a decision group, which integrates simultaneously several attributes in the analysis and having different preference levels, thus the farmers can carry out the evaluation process by themselves. The model is validated through a case study applied to the selection of an agricultural tractor, which is evaluated by four members of an agricultural cooperative, including two types of attributes. On the one hand, tangible attributes: initial cost, maintenance cost and engine power. On the other hand, intangible attributes: after-sales service and maintainability. Currently, the model is being integrated in a software to facilitate applications by farmers, avoiding assigning this task to third parties.

Keywords: Tractor selection · Multicriteria evaluation · TOPSIS · NGT

1 Introduction

Currently, the food industry has shown important technological advances so the managers of this type of companies frequently require purchasing modern technologies applied to the agricultural fields and the production processes. The purpose of these modern technologies is to increase productivity and efficiency, but also quality, which includes many government restrictions, regulations and standards because food products are handled [1, 2].

However, investing in advanced technology is not the only source of competitiveness, since it requires highly skilled and trained personnel who must have knowledge related to technology for its proper usage and commonly, technology purchases are accompanied by training programs. Thus, the combination of technologies and human resources can be one of the main sources of agro-industry competitiveness allowing the participation of firms in the globalized world.

Once farmers have decided to invest in innovative technologies, they face new challenges. The first is that in the market there are usually many possible alternatives

© Springer International Publishing AG 2017
R. Valencia-García et al. (Eds.): CITI 2017, CCIS 749, pp. 319–331, 2017.
DOI: 10.1007/978-3-319-67283-0_24

that meet the expected requirements, but also, these technologies are almost always characterized by more than one attribute [3, 4]. For example, if a tractor must be purchased, the first observed characteristic is associated with the initial cost or investment required, however, there are many attributes that must be integrated such as maintainability and quality of service. That quantity of attributes makes the decision-making a complex problem and a complicated process for farmers.

According to the number of available alternatives for tractors, for example, currently in Mexico, there are many brands available in the market and all of them include foreign technologies, which have been designed with different capacities. For this reason, it is important that during the planning stage, the terrain features be clearly defined, so the needs and characteristics that these possible alternatives must meet, can be defined.

1.1 Attributes in Agricultural Tractors

In tractors, these attributes are classified per their nature: attributes that are objective, can be quantified, and generally are associated with economic or engineering aspects. The most classical examples could be the initial investment, engine power, the number of accessories that can be adapted, among others, and usually the technology that the vendor provides them. The second category refers to those of a qualitative nature, which are not easy to quantify, so to integrate them into the evaluation process, a decision group should be asked to make a series of assessments per a pre-established Likert scale. Examples of this type of attributes are the quality of the service, the safety and the tractor maneuverability, among others [5–7].

1.2 Techniques in Agricultural Tractors Evaluation

After identifying all tractors that can meet the farmers' needs and their attributes, then, the problem is to choose the most optimal, and it means that it is necessary to carry out an evaluation process. In that sense, literature shows three types of techniques used for evaluation process: economic, strategic and analytical [8].

First category, economic techniques represent the industrial practice and all methodologies taught in Engineering Economics seminars such as net present value, internal rate of return, equivalent uniform annual cost, payback period, cost-benefit analysis, among others. However, these techniques have limitations because only integrate economic attributes, so they are widely criticized for not including qualitative attributes.

Second category, strategic techniques are the less used and widespread, since they refer to techniques used by top management, which do not include economic aspects in the analysis and are only based on the experience and knowledge about the strategic objectives of the company. These techniques can be rejected by lower levels of the organizational structure because they do not understand the decision-making process, since sometimes it is hard to make decisions considering all different scenarios.

Finally, the analytical techniques, which are still unknown to the industrial sector, but are widely recommended due to their ability to integrate qualitative and quantitative attributes. Thus, they are considered multi-attribute and multi-criteria, since they allow evaluating simultaneously several attributes and it is a group of decision makers who carry out the analysis. The most common techniques are: the analytic hierarchy process (AHP) [9], the technique for order of preference by similarity to ideal solution (TOPSIS) [10], the dimensional analysis [11], the additive linear model [12], among others.

The applications of analytical techniques are broadly reported in the industrial sector for the evaluation of robots [13] and manipulation systems [14, 15]. However, much research and applications are required in the agro-industrial sector, there exist reports such as the evaluation of machinery to harvest forages [16], proper use of available infrastructure [17], identify and pursue opportunities for process automation [18]. For instance, in Camarena et al. [19] an integer linear model is used to evaluate agricultural machinery. Likewise, using multi-attribute techniques, water use policies have been defined and risk analysis in investments have been performed. [20]. In addition, there are reports of multi-attribute applications to determine financial policies for forest conservation and products optimization [21, 22].

1.3   Research Problem and Objective

Due to the number of attributes involved in the evaluation and selection of agricultural tractors, choosing a single alternative becomes a complex problem that is not properly structured, the common action is to apply quantitative techniques that only integrate economic aspects. In addition, more integrative models and techniques are difficult to understand by managers and farmers, and these decisions are delegated to third parties, who do not know the needs of farmers or agro-industrial enterprise [23].

Investing in a new tractor may require the disbursement of a large amount of money for a single farmer, so in many cases they are grouped into small rural production cooperatives, which allows them to join economic efforts, but all require to play a role in the decision group that performs the analysis.

In general, to make a right decision, it is necessary to consider multiple aspects that can sometimes jeopardize the farmer's economic stability, so if a new tractor is going to be bought, it is crucial to choose the one which meets all expected requirements. Even though there are different alternatives only one must be selected [24]. The alternatives are represented by several attributes and certain farmers integrate the decision group.

For this reason, the objective of this article is to present a multicriteria and multi-attribute model that solves this problem of tractor selection, which is currently been integrated into a software to facilitate calculations, avoid errors, speed up and provide a democratic sense to the decision-making process.

2   Proposed Model

The model integrates two techniques widely known in the manufacturing field and they will be adapted to the agro-industrial sector to facilitate their application by farmers and managers. The techniques used are the Nominal Group Technique (NGT) and the Technique for Order Preference by Similarity to Ideal Solution (TOPSIS), which are described below, but, first the matrix approach to decision making is explained.

2.1   Matrix Approach to Decision-Making

It is assumed that a set of K tractors has a total of J objective attributes that can be quantified and L subjective attributes which are obtained by the evaluations of a decision group, being evaluated by a total of P members. The quantitative attributes are called X_1, X_2, ... X_J, and the qualitative attributes are represented by X_{J+1}, X_{J+2}, ... X_{J+L}, as indicated by Rudnik, Kacprzak [25].

These objective attributes are represented per Eq. (1) as **OV**. Whereas the subjective attributes come from the evaluation of the decision group affiliates and here is where the nominal group technique is used, since each of the members generates, in a secret way, a matrix to present their opinions which can be represented by **SV^P** as indicated in Eq. (2) [26].

$$OV = \begin{array}{c} T^1 \\ T^2 \\ . \\ . \\ T^k \end{array} \begin{bmatrix} X_1^1 & X_2^1 & . & . & X_J^1 \\ X_1^2 & X_2^2 & . & . & X_J^2 \\ . & . & . & . & . \\ . & . & . & . & . \\ X_1^k & X_2^k & . & . & X_J^k \end{bmatrix} \tag{1}$$

where:

X_j^k = attribute value j on tractor k

$j = 1, 2...J$

$k = 1.....K$

$$SV^p = \begin{array}{c} T^1 \\ T^2 \\ . \\ . \\ T^k \end{array} \begin{bmatrix} X_{J+1}^{1P} & X_{J+2}^{1P} & . & . & X_{J+L}^{1P} \\ X_{J+1}^{2P} & X_{J+2}^{2P} & . & . & X_{J+L}^{2P} \\ . & . & . & . & . \\ . & . & . & . & . \\ X_{J+1}^{KP} & X_{J+2}^{KP} & . & . & X_{J+L}^{KP} \end{bmatrix} \tag{2}$$

where:

x_{J+i}^k is rating of the expert P for tractor $\mathbf{T}^k$ according to attribute X_{J+i}.

$k = 1,... K$

$i = 1,...L$

Given that, a single matrix of subjective values must be obtained, the opinions provide by each expert in **SV^P** must be unified. Then, Eq. (3) is proposed to obtain their mean, and this is called total matrix of subjective values represented by **TSV**.

$$TSV = \sum_{P=1}^{P} SV^P / P = \begin{array}{c} S^1 \\ S^2 \\ . \\ . \\ S^k \end{array} \begin{bmatrix} X_{J+1}^1 & X_{J+2}^1 & . & . & X_{J+L}^1 \\ X_{J+1}^2 & X_{J+2}^2 & . & . & X_{J+L}^2 \\ . & . & . & . & . \\ . & . & . & . & . \\ X_{J+1}^K & X_{J+2}^K & . & . & X_{J+L}^K \end{bmatrix} \tag{3}$$

where:

$x^k_{J+i} = \frac{\sum_{p=1}^{P} x^{kp}_{J+i}}{P}$ is the average rating that the experts have assigned to tractor T^k according to the attribute X_{J+i}.

$k = 1, \dots K$

$i = 1, \dots L$

Having the **OV** and **TSV** matrices, the final decision matrix (**FDMM**) is integrated, which is used to carry out the evaluation of the tractor [25].

$$FDMM = [OV, TSV] = \begin{matrix} S^1 \\ S^2 \\ \cdot \\ \cdot \\ \cdot \\ S^k \end{matrix} \begin{bmatrix} x^1_1 & \cdots & x^1_J & x^1_{J+1} & \cdots & x^1_{J+L} \\ x^2_1 & \cdots & x^2_J & x^2_{J+1} & \cdots & x^2_{J+L} \\ \cdot & & \cdot & \cdot & & \cdot \\ x^K_1 & \cdots & x^K_J & x^K_{J+1} & \cdots & x^K_{J+L} \end{bmatrix} \tag{4}$$

2.2 TOPSIS Technique

TOPSIS is a technique that considers tractors as vectors located in a $J + L$-dimensional Euclidean space, as indicated in Eq. (5). Also, this technique considers the attributes as vectors in k-dimensional space, such as illustrated in Eq. (6) [27].

$$T^i = (x^i_1 \dots \dots x^i_{J+L}) \text{ for } i = 1, 2, \dots k \tag{5}$$

$$X_n = (x^1_n \dots \dots x^k_n) \text{ for } n = 1, 2, \dots J + L. \tag{6}$$

TOPSIS assumes that there is always an ideal tractor, which is composed of the highest nominal values in each attribute, represented by T^+; however, it is also considered a non-ideal alternative that is represented by the worst nominal values in the attributes which is illustrated by T^-. The alternatives are represented by Eqs. (7) and (8) respectively [28].

$$A^- = (x^-_1, x^-_2, \dots \dots x^-_{J+L}) \tag{7}$$

$$A^- = (x^-_1, x^-_2, \dots \dots x^-_{J+L}) \tag{8}$$

Based on the concepts stablished before, it is sought to choose a tractor that is located a shortest Euclidean distance from T^+, but with the greatest distance from T^-. However, TOPSIS is a technique that considers both distances in the estimation of a decision index. Thus, the TOPSIS technique is summarized as follows.

2.2.1 Stage 1. Normalization of Attributes

It is possible that the attributes evaluated on the tractor are expressed in different scales of measurement, for example, the cost in Mexican pesos or US dollars, but the fuel consumption is expressed in liters or gallons per hour, among others. In order to perform any operation with data, it is convenient to convert the attributes in **FDMM** into dimensionless, which is completed through the normalization process, by dividing each value into the attributes by their respective Euclidian norm, as is indicated in Eq. (9) [29].

$$TX_n = \frac{X_n}{\|X_n\|} = \left(\frac{x_n^1}{\|X_n\|}, \ldots \ldots \frac{x_n^k}{\|X_n\|} \right) \tag{9}$$

Where $\|X_n\|$ represents the Euclidean norm of each attribute which is obtained according to Eq. (10).

$$|X_n| = \sqrt{\sum_1^x x_i^2} \tag{10}$$

A straightforward way of performing the normalization process for the ideal tractor and non-ideal tractor is illustrated below.

$$T^k = (t_1^k, \ldots \ldots, t_n^k) = \left(\frac{x_1^k}{\|X_1\|}, \ldots \ldots, \frac{x_n^k}{\|X_n\|} \right) \tag{11}$$

$$TA^+ = (t_1^+, \ldots \ldots, t_n^+) = \left(\frac{x_1^+}{\|X_1\|}, \ldots \ldots, \frac{x_n^+}{\|X_n\|} \right) \tag{12}$$

$$TA^- = (t_1^-, \ldots \ldots, t_n^-) = \left(\frac{x_1^-}{\|X_1\|}, \ldots \ldots, \frac{x_n^-}{\|X_n\|} \right) \tag{13}$$

2.2.2 Stage 2: Calculation of Distances

Since TOPSIS considers the distance to T^+ and to T^-, both must be calculated; however, there is another problem, the importance levels of the attributes, which may be different from each other. In order to know the distance to the ideal tractor, Eq. (14) is used, whereas Eq. (15) is used to estimate the distance to the non-ideal tractor [30].

$$\rho(A^k, A^+) = \|w * (TA^k - TA^+)\| \tag{14}$$

$$\rho(A^k, A^-) = \|w * (TA^k - TA^-)\| \tag{15}$$

Where w represents the importance level of the attributes in evaluation, whose sum must be equal to one and is obtained using the NGT.

2.2.3 Stage 3. Calculation of the Decision Index

It has been mentioned previously that one of the advantages of TOPSIS is that considers the two distances, ideal and non-ideal, therefore, the decision index is estimated based on both distances as is shown in Eq. (16) [30].

$$RC(A^+, A^i) = \frac{\rho(A^k, A^+)}{\rho(A^k, A^+) + \rho(A^k, A^-)} \tag{16}$$

3 Case Study

An agricultural cooperative must acquire a new tractor, which will be used by the different members, so it has been decided to organize a research group integrated by four people.

3.1 Attributes Evaluated

The attributes to be evaluated are the following:

- *Initial cost ($):* This attribute is objective, represents the total amount payable for the tractor, and includes financing expenses. It is expressed in Mexican pesos and it is required to minimize it.
- *Annual maintenance cost ($):* It refers to the annual cost of maintenance, which includes mechanical parts purchase, specialist inspection services and annual investment insurance. This attribute is objective, expressed in Mexican pesos and low values are expected.
- *Engine power or horsepower (HP):* This attribute refers to the power of the engine, expressed in horsepower (HP); it is an objective attribute that must be maximized.
- *After-sales service:* This attribute is subjective and refers to the quality of the service that farmers received from the supplier after purchasing a product. It is' obtained by subjective valuations and is desired to maximize.
- *Maintainability.* It refers to the ease and rapidity with which maintenance activities can be performed to the tractor. This is a subjective attribute obtained through experts' valuations which is desired to maximize.

3.2 The Final Decision Matrix

Several technical data sheets of tractors have been identified because they may be alternative solutions; however, it is considered that only six suppliers have influence in the region, so these are considered in this analysis. It is worthy to mention that the objective values of the tractors are codified in order to ensure the suppliers' anonymity. The final decision matrix that includes objective and subjective attributes is illustrated in Table 1, which also shows the ideal and non-ideal tractors.

Table 1. Final decision matrix

T^k	Attributes				
	Initial cost ($)	Annual maintenance cost ($)	Power (HP)	After-sales service	Maintainability
T^1	738,223	70,000	255	8.5	8.3
T^2	510,730	65,000	275	7.4	7.6
T^3	415,232.50	72,000	285	6.8	5.9
T^4	639,477.50	91,000	241	7.5	6.8
T^5	570,305	82,000	180	8.3	8.4
T^6	680,370	110,000	210	8.5	8.5
T+	415,232.50	65,000	285	8.5	8.5
T-	738,223	110,000	180	6.8	5.9
Opt	Min	Min	Max	Max	Max
w	0.23857	0.08151	0.12869	0.17696	0.37427

In this case, it is observed that the ideal solution would be a tractor whose initial cost was 415,232.50 Mexican pesos, an annual maintenance cost of 65,000 Mexican pesos, with 285 horsepower, the supplier's reputation of 8.5 and maintainability score of 8.5. In the same way, the worst scenario when buying a tractor includes a cost of 738,223 Mexican pesos for initial investment, an annual maintenance cost of 111,000 Mexican pesos, an engine power of 180 horsepower, but also, the supplier's reputation only 6.8 and the maintainability of 5.9 on a scale from 1 to 9.

In addition, the last row in Table 1 illustrates the weight or importance level that farmers have provided to each attribute from a subjective assessment performed by them. Note that maintainability is the attribute that shows the highest weight value, which means it is the most valued by the decision group, since once the warranty has expired, farmers are the ones who perform the tractor maintenance.

3.3 Normalization of Attributes

Table 2 shows the normalization process for attributes, performed per Eqs. (9), (11), (12) and (13). However, the last row presents the norm value for each attribute, obtained by the Eq. (10). The values in Table 2 are already dimensionless thus additive operations can be performed.

3.4 Attributes Weighting

After the standardized attributes were obtained, the next step was to weight the attributes according to the preference levels as is shown in Table 1. In that sense, Table 3 illustrate the weighting process.

Table 2. Normalization of attributes

T^k	Attributes				
	Initial cost ($)	Annual maintenance cost ($)	Power (HP)	After-sales service	Maintainability
T^1	0.5005	0.3440	0.4271	0.4415	0.4433
T^2	0.3463	0.3194	0.4606	0.3844	0.4059
T^3	0.2815	0.3538	0.4774	0.3532	0.3151
T^4	0.4336	0.4472	0.4037	0.3896	0.3632
T^5	0.3867	0.4029	0.3015	0.4311	0.4487
T^6	0.4613	0.5405	0.3517	0.4415	0.4540
T+	0.2815	0.3194	0.4774	0.4415	0.4540
T-	0.5005	0.5405	0.3015	0.3532	0.3151
Norma	1474896.255	203504.2997	597.0393	19.2520	18.7219

Table 3. Attributes Weighting

T^k	Attributes				
	Initial cost ($)	Annual maintenance cost ($)	Power (HP)	After-sales service	Maintainability
T^1	0.1194	0.0280	0.0550	0.0781	0.1659
T^2	0.0826	0.0260	0.0593	0.0680	0.1519
T^3	0.0672	0.0288	0.0614	0.0625	0.1179
T^4	0.1034	0.0364	0.0519	0.0689	0.1359
T^5	0.0922	0.0328	0.0388	0.0763	0.1679
T^6	0.1101	0.0441	0.0453	0.0781	0.1699
T+	0.0672	0.0260	0.0614	0.0781	0.1699
T-	0.1194	0.0441	0.0388	0.0625	0.1179

3.5   Calculation of Distances to Ideal and Non-ideal Tractor

With the standardized and weighted attributes, it is necessary to calculate the distances for each evaluated tractor to the ideal and non-ideal tractors using Eqs. (14) and (15), respectively. The results obtained are illustrated in Table 4, where last column indicates the distance and the order of alternatives if only one of them is considered. Note that if is only considered the distance to the ideal tractor, it must be chosen T^2, but if is considered the distance to the non-ideal, the best option is T^5.

3.6   Calculation of the Decision Index

However, TOPSIS is a technique that considers the distance to the ideal and non-ideal alternative, so that the decision index and its calculation are illustrated in Table 5, which shows that the alternative T^2 must be selected, since it is the lowest value.

Table 4. Distance to ideal and non-ideal solutions

Distance to ideal tractor

T^k	Initial cost	Annual maintenance cost	Power	After sales	Maintainability	Distance	Order
T^1	0.002730	0.000004	0.000042	0.000000	0.000016	0.0528	5
T^2	0.000239	0.000000	0.000005	0.000102	0.000324	0.0259	1
T^3	0.000000	0.000008	0.000000	0.000244	0.002702	0.0543	6
T^4	0.001316	0.000108	0.000090	0.000084	0.001155	0.0525	4
T^5	0.000629	0.000046	0.000512	0.000003	0.000004	0.0346	2
T^6	0.001839	0.000325	0.000261	0.000000	0.000000	0.0492	3

Distance to non-ideal tractor

T^k	Initial cost	Annual maintenance cost	Power	After sales	Maintainability	Distance	Order
T^1	0.000000	0.000257	0.000261	0.00024	0.002302	0.0554	5
T^2	0.001354	0.000325	0.000419	0.00003	0.001155	0.0573	3
T^3	0.002730	0.000232	0.000512	0.000000	0.000000	0.0589	2
T^4	0.000255	0.000058	0.000173	0.000041	0.000324	0.0292	6
T^5	0.000738	0.000126	0.000000	0.000190	0.002498	0.0596	1
T^6	0.000088	0.000000	0.000042	0.000244	0.002702	0.0555	4

Table 5. Decision index

T^k	Dist. to Ideal	Dist. to no Ideal	Index	Order
T^1	0.0528	0.0554	0.4883	5
T^2	0.0259	0.0573	0.3110	1
T^3	0.0543	0.0589	0.4797	4
T^4	0.0525	0.0292	0.6427	6
T^5	0.03456	0.0596	0.3671	2
T^6	0.0492	0.0555	0.4704	3

4   Discussion

This paper presents a case study of the evaluation and selection process of agricultural tractors through a multicriteria approach, allowing the analysis of several attributes by a decision group integrated by four farmers, which gives a sense of democracy to that decision process, which was not limited evaluating only aspects associated with costs, and integrating objective and subjective attributes. In addition, it integrates an important aspect that refers to the maintenance cost from a quantitative perspective and the facility to perform it from a qualitative approach [31], this activity is crucial for rural areas which are located away from the service centers from providers. The model was applied by the farmers themselves, who know the problem of their environmental context needs which must be met, thus avoiding the personnel outsourcing for that activity and saving money [32].

However, it is possible that the best decision is buying none of the alternatives, as described by Andrabi et al. [33], who states that when the use of a tractor is low, an alternative is to rent a tractor and not to invest a large amount of financial resources.

In addition, the use of specialized software has not been required, as in evaluations performed with other techniques, such as AHP (Analytic Hierarchy Process) [32], which allows farmers to save money [34].

5 Future Research

At this time, the research group is integrating the model into a software that has been distributed for free, as in India according to the case reported by Mehta et al. [35]. Likewise, sensitivity tests are being conducted to determine the ranges in which one solution remains preferable to others. Also future research, will integrate financing attributes because sometimes the due date for payment of tractors is a long period, as is reported by Bojnec and Latruffe [36] for the case of Slovenian farms and Papageorgiou [37] in Greece.

References

1. Kimoto, R., Ronquillo, D., Caamaño, M.C., Martinez, G., Schubert, L., Rosado, J.L., Garcia, O., Long, K.Z.: Food, eating and body image in the lives of low socioeconomic status rural Mexican women living in Queretaro State, Mexico. Health & Place **25**, 34–42 (2014). http://dx.doi.org/10.1016/j.healthplace.2013.10.004
2. Zeng, D.-Z., Zhao, L.: Globalization, interregional and international inequalities. J. Urban Econ. **67**(3), 352–361 (2010). http://dx.doi.org/10.1016/j.jue.2009.11.002
3. Hua, Y.: Influential factors of farmers' demands for agricultural science and technology in China. Technol. Forecast. Soc. Chang. **100**, 249–254 (2015). http://dx.doi.org/10.1016/j.techfore.2015.07.008
4. Carter, M.R., Cheng, L., Sarris, A.: Where and how index insurance can boost the adoption of improved agricultural technologies. J. Dev. Econ. **118**, 59–71 (2016). http://dx.doi.org/10.1016/j.jdeveco.2015.08.008
5. Sun, B., Ma, W.: An approach to consensus measurement of linguistic preference relations in multi-attribute group decision making and application. Omega **51**, 83–92 (2015). http://dx.doi.org/10.1016/j.omega.2014.09.006
6. Chuu, S.-J.: Selecting the advanced manufacturing technology using fuzzy multiple attributes group decision making with multiple fuzzy information. Comput. Ind. Eng. **57**(3), 1033–1042 (2009). http://dx.doi.org/10.1016/j.cie.2009.04.011
7. Evans, L., Lohse, N., Summers, M.: A fuzzy-decision-tree approach for manufacturing technology selection exploiting experience-based information. Expert Syst. Appl. **40**(16), 6412–6426 (2013). http://dx.doi.org/10.1016/j.eswa.2013.05.047
8. Ilgin, M.A., Gupta, S.M., Battaïa, O.: Use of MCDM techniques in environmentally conscious manufacturing and product recovery: State of the art. J. Manuf. Syst. **37**, Part 3, 746–758 (2015). http://dx.doi.org/10.1016/j.jmsy.2015.04.010
9. Veisi, H., Liaghati, H., Alipour, A.: Developing an ethics-based approach to indicators of sustainable agriculture using analytic hierarchy process (AHP). Ecol. Ind. **60**, 644–654 (2016). http://dx.doi.org/10.1016/j.ecolind.2015.08.012

10. Yue, Z.: Extension of TOPSIS to determine weight of decision maker for group decision making problems with uncertain information. Expert Syst. Appl. **39**(7), 6343–6350 (2012). http://dx.doi.org/10.1016/j.eswa.2011.12.016

11. Braglia, M., Gabbrielli, R.: Dimensional analysis for investment selection in industrial robots. Int. J. Prod. Res. **38**(18), 4843–4848 (2000). doi:10.1080/00207540050205668

12. Goh, C.-H., Tung, Y.-C.A., Cheng, C.-H.: A revised weighted sum decision model for robot selection. Comput. Ind. Eng. **30**(2), 193–199 (1996). http://dx.doi.org/10.1016/0360-8352 (95)00167-0

13. Knott, K., Getto, R.D.: A model for evaluating alternative robot systems under uncertainty. Int. J. Prod. Res. **20**(2), 155–165 (1982). doi:10.1080/00207548208947757

14. Wei, C.-C., Kamrani, A.K., Wiebe, H.: Animated simulation of the robot process capability. Comput. Ind. Eng. **23**(1–4), 237–240 (1992). http://dx.doi.org/10.1016/0360-8352(92) 90107-U

15. Offodile, O., Lambert, B., Dudek, R.: Development of a computer aided robot selection procedure (CARSF). Int. J. Prod. Res. **25**, 1109–1121 (1987)

16. Russell, N.P., Milligan, R.A., LaDue, E.L.: A stochastic simulation model for evaluating forage machinery performance. Agric. Syst. **10**(1), 39–63 (1983). http://dx.doi.org/10.1016/ 0308-521X(83)90015-X

17. Elhorst, J.P.: The estimation of investment equations at the farm level. Eur. Rev. Agric. Econ. **20**(2), 167–182 (1993). doi:10.1093/erae/20.2.167

18. Søgaard, H.T., Sørensen, C.G.: A model for optimal selection of machinery sizes within the farm machinery system. Biosyst. Eng. **89**(1), 13–28 (2004). http://dx.doi.org/10.1016/j. biosystemseng.2004.05.004

19. Camarena, E.A., Gracia, C., Cabrera Sixto, J.M.: A mixed integer linear programming machinery selection model for multifarm systems. Biosyst. Eng. **87**(2), 145–154 (2004). http://dx.doi.org/10.1016/j.biosystemseng.2003.10.003

20. Bartolini, F., Bazzani, G.M., Gallerani, V., Raggi, M., Viaggi, D.: The impact of water and agriculture policy scenarios on irrigated farming systems in Italy: an analysis based on farm level multi-attribute linear programming models. Agric. Syst. **93**(1–3), 90–114 (2007). http:// dx.doi.org/10.1016/j.agsy.2006.04.006

21. Hayashida, T., Nishizaki, I., Ueda, Y.: Multiattribute utility analysis for policy selection and financing for the preservation of the forest. Eur. J. Oper. Res. **200**(3), 833–843 (2010). http:// dx.doi.org/10.1016/j.ejor.2009.01.035

22. Manos, B., Chatzinikolaou, P., Kiomourtzi, F.: Sustainable optimization of agricultural production. APCBEE Procedia **5**, 410–415 (2013). http://dx.doi.org/10.1016/j.apcbee.2013. 05.071

23. Leicht, K.T., Jenkins, J.C.: State investments in high-technology job growth. Soc. Sci. Res. **65**, 30–46 (2017). http://dx.doi.org/10.1016/j.ssresearch.2017.03.007

24. Lee, H., Choi, H., Lee, J., Min, J., Lee, H.: Impact of IT investment on firm performance based on technology IT architecture. Procedia Comput. Sci. **91**, 652–661 (2016). http://dx. doi.org/10.1016/j.procs.2016.07.164

25. Rudnik, K., Kacprzak, D.: Fuzzy TOPSIS method with ordered fuzzy numbers for flow control in a manufacturing system. Appl. Soft Comput. **52**, 1020–1041 (2017). https://doi. org/10.1016/j.asoc.2016.09.027

26. Akbaş, H., Bilgen, B.: An integrated fuzzy QFD and TOPSIS methodology for choosing the ideal gas fuel at WWTPs. Energy **125**, 484–497 (2017). https://doi.org/10.1016/j.energy. 2017.02.153

27. Ertuğrul, İ., Karakaşoğlu, N.: Comparison of fuzzy AHP and fuzzy TOPSIS methods for facility location selection. Int. J. Adv. Manuf. Technol. **39**(7), 783–795 (2008). doi:10.1007/ s00170-007-1249-8

28. Li, X., Chen, X.: Extension of the TOPSIS method based on prospect theory and trapezoidal intuitionistic fuzzy numbers for group decision making. J. Syst. Sci. Syst. Eng. **23**(2), 231–247 (2014). doi:10.1007/s11518-014-5244-y
29. Mavi, R.K., Goh, M., Mavi, N.K.: Supplier selection with shannon entropy and fuzzy TOPSIS in the context of supply chain risk management. Procedia – Soc. Behav. Sci. **235**, 216–225 (2016). https://doi.org/10.1016/j.sbspro.2016.11.017
30. Mohamed, H., Omar, B., Abdessadek, T., Tarik, A.: An application of OLAP/GIS-Fuzzy AHP-TOPSIS methodology for decision making: location selection for landfill of industrial wastes as a case study. KSCE J. Civ. Eng., 1–11 (2016). doi:10.1007/s12205-016-0114-4
31. Lorencowicz, E., Uziak, J.: Repair cost of tractors and agricultural machines in family farms. Agric. Agric. Sci. Procedia **7**, 152–157 (2015). https://doi.org/10.1016/j.aaspro.2015.12.010
32. Amini, S., Asoodar, M.A.: Selecting the most appropriate tractor using analytic hierarchy process – an Iranian case study. Inf. Process. Agric. **3**(4), 223–234 (2016). https://doi.org/10.1016/j.inpa.2016.08.003
33. Andrabi, T., Ghatak, M., Khwaja, A.I.: Subcontractors for tractors: theory and evidence on flexible specialization, supplier selection, and contracting. J. Dev. Econ. **79**(2), 273–302 (2006). https://doi.org/10.1016/j.jdeveco.2006.01.012
34. Malaga-Toboła, U., Tabor, S., Kocira, S.: Productivity of resources and investments at selected ecological farms. Agric. Agric. Sci. Procedia **7**, 158–164 (2015). https://doi.org/10.1016/j.aaspro.2015.12.011
35. Mehta, C.R., Singh, K., Selvan, M.M.: A decision support system for selection of tractor-implement system used on Indian farms. J. Terramech. **48**(1), 65–73 (2011). doi:https://doi.org/10.1016/j.jterra.2010.05.002
36. Bojnec, Š., Latruffe, L.: Financing availability and investment decisions of slovenian farms during the transition to a market economy. J. Appl. Econ. **14**(2), 297–317 (2011). http://dx.doi.org/10.1016/S1514-0326(11)60016-0
37. Papageorgiou, A.: Agricultural equipment in greece: farm machinery management in the era of economic crisis. Agric. Agric. Sci. Procedia **7**, 198–202 (2015). https://doi.org/10.1016/j.aaspro.2015.12.017

Author Index

Printed in the United States
By Bookmasters